On Making in the Digital Humanities

On Making in the Digital Humanities

The scholarship of digital humanities
development in honour of John Bradley

Edited by
Julianne Nyhan, Geoffrey Rockwell,
Stéfan Sinclair and Alexandra Ortolja-Baird

⌂UCLPRESS

First published in 2023 by
UCL Press
University College London
Gower Street
London WC1E 6BT

Available to download free: www.uclpress.co.uk

A CIP catalogue record for this book is available from The British Library.

ISBN: 978-1-80008-422-3 (Hbk.)
ISBN: 978-1-80008-421-6 (Pbk.)
ISBN: 978-1-80008-420-9 (PDF)
ISBN: 978-1-80008-423-0 (epub)
DOI: https://doi.org/10.14324/111.9781800084209

Contents

Contributors   vii
List of figures and table   xi

Introduction: On making in the digital humanities   1
Julianne Nyhan and Geoffrey Rockwell

1   Four corners of the big tent: a personal journey through
    the digital humanities   14
    John Bradley

Part I: Making Projects   49

2   Prosopography meets the digital: PBW and PASE   51
    Charlotte Roueché, Averil Cameron and Janet L. Nelson

3   Braving the new world: REED at the digital crossroads   66
    Sally-Beth MacLean

4   Sustainability and modelling at King's Digital Lab:
    between tradition and innovation   78
    Arianna Ciula and James Smithies

5   The *People of Medieval Scotland* database as history   105
    Dauvit Broun and Joanna Tucker

Part II: People Making   127

6   The history of the 'techie' in the history of digital humanities   129
    Julianne Nyhan

7 Jobs, roles and tools in digital humanities   148
   Julia Flanders

8 The politics of digital repatriation and its relationship
   to Rongowhakaata cultural data sovereignty   162
   Arapata Hakiwai, Karl Johnstone and Brinker Ferguson

Part III: Making Praxis   177

9   Towards an operational approach to computational
    text analysis   179
    Dino Buzzetti

10 From TACT to CATMA; or, a mindful approach to text
    annotation and analysis   213
    Jan Christoph Meister

11 Pursuing a combinatorial habit of mind and machine   251
    Willard McCarty

12 Historians, texts and factoids   267
    Manfred Thaller

Part IV: In Memoriam   275

13 If Voyant then Spyral: remembering Stéfan Sinclair   277
    Geoffrey Rockwell

Index   289

Contributors

Alexandra Ortolja-Baird is a Lecturer in Digital History and Culture at the University of Portsmouth. Her research intersects digital humanities, early modern intellectual history, and cultural heritage and archival studies. She has previously held positions at King's College London, University College London and the British Museum. Her current work explores digital approaches to archival silences.

John Bradley worked in the digital humanities from the early 1970s until 1997, first at the University of Toronto and then at the Department of Digital Humanities at King's College London, continuing past his retirement in 2015. Most of his posts were 'academic-related' until he was made an academic by King's in 2011. His work includes the development of the text analysis software TACT and the experimental software platform *Pliny*. He has collaborated on more than 20 public humanities-oriented digital resources.

Dauvit Broun has been lecturing at the University of Glasgow since 1990, and since 2009 as Professor of Scottish History. He was Principal Investigator of projects centring on the creation and development of the PoMS database (two funded by the AHRC, 2007–13, with John Bradley as a Co-Investigator, and one funded by the Leverhulme Trust, 2013–17, with John Bradley as Co-Investigator).

Dino Buzzetti taught history of philosophy, mainly medieval, at the University of Bologna. For several years he ran a course on documentation and historical document processing at the Faculty of Preservation of Cultural Heritage and a course on humanities computing for philosophy students. His main research topic was the history of logic in relation to contemporary developments in philosophical and theological doctrines.

Averil Cameron is a historian of late antiquity and Byzantium. She taught at King's College until 1994 and chaired the Humanities Research Centres. As a Fellow of the British Academy she was instrumental in bringing the *Prosopography of the Byzantine Empire* (PBE, later PBW) to King's and was the founding director of the Centre for Hellenic Studies. In relation to PBE and PBW she worked closely with Harold Short and John Bradley.

Arianna Ciula is Director and Senior Research Software Analyst at King's Digital Lab (King's College London, UK). She has broad experience in digital humanities research and teaching, research management, and digital research infrastructures. Her personal research interests focus on the modelling of scholarly digital resources related to primary sources. She has lectured and published on humanities computing, in particular on digital manuscript studies and editing, and is an active member of the digital humanities international community.

Brinker Ferguson is the manager of the Digital Humanities and Social Engagement (DHSE) cluster and directs the Digital Cultural Heritage Lab at Dartmouth College. She is also an adjunct professor, lecturing on digital heritage and oceanic studies in the Anthropology Department. Her research focuses on cultural heritage conservation, computational photography and indigenous agency. She completed her PhD in 2018 in digital heritage at UCSC on the 3D documentation of a Maori meetinghouse, currently at the Museum of New Zealand, Te Papa.

Julia Flanders is Professor of the Practice in English and Director of the Digital Scholarship Group in the Northeastern University Library. She also directs the Women Writers Project and serves as editor in chief of *Digital Humanities Quarterly*. She is the co-editor, with Neil Fraistat, of the *Cambridge Companion to Textual Scholarship* (Cambridge University Press, 2013), and the co-editor, with Fotis Jannidis, of *The Shape of Data in Digital Humanities* (Routledge, 2019).

Arapata Hakiwai shares the strategic leadership of Te Papa as Kaihautū. His leadership encompasses the Iwi Relationship Programme, the Karanga Aotearoa Repatriation Programme, iwi in residence, and the Rongomaraeroa marae. During his 20 years in the museum sector he has been involved in the repatriation of Māori and Moriori kōiwi tangata. He currently leads a worldwide research project to identify and create a global digital database of Taonga Māori and Moriori in museums and galleries.

Karl Johnstone is the owner of Haumi (NZ) Ltd, a specialist cultural development business developing projects of national and international significance in partnership with a network of organisations. He has previously worked at Te Papa and was director of the New Zealand Māori Arts and Crafts Institute. In his perpetuation of Māori arts and culture, he considers the interface of tikanga and technology to be a critical area to further unlock Māori potential and expand opportunities into the future.

Sally-Beth MacLean is Director of Research/General Editor of the Records of Early English Drama and Professor Emerita of English, University of Toronto. She is co-author of *The Queen's Men and Their Plays* (1998) and *Lord Strange's Men and Their Plays* (2014). She has directed the development of REED's Patrons and Performances and Early Modern London Theatres websites, and most recently REED Online, the portal for REED's digital editions.

Willard McCarty is Professor Emeritus, King's College London; Editor of *Interdisciplinary Science Reviews* (2008–) and the online seminar *Humanist* (1987–); and with G.E.R. Lloyd and Aparecida Vilaça co-organiser of the workshop series 'Science in the Forest, Science in the Past' (Cambridge, 2017–). His current book project is a historical, anthropological and philosophical study of the relation between digital computing and the human sciences. See www.mccarty.org.uk.

Jan Christoph Meister was Professor of Digital Humanities and German Literature at the University of Hamburg, Germany until his retirement in 2020. He has been active in humanities computing and digital humanities since 1990 and served as Chair and Exec member in various digital humanities organisations, including the European Association for Digital Humanities (EADH), the Alliance of Digital Humanities Organizations (ADHO) and Digital Humanities im deutschsprachigen Raum (DHd). His digital humanities research focuses on text analytics and markup; in this context he and his team have developed and maintained the web service CATMA since 2008.

Janet Nelson is Professor Emerita of Medieval History at King's College London. She has published extensively on early medieval Europe, including Anglo-Saxon England. Her research focus has been on kingship, government and political ideas, on religion and ritual, and increasingly on women and gender. She is currently Co-Investigator on the AHRC-funded *Making of Charlemagne's Europe* project. She co-directed with Simon Keynes (Cambridge) and Stephen Baxter (KCL) the AHRC-funded project *Prosopography of Anglo-Saxon England* (PASE and PASE2).

Julianne Nyhan is Professor of Humanities Data Science and Methodology at Technische Universität Darmstadt. Until 2022 she was Professor of Digital Humanities at UCL and Director of the UCL Centre for Digital Humanities. She is the Principal Investigator of the AHRC Towards a National Collection Discovery Project *The Sloane Lab: Looking back to build future shared collections*. She has published widely on the history of digital humanities, including *One Origin of Digital Humanities: Fr Roberto Busa in his own words* (2019).

Geoffrey Rockwell is Professor of Philosophy and Humanities Computing at the University of Alberta, Canada. He is currently Director of the Kule Institute for Advanced Study. Geoffrey has published on textual visualisation and analysis, and computing in the humanities including a book for the MIT Press, *Hermeneutica: Computer-assisted interpretation in the humanities* (2016). He is a co-developer of Voyant Tools and leads the TAPoR project documenting text tools.

Charlotte Roueché is Professor Emeritus of Digital Hellenic Studies at King's College London. Charlotte works on texts – inscribed or in manuscripts – from the Roman, late Antique and Byzantine periods. She is particularly interested in the interface between digital humanities and classical and byzantine studies, exploring how digital tools and digital publication can be used to break down barriers between disciplines, and between scholars across the world.

James Smithies is Professor of Digital Humanities in the Department of Digital Humanities, King's College London. He was previously founding director of King's Digital Lab. Before working at King's, James worked at the University of Canterbury (New Zealand) as Senior Lecturer in Digital Humanities. He has also worked as a technical editor, business analyst and project manager. His approach to digital humanities is presented in *The Digital Humanities and the Digital Modern* (2017).

Manfred Thaller was born in Austria in 1950. He holds a PhD in modern history from the University of Graz (1975) and a postdoctoral degree in social studies from the Institute for Advanced Studies, Vienna (1978). He was Professor of Historical Computer Science at the University of Bergen from 1995 to 2000. Until his retirement in 2015 Manfred held a professorship for Humanities Computer Science at the University of Köln.

Joanna Tucker is Lecturer in History at the University of Glasgow. Her research focuses on approaches to medieval charters and cartulary manuscripts, especially developing a new methodology for analysing scribes and their work in *Reading and Shaping Medieval Cartularies: Multi-scribe manuscripts and their patterns of growth* (2020). She has engaged in digital humanities approaches to manuscripts and texts as Co-Director of www.modelsofauthority.ac.uk and Co-Investigator on the research network *A Digital Framework for the Medieval Gaelic World* (AHRC-IRC 2020–2021).

List of figures and table

Where no source is provided, these are author images.

Figures

1.1	TACT's KWIC display showing the use of *'moon'* in *A Midsummer Night's Dream*	18
1.2	Correspondence Analysis: dimensions 1 and 2 of words in Hume *Dialogues*	22
1.3	An entity relationship diagram for PASE	30
1.4	PASE, Cenburg 1: an Abbess, found through the *Office* facet	36
1.5	*Pliny* in operation	41
4.1	RSE team, data, models and systems are entangled with each other. Concentric circles denote co-constitution as opposite to exogenous relations. The socio-technical system is multilayered	82
4.2	KDL solution development architecture by Brian Maher, Tiffany Ong, Miguel Vieira and Tim Watts	84
4.3	KDL core development stack by KDL solution development team	85
4.4	Integration of KDL SDLC with the lab operational methods by Tiffany Ong (based on Smithies and Ciula 2020, fig. 3)	97
4.5	Models mediate and bridge team expertise, data and technical systems. Models are of different kinds and produced in different phases of the SDLC as part of the team's processes and methods	98
9.1	The markup loop (cf. Buzzetti and McGann 2006, 68)	200
9.2	The conversational cycle (see Parker-Rhodes 1978, 16). Used with permission of the author's estate	202
9.3	The helicoidal cycle (cf. Gardin 1980, 45). From *Graphic Representations of the Periodic System During One Hundred Years* by Edward G. Mazurs. Used with permission of University of Alabama Press	203

9.4 Subjectivity and objectivity in the speech process
(cf. Parker-Rhodes 1978, 16)   205

9.5 Recursiveness of the subjective/objective distinction   206

9.6 Chiastic self-referentiality of the subjective/objective
distinction   206

10.1 Prototypical variants of digital annotation as data
modelling   228

10.2 The three axes of digital text annotation   229

10.3 CATMA's hermeneutic data model   232

10.4 Instance of a rhetorical 'claim' tag with 'Plausibility'
property set to 'medium' and a free-text comment
by the annotator ('to be revisited: priming effect')   235

10.5 Expandable Double Tree visualisation of a keyword
in context in CATMA   237

10.6 *Stereoscope*, a 3DH-compliant prototype that
supports the generation, critique and discursive
organisation of CATMA-generated annotation
and meta-annotation data   240

10.7 VEGA code editor in CATMA 6 (prototype)   240

10.8 CATMA 6 System Architecture   249

11.1 Notes written on a 3x5 paper slip while reading
a book   260

11.2 Notes copied from a digitised article into NoteCards   260

11.3 Printed notes cut into 3x5 slips   261

11.4 Slips sorted and gathered into thematic groups   261

11.5 Transcription of groups onto pages   262

11.6 Transcribed notes physically reorganised,
photocopied and printed   263

13.1 Rembrandt's *Philosopher in Meditation*   277

13.2 Spyral notebook from the Art of Literary Text
Analysis series   283

13.3 Mathematica notebook   284

13.4 Voyant Export panel   285

13.5 Engraving of the *Philosopher in Meditation*
by Devilliers l'aîné after Rembrandt (1814)   286

Table

7.1 Roles and their characteristic metaknowledge
and skills   154

Introduction:
On making in the digital humanities
Julianne Nyhan and Geoffrey Rockwell

John Bradley and the scholarship of digital humanities development

The making of digital scholarly artefacts has distinguished the digital humanities since Father Busa decided to use information processing technology as an alternative way to make concordances in the late 1940s (Jones 2016; Nyhan and Passarotti 2019). One story we tell about the digital humanities is that it is a field that values practices of making digital artefacts as scholarship. These artefacts might be, inter alia, scholarly digital editions, historical databases, tools for analysing a text or 3D models of cultural heritage artefacts (Rockwell 2011). Though the digital resources that digital humanities makes have global reach, they are invariably made in situated contexts (Hauswedell et al. 2020) by teams of individuals that include both traditionally trained scholars and computing professionals (Nyhan and Flinn 2016).

Yet we rarely hear from these hybrid teams about the messy business of making together. For all of digital humanities' attention to the artefacts it makes, and its computational techniques of making, it has given less attention to the processes, actors, ecologies, histories and ideologies of making. This volume presents chapters on the practices of making in the digital humanities organised around and inspired by the interdisciplinary career of John Bradley. This volume is not a traditional *festschrift* in the sense of a collection about Bradley; it is a feast or celebration made up of essays about the type of modelling and software development that epitomises John Bradley's life's work. We begin by setting out some of the most salient understandings of making, and its contexts, that informed our approach to this volume. We continue by reflecting on the particular contributions to understandings of making included in this volume's chapters and we close by reflecting on the career of John Bradley, maker and pioneer of digital humanities.

Why making?

The field of inquiry called digital humanities, which sits at the intersection of computing and the humanities, has gone from strength to strength in recent years. There have been many attempts to define this field (Terras et al. 2013). One story that has consistently been told is that digital humanities is a field of practices that involve making digital artefacts as scholarly interventions on questions of interest to humanists. Making – used here in the sense of an activity that creates new knowledge, interpretations and/or new questions through the process of building in its widest sense, and which is not limited to the type of building that is synonymous with, for example, maker spaces – is an activity that is both central to and distinctive of digital humanities and humanities computing, as it was known in the last millennium. Initially, with devices like electromechanical accounting machines (Roberto Busa), early digital computers (John W. Ellison) and even pen and paper (Josephine Miles), early pioneers interfolded algorithmic and humanistic thinking and action to make humanities research tools, like concordances, in new ways, and to devise new methods, like quantitative analysis of poetry, remaking texts to analyse them in new ways (Burton 1981; Oakman 1980; Buurma and Heffernan 2018). Today, the continued relevance and expanded breadth of making's arena of operation is suggested by analyses of 'the relationship of humanities and technology as a tool, a study object, an expressive medium, an experimental laboratory, and an activist venue' (Thomson Klein 2017, drawing on Svensson 2010). Through making, the digital humanities have engaged in, for example, collaborations across disciplinary and institutional boundaries (Deegan and McCarty 2012), participated in projects that entwine physical and digital computing, humanistic fabrication and the study of history (Elliott et al. 2012; Boeva et al. 2017); and participated in a recent turn towards 'critical making' (Resch et al. 2018). So too, making continues to feature in debates about digital humanities' disciplinary identity and the modalities of scholarship and communication that it values, as suggested by the long-running controversy over the place of 'hack and yack' in digital humanities (Nowviskie 2016; Liu 2012).

For all this, Thomson Klein reminds us that making has sometimes been dismissed as a purely mechanical activity (Thomson Klein 2017), as a predilection that testifies to the digital humanities flight from theory and interpretation (Kirsch 2014). Not only has this been refuted by, for example, Rockwell and Sinclair, who have elaborated and theorised text analysis tools as hermeneutic interventions (Rockwell and Sinclair 2016; also Galey and Ruecker 2010), but enriched understandings are also emerging of how making can alert us to the complexities of the digital itself and the computational infrastructures and systems on which the digital humanities is built.

Digital artefacts and systems have been conceptualised as, among other things, sites of assemblage (Thylstrup 2018) where labour, infrastructure, affect, funding, ideology and more converge in configurations that are not always detectable on the surface level of the interface. Digital artefacts are created through often occluded technical workflows, collaborative teams, ethical decisions, critical and imaginative interventions and the varying cultural contexts and histories that underpin and support them (Fyfe 2016). Because those processual layers are often not manifested in the interface that appears on the silicone screens of our devices, they can be assumed not to exist (Galey and Ruecker 2010). The consequence of this invisibility can be the false impression that digital collections, for example, 'have not only been protected from editorial intervention, but may even function outside traditional infrastructures of production' (Mak 2014, 1520).

So too, the digital infrastructures with which the digital humanities makes, mediates and disseminates artefacts are increasingly understood to partake of, and give rise to, deeply problematic social asymmetries and inequalities. These include the devalued labour that underpins dominant areas of the world wide web, like social media content moderation (Roberts 2019), the economies of exploitation that operate through platform capitalism (Zuboff 2019) and the environmental, individual and societal damage of computing (Noble 2019).

As such, the complexities of making in the digital humanities are in the process of being better understood. Hackneyed rejoinders that 'the computer is just a tool' are being problematised with theorisations of making that show how it can be implicated in acts of liberation and oppression, creativity and constriction, and thinking and doing (Losh and Wernimont 2018; Risam et al. 2021; Risam 2018). Making in the digital humanities is increasingly understood to be a rich, complex and sometimes even dark process, that can be used to create or imagine lost and new worlds, to sometimes reamplifying the worst tendencies of the digitally mediated world we already have, as well as offer new spaces for the inclusion and agency of communities and individuals previously excluded.

This volume accordingly positions making as a category of analysis and discussion because it is a core and longstanding activity of the digital humanities that functions as a lens through which to explore many pressing questions of the wider field, including its interrelationship with the humanities, while navigating dimensions that range from the individual contribution to the large-scale project. In this volume we seek to contribute to ongoing conversations with chapters from emerging, established and retired scholars who can offer rich and situated insights into the processes and entanglements of making in the digital humanities and digital cultural heritage.

In this set of essays from scholars who have worked in hybrid teams and who can offer situated, self-reflective perspectives on the praxis of modelling and the development of scholarly work in the digital humanities, we learn more of the cultural, technical, critical, human and historical contexts that shape digital humanities and its praxis- and data-led research and uncover more about the many processes that give rise to digital humanities artefacts. Self-reflection is to be expected in an emerging field; one would expect the digital humanities to have to explain its status and relationship to parent disciplines both as a way of negotiating what the field is (and is not) and as a way of legitimising itself. What is interesting is the different forms these reflections take in this volume, from technical reflections about how to best use computing for a particular task, to the more critical reflections on the very nature of making, and, in turn, digital humanities. That is not to say that other types of reflections are not warranted; it is simply to offer through this volume a space for reflections on the praxis of digital projects. Nor is it to say that these contributions are not theoretical; rather it is to say that the projects focalised in this volume are themselves part of what bears theory including reflection. From this volume, the following perspectives on making emerge.

1. Projects have primacy: This volume gathers many reflections that are grounded in particular projects, including *Prosopography of the Byzantine World*; *Prosopography of Anglo Saxon England*; *Clergy of the Church of England Database*; *People of Medieval Scotland*; the *Digital Repository of Te Hau-Ki-Turanga Data*; the *Julfa Cemetery Digital Repatriation Project*; *Sudan Memory* project; *Records of Early English Drama* (REED) project; and CATMA. Making in the digital humanities, as in many other fields, is often conceived as something that takes place in a project. Thus, the project has primacy in the *poiesis* of the digital humanities. Yet the unit of a project is at once both distinct from the wider discipline and constitutive of it.

A project, unlike a discipline, should have an identifiable start, an articulated goal, which includes that which will be made, and a projected end. The end marks a transition in making and often leads to the beginning of a follow-on project – 'project 2.0'. A discipline like the digital humanities, by contrast, should be capable of adapting and maintaining itself through time in the training of 'disciples' or students. Disciplines should be capable of *autopoiesis* or self-creation and self-maintenance. The connection is that, paradoxically, this ongoing self-making often takes place through time-limited projects. Projects come and go in a healthy discipline and this volume is partly about the launching and pacing of projects. It is about the imagining, care and repair of the objects of making so that they can come and go in ways that advance our knowledge. Perhaps the most direct engagement with this idea in this volume is Ciula and Smithies' chapter, which sets out the technical, financial and social pathways towards the sustainability and archiving of projects that have been devised by King's Digital Lab (KDL).

The other chapters brought together here can also be understood as a dialogue on the sustainability and impact of the digital humanities project. Those applying computing technology to research challenges in the humanities have had to struggle not only *with* the machines, but also *for* recognition in the humanities if their work is to contribute to the humanities. Digital humanists have had to both do the work and convince their humanities peers that this was work worth doing, because it rarely resulted in anything like a book. Thus, the digital humanities, or humanities computing, has a tradition of reflecting back on what it was doing in order to justify itself to fields that are anchored in discourse and that primarily value publication practices. This is evinced by, among others, Thaller's chapter, which finds that databases have still not made the inroads into historical studies that one might have expected, and which suggests attention to the modelling of the factoid as a way to remedy this.

2. Making involves people: The making of digital artefacts, especially complex ones, takes many skills which range from grant writing to content expertise, to programming, to infrastructure support, to interface-design and on to training and technical writing. It is rare indeed to find a project imagined, developed, run and communicated by only one person, no matter how broad their skills. This is in part because digital humanities projects involve not only the novel design of content, but also the development of the means of distribution. You are not just writing a new kind of book, you are also building a publishing tool and associated infrastructure.

For this reason, most projects are developed by teams that involve people trained in different traditions who have to communicate across their disciplines. For example, it is common for digital humanities projects to bring together 'content specialists' trained in a humanities discipline and 'developers' trained in computing (science or engineering). This dialogue has been a source of interdisciplinary reflection in the field itself, and in this collection we see such collaborations across disciplines. If digital humanities (DH) is an 'interdiscipline', it is so partly in the sense that it is a space where the ideas of computing, the arts and the humanities intermingle. This space tries to be inclusive of different disciplines in ways that support innovation.

The challenges of creating and maintaining digital scholarly artefacts has also led to the emergence of the hybrid DH specialist who can bridge relevant disciplines. These people do not fit nicely into traditional departments, which is why they are often in 'alternative-academic' positions.[1] Ciula and Smithies' chapter in this volume evokes a sense of both the mystery and the independence that can be associated with these positions, held by people like John Bradley. They require a 'type of expert – consciously not a humanist, nor a technical support professional – who works closely with academics but retains a separate identity and an awareness that they inhabit different career paths', thus evoking the negotiations that are also crucial to the digital humanities. John Bradley and many of the other authors in this collection, such as Rockwell, were in alternative positions at one time or another. They and many others worked in 'centres', which remained for many years the most prominent institutional instantiations of the digital humanities (Nyhan and Flinn 2016).

Flanders' contribution to this volume reflects on the ways that individuals, instruments, modes of knowledge production and modes of action are interwoven to make digital humanities centres:

> unpick[ing] the relationship between the visible 'jobs' (formal employment categories within an institution), 'roles' (functional spaces of action within a working organisation), 'skills' (the actual competencies carried by specific individuals), and 'tools' (the implements through which those competencies are exercised in the course of actual quotidian work).

This collection recognises the importance of many voices and welcomes perspectives from those who have faculty responsibilities and from those in other types of DH positions. Julia Flanders' chapter reflects on the professional roles involved in projects and the skills and knowledge expected of different roles.

When reading the chapters assembled in this volume, such as that of Broun and Tucker, one is struck by the references they contain to the many people who were and are involved in making and maintaining. Those individuals include people who work directly on and with the computer. They can also include the individuals and communities for whom the objects being modelled in digital humanities projects are 'integral to their identity and heritage', as Hakiwai, Johnstone and Ferguson's chapter explores. Indeed, in their chapter the depth of those interrelationships, between computing, cultural heritage objects, culture, identity and memory is exemplified. Hakiwai, Johnstone and Ferguson's chapter powerfully evokes the significance of such interrelationships in the course of problematising digital repatriation projects, showing how those interrelationships can go beyond the individuals who work directly on digital humanities projects themselves and reach individuals for whom the objects at the centre of those projects are connected with questions of identity, heritage and memory.

Nyhan's chapter turns the lens back to the teams of staff who have worked on digital humanities projects directly. She argues that few of the individuals who actually made the digital humanities work on a day-to-day basis have been given detailed attention in the historiography of the field. She argues that more critical and detailed histories of the origins and development of the often overlooked and devalued role of the 'techie' in the digital humanities is needed to reverse engineer knowledge-making in the digital humanities and to interrogate some of the power dynamics that have shaped the development of the field.

3. **Making shifts praxis:** This collection raises important issues about what making is in the digital humanities and its relationship to theory in the humanities. In this collection we take the view that making is also a way of expressing and testing theories in the humanities. Many of the papers here describe how theories or models of humanities phenomena led to and tested design decisions. Meister, for example, moves from theories of interpretation to the design of CATMA. By its very nature, a collection of essays is more 'yack' than 'hack', but in this case it is yack about hack, or reflection on making and prototyping – an important part of any engagement between the humanities and computing that integrates traditions.

Another important contribution of the collection is to confront what this shift in praxis means for the humanities and other disciplines. What the chapters in this collection have in common is the experience of creation and ongoing maintenance though constant reflection on and redesign of time-limited projects. We can say that projects as imagined and maintained are the cross-threads in the weft of the digital humanities. Many are announced but not really launched. Many reinvent themselves, adapting to grant opportunities. Others languish, forgotten by the discipline. Yet others are cared for and repaired. Some are even recovered later as a way of understanding our history. This collection therefore looks not only at the starts or *principi* of projects, but also at their care, repair and return. It does this in order to benefit those working on their own projects: we look at the ways projects reach across boundaries to connect with the challenges of the humanities, the warp of the field woven.

MacLean's chapter looks at how a long-running project, REED (Records of Early English Drama), is shifting from print volumes as outcomes to a prosopographical database. An important part of this shift is the building and evaluation of a prototype developed with John Bradley. Broun and Tucker's chapter reflects on John Bradley's role in designing the *People of Medieval Scotland* database (PoMS) and on how the resource 'could be seen to exemplify a form of historical enquiry which is active and personal, and is open to different kinds of user, to a greater or lesser extent'.

4. Making is collaborative and more than programming: The jumping-off point of Bradley's chapter is that the digital humanities has usefully been conceptualised as an inclusive 'big tent' that has always welcomed different types of contributions (Bianco 2012). They include all sorts of making, from the marking up of electronic texts, to the modelling of phenomena, to developing tools, to administering projects. Even writing papers and theorising in discourse is a making especially useful in the reflection that characterises DH. What matters in the digital humanities is the breadth of possible contributions through making, and recognition that it is not discourse alone that is scholarship.

As mentioned above, digital humanities projects tend to be collaborative and involve teams with different skills. DH has therefore had to adapt tools and create sites for communication from Humanist (the discussion group) to the DH conference. Flanders connects her discussion of roles and skills to the issue of tools, including the tools needed by different roles to support projects, such as administrative tools or communications tools. She points out how a tool can be a method or even an irritant that provokes discussion in a collaboration.

Reflection on collaboration has been especially important to DH, especially collaboration across disciplines and across roles like faculty and library (Deegan and McCarty 2012). We have had to talk about and build for collaboration in order to find ways to make it work. Many of the contributions in this collection are multi-authored, thus reflecting the praxis of collaboration and reflecting on collaboration. And yet, collaborative ownership of the resource created in the process of making cannot and should not be assumed.

5. Making involves maintaining: Digital resources need to be maintained in ways that print resources do not. Where we have an extensive infrastructure of people, publishers, archives and libraries that circulate and maintain print resources, DH has engaged in experimenting with new forms of infrastructure to sustain digital scholarship. Thus, sustainability has become an important issue for DH, especially after many early centres and associated projects began to disappear. While some projects imagine themselves as developing prototypes that need not be sustained as long as the ideas are in circulation (Galey and Ruecker 2010), others have had to develop sustainability strategies. Such strategies have then become a subject of discussion, as has the idea and importance of care and carework (Klein 2015). Further to this, Ciula and Smithies outline the numerous digital resources that have been developed at King's College London from c.1997–2016, with special emphasis on those resources to which John Bradley contributed, and reflect on the challenges and gains of their maintenance and care.

6. Making takes infrastructure: Both the creation of digital resources and especially their maintenance takes infrastructure, and the humanities have not, until recently, had access to computing infrastructure to support the ongoing creation and maintenance of digital things like software. We were supposed to be monk-like scholars who just need a good library and a quiet office. Historically, the absence of DH research and learning infrastructure led to the creation of humanities computing centres in faculties and libraries that could provide centralised support and promote best practices. The infrastructure needed now goes beyond the obvious network and server infrastructure required for an online resource to be available and we have found that what we need is often a need shared across disciplines. Willard McCarty's reflections on note-taking is an example of a need that goes beyond the humanities, and John Bradley's discussion of *Pliny*, a note-taking tool, is an example of how software can act as a way of thinking through such a need. Now making has gone beyond text resources and text tools to include creative making across the arts, which calls for labs where one can create new media works or use 3D printers to make physical prototypes.

Interestingly, many of the digital projects described in this collection are of the sort that become infrastructure themselves for further research. Jan Christoph Meister's chapter on CATMA talks about how influential John Bradley's earlier text analysis tool, TACT (Text Analysis and Concording Tool), has been. Bradley likewise discusses TACT in his chapter. CATMA reimplemented many of the ideas of TACT, including support for the COCOA markup language that pre-dates XML, and CATMA in turn supports a hermeneutic approach to markup and analysis. CATMA is now infrastructure for other projects closely interpreting texts with exploratory markup. Likewise Voyant, whose development is described in Rockwell's chapter, has become infrastructure for thousands of users. The paradigm is not that of scientific progress which builds on earlier work, but closer to a dialogue of primary and secondary sources where tools make projects possible. What many of the digital humanists in this collection describe is the creation of digital resources and tools which others can use as 'editions' of primary sources. Reflecting on the maintenance of such resources has in DH led to reflection on research infrastructure in general.

7. Making is neither neutral nor without history: Each project discussed in this book has its own history of making. Projects like Voyant, described in Rockwell's chapter on making with Stéfan Sinclair, grew out of a particular approach to making a tool through experiments. But we also need to confront how making is shaped by complex and sometimes problematic historical entanglements, like the colonial and imperial origins of the western museum and the information biases and asymmetries that have shaped its collections and collection records. As explored in Hakiwai, Johnstone and Ferguson's chapter, the digital repatriation of objects extracted from indigenous people by museums across the globe opens fundamental questions about '[i]ndigenous cultural data sovereignty . . . [and] the multifaceted legal and ethical dimensions of data storage, ownership, access and consent to intellectual property rights and practical considerations regarding how data are used in the context of research, policy and practice'.

8. Making takes change: Given that digital resources are typically built on a stack of computing infrastructure, DH is particularly sensitive to changes in that underlying computing. DH takes advantage of, adapts and transforms new solutions in computing, but it is also potentially distracted by fashions in computing that may or may not survive and be genuinely useful to computing. How many humanists have started blogs that now are moribund? Further, the challenges of sustaining resources built on an unstable stack of rapidly changing infrastructure are significant. Without a written record of manuals, project reports, journals and books like this one we would have few documentary sources to draw on when writing histories of the field. Precious few projects survive long after the last grant funding is spent. Few projects can afford to re-implement when the software platform is outdated. It is partly for this reason that projects like the Text Encoding Initiative (tei-c.org) focused on open and sustainable guidelines for text encoding. It is also in this context that Meister's chapter can be read as a discussion of resistance to change, in particular resistance to developments in standoff markup.

Why John Bradley?

So many of the chapters included in this volume converse with the scholarship and making of John Bradley. As a scholar active at the crossroads of computing and the humanities since the 1970s, Bradley is truly one of the pioneers of contemporary digital humanities. John's career spanned decades and continents. Some of his most widely recognised work includes leading the development of the Text Analysis Computing Tools (TACT) system while at the University of Toronto. TACT was released at the first joint ACH-ALLC conference in Toronto in 1989 (the conference that became the DH conference with the formation of the Alliance of Digital Humanities Organisations). It was one of the best of a new breed of usable text analysis environments that enabled researchers to study electronic texts on their PCs. Developed for IBM PCs, it nonetheless incorporated ideas drawn from the then new Graphical User Interface (GUI) of the Apple Macintosh.

Throughout his career Bradley continued to think through software design, development and how humanists might think, and he later developed a personal note management system called *Pliny*, which in 2008 was awarded an Andrew W. Mellon foundation Technology Collaboration award (MATC). He has also been a collaborator and contributor to countless projects in Europe and North America, ranging in subject from visualisation to music to history. He focused on issues that arise from the modelling, collecting and presenting of highly structured data and text from complex humanities sources.

Digital technologies are often presented as prototypes that are full of promise, turning our attention to a future. This collection often looks at the past of a field that is now being taken to task as a discipline. The digital humanities as a field is no longer new and John Bradley has been developing working systems for over 30 years. But John Bradley not only made things, he also reflected as a master maker on the making with others. He was 'il miglior fabbro' or 'the better craftsman', to borrow T.S. Eliot's dedication from *The Waste Land,* which in turn is borrowed from Dante's *The Divine Comedy*.

Following Bradley's lead, this collection contributes to a reflective turn in the digital humanities as we attempt to use the perspectives of the humanities to reflect on our computing. This volume fills a gap in our understanding of projects and digital humanities craft by focalising the interwoven layers of human and technological textures that constitute our disciplinary past. To do this the collection has assembled an international group of experienced scholars in the digital humanities to reflect on various forms of *making* precisely because John Bradley's work is fundamentally characterised by reflection on the practices of making. These essays are individually important, but together provide a very human view on what it is to do digital humanities, and on what it is to *make* the digital humanities.

Note

1. #Alt-Academy: http://mediacommons.org/alt-ac/ (accessed 6 September 2022).

References

Bianco, Jamie 'Skye'. 2012. 'This Digital Humanities which Is Not One'. In *Debates in the Digital Humanities*, edited by Matthew K. Gold, 96–113. Minneapolis, MN: University of Minnesota Press.

Boeva, Yana, Devon Elliott, Edward Jones-Imhotep, Shezan Muhammedi and William J. Turkel. 2017. 'Doing History by Reverse Engineering Electronic Devices'. In *Making Things and Drawing Boundaries: Experiments in the digital humanities*, edited by Jentery Sayers, 163–76. Minneapolis, MN: University of Minnesota Press.

Burton, D.M. 1981. 'Automated Concordances and Word Indexes: The fifties', *Computers and the Humanities* 15(1): 1–14.

Buurma, R.S. and L. Heffernan. 2018. 'Search and Replace: Josephine Miles and the origins of distant reading', *Modernism/Modernity* 3(1). Accessed 5 September 2022.

Deegan, M. and W. McCarty (eds). 2012. *Collaborative Research in the Digital Humanities*. Farnham: Ashgate.

Elliott, Devon, Robert MacDougall and William J. Turkel. 2012. 'New Old Things: Fabrication, physical computing, and experiment in historical practice', *Canadian Journal of Communication* 37: 121–8.

Fyfe, Paul. 2016. 'An Archaeology of Victorian Newspapers', *Victorian Periodicals Review* 49: 546–77.

Galey, A. and S. Ruecker. 2010. 'How a Prototype Argues', *Literary and Linguistic Computing* 25(4): 405–24.

Hauswedell, Tessa, Julianne Nyhan, M.H. Beals, Melissa Terras and Emily Bell. 2020. 'Of Global Reach Yet of Situated Contexts: An examination of the implicit and explicit selection criteria that shape digital archives of historical newspapers', *Archival Science* 20: 139–65.

Jones, S.E. 2016. *Roberto Busa, S. J., and the Emergence of Humanities Computing: The priest and the punched cards*. New York: Routledge.

Kirsch, Adam. 2014. 'Technology is Taking Over English Departments', *The New Republic*, 2 May. Accessed 5 September 2022. https://newrepublic.com/article/117428/limits-digital-humanities-adam-kirsch

Klein, L. 2015. 'The Carework and Codework of the Digital Humanities', *The Digital Antiquarian 2015*. Republished in *Digital Humanities Now*. Accessed 5 September 2022. http://digitalhumanitiesnow.org/2015/06/editors-choice-the-carework-and-codework-of-the-digital-humanities-lauren-klein/

Liu, Alan. 2012. 'Where is Cultural Criticism in the Digital Humanities?'. In *Debates in the Digital Humanities*, edited by Matthew K. Gold, 490–509. Minneapolis, MN: University of Minnesota Press.

Losh, Elizabeth M. and Jacqueline Wernimont (eds). 2018. *Bodies of Information: Intersectional feminism and digital humanities*. Minneapolis, MN: University of Minnesota Press.

Mak, B. 2014. 'Archaeology of a Digitization', *Journal of the Association for Information Science and Technology* 65: 1515–1526. https://doi.org/10.1002/asi.23061

Noble, S.U. 2019. 'Toward a Critical Black Digital Humanities'. In *Debates in the Digital Humanities*, edited by Matthew K. Gold and Lauren F. Klein, 27–35. Minneapolis, MN: University of Minnesota Press.

Nowviskie, B. 2016. 'On the Origin of "Hack" and "Yack"'. In *Debates in the Digital Humanities 2016*, edited by Matthew K. Gold and Lauren F. Klein, 66–70. Minneapolis, MN: University of Minnesota Press.

Nyhan, Julianne and Andrew Flinn. 2016. *Computation and the Humanities: Towards an oral history of digital humanities*. Cham, Switzerland: Springer.

Nyhan, Julianne and Marco Passarotti (eds). 2019. *One Origin of Digital Humanities: Fr Roberto Busa in his own words*. Cham, Switzerland: Springer Nature.

Oakman, Robert L. 1980. *Computer Methods for Literary Research*. Columbia, SC: University of South Carolina Press.

Resch, Gabby, Dan Southwick, Isaac Record and Matt Ratto. 2018. 'Thinking as Handwork: Critical making with humanistic concerns'. In *Making Things and Drawing Boundaries: Experiments in the digital humanities*, edited by Jentery Sayers, 149–61. Minneapolis, MN: University of Minnesota Press.

Risam, Roopika. 2018. *New Digital Worlds: Postcolonial digital humanities in theory, praxis and pedagogy*. Evanston, IL: Northwestern University Press.

Risam, Roopika and Kelly Baker Josephs. 2021. *The Digital Black Atlantic*. Minneapolis, MN: University of Minnesota Press.

Roberts, Sarah T. 2019. *Behind the Screen: Content moderation in the shadows of social media*. New Haven, CT: Yale University Press.

Rockwell, Geoffrey. 2011. 'On the Evaluation of Digital Media as Scholarship', *Profession* 2011: 152–68.

Rockwell, Geoffrey and Stéfan Sinclair. 2016. *Hermeneutica: Computer-assisted interpretation in the humanities*. Cambridge, MA: MIT Press.

Svensson, Patrik. 2010. 'The Landscape of Digital Humanities', *DHQ: Digital Humanities Quarterly: The Landscape of Digital Humanities* 4:1.

Terras, Melissa M., Julianne Nyhan and Edward Vanhoutte (eds). 2013. *Defining Digital Humanities: A reader*. Farnham: Ashgate.

Thompson Klein, Julie. 2017. 'The Boundary Work of Making in Digital Humanities'. In *Debates in the Digital Humanities*, edited by Jentery Sayers, 21–31. Minneapolis, MN: University of Minnesota Press.

Thylstrup, Nanna Bonde. 2018. *The Politics of Mass Digitization*. Cambridge, MA: MIT Press.

Zuboff, Shoshana. 2019. *The Age of Surveillance Capitalism: The fight for a human future at the new frontier of power: Barack Obama's books of 2019*. London: Profile Books.

1
Four corners of the big tent: a personal journey through the digital humanities

John Bradley

For many years Professor Stanley Fish (the Davidson-Kahn Distinguished University Professor of Humanities and Law at Florida International University at the time of writing) seems to have had it in for the digital humanities. In his piece 'Mind Your P's and B's: The digital humanities and interpretation' (Fish 2012) he claimed that he intended to explore 'how . . . the technologies wielded by digital humanities practitioners either facilitate the work of the humanities, as it has been traditionally understood, or bring about an entirely new conception of what work in the humanities can and should be'; in the end he went on to say: 'But whatever vision of the digital humanities is proclaimed, it will have little place for the likes of me and for the kind of criticism I practice.' In a more recent piece Fish states that digital humanists claim that their field will 'improve our traditional interpretive activities . . . [and] will bring humanities activities in line with the more culturally privileged activities of science and mathematics' (Fish 2018). In his view, the digital humanities is in fact 'an anti-humanistic project . . . [based on] the hope that a machine, unaided by anything but its immense computational powers, can decode texts produced by human beings'.

Fish's thoughts have stimulated considerable push-back from a segment of the digital humanities (DH) community, but some of it contains more heat than light. For me, one of the best responses came from Willard McCarty in *Humanist* (2018), where he claims that although part of Fish's attack on some of the currently prominent parts of the digital humanities is 'right again, painfully so in my opinion', in fact there are other areas of digital humanities research that are both 'quieter' and 'exciting'.

In spite of McCarty's observations, Fish is not the only one to mistake a particular part of the admittedly broad domain of the digital humanities for the whole. His views, and the views of others like him, arise out of the explosion of interest in the methods of Textual Big Data that started in 2008 or thereabouts. Stephen Marche (2012) started his piece in the *Los Angeles Review of Books* with the alarming words 'BIG DATA IS COMING for your books. It's already come for everything else', and went on to challenge any 'big data' model of textual studies by observing that big data methodologies must treat the materials they are working with as data. As a consequence, in his view, the digital humanities' deeper problem is that '[l]iterature cannot meaningfully be treated as data . . . literature is the opposite of data'. Another example: Anthony Mandal's very fine review of what he considers to be important work in the digital humanities for 2017 (Mandal 2018), made in the context of critical and cultural theory, also appears (perhaps understandably, given the context for his review) to focus on certain kinds of activities in the DH (big data, humanity and machines, and 'new inflections' that respond to the challenges these activities represent) and ignore others. There are many other writers who do the same, and many focus on the recent developments that come out of textual big data as if they were the entire field of the digital humanities.

Not everyone in the DH is focused on textual big data in this way, of course. See Klein and Gold's article in *Debates in the Digital Humanities*:

> Along with the digital archives, quantitative analyses, and tool-building projects that once characterized the field, DH now encompasses a wide range of methods and practices: visualizations of large image sets, 3D modelling of historical artefacts, 'born digital' dissertations, hashtag activism and the analysis thereof, alternate reality games, mobile makerspaces, and more. (Klein and Gold 2016)

They go on to observe that 'in what has been called "big tent" DH, it can be difficult to determine with any specificity what, precisely, digital humanities work entails'.

In this chapter I would like to explore a broader range of activities that fit into the digital humanities than that part of DH of which Stanley Fish is apparently aware. Indeed, perhaps I am well suited to drawing attention to various aspects of the digital humanities, since I have worked in it (and its precursor, 'humanities computing') since its relatively early days in the mid-1970s (see Bradley and Nyhan 2017). I was first involved in DH as a part of my work at the University of Toronto from 1978 until

1997, and then I became even more truly centred on the digital humanities when I moved in 1997 to King's College London's Department of Digital Humanities (then the Centre for Computing in the Humanities), directed by Harold Short. Not surprisingly, my job has changed since the 1970s: I started my work in the digital humanities in Toronto as a programmer (although even then I was not someone who wrote code based solely on instruction from others, but someone who engaged sufficiently with the domain in which the code was going to be used to take on some understanding of that as well). By the end of my career at King's I was into the lower-middle range of academia, having been transferred from a non-academic post to an academic one of Senior Lecturer (which at King's is somewhere at the lower end of what in North America would be considered Associate Professor) in 2011. Having in 2015 come out the other end of this career into retirement, I thus find myself writing a kind of valedictory presentation in this paper.

Over these many years, as my work changed in character, I found myself exploring perspectives of what I now consider the digital humanities that sometimes were, and sometimes were not, captured by the 'digital humanities as digitally assisted text analysis' perspective which is the focus of Stanley Fish and others. Indeed, because of these changing connections with DH over the years I have truly been engaged with the DH's 'big tent' as Klein and Gold described it. As a consequence, I would like to present here four corners, let's call them (or perhaps 'perspectives'), of this DH tent that I have been in myself. Furthermore, as well as representing my personal engagement with the DH over the many years of a personal career, I believe they also happen to represent the several different ways that other staff in the Department of Digital Humanities at King's have worked when they believe they are 'doing DH'.

So, what are the four corners? I will label them as:

1. Traditional scholarship about digital things in society
2. Data analysis using digital tools
3. Data representation using digital tools
4. Making digital tools

As you can see, they are arranged here from what is perhaps the most 'conservative' kind of DH work – that which stays closest to traditional academic humanist approaches – to more radical challenges to what research and scholarship can be.

At various points in my career in DH, I have worked in all four of these corners; indeed one of them – making digital tools – twice. I think it is most useful to explore them in the order in which they occurred in my working life since that ordering makes evident the different ways in which I fitted into a digital humanities perspective as my career developed.

COGS and TACT: making digital tools

It is hard today to recall what computing was like in the 1970s. The personal computer was not yet available. Certainly, the University of Toronto's computer centre, where I worked, was focused almost entirely on their IBM 370 mainframe, and although many science and engineering departments had mini computers like the PDP-11, in those days a significant amount of the University of Toronto's academic computing was indeed carried out on this machine. My job, like many others at the computer centre, was to be a go-between from the academic concerns of the user community to the university's mainframe computer. This needed specialist training of the kind I had received to make it work. Although I ended up being associated with the needs of the humanities it is worth noting that I did not come to my post at Toronto from a background in the humanities. I had been trained in computer science, particularly programming.

In the 1970s, with the exception of statistical software such as SPSS and SAS, there was relatively little off-the-shelf commercial or free academic software in use at Toronto's computer centre. The computer centre had tried to make the Oxford Concordance Program (OCP) work for humanists, but had not had much success. As a consequence I was asked to create a concordance generating system, and from this work the concordance program COGS (Concordance Generating System) was born. It was written in IBM's PL/I programming language, ran on the 370 mainframe, and produced only KWIC concordances, but it could handle quite large (for its day) source texts. It was through COGS that a partnership with Toronto's Professor Ian Lancashire first emerged, as well as what was to become an enduring connection with Toronto's Records of Early English Drama (REED) project.

Although in the recent past there has been discussion about whether tool building can, on its own, be considered a 'scholarly act' (see, for instance, Ramsay and Rockwell 2012), at the University of Toronto in the 1970s there was no humanist academic that I knew who took up the task of writing software as part of their academic activities, and certainly no one would have thought of it as scholarly work. Nonetheless, it was recognised that work such as the development of COGS was at least a 'somewhat scholarly' activity. The software needed to serve the interests of its humanities user, and for it to do so, some degree of understanding of what was needed was necessary.

James Feibleman, in his *Philosophy of Tools*, notes that '[a] tool is, so to speak, an objectified idea . . . It is thought in action' (Feibleman 1967, 332). In 1967 Feibleman was not thinking of software as tool here – but his observation that a tool is an objectified idea also applies to software, and it was through this connection that even COGS, with all its limitations, could be considered at least a product of thought – an 'objectified idea' – about some scholarly concerns. With COGS I had my first experience of being thought of as a partner with some of its academic users, even if I was not considered to be in an academic post myself. There is more to say about this issue later in this chapter.

A number of years later I became the main architect and significant programmer, with colleague Lidio Presutti, of TACT (Text Analysis Computing Tools), which has been described as 'a historically important text analysis and retrieval system'.[1] It grew out of a partnership that had been arranged by Ian Lancashire between IBM and the university, which aimed to explore the use of IBM personal computers in a humanities environment. As a consequence, TACT was designed to run in MS-DOS which, at the time, imposed what now would seem amazing constraints. In particular there was the 640K limitation, which was the RAM space made available for software like TACT in which it and its data had to fit. You can see a screen capture of TACT in operation in Figure 1.1.

TACT was first released at the Toronto ALLC/ICCH conference in 1989, and went on to be used for much longer than I had originally

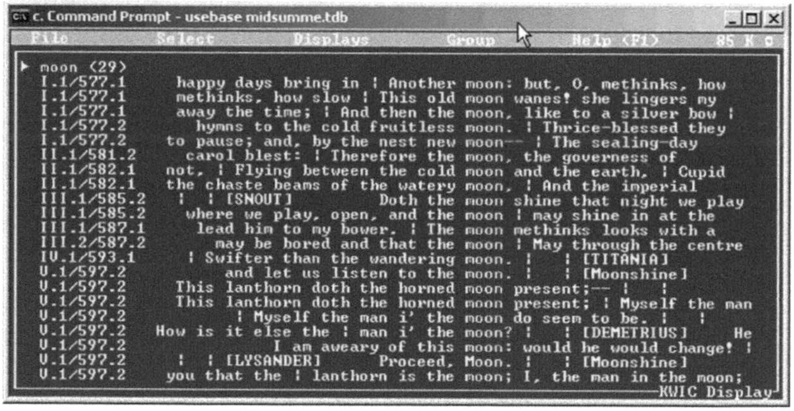

Figure 1.1 TACT's KWIC display showing the use of '*moon*' in *A Midsummer Night's Dream*.

expected: it remained in use by at least a small community of active users until well after the year 2000. During that time TACT had some significant impact on the thinking about what software for what was then called 'text analysis' should look like. A brief article that describes its use in teaching (of Machiavelli's *Il Principe*) can be found in Armstrong 1996. Mark Hawthorne's 1994 article in *Computers and the Humanities* (Hawthorne 1994) gives a more elaborate analysis of the potential for the software to be useful for text analysis work,[2] and there is a brief but interesting description of TACT in Rockwell and Sinclair (2016, 58–60).

Broadly speaking, TACT's functionality came out of my observation of the functionality of software like the Oxford Concordance Package, and John B. Smith's ARRAS. Indeed, from a text analysis perspective, TACT's display capabilities were not in fact substantially advanced over what these pieces of software could do (although Rockwell and Sinclair, who have spent some considerable time carrying out a historical analysis of text analysis systems like TACT, claim that some aspects of TACT's functionality 'has not been surpassed' (Rockwell and Sinclair 2016, 60). What, then, made TACT innovative at its time?

I believe that some part of TACT's innovation came out of the impact of the then emerging personal computer revolution, and the substantial rethinking of human–computer interaction (HCI) that was represented by Apple's Macintosh and by software like the earliest spreadsheets (for DOS machines) that exploited the computer screen's spatial and potentially object-oriented nature. Like these early spreadsheets, TACT was built for the IBM computer's DOS-based screen, which was amazingly limited to 80 by 24 fixed-size characters, but it did provide a user interface that exploited this limited spatial representation through direct interaction.

Thus, with TACT I was aiming to join together much of the functionality of older systems such as ARRAS with the new thinking represented by the Macintosh and the spreadsheet. ARRAS's implementation on a mainframe CMS system, as Rockwell and Sinclair note (Rockwell and Sinclair 2016, 55), allowed for the kind of interaction between user and machine that was like a *conversation*: the user asks for something through a command and ARRAS responds. Then, having seen the response, the user issues another command. TACT's interface was meant to promote not a feeling of *conversation*, but instead one of *exploration*, enabled by the object-oriented, direct manipulation approach. By virtue of being on a personal computer, this direct manipulation kind of interaction that I was beginning to imagine for TACT was something quite different from what pre-existing text analysis software had been able to offer.

Ramsay and Rockwell (2012) speak of text analysis tools as 'telescopes for the mind', and perhaps TACT's attempt to provide an exploration-oriented interface for its text analysis may parallel some of the sense of exploration that the development of the telescope and microscope afforded. The telescope substantially furthered our understanding of astronomy; the microscope furthered our understanding of the life sciences. However, it is important to understand that for these instruments the scientific theory upon which both were based was not the theories within astronomy or the science of life, but on an entirely different field of science: optics. Perhaps in a somewhat similar way, a tool like TACT was successful to the extent that it combined a suitable presentation of the materials of study (involving, therefore, models for representing text) with models that come out of other domains entirely – such as those of human–computer interaction (HCI).

As a consequence of the user-interaction aspect of TACT, it was evident that it needed not only a formal model for the text – what kinds of things were represented about a text and how they interacted; it also needed models for the user interaction too: what kinds of things were represented there on the screen, how did users interact with them, what structures supported this in the software, and how did what the user saw and what s/he did connect to the textual model that had to sit behind everything else? As a developer of TACT, then, my interest came from issues related to models not only for the text, but also for models of the interaction.

From my perspective was TACT development also digital humanities work? Thinking about how to represent text inside TACT seemed to be clearly so, but what about the HCI component of TACT? Discussions with academics at the University of Toronto about the HCI side of TACT did not seem at the time to engage their interest explicitly, although I think that subconsciously, as it were, it had an important effect on how they viewed TACT. Perhaps it is true that new ideas arise from working in an area that involves some interaction between two quite different domains. If that is so, then perhaps it was not only TACT's model of text but also its models for HCI that made TACT more properly an example of DH work.

Using digital tools for research

Way back in the late 1980s and early 1990s at the University of Toronto I found myself working with friend and colleague Geoffrey Rockwell, who was at the time – nominally at least – reporting to me within the Computer Centre. As my involvement in TACT gradually reduced,

Geoffrey and I began to think about what other aspect of computing in the humanities we could explore. Among the various interests that emerged was one of looking at how digital methods could present new kinds of insights about texts that would be relevant to a humanist's perspective. I was also interested in how bits and pieces of TACT code could be reused and reassembled into new mechanisms.[3] Geoffrey was working on his PhD thesis at the time, which was about philosophical dialogue, and as a consequence of this we acquired David Hume's *Dialogues Concerning Natural Religion* in electronic form. What could we do with this through digital humanities techniques?

Various things were explored, and at some point we became interested in Alastair McKinnon's article (1989) in which he used the statistical technique called Correspondence Analysis (CA) to try to locate overarching themes in the work of philosopher Søren Kierkegaard. McKinnon provided a good introduction to the concept of CA and how he applied it to texts in his article, and we used a very similar conceptual approach to look at Hume's *Dialogue* text by creating a multidimensional *profile* for each word in the dialogue which reflected its distribution across the 13 parts of the text, and then giving these collections of 13-dimension numeric data to Michael Greenacre's CA software to distribute these words across a multidimensional space.[4] Like McKinnon with his data from Kierkegaard, we worked to interpret CA's resulting dimensions as possible themes that the words suggested in the text. Some of the result of this interpretation can be found in Bradley and Rockwell (1996, 39–42).

Figure 1.2 shows the projection of the first two (of 13) transformed dimensions produced by the CA application for the words of Hume's *Dialogues*. One way of exploiting the analysis (suggested by McKinnon) is to look at the words at the extremes of each dimension. For dimension 0 they are 'science' and 'generation', for dimension 1 they are 'science' and 'ills'. What themes might these words suggest? We created an online tool for this data, which is the source of Figure 1.2. SIMWEB allowed a user to select, zoom in, and change what spatial dimensions were being projected. One could also click on a word to get a KWIC display of its appearances in the *Dialogues* text.

This work was carried out in the 1990s, but I believe that our CA experiment resonates well with the current interest in big textual data's numerically based techniques, even though it was carried out well before the phenomenon of big textual data had emerged. Back then our work was inspired not only by McKinnon's direct example, but more generally by the whole approach of using statistical, numeric methods to support

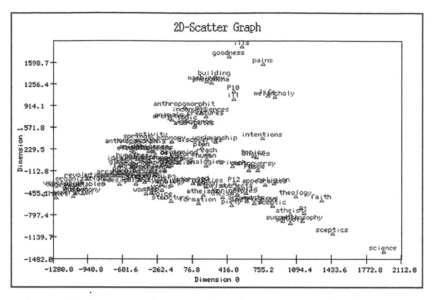

Figure 1.2 Correspondence Analysis: dimensions 1 and 2 of words in Hume *Dialogues*.

critical analysis described in Rosanne G. Potter's article in *Computers and the Humanities* (1988), and then in her influential book *Literary Computing and Literary Criticism* a year later (Potter 1989). Back in the late 1980s, Potter was already observing that 'Literary criticism may be at a crossroads, a moment when vision is extended into scientific areas, not just to ransack them for useful metaphors but' (in our view the most important point) 'to use their ways of seeing in order to see better *what literary critics are interested in seeing*' (Potter 1989, xxix).

Rockwell and Stéfan Sinclair continued work in this area, exploring how the use of digital tools can work to reveal things relevant to literary criticism about texts. Much of this work centred on the development of their remarkable web platform *Voyant Tools*.[5] A recent development is the interesting idea of these tools as 'hermeneutica', described in the book of the same name (Rockwell and Sinclair 2016, 2) as 'small embeddable "toys" that can be woven into essays published online'. They demonstrated in the book's four 'interludes' how this weaving together of results often with even basic text analysis tools can be effective, and thereby illustrated how this 'hermeneutica approach' explores some texts in ways that, as Potter suggested, might interest a literary critic.

Correspondence Analysis is a particular kind of statistical method, and when applied to texts (as McKinnon, and subsequently Rockwell and

I did) was perhaps an example of exactly the kind of thing that Stanley Fish objected to in his 2012 blog entry 'Mind Your P's and B's' that I mentioned earlier. As he states, 'first you run the numbers, and then you see if they prompt an interpretive hypothesis. The method, if it can be called that, is dictated by the capability of the tool.' With CA you indeed first give it the data from the text without assuming in advance what result you are going to get. The analysis is an approach 'that can bring to analytical attention patterns of sameness and difference undetectable by the eye of the human reader' (Fish 2012). In Fish's view, the traditional humanities analytical approach, including his own, is a kind of opposite: 'first the interpretive hypothesis and then the formal pattern, which attains the status of noticeability only because an interpretation already in place is picking it out.' Indeed, his scholar-perception approach seems to be exactly the kind of thing that Potter (1988) is aiming to challenge! She claims that assertions about texts from traditional scholarly methods such as Fish's produce assertions 'based on insight and intuition' which, although 'spectacular as they sometimes were', in the end seemed to be 'acts of sorcery' (Potter 1988, 92). Both Potter and Fish would seem to acknowledge that their two approaches are in a kind of conceptual conflict.

This character of CA – the methodological opposite of that followed by Fish – has been noted by statisticians who are familiar with it as well, although their view of its significance is not as negative as Fish's appears to be. Note, for example, Micheloud's *Correspondence Analysis* (1997), where he describes CA as an 'inductive approach' where the analyst goes 'from the data itself' and uses CA 'to see patterns in the data'. Micheloud labels this approach 'Exploratory Data Analysis' (Micheloud 1997, section 1A). When Micheloud wrote his introduction to CA in 1997 this approach was apparently still a relatively recent development in statistics. More recently, developments out of big data analysis techniques, such as Topic Modelling, work in a similar way. One can apply the Topic Modelling approach to a text structured as a large set of short texts (such as a set of letters in a collection of correspondence) without needing to have an already defined sense of what one is looking for. The mathematical/statistical techniques of Topic Modelling group words according to their pattern of collocation in these short texts, and generate a set of proposed clusters of words that can subsequently be interpreted as possible themes that might appear in the text. One can see an example of this being tried with humanities materials in Blevins 2010, where it was applied to the diary of American historical figure Martha Moore Ballard (1734–1812). Two of the six groupings Blevins shows as the output (with a label provided by Blevins suggesting a possible semantic interpretation of the cluster) give the idea:

- **MIDWIFERY**: birth deld safe morn receivd calld left cleverly pm labour fine reward arivd infant expected recd shee born patient
- **CHURCH**: meeting attended afternoon reverend worship foren mr famely performd vers attend public supper st service lecture discoarst administred supt

I have already mentioned Ramsay and Rockwell's comments about text analysis tools as 'telescopes for the mind', showing us something in a new light (Ramsay and Rockwell 2012, 79). Perhaps that is what is going on here. However, at present at least it is not clear how one can operate this kind of tool in ways that are as convincing to a sceptical viewer (here, a literary critic like, say, Fish) in the way that looking through a telescope became. For at least several hundred years we have been able to trust, to assume even, that what we see through an optical telescope is actually there in nature. But, can we trust what Correspondence Analysis or Topic Modelling is doing to our text? How do we know that the outputs from these techniques are not merely 'artefacts' of the mathematical process that do not, in fact, correspond to a human interpretation of the same text?

Ian Hacking, the well-known philosophy of science scholar, explores essentially the same issue in the context of those powerful scientific tools – the microscope and the telescope – in Hacking 1981, with its provocative title 'Do we see through a microscope?'. In Hacking's view both microscopes and telescopes began to affect scientific thinking before they had a solid theoretical basis regarding how they worked. Galileo's claim that he saw the four moons of Jupiter was made long before the science of optics, which explained how a telescope operated, was fully worked out. Indeed, according to Hacking, Galileo's interpretation is so poorly grounded theoretically that he dares to call Galileo more of a 'con man, not an experimental reasoner' (Hacking 1981, 305). Concerns about whether what one saw corresponded to what was there turned out to be even stronger with the microscope: according to Hacking, early microscopes led to speculation that life was tied up with 'globules' that appeared to be visible. When better glass was available as late as the 1860s, these globules that had seemed apparent disappeared. Hacking claims that it was not until 1873 that one could read in print how a microscope actually worked (Hacking 1981, 315–16). And, as Hacking reminds us, it was not only theories of optics in glass that needed to develop to justify interpretation with a microscope; an understanding was also necessary of how, for instance, dyes work when they stain the object so that its parts become visible. It becomes a non-trivial matter to know how to interpret what one is seeing through a microscope in such a way that one can make a convincing case about what is actually there in the specimen.

I believe we have similar issues with numeric-based digital techniques such as Correspondence Analysis or Topic Modelling when applied to a text. As Hacking reminds us, 'One needs [optical] theory to make a microscope. You do not need theory to use one' (Hacking 1981, 313). This might be so, but the theory is in the background nonetheless. Biological assertions are made, based on a long history of learning by a professional microscope user, about how the microscope itself affects the image we see through the eyepiece. Our digital tools can also produce what might appear to be thought-provoking results, but without a proper understanding of the theoretical basis upon which the results have been generated, how can we know what to trust about them? The issue here is, of course, one of objective solidity.

Although objectivity of observation and deduction is often stated to be one of the pillars of science, it isn't so clear that it operates in the same way in the humanities – particularly in textual criticism. As I mentioned earlier, by introducing numeric methods into textual analysis back in the 1980s it was Potter's aim to introduce approaches into textual criticism that were more objective. However, the use of sophisticated mathematical techniques (such as Topic Modelling) to buttress a literary argument is likely, in fact, to bring subjective interpretation in by the back door. Potter notes (1998, 93) that literary criticism has often been 'enriched by new ideas from related humanistic fields'. She then mockingly quotes John Ellis's label of 'wise eclecticism' for this process: 'a general tendency to believe that if you can compose an interesting argument to support a position, any well-argued assertion is as valid as the next one.' Although she claims that mathematical methods act against this approach by being objectively assessable, I believe that the ungrounded use of complex numerical methods in fact risks exactly this same kind of tendency too.

Building digital resources: highly structured data

My move in 1997 to what was then the Centre for Computing in the Humanities (CCH) at King's College London marked a substantial change in my relationship to humanities computing. Humanities computing had been only one domain under the very broad area of digital

Academic Technology for which I was responsible at the University of Toronto. Furthermore, at Toronto I had worked with the very different needs for computing for the sciences and the professional schools as well as the humanities. In the end, my work as a manager at the University of Toronto became so broad as to become, for me, almost completely devoid of interest. My new post under Harold Short at CCH at King's, in contrast, was intended to focus primarily on the place of computing in the humanities. At King's I was no longer a manager, but for me this was a plus since I was now able to focus close-up on the technical and intellectual issues that came my way. I was able to set up my own Linux computer, learn Perl, explore relational databases, enrich my understanding of the still-emerging WWW – all sorts of engaging things.

As time went on at King's it became evident that much could be achieved by partnering with humanities academics in multi-year funded digital projects, and Harold Short led the way into what became for me one of the most rewarding aspects of my work. The *Prosopography of the Byzantine Empire* (PBE) was already well underway when I joined CCH, where my involvement was centred in the development of a web-based access mechanism for displaying its contents.[6] PBE was the first of a set of more than 20 highly collaborative academic projects in which I was involved over my almost 20 years at King's that combined academic and technical innovation in ways that were stimulated by the potentials of digital/web publication. These included projects such as the *Clergy of the Church of England* database, *People of Medieval Scotland*, *Art of Making in Antiquity*[7] and many others (a few of which shall be mentioned later). Over the almost 20 years, my involvement ranged from being a junior project team member to co-investigator. Time and time again we have been told that the digital resources we created were of significant value to their particular research communities. However, there was also a specifically digital humanities component in the work. These were all projects that centred on the development of highly structured data as the basis for representing the material being worked on. This was not, and remains not, an approach to representation that has been much explored in the DH community. Indeed, one could argue that there has been in particular a bias against that quintessential highly structured data paradigm: the relational database. By being based on this highly structured data paradigm these projects created resources that demonstrated new methods of interaction with humanities materials and seemed to me to be in this way clearly work in the digital humanities.

One cannot speak at length about the creation of digital resources in the digital humanities without mentioning what is perhaps the most prominent product of computers in the humanities work over the past 20 years or so: the *Text Encoding Initiative* (TEI 2018). From its beginnings decades ago, TEI's focus has primarily been on the issues that arise from the preparation and representation of a scholarly interpretation of texts, and TEI's 'text and document orientation' is surely not surprising given that many parts of the humanities are grounded in the study of texts. Indeed, the large number of digital edition projects that have been influenced by TEI can be seen by looking at Patrick Sahle's *Catalogue of Digital Editions* (Sahle 2008/2018). Perhaps as a consequence of this primacy of digital editions and TEI, often the assumptions of even prominent digital humanities thinkers have centred on digital editions as quintessential digital humanities resources to the exclusion of other possible kinds. Even when Bethany Nowviskie, for example, is aiming to think broadly about digital resources, she makes claims like this one: that practitioners will be exploiting 'born-digital contemporary data and *digitized historical corpora* to answer hitherto unanswerable questions' (Nowviskie 2014, 5, emphasis mine). In contrast, we at DDH believed that our resources, which are neither made up of contemporary data nor were historical textual corpora, also enabled this asking and answering of new questions.

Given the prominence of thinking about digital editions as digital resources, I would like to direct the reader to Elena Pierazzo's very fine ebook (Pierazzo 2014) which gives a good summary of many of the issues that arise there. My aim in this section, however, is to explore some of the issues that arise out of the work we did at King's to construct the digital resources that could *not* be described as textual editions. In particular, I will point out here some of the issues that Pierazzo describes with regard to digital edition creation that have something of a different spin on them in our projects. I will explore (a) why non-textual resources for humanists – primarily historians – became prominent to us, (b) how their development affected the tasks associated with modelling, and (c) how their development affected user presentation.

The great majority of these 'non-textual resource building projects' in which I was involved at CCH/DDH were historical. However, obviously much historical scholarship *is* text based. As American modern historian David Bodenhamer claimed in 2008, '[d]espite a flurry of interest in quantitative history in the 1960s and 1970s, historians as a group have remained more comfortable with manuscripts than databases' (Bodenhamer 2008, 220). So, it is obviously entirely reasonable to carry out a digital humanities historical project that involves the preparation of a digital edition of an important historical source that is based, presumably, on the TEI. Given that this is so, it is striking that in spite of the significant weight of DH thinking that encourages one to 'think textually' about digital projects, the great majority of historically based projects in which I was involved at DDH did *not* involve the preparation of digitised historical corpora. Instead, they largely fell into two kinds. One kind could be classified as specialised image archives. I shall return to them briefly later. The other kind can be classified as prosopographies, such as PBE, PoMS and CCEd (mentioned earlier), and *Prosopography of the Byzantine World* (PBW), *Prosopography of Anglo-Saxon England* (PASE), *Making of Charlemagne's Europe*, and most recently *Digital Prosopography of the Roman Republic* (DPRR).[8] These were all multi-year, multi-person funded projects producing large and complex prosopographical resources. One example of their size will suffice: at the time of writing the published online version of *People of Medieval Scotland* had identified over 15,000 people and institutions, from over 6,000 sources (mainly legal charters), and had made more than 68,000 complex multi-faceted assertions about these people. PoMS is still growing in size.

Even though the prosopographer's focus is not so much on the primary historical sources themselves but on what these sources have to say about historical people, traditional prosopography published in print form certainly looks like a text-oriented enterprise. The sources are almost always historical texts, the published product is further text in the form of articles about the historical individuals the prosopographers have identified; a type of humanities research that I have classified elsewhere as 'text in, text out'. Our prosopographical projects, however, did not engage in the writing of articles about their historical people: they created highly structured data about them instead. Along with this shift in focus from text to data came some thinking about which historical objects needed to be more formally conceptualised into data: people, obviously, and sources too – but what else? Well, of course, there were the other things the sources mentioned: places (including places as property), titles and offices people held, etc. The work to create King's first digital prosopography (PBE) in the 1990s in terms of a highly structured, rather than a textual, object required these entities and the relationships between them to be formally represented as data, but the data structure also had to work in ways that were understood by PBE's historians. Thus, the idea of what came to be called, intentionally ironically, the *factoid* came out of the design work for PBE. An object was clearly needed that represented a spot in a text that said something about a person or persons, and the PBE historians ended up calling this the factoid. The ironic character of the name of this object was appropriate because, of course, historians know how tricky it can be to take an assertion in a historical source and map it to a seemingly 'factual' sense of what actually happened at the time. Nonetheless, in spite of this, the idea of the factoid has proven to be good enough that it has been used as a central design component in the great majority of King's subsequent structured prosopographies, and I have often been told that it has been taken up by other prosopographical projects that do not involve King's. There is more on the idea of the factoid in Bradley 2017.

Not all the structured data resources in which I was involved were prosopographies. Several looked significantly like digital image archives.[9] However, they were not conventional digital image archives, where the role of the archive makers was to digitise and then catalogue the created materials using conventional cataloguing structures such as, say CIDOC or METS.[10] This is because our partners in these and other similar projects were not librarians, curators or archivists but academics with a particular perspective on what these images showed: concerns that fell outside the interests of library or museum cataloguers. Our partners wanted to record these academic, often somewhat subjective, interpretations about the things showing in the images. In the case of *Art of Making*, for example, they were interested in recording evidence showing on the sculptures of what tools were used to create the work. Conventional cataloguing models like CIDOC or METS are exactly formal in the sense that our projects were, and are, fully compatible with storage in a relational database. But they do not contain structures that on their own can record the scholarly issues that our partners wished to record about the materials. Thus, as in our work on prosopography, we needed to develop a more bespoke model of how to organise the data rather than restrict oneself to what METS or CIDOC could say about the materials.

The process of creating these online digital resources with our historian partners for both our prosopographical and non-prosopographical structured data projects grew out of, on the one hand, the need to reflect in them the interests of the historians in each project, and, on the other, the nature and constraints of the kind of formal modelling that is needed to allow the technology to do anything useful with the material. Thus, before anything was built it was necessary to begin with a modelling activity: to bring the historical and technological understanding together in rather intensive discussions that aimed to ensure that (i) as much as possible, the software structures represented the interests and concerns of the historians, and (ii) the historians understood both the limitations and the potential inherent in expressing their interests in this way. Only after there was a reasonable degree of shared understanding of both

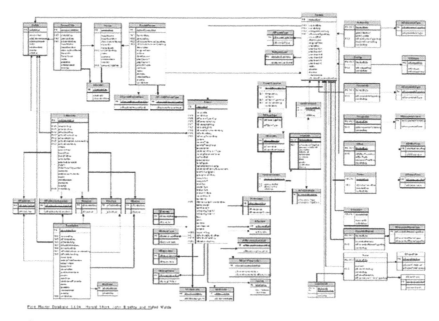

Figure 1.3 An entity relationship diagram for PASE.

perspectives was anything built. Since we were using relational databases as the storage mechanism for the material, the ideas the project wanted to record had to be expressed in terms of the *entities, attributes* and *relationships* that characterised this kind of representation. Consequently, our modelling work generally resulted in a structured data diagram similar to that shown in Figure 1.3. Here, the boxes represent the entities in the model, the lists in the boxes are the attributes associated with those entities, and the arrowed lines are the relationships between them. If the process was successful, both the historians and the technologists had sufficient common understanding of the model captured in the diagram for useful discussion about it to be possible.

Having created the model and from it the database, mechanisms were then created to allow the material to be entered. For the last 15 years or so these tended to be in the form of rather complex data entry forms that were accessed through a web browser (in a number of our recent projects, we used the form mechanisms provided by the Django framework.[11] Usually, once the historians were presented with these data entry forms and began to use them, the nature of the representation they were working with became abundantly clear. Thus, it was often necessary, once close-up engagement with the material that the forms required was underway, to tweak the database design to deal with issues that then emerged.

I have labelled this significant component in the building of these structured data resources as a *modelling* one, and as it turns out there has been considerable interest in recent years in modelling by digital humanists. Indeed, Pierazzo claims that modelling is 'the key methodological structure of digital editing' (Pierazzo 2014, 11), and, not surprisingly, much of the discussion in the DH about the kind of modelling we are speaking about here has been in a context of digital editions (see Pierazzo's summary of this in Pierazzo 2014, 44–83), where the text being edited is the central focus of the edition, and consequently of the model too. After all, as Sahle says (2008/2018, page 'about'), information 'without reproduction' of this central textual object as the primarily focus is not a critical edition.

This text-centred modelling approach for digital editions is, in good part, a consequence of the base technology used to capture structure in a text: TEI as expressed through XML. As Pierazzo reminds us (Pierazzo 2014, 32) XML (and its precursor, SGML) was designed from the beginning as an approach to markup that was to be layered on top of a text. With all of the problems XML has for scholarly markup, particularly because of its hierarchical nature (see Pierazzo's critique of the problem in her discussion of the OHCO model: Pierazzo 2014, 69–72), the fact that it is a technology that can add an interpretative structure by layering it on top of a text makes it particularly well-suited to textual editing: XML and thus TEI recognise the centrality of the text by using the intimate connection of markup to represent the interpretation.

In contrast, since for pretty much all of *our* non-textual projects the major technology was the relational database, in that context there was not, and did not need to be, a single central object (like the text in a digital edition) around which the rest developed. What thinking goes into the modelling process for these 'un-centred' projects? In this issue we can find interesting points in common and in contrast between modelling for a digital edition and the modelling involved in our non-textual projects, and again I draw on Pierazzo's insights into the issue. She states that 'by modelling we intend here the analytical process of establishing the kind and purpose of the edition, its implied community of users and what features best represent their various needs'. She also refers to Rehbein (Pierazzo 2014, 115), who claims that to do a digital edition the editor has to change their thinking from how the text will look on the printed page to thinking about what 'functional and semantic' materials are to be represented (Rehbein 2010, 5); a shift he reports as a change 'from output-driven to input- and user-driven design' (Rehbein 2010, 2).

That part of model development that is end-user driven has been a component for our structured data resource-building projects too, but this aspect is not the whole story. Instead, the other part of Rehbein's characterisation, that of 'input-driven', is closer to what goes on in much of the modelling for our projects. By the phrase 'input-driven' I have assumed that Rehbein means to refer to that part of the modelling process that decides what aspects of the text are to be expressed in the markup – based on what the editor thinks is there and what s/he thinks is interesting to record. Our non-textual projects have something like this side of things too, since the structure that emerges will also need to represent a formalisation of some aspects of the historical world it represents as filtered through the modern perspective of the project's historians.

An important difference, however, between our modelling for our data-driven project and that for textual editions is that often in our work the objects being represented will be those that are better characterised as being 'in the world' rather than 'in the text'. In our all non-textual projects each project team has needed to think, from the ground up as it were, about what in-the-world objects are being represented in the structure that will be built and how they connect together. Because of the lack of an essential structural centre in these projects – a text – the model that emerges tends to focus instead on relationships *between* these objects. You can see these presented in the lines between the boxes in Figure 1.3, which represent these relationships as semantic connections. Thus in our factoid prosopographical projects factoids can be thought of as the objects that *link* historical persons with their appearances in historical sources and with our conceptions of other things in that historical world, such as places or pieces of property, or titles they held. Our experience has shown us that this kind of linked web of in-the-world objects can be very effectively represented using the relational model (and also, more recently, the technologies of the Semantic Web). The nature of this approach to representation in the model, and the interaction it produces between objects 'in the text' and objects 'in the world', has been explored in more detail in the context of three of our projects that took this approach, rather than a textual one, to online resources drawing on historic legal charters in Bradley et al. 2019.

This kind of data modelling is essential to structured data representation, since the abstract concepts of entity, attributes and relationships that form the basis for relational database modelling theory are, deliberatively, too abstract to represent materials directly. However, it is through associating these abstract ideas with the items being represented, based on the relational paradigm's underlying entity-attribute-relationship concepts, that the DB technology is enabled to do useful things with them, and do them in ways that then correspond to our understanding of the world being modelled. It was through the definition and expression of structures in terms of these relational database abstract concepts in ways that could represent ideas of interest to our humanist colleagues that made this significant intellectual and creative work. It seems clear to me that the creation of these models generates products that represent some aspects of historical thinking and thus they should be considered products that are worthy of discussion in a historical community. However, each individual model – for PBE, say, or CCEd – is less obviously something that will generate discussion in the digital humanities community, unless ideas that go beyond the range of each individual project emerge.

In what way, then, does this kind of modelling work generate substantial contributions to the digital humanities? An example of such an intellectual product from this kind of work that fits as much in the digital humanities sphere as it does in the traditional scholarly one is the *factoid prosopography* modelling approach itself. It is grounded in the abstractions and requirements of highly structured data design, and yet aims to provide a vehicle that represents materials of interest to historians in ways that fit with their approach to scholarship – even to the extent of acknowledging, through the ironic character of the name, the kind of simplification of representation that the approach represents. As a proof of concept it served the needs of a number of prosopographical projects in which we were involved, and has been apparently influential in the design of prosopographical projects created elsewhere. It sits as a level of abstraction that is outside any one of our particular projects, and is meant to instead capture formally a way of historical thinking about prosopography that is enabled by a digital representation. Thus, it has a digital humanities side as well as a historical one.

By this stage we were able to create models for these projects that could usefully capture the interests of our humanist colleagues. Now it was necessary to think about how this material could be made available to other scholars to support their research. Is the database, in and of itself, sufficient?

It is interesting to note that in the context of digital editions there has always been a minority view that the marked-up text could be thought of as the end point of the resource creation work. Once the marked-up text (with TEI) was completed, simply making it available was all that was required, and no further 'user interface' was necessary. The problem with this, of course, was that there was then only a very small minority of textual scholars who were technically equipped to usefully exploit the TEI/XML for their own research. The arrival of the world wide web, and its eventual penetration into the working practice of a broad range of humanist scholars, has made it evident that an edition created by using TEI markup could be presented – transformed – into a set of web pages that would be accessible to a much larger community of users as HTML/web pages. Furthermore, the arrival of the XSLT[12] transformation language made it fully practical to create transformation processes for this purpose. Indeed, because of the nature of what is being done in the preparation of a digital edition, transformation can usefully become one of the central ways of thinking about how to represent a text digitally. As Rehbein says at the very beginning of his article (Rehbein 2010, 1), edition building is always about 'a transformation from something into something different, at least as regards a text'. Furthermore, a web-based publication has to be thought of in terms of *user interaction*. Indeed, Sahle makes the claim in his catalogue (Sahle 2008/2018, 'about') that 'an edition cannot be called truly digital if by printing it we do not have a loss of functionality'. The nature of interaction by users is a key issue for our non-digital-edition resources too.

Of course a web-based digital edition interface will contain some pages that were not direct representations of the source text (for example, pages that acted as table of contents, or indexes), but at the bottom of it all, a major element of the interface design must be to sort out how to present the textual material of the source with the enhancements that came out of the markup added to it through the editorial process. In the end, the text-plus-markup itself provided the basis for much of the thinking about what the user interface should be (Pierazzo 2014, 115–16). As a consequence, in this part of her book Pierazzo praises the wireframe approach – where early in the design process one creates a mocked-up layout of the material to be displayed as an aid to designing the subsequent presentation in the website itself. She claims that it allows one to more clearly 'embody visions and imagine the future' (Pierazzo 2014, 117).

To *some* extent we found that thinking through wireframe design in our non-textual edition projects was helpful too. However, a wireframe of a page could only be undertaken once one had a general sense of what that a page was going to contain. For a digital edition project, a wireframe that shows how the text and apparatus attached to it is going to be shown could usefully be undertaken early on. For our non-textual structured data resources, however, this sense of what the core web pages were going to be, and what they should contain, was not so clear early on.

For our projects, which did not have a text as a central component for presentation, one had to first conceive of what kinds of materials were to be displayed, and how they were to be linked together before you could take up the wireframe stage of designing them. Stan Ruecker's work on Rich Prospect Browsing (Ruecker et al. 2011) comes close to dealing with the issues that we had to confront too. Ruecker needed to imagine how his materials – images of objects, and metadata about them – could be presented in ways that empowered the user but was true to what was available. In a similar way, we found ourselves drawn back to our data model to establish individual classes of web pages which could be designed for the resource's presentation website.

Pierazzo does not talk much about the design of those pages that do not represent the text itself, such as navigational ones. Navigation mechanisms that allow the user to find their way through an online resource is an issue that is, of course, important for all web resources. It seems that in digital editions navigation is often grounded in terms of concepts such as table of contents or indexes. Instead, Pierazzo's discussion on this subject seems to focus, naturally enough, on conceptions of 'reading' and the different kinds of reading for different purposes (Pierazzo 2014, 163–70).

However, for our projects, since we had no text to ground our websites, the issue of navigation became very prominent in our thinking. As appropriate as concepts such as table of contents or index are for navigation of digital editions, they cannot be the central navigation ones for highly structured data resources such as our online prosopographies. Instead, we have found that the best way of thinking about navigation is in terms of *search* or *query*, and this seems to parallel the nature of structured data as well where query languages (SQL for relational database, SPARQL for RDF-graph-based representations) provide the principal mechanisms for getting access to what a data collection holds. Although querying might provide a good basis for thinking about navigation through structured data, these querying languages such as SQL or SPARQL are far too formal and foreign to our expected non-technical web users to provide a suitable platform to give them directly. Instead, after several years of working on the issue, we started in about 2005 to think in terms of *facetted searching* – an approach related to the concepts of *facetted classification*. There is a good introduction to facetted classification for our purposes in Denton 2003. Figure 1.4 shows one screen in PASE that has facetted searching in operation.

Whereas facetted classification grew out of the interests of those in library science, and developed from the ideas of the great library science scholar Siyali Ramamrita Ranganathan for the purpose of classifying books in libraries, our interests turn some of the central ideas of facetted classification into *facetted browsing*. We do not have a focus on organising

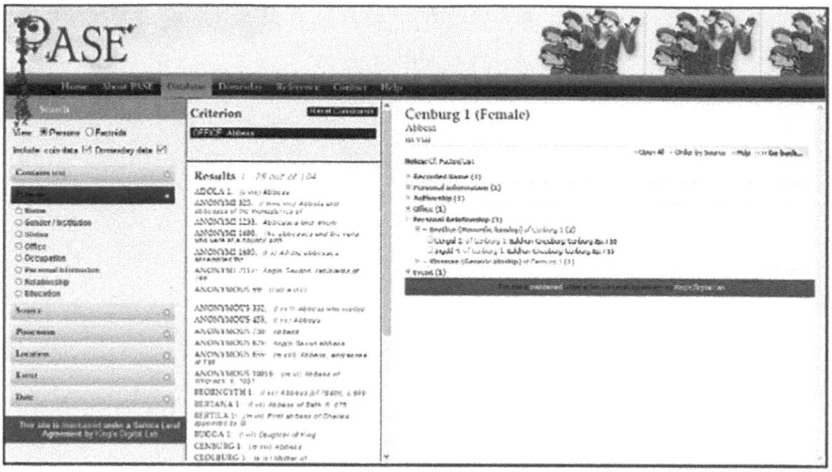

Figure 1.4 PASE, Cenburg 1: an Abbess, found through the *Office* facet.

books or libraries in our structured data, and as a consequence we do not need to think about a universal classification system for them. Instead, facetted browsing arises as a user interface mechanism out of the structures that, by the time we get to thinking about these matters, are already defined in the data model: they represent the semantics of the data collection that is of interest to our historian partners. These provide the facets that the user sees and they allow them to create multifaceted queries against the data such as 'show me all women who appear in narratives about weddings who were not the bride'.

Denton provides some basic principles for facetted classification (Denton 2003, 4.2) that we have found to apply to facetted browsing too.

1. The user should not be able to form a query that is known to have no results.
2. Users must always know where they are in the classification.
3. Users must always be able to refine their query or adjust their navigation to see what is nearby in the classification.
4. The URL is the notation of the classification.

At the time this article was written, our work with facetted browsing approaches had gone on for well over 10 years. During this time we have thought considerably about the user experience issues that arose from its use, and as a result our newer facetted browsing interfaces can look substantially different from our earliest ones. Thus, because there was considerable intellectual effort put into these interfaces, one can ask whether this conceptual development of facetted browsing for user interface constitutes work in the digital humanities. The fundamental idea that complex structured data of the kind we have here can usefully be made available to users through facetted browsing techniques might qualify. However, the detailed specific work in making the interface work as well as possible for each individual project does *not* seem to me to have produced general principles in ways that constitute 'digital humanities' work.

Finally, my most recent work with the publishing of digital resources has been in the area of open, highly structured data. This was in response to the growing interest in what has been called Linked Open Data (LOD). Since there had been particular interest in LOD in the digital classics community – a group who seemed to be ready to explore it – it made sense to begin to explore the issues LOD raises by publishing the structured data behind our recently completed *Prosopography of the Roman Republic* (DPRR) project as open data. We chose to do this in the form of the Semantic Web's RDF and associated technologies. You can see the result of this work at http://romanrepublic.ac.uk/rdf (with documentation at http://romanrepublic.ac.uk/rdf/doc). Publishing data as LOD is somewhat similar to directly publishing the TEI files for a digital edition project, and raises similar questions about who can make use of them. The issues I was exploring with DPRR as LOD were: (a) how readily could our relational data be transformed into RDF; (b) how did the Semantic Web's ontology technology OWL add to what was published; (c) how could classical Roman historians take advantage of material published in this way – in particular could they exploit the data in DPRR in ways other than that facilitated by DPRR's facetted browsing interface?

Was this digital humanities work? As far as I was aware, very little work had been carried out in the DH domain to expose significant amounts of highly structured data in terms of LOD technologies like RDF. To the extent that new insights might arise from this venture into how this kind of LOD could affect humanities scholarship it seems to me to be a more digital humanities undertaking then, say, an AI or historical one. However, this is still early days for this work, and it is going to be some time, if ever, before appropriate insights might be gained. Some of my preliminary thoughts can be found in Bradley 2019.

Software development again: *Pliny*

In 2005, after passing through a number of years of work that focused on digital resource construction of the kind we have just described, the chance came for me to again spend some time thinking about tools and toolmaking, and to actually build tools myself. When I first came to King's in 1997 I had originally thought that it might be possible to continue work along the lines of TACT – centred on tools for textual analysis. However, it quickly became evident that the WWW had opened up plenty of potential for work in digital resource development, and that this should be where most of my efforts could go most usefully.

Furthermore, by 2005 my interest in tool building had taken a turn away from TACT-like tools for textual analysis for several reasons, one of them being that it had seemed evident to me at that time that these kinds of tools were destined to serve the interest of relatively few human-ist scholars. Instead, Fish's view, as presented in his 2012 article – that reading 'with intentionality' was central to scholarship – still seems to me to be much closer to mainstream humanities scholarly activity. This view seemed to be confirmed in the writings of those who had studied humanities scholarly practice, such as what was reported in what was for me the very influential work by Brockman, Neumann, Palmer and Tidline (Brockman et al. 2001). It described practices used by humanists that in fact seemed rather well aligned with Fish's example of thinking about the occurrence of 'B' and 'P' words in Milton's *Areopagitica* and then else-where. What kind of digital tool could fit with his practice, and what with the practices of other humanist scholars? Fish does not, and perhaps can-not, imagine the kind of computer tool that would support the work he wanted to do. This was fair enough; after all, it was bound to be very dif-ferent from the kind of tools which he had seen and which represented to him the digital humanities.

The eventual product of this interest of mine (and the work that followed from it through a year's sabbatical provided to me through the generosity of the head of DDH at the time, Harold Short) until about 2014 was *Pliny*. *Pliny* was both a piece of software and a project aimed at sup-porting what, in a past version of their website, the Arts and Humanities Research Council (UK) claimed was '[i]n many subjects and disciplines' the primary research activity: 'the synthesis and analysis of material [which] takes place within an individual mind'. The site went on to say that 'the process and the outcome [was] distinctive precisely because it has emerged from the critical and reflective processes of that individual mind', and that this methodological approach 'may be a special charac-teristic of the arts and humanities'. *Pliny* software aimed to explore the significance of annotation and note-taking as a part of this synthesis and analysis and it provided an environment which supports the further thinking that emerges from these activities. As Ann Blair, a historian who has looked at scholarly practice in Europe in the past, claims, 'Note taking constitutes a central but often hidden phase in the transmission of knowledge' (Blair 2004, 85). So the question was not only about how digital technology could support note-taking, but how it could then help the note-taker make use of their notes in further work.

The *Pliny* project had four aspects to it:

1. First, it was a prototype software tool to support note-taking and interpretation development in traditional humanities research.
2. In addition, the software became for me a device to help think about some aspects of what interpretation is about in the humanities.
3. It was built in a platform called *Eclipse*,[13] which provided a particular way of handling tool integration, and therefore supported a particular approach to thinking about software development for digital humanities tools too, one that promotes interaction between diverse tools, such as, say, a text analysis environment and a geographic information system through the mechanisms of interpretation development in the humanities. Because of *Eclipse*, *Pliny* was able to demonstrate a technical model of how these tools might thereby link into traditional scholarship.
4. Finally, it was a prototype, and as such, provided a situation where one could think about how tool building of *Pliny* could act itself as a kind of 'practice-led research'. How might 'practice-led research' be carried out, and how could it connect with the digital humanities?

I have often described *Pliny*, as a piece of software, as 'Engelbartian'. By this I mean to reference the work of Douglas Engelbart, a key thinker early in the development of the personal computer (his team invented the mouse, for example, and through it a way of thinking about the computer screen as a 2D spatial entity). In his early work, which dates from the early 1960s, he proposed his *H-LAM/T* approach – a way of thinking about humans with their technology that focuses on the way that one could enhance human cognitive abilities by improving the tooling available to support it. H-LAM/T stands for 'Human, using language, artefacts, and methodology in which he is trained' (Engelbart 1962, 9, 11), and it provided a way of thinking about how new technology that suggested that the best way to help intellectual work was to have that technology integrate closely with *existing* practice, and thereby augment how this practice could be carried out. Because of this, Engelbart's project to develop this kind of software tool was named 'Project Augment'. The aim was to have software that could enhance or augment what humans can deal with in their own minds, and thus what this software did need not take away or reduce humans' involvement in the material that represents the problem they are interested in.

Through *Pliny* I proposed a way to think about how a computing tool might augment the traditional acts of note-taking and subsequent development of ideas from them that are central to many academics' research practice. It provided an environment for taking notes attached to a range of different media (for example, web pages, PDF documents, images). The idea of annotation and note-taking was perhaps obvious, but the question then arose, once personal annotations were made, of what the annotator was to do with them. How could software provide an environment where these notes could subsequently be reused to develop set of ideas in the mind of the user – to, in effect, augment the user's ability in the sense meant by Engelbart?

You can see *Pliny* in operation in Figure 1.5. There is, of course, no room here to go over the ideas that were explored during the development of *Pliny* in detail. *Pliny*'s website[14] lists 13 presentations and papers given between 2006 and 2017 that present these ideas. The important point was that I had intended the *Pliny* project to:

1. Show, through a prototype tool, how computing could fit with the humanities in ways that were different from what others were exploring.
2. Explore how this tool, and this type of support for humanities research, could usefully support and connect with the more familiar aspects of the digital humanities, such as text analysis tools.
3. Develop an interested user community who could, through their use of *Pliny*, discover ways in which the program, and the ideas behind it, could be improved and further developed.
4. Develop a discussion that, even if *Pliny* was wrong-headed in various ways about what traditional research was about, would encourage thinking about what constituted the digital humanities so that it could include this kind of work. Incidentally, *Pliny* shows a way to support a research practice digitally, which is almost exactly the kind of work Fish is describing to us in his 2012 piece where he complains that the digital humanities has nothing to offer the likes of him.

In spite of the many years of work on *Pliny*, I think it is fair to say that in many ways the project has been a failure. I believe that it certainly demonstrated items 1 and 2 above. There seemed to be some early excitement from some parts of the DH community when I demonstrated and spoke

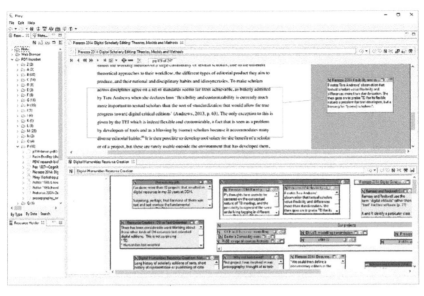

Figure 1.5 *Pliny* in operation.

about *Pliny*, and the fact that a succession of papers about *Pliny* were accepted through a peer review process also suggests that some could see that there was something in it. The Mellon Foundation even awarded it a MATC prize in 2008. On the other hand, there has never been a community of any size of *Pliny* users. At some point it became clear that there was a User Experience problem: a user on their own was not able to sort out from *Pliny* itself how to use it effectively (this is probably evident in Figure 1.5) – it was, after all, quite a different kind of application from the well-established applications of word processor, web browser, spreadsheet, etc. Furthermore, it did not fit into what is the now well-established practice of centring user software on the web browser. *Pliny* aimed to incorporate web resources into itself, but was not, itself, a web application. Finally, my wish to see *Pliny* start further thinking within the DH community about the place of technology to augment the work of humanities scholarship – in the way that both opened up a new area of discussion and developed new insights into formal digital models to support conceptual thinking in the humanities – simply failed to occur.

In the end, then, *Pliny* has produced primarily a body of writing by myself and some colleagues that described what *Pliny* was about, and attempted to open up some new thinking about a broader place for the digital humanities in humanities research practice. To the extent that articles derived from the *Pliny* work did get published in peer review journals, there was some degree of success. However, the lack of response of which I am aware to any of them suggests that in spite of this, *Pliny* did not in fact play the role of redirecting some effort and interest in the digital humanities community that I had hoped for.

Which brings me to my final 'corner' of the digital humanities tent.

Writing about digital things: traditional scholarship about digital things in society

Since my retirement from King's in 2015, things have changed at the Department of Digital Humanities (DDH), and these changes seem to reflect, from where I now sit, an altered view of what constitutes the 'digital humanities' both at King's and in the broader academic world. The department has grown substantially, to accommodate the demands of its recently launched undergraduate programme, which is called a 'Digital Culture BA' and which focuses (according to a recent version of the department's undergraduate webpage) on 'provid[ing] rigorous and critical insight into how technological innovations are bringing about new challenges and opportunities in our societies'.[15] As a consequence, much of the department's teaching, many of its academic staff, and much of its research is now in the field of cultural and media studies and related fields. Some of the work in this research is done using data-driven methodologies, but much of it obviously is not. It is, of course, instead based on traditional humanities and social science approaches of reading (or watching) primary and secondary sources and conducting interviews with people in contemporary society, and writing about insights that come from that engagement. A book published recently by a member of the department, Paolo Gerbaudo, entitled *The Digital Party* is perhaps a good example of this orientation. According to Gerbaudo's announcement of it on HUMANIST:

> The book looks at the transformation of political parties in the digital era focusing on the cases of Podemos, the Five Star Movement, Pirate Parties, France Insoumise and Momentum. It is based on 4 years of research and 30 interviews with politicians, organisers and developers of participatory platforms and observations of rallies, campaigns, party offices and events. (Gerbaudo 2018)

Gerbaudo doesn't say, but although perhaps some of the research he carried out for his book uses DH methods, clearly much of the research is seemingly traditional humanities and social science scholarship.

What makes it digital humanities is not so much the methodology, but the things that are being studied, which arise out of recent digital phenomena such as social media.

I described this kind of digital humanities work early in this paper as the most conservative kind of digital humanities, but it is important to understand that it is also a widespread component of the scholarly work of many who are operating in the less traditional components of the DH as well. Indeed, some of our leading and best-known theorists of the digital humanities, such as Willard McCarty, Stephen Ramsay, Bethany Nowviskie and Jerome McGann, have published important works that, although drawing to some significant extent on observations that come out of engagement in the broader DH, in the end reach their conclusions through entirely conventional humanities scholarship methods. Think of McGann's *Radiant Textuality* (2001) for instance. The ideas in it about creative text are radical and perhaps in the best spirit of the more extreme edge of the digital humanities. However, the *method* used to get there – which is what I am speaking about here – is essentially conventional: a single scholar observes, thinks/struggles, then writes.

I did not think of myself as an academic when I was working on TACT in Toronto, and perhaps for this reason I wrote very little about it except for its first User's Guide (and one article – see Bradley 1991). However, for perhaps similar reasons to those of other researchers, since coming to King's I found myself not only making things like the many digital online resources I discussed earlier, or *Pliny*, but also writing about them. Perhaps the objects created could have stood on their own two feet, and did not need any further supporting justification, and, indeed, the historian users of, say, the *Prosopography of Anglo-Saxon England* (PASE) are most likely not interested in what I wrote about PASE and the act of doing structured, factoid prosopography more generally. For them hopefully PASE stands on its own two feet without this. However, I was a member of the digital humanities community, not an Anglo-Saxonist. For me, what was interesting about PASE was how its structured, digital representation affected the way our historian researchers worked with their material, how they chose to represent it, and how comfortable they were with the resulting highly structured, semi-mathematically formal result. In this sense, my writings about structured prosopography share a common aim with the publication of academic papers in computer science. There it is rarely, if ever, considered sufficient to just build new digital tools that explore new ideas about what the tools can do – it is necessary to subsequently publish something that describes the tool and the new thinking that it has stimulated in computer science. Indeed, this writing-up element of research is common across all the sciences; it is not enough to perform the experiment, it is not enough to even interpret the results for yourself – the experiment and its interpretation have to be published.

In the end, then, while answering Fish and others' worries about the impact of the digital humanities on the humanities more generally, I think it useful to quote James Smithies:

> As unsophisticated as they may sometimes be, the digital humanities do not threaten the future of the humanities. They merely reflect a belief that contemporary experience (digital or otherwise) is relevant to academic research and sometimes offer opportunities to gain new perspectives on human experience. (Smithies 2017, 6)

Fish's evident worry that the digital humanities damage the humanities because it approaches its work with an inadequate critical attitude and methodology is perhaps closely related to the concerns raised in McCarty's comments that I mentioned early in this paper. I think they can best be answered by digital humanists themselves, taking up the challenge of critically thinking about what they are doing and then presenting these considerations to the broader DH community, and to the humanities more generally. At present, it would appear that the best way to do this continues to be through the medium of writing and publishing.

Conclusion: my 'so-called career' and the digital humanities

So, in the end, what is the point of all this rambling around though different kinds of work I have identified as belonging to the digital humanities?

Near the end of Melissa Dinsman's interview of Bethany Nowviskie in the *LA Review of Books* 2016 series *The Digital in the Humanities*, Nowviskie turns the interviewer/interviewee tables to ask a question of the interviewer:

> One thing I noticed about your questions is that, while they are definitely forward-looking, they kind of run in a channel in which the humanities is an academic enterprise, concerned with its own disciplinarity, firmly embedded in the university, and focused – or at

least I've taken you to mean focused – on fairly traditional departments and subject areas. (Nowviskie and Dinsman 2016)

Looking back over what I often call 'my so-called career' I have noted here the range of different kinds of posts and work that it has entailed. I never had an academic post at the University of Toronto. Although I did finally end up at King's in an academic post with a modest academic title, most of my work there was carried out in posts that were not seen as academic ones. Nonetheless, my career was essentially entirely within an academic context and a part of an academic enterprise. However, it was not quite so clearly focused, as Nowviskie observes, on traditional departments and subject areas. At Toronto there was a 'service', 'academic-related' orientation within the computer centre, and then at King's I found myself in a centre and subsequently a department which placed itself consciously simultaneously both outside and inside the traditional humanities academic world, and where I was reconfigured only late in the day (2011) into an academic post.

Perhaps, I think, the best way of understanding what the digital humanities might be starts with trying to develop a model of it that encompasses this broad range of tasks and products. The digital humanities might best provide a challenge to the model of traditional humanities not through any single part of what it does, but by the broad range of activities that it encompasses, all of which are seemingly carried out in the big tent of a modern academic institution.

Notes

1. http://tapor.ca/tools/199. All websites cited in the notes below were accessed and checked 6 September 2022.
2. Thanks to TAPoR (http://tapor.ca) for these two references.
3. Out of this, plus an interest in the then-emerging potential of the WWW, came the work on *TACTweb*: see http://tapor.ca/tools/231.
4. See a more detailed description of what we did in the Appendix to Bradley and Rockwell 1996, 44–46
5. https://voyant-tools.org
6. See http://www.pbe.kcl.ac.uk
7. http://theclergydatabase.org.uk/; http://www.poms.ac.uk; http://www.artofmaking.ac.uk
8. https://www.pbw.kcl.ac.uk/; http://www.pase.ac.uk; http://www.charlemagneseurope.ac.uk/; http://romanrepublic.ac.uk/
9. *BPI1700* (http://www.bpi1700.org.uk/index.html), a collection of images showing British printed images before 1700; *Art of Making* (http://www.artofmaking.ac.uk/), showing images of classical Roman sculpture; *CVEO* (http://www.chopinonline.ac.uk/ocve/), providing images of pages of Polish composer Fryderyk Chopin's first editions.
10. http://network.icom.museum/cidoc/; http://www.loc.gov/standards/mets/
11. http://django.org

12. https://www.w3.org/TR/xslt/all/
13. https://www.eclipse.org/
14. At http://pliny.cch.kcl.ac.uk in the section 'Publications'.
15. https://www.kcl.ac.uk/ddh/undergraduate/undergraduate.aspx

References

Armstrong, Guyda. 1996. 'Computer-Assisted Literary Analysis Using the TACT Text-Retrieval Program', *Computers & Texts* 11. Accessed 6 September 2022.

Blair, Ann. 2004. 'Note Taking as an Art of Transmission', *Critical Inquiry* 31: 85–107.

Blevins, Cameron. 2010. 'Topic Modelling Martha Ballard's Diary'. Accessed 6 September 2022. http://www.cameronblevins.org/posts/topic-modeling-martha-ballards-diary/

Bodenhamer, David J. 2008. 'History and GIS: Implications for the discipline'. In *Placing History: How maps, spatial data, and the GIS are changing historical scholarship*, edited by Anne Kelly Knowles. Redlands: Esri Press.

Bradley, John. 1991. 'TACT Design'. In *A TACT Exemplar*. In Series *CCH Working Papers*, edited by T. Russon Wooldridge, 7–14. Centre for Computing in the Humanities, University of Toronto.

Bradley, John. 2017. *Factoid prosopography*. Accessed 6 September 2022. https://factoid-dighum.kcl.ac.uk/

Bradley, John. 2019. 'DPRR as Linked Open Data: Some implications', *Digital Humanities Quarterly* 14(2). Accessed 6 September 2022. http://digitalhumanities.org/dhq/vol/14/2/000475/000475.html

Bradley, John, Alice Rio, Matthew Hammond and Dauvit Broun. 2019. 'Exploring a Model for the Semantics of Medieval Legal Charters', *International Journal of Humanities and Arts Computing* 13(1): 136–54. https://doi.org/10.3366/ijhac.2017.0184

Bradley, John and Julianne Nyhan. 2017. 'Getting Computers into Humanists' Thinking'. In *Computation and the Humanities: Towards an oral history of digital humanities*, edited by Julianne Nyhan and Andrew Flinn. Cham, Switzerland: Springer. https://doi.org/10.1007/978-3-319-20170-2_14

Bradley, John and Geoffrey Rockwell. 1996. 'Watching Scepticism: Computer-assisted visualization and Hume's *Dialogues*'. In *Research in Humanities Computing*, edited by Susan Hockey and Nancy Ide, 32–47. Oxford: Oxford University Press.

Brockman, W.S., L. Neumann, C. Palmer and T.J. Tidline. 2001. *Scholarly Work in the Humanities and the Evolving Information Environment*. Washington, DC: Council on Library and Information Resources. Accessed 6 September 2022. https://www.clir.org/pubs/reports/pub104/

Denton, William. 2003. 'How to Make a Faceted Classification and Put it on the Web'. Accessed 6 September 2022. https://www.miskatonic.org/library/facet-web-howto.html

Engelbart, Douglas C. 1962. *Augmenting Human Intellect: A conceptual framework*. Stanford Research Institute Report AFOSR-3223. Accessed 6 September 2022. http://dougengelbart.org/content/view/138/000/

Feibleman, James K. 1967. 'The Philosophy of Tools', *Social Forces* 45(3): 329–37.

Fish, Stanley. 2012. 'Mind Your P's and B's: The digital humanities and interpretation', *New York Times*. Accessed 6 September 2022. https://opinionator.blogs.nytimes.com/2012/01/23/mind-your-ps-and-bs-the-digital-humanities-and-interpretation

Fish, Stanley. 2018. 'Stop Trying to Sell the Humanities', *Chronicle of Higher Education*, 17 June.

Gerbaudo, Paulo. 2018. 'New Book/The Digital Party: Political organisation and online democracy', *Humanist Discussion Group* 32: 264.

Hacking, Ian. 1981. 'Do We See Through a Microscope?', *Pacific Philosophical Quarterly* 62(4): 305–22.

Hawthorne, Mark. 1994. 'The Computer in Literary Analysis: Using TACT with students', *Computers and the Humanities* 28(1): 19–27.

Klein, Lauren F. and Matthew K. Gold. 2016. 'Digital Humanities: The expanded field'. In *Debates in the Digital Humanities*. Accessed 6 September 2022. https://dhdebates.gc.cuny.edu/read/untitled/section/14b686b2-bdda-417f-b603-96ae8fbbfd0f

McCarty, Willard. 2018. 'Fish'ing for Fatal Flaws', *Humanist Discussion Group* 32(102). Accessed 6 September 2022. http://lists.digitalhumanities.org/pipermail/humanist/2018-June/015 669.html

McGann, Jerome. 2001. *Radiant Textuality*. New York: Palgrave Macmillan.

McKinnon, Alastair. 1989. 'Mapping the Dimensions of a Literary Corpus', *Literary and Linguistic Computing* 4(2): 73–84.

Mandal, Anthony. 2018. 'Digital Humanities'. In *The Year's Work in Critical and Cultural Theory*. The English Association and Oxford University Press. https://doi.org/10.1093/ywcct/mby016

Marche, Stephen. 2012. 'Literature is not Data: Against digital humanities', *Los Angeles Review of Books*, 28 October. Accessed 6 September 2022. https://lareviewofbooks.org/article/literat ure-is-not-data-against-digital-humanities

Micheloud, François-Xavier. 1997. *Correspondence Analysis*. Accessed 6 September 2022. http:// www.micheloud.com/fxm/cor/e/index.htm

Nowviskie, Bethany. 2014. *Speaking in Code: An NEH summit on social and intellectual implications of tacit knowledge exchange in digital humanities software development*. University of Virginia Library Scholars' Lab. Accessed 6 September 2022. https://libraopen.lib.virginia.edu/public_ view/d217qp50k

Nowviskie, Bethany and Melissa Dinsman. 2016. 'The Digital in the Humanities: An interview with Bethany Nowviskie', *Los Angeles Review of Books*. 9 May. Accessed 6 September 2022. https:// lareviewofbooks.org/article/digital-humanities-interview-bethany-nowviskie

Pierazzo, Elena. 2014. *Digital Scholarly Editing: Theories, models and methods*. Accessed 6 September 2022. http://hal.univ-grenoble-alpes.fr/hal-01182162

Potter, Rosanne G. 1988. 'Literary Criticism and Literary Computing: The difficulties of a synthesis', *Computers and the Humanities* 22: 91–97.

Potter, Rosanne G. (ed). 1989. *Literary Computing and Literary Criticism: Theoretical and practical essays on theme and rhetoric*. Philadelphia, PA: University of Pennsylvania Press.

Ramsay, Stephen and Geoffrey Rockwell. 2012. 'Developing Things: Notes toward an epistemology of building in the digital humanities'. In *Debates in the Digital Humanities*, edited by Matthew K. Gold, 75–84. Minneapolis, MN: University of Minnesota Press.

Rehbein, Malte. 2010. 'The Transition from Classical to Digital Thinking: Reflections on Tim McLoughlin, James Barry and collaborative work', *Computerphilologie* 10: 55–67.

Rockwell, Geoffrey and Stéfan Sinclair. 2016. *Hermeneutica: Computer-assisted interpretation in the humanities*. Cambridge MA: MIT Press.

Ruecker, Stan, Milena Radzikowska and Stéfan Sinclair. 2011. *Visual Interface Design for Digital Cultural Heritage: A guide to rich-prospect browsing*. Aldershot: Ashgate.

Sahle, Patrick. 2008/2018. *A Catalog of Digital Scholarly Editions*. Accessed 6 September 2022. http://www.digitale-edition.de/

Smithies, James. 2017. *The Digital Humanities and the Digital Modern*. Aldershot: Palgrave Macmillan.

TEI. 2018. *TEI: Text Encoding Initiative*. Accessed 6 September 2022. http://www.tei-c.org/

Part I:
Making Projects

2
Prosopography meets
the digital: PBW and PASE*
Charlotte Roueché, Averil Cameron and Janet L. Nelson

Prosopography

Which comes first – the person or the source? One of the first major endeavours to develop a formal prosopography was undertaken in response to the impact on the study of Roman history of the discovery of ever-increasing numbers of inscribed texts; a narrative which had been driven by the analysis of literary sources was suddenly confronted with a flood of data about individuals – some previously known, but many more newly revealed. It was the German scholar Theodor Mommsen (1817–1903), who was responsible for the organisation and publication of the major collection of Latin inscriptions, *Corpus Inscriptionum Latinarum* (CIL), who initiated the accompanying *Prosopographia Imperii Romani* (PIR). To begin with, this was partly an exercise in organising the data (Eck 2003).

While historical biography and biographical dictionaries had a long history, and continue to be written, PIR represented a publication which was driven by the data in the sources, not by the historian's selection of 'interesting' people. Although book publication meant that not everyone could be included, the tendency of the Romans to describe a man's career – with a list of offices held – now enabled the editors to accept for inclusion all persons who had held an office of some kind. That approach, eminently manageable, established a model for later studies and determined the kind of information included; among the people excluded perhaps the most obvious are women, who qualified for inclusion only through their relationships to men. The resultant assemblage provided valuable new resources for historians examining political structures and the interactions of elite groups; it also stimulated further work of the same kind. The first edition of PIR, recording people in the Roman imperial period, appeared in 1898; in 1912 Matthias Gelzer published a study, based on prosopographical research, of the Roman Republic (Gelzer 1912); Friedrich Münzer was to use PIR in extending this approach (Münzer 1920); and for English readers Ronald Syme's *Roman Revolution* exemplified the value of tracing individual relationships (Syme 1939). Lewis Namier was to apply similar analysis to members of the British parliament in the eighteenth century, another very well-documented group; it is interesting to note that the *Oxford Dictionary of National Biography* article, in including the evidence for his wealth at death from the Calendar of the Grants of Probate and Letters of Administration, is adopting precisely the methodology which he espoused of gathering materials from a very wide range of sources (Cannon 2004).

During the twentieth century contemporary populations and their statistics were increasingly recorded and measured, for a host of reasons. Historians of earlier periods were also considering how to extend analyses of persons beyond the study of a ruling elite. While there were lively discussions of methodologies, one fundamental challenge was that of volume. The question of defining the appropriate format for social history was raised by Lawrence Stone, but all analyses needed to conform with the constraints of print publication (Davies 2004). The only way to combine detail with volume was to focus on a clearly defined and limited place or time, as in the groundbreaking study of Montaillou; such an approach was simply not scalable in print (Le Roy Ladurie 1975).

Prosopography in Roman and late Roman studies

PIR covers the period to AD 284, after which the nature of the sources changes substantially; the proportion of inscriptions is much reduced and careers within the church come to parallel those within the state. Mommsen envisaged a continuation into the later Roman empire and some data were collected which were recovered at the end of the Second World War and brought to London. A new British Academy Prosopography Committee met for the first time on 4 October 1949 (Martindale 2003). In 1950 the newly created Fédération internationale des associations d'études classiques / International Federation of the Societies of Classical Studies (FIEC) held its first Congress;[1] on that occasion the British, represented by A.H.M. Jones (1904–70) (Brunt 2004), and the French, represented by H.I. Marrou (1904–77), decided to undertake the prosopography of the later Roman period, leaving the secular individuals to the British and the ecclesiastical persons to the French (Mathisen 2003). Any such undertaking required defined limits: the inheritance from PIR meant that the *Prosopography of the Later Roman Empire* (PLRE) would cover only holders of central government offices, which also reflected the research interests of Jones. This rather artificial division reflects the greater volume of material for this period, and also the need for different systems of organisation. PIR orders individuals alphabetically and covers the period 31 BC–284 AD. For the later Roman Empire (defined here as AD 250–640) the ecclesiastical materials have been treated by geographical region and work still continues (by Mandouze et al., 1982–2013);[2] the secular materials were divided by period (Jones et al. 1971–92). This division again reflected the problems of working within the printed book structure, but it is also true that PLRE enormously improved our understanding of late Roman administration.

Prosopography in medieval history

In 1980 the Medieval Institute at the University of Michigan launched a new journal, *Medieval Prosopography*. The founding co-editors were the godparents of the new journal and George T. Beech has served medieval prosopography for nearly 40 years in both editorial and godparental capacities, as well as being a very active founding member of the celebrated Medieval Studies Congresses at Western Michigan University, Kalamazoo, from 1962 to the present. In 1980 he observed that 'large-scale lists of data on occupational, religious or political groups' were taking the place of earlier monographs on individuals and families, and – *en passant* – that scholars 'now' were 'sometimes working in teams', and that 'the application of electronic data-processing techniques to the analysis of masses of names . . . has contributed still further to the advancement of medieval prosopography' (Nelson et al. 2003, 155–9).

First steps towards the digital

PLRE I (edited by Jones and others) and II (edited by J.R. Martindale) were published by Cambridge University Press in 1971 and 1982. PLRE III, edited by Martindale, was nearing completion in the early 1980s; it went to press in 1987 and was published in 1992. In 1981 a provisional British Academy planning committee was established to discuss a possible

Byzantine continuation; it included two members of the PLRE committee of the British Academy, Cyril Mango (Bywater and Sotheby Professor of Byzantine and Modern Greek Language and Literature at the University of Oxford), who chaired the Committee, and Averil Cameron (Department of Classics, King's College London). The initiative for a *Prosopography of the Byzantine Empire* (PBE) came from within the Academy and with the support of the publisher, and it had a long gestation. It was urged from the beginning, including by Cambridge University Press (CUP) as publisher (represented by Pauline Hire, the editor of PLRE for CUP), that such a project must be computerised, and as discussions proceeded this was interpreted as meaning more than 'done on a word processor' (contrast 'the use of a computer ought to be considered', as Mango put it during the discussions). At the time, the use of computers in the humanities was largely focused on the stylistic and literary analysis of texts (Marriott 1979; Sansone 1990). While initially there was little awareness of the possibilities offered by a digitised prosopography, this understanding changed over the several years during which the project was in the planning stage; understanding of what computing might mean was changing over the same period, as were the available tools. The committee decided that the new prosopography would provide continuous coverage from AD 641 (the end-date of PLRE III) to the mid-thirteenth century (the start-date of the *Prosopographisches Lexikon der Palaiologenzeit*) (Trapp 1976). Martindale, with his long experience from working on PLRE, would be central to the project; he was 'exceptionally well qualified', Mango maintained. The location would be either London (King's) or Oxford; Martindale was Cambridge-based and that was a practical consideration. The project was announced at the International Congress of Byzantine Studies, Washington DC, in 1986.

Also at the British Academy, on 24 October 1985, the late Donald Bullough hailed the 'massed computers of Franco-German prosopographical research' (Bullough 1985). He did so with more than a touch of irony and paradox. The application of digital humanities to prosopography involved no magic wands. The machines that could provide masses of names and sometimes their kin-groups could at the same time, Donald thought, 'further dim their individuality'. Bullough's aim, far from dimming individuality, was of course to evoke Charlemagne's court and the world of the court – which reproduced itself from one generation to the next – not through simple replication but by evolution. This can be imagined working vertically and horizontally: the men of the 770s acquired new and elaborate cultural traits, and from the 780s through to the imperial years after 800, there was (to borrow Walter Ullmann's borrowed term) a collective social Carolingian re-naissance (Ullman 1979). Over the same period a horizontal process re-formed the court as an organism that grew tentacularly, so that there was a spatial spread (to follow through Bullough's line of thinking) of 'literacy . . . and patterns of formal loyalty without which it would have been impossible to govern the extended *regnum*, and the political and institutional cohesiveness which followed from this' (Bullough 1985, 132). Bullough left it at that. Had he lived (he died, alas, in 2002), he might have become interested in applying massed computers to prosopography, but that was not to be.

Just how far Franco-German prosopographical research had come was signalled by Michael Borgolte's publication in 1986 of *Die Grafen Alemanniens in merowingischer und karolingische Zeit: ein Prosopographie*. Massed computers were not in evidence. The reader was presented instead with an encyclopedic biographical dictionary of a regional elite. Some 10 years later, in 1997, Philippe Depreux regaled francophone scholars with *Prosopographie de l'entourage de Louis le Pieux (781–840)*, which offered mini-biographies of 280 persons (including just two women, both empresses).[3] In the UK, meanwhile, although many prosopographers stuck to their card-files, many more were starting to construct databases capacious enough to include – along with institutional structures – communities with ideas and ideals, and quantities of individuals that prosopography could help organise and interpret, search and relate. The result was to widen the scope of medieval history hugely, by exploring not just rarefied coteries but social worlds that overlapped and interacted. *The New Dictionary of National Biography* (published on 23 September 2004, in 60 volumes) still exuded a whiff of the great and the good. A prosopographical project 'allows, in principle, a universal record', asserted one rather unrealistic historian in 2000 at a symposium at the British Academy. Another, wiser, historian (on the same occasion) reminded the audience that a database was 'only as comprehensive as the available data themselves'.[4] Such a project's target material consisted very largely of '"new", i.e. hitherto hidden, men and women' (Nelson et al. 2003, 158). Digital technology, and changes in national research funding policies (see below), could together make a database relational and adaptable.[5]

Meanwhile, at KCL

'Humanities computing' began at King's College London in the early 1970s, with Computing Services staff assisting humanities academics to generate concordances and create thesaurus listings in a manner typical of the period. In 1971 the arrival of Roy Wisbey as Professor of German gave the activity a particular boost; in 1964, while at Cambridge, Wisbey had started the Centre for Literary and Linguistic Computing. The inaugural meeting of the Association for Literary and Linguistic Computing (ALLC) was held at King's in 1973, with attendees from a number of countries across western Europe, and Wisbey was elected as its first chair.

In part because computing services' support for humanities research was already established at King's, Wisbey did not feel it necessary to create a new humanities computing centre when he arrived. In 1985, however, when he was Vice-Principal of the College, a series of institutional mergers gave him the chance to propose the formation of a 'Humanities and Information Management' group (HIMG) in the restructured Computing Centre (Siemens et al. 2008). Gordon Gallacher moved to the new Centre from Imperial College and worked as Acting Assistant Director of HIMG, while the College advertised for a Director; this attracted an application from Harold Short, who was appointed to the post in August 1988.

Increasingly scholars at King's were examining new ways of exploiting these new possibilities, going well beyond the original traditions of textual analysis. One group of scholars who had been considering the use of digital tools were those interested in the large collections of papyri from Roman Egypt, and the possibilities for using computers to handle this abundant material had been explored as early as the 1960s (Tomsin 1966). In 1985 Dominic Rathbone arrived as a lecturer in the Department of Classics at King's. He was completing a thesis on the economic history of Roman Egypt and started to discuss with colleagues the possibility of a digital prosopography of Roman Egypt. The project, *Computerised Prosopography of Roman Egypt* (CPRE), received funding from the Leverhulme Trust and Rathbone started to work with Mark Stewart in HIMG. The first system they used was STATUS, and they later transferred to the more powerful TRIP; the major challenge at this stage was mastering over-complex software, which left little time for actual data input.[6] This project was later subsumed into a larger international undertaking (Strassi 2015; Fiorillo 2015).[7] In 1987 a medievalist with extensive computing experience, Susan Kruse, joined the HIMG, and, with Janet Nelson in the Department of History, designed and co-taught an optional introductory computing course for undergraduates

Prosopography comes to KCL

These various developments came together in 1988, when the PBE planning committee met in March. The meeting was chaired by Cyril Mango, and those present were Robert Browning, A.A.M. Bryer, Donald Nicol, Averil Cameron, John Martindale, Peter Brown, Michael Evans and Peter Williams (the last three from the British Academy). The decision was made, in the light of developments at KCL, to base the project there, although the chair of the committee, Cyril Mango, dissented. Following this meeting PBE was formally set up as a British Academy Research Project. Mango withdrew from the project, and Professor Robert Browning became chair of a new British Academy PBE management committee; the first meeting took place in July 1988.

Work started immediately at King's; John Martindale collaborated on the design with Gordon Gallacher, in HIMG, working in parallel, and in discussion, with the CPRE project, and using the same TRIP software. The initial format was a flat-file database on a mainframe server. The challenge that the two projects shared was the fundamental challenge posed by the new medium; there was no longer a rationale for excluding people. For Roman Egypt this meant tackling, for the first time, all the thousands of people briefly mentioned in the papyri. For the PBE it meant abandoning the model which had continued from PIR to PLRE – and which was imposed by print publication – of selecting only office-holders to record; this would come to transform the structure in which the information was presented.

KCL: further developments

Meanwhile, the interest in humanities computing in the College, with the growth of optional extra courses, such as the one taught by Kruse and Nelson, led to the introduction in 1989 of an undergraduate 'minor' programme in which students gained the degree title 'French/Spanish/ Music/. . . with Applied Computing'. This course was designed and taught by members of the new Humanities and Information Management group. Over the same period, the group was developing further research collaborations. The increasingly academic focus of the work led to the creation in 1992 of the Research Unit in Humanities Computing (RUHC) as a joint development of the School of Humanities (which established a 'Lecturer in Humanities Computing' post), and the Computing Centre, which funded two posts (Director and Senior Analyst). The RUHC further developed the teaching programme, introducing courses for humanities graduate students and a special course for historians, and became involved in an increasing range of major research projects in the humanities, joining the *Prosopography of the Byzantine Empire*.

During the 1980s universities were increasingly looking to formalise and develop research processes and projects; in the humanities, as already in the sciences, there was a move towards large, collaborative and interdisciplinary projects. While interdisciplinarity always presents practical challenges, the School of Humanities at KCL was already relatively close-knit, with collaborations across departmental lines. In 1988–9 the College was in the process of developing interdisciplinary research centres, a model which many institutions have followed; the two first Centres were the Centre for Late Antique and Medieval Studies, established and led by Roy Wisbey, and the Centre for Hellenic Studies, established and led by Averil Cameron, who was also a member of the PBE committee. The new PBE project fitted very well into this environment.

By 1996 it was clear that additional resources were needed to cope with increasing demand for computing in the humanities, and with the backing of the Head of School, Professor Barry Ife, the RUHC was transformed into another Research Centre, the Centre for Computing in the Humanities (CCH). The Centre differed structurally from other Research Centres at King's and continued to be jointly funded by Computing Services and the School of Humanities. The complement of full-time staff went from three posts – held by Harold Short (Director), Lynne Grundy, and the shared post held by Gordon Gallacher and Susan Kruse – to five, bringing in John Lavagnino and Willard McCarty. In 1996 Gallacher and Kruse moved to Scotland and in 1997 John Bradley arrived to fill their post. CCH continued to grow, and in 2002 moved out of Computing Services to become an academic department, the first in the world in this field. The CCH name, however, was retained until 2010, when it was changed to Department of Digital Humanities.

The birth of the factoid

In 1993 Dion Smythe joined John Martindale in working on the PBE. He and Gordon Gallacher began to reassess the materials which had been collected, and reconsider how they should be presented. In the same year, 1993, discussions with the recently reconstituted Berlin-Brandenburg Academy, where it had become clear that work on Byzantine prosopography was also in hand, resulted in an official agreement to collaborate; the *Prosopographie der mittelbyzantinischen Zeit* (PmbZ) would cover the first period (642–867) and also the second (868–1024); the British team would continue their work on the first period, incorporating references to the PmbZ, and would then deal with the period from 1025.

This provided a reason to reassess the approach of the British project, to consider what it could usefully contribute. The PmbZ was intended as a print publication, with the data presented in articles, although the material is now also available online. But the huge crowd of people who could now be included in a digital resource were not most usefully presented in the traditional long article form; while this is entirely suitable for a collection of elite people, as in the early prosopographies, it is not a useful way to include butchers, bakers and candlestick makers. This kind of approach also meant processing the sources in a slightly different way. The researchers worked systematically through each source, recording all statements about individuals, and attaching such statements to person records. The information for an individual is not reconciled, as in an article-based prosopography, and in the PmbZ: though some sources are clearly more accurate than others, all available testimony is recorded. The PBE dataset is a guide to what is said in the sources; it has not set itself the task of source criticism, establishing which sources are more 'valuable', 'accurate' or 'true'.[8] This was a radical new approach, made possible by working in a digital environment.

The first requirement was to define the data, which were statements made in a wide range of sources. It was not possible to treat every such statement as a 'fact'; the team originally conceived them as hypotheses and used the term Hyp-id. This understanding produced the concept of the 'factoid', which was to become a bedrock of all the subsequent prosopography projects at KCL. A factoid is an assertion, in an earlier source, as interpreted by a modern scholar (Bradley n.d.). This wealth of information was both too irregular and also too rich to be adequately expressed in a flat-file structure. The technical change needed to accommodate this methodological change was to develop the system in a relational database. It was Gordon Gallacher who responded to this by undertaking the initial relational design for a database which deployed factoids, which remained fundamental to all future projects; he worked in the INGRES software recently purchased by King's.

John Bradley at KCL

Working first with PBE, John embraced the 'factoid' concept and started to refine it. The team were already working on the first phase of the project – people recorded in Byzantine sources from the period 642–867. Since the original work had been designed in article format, this was retained in the publication. The persons in PBE I are described in articles, with even some references to modern scholarly discussion; but the indices and search aids were generated by the factoid database, covering a relatively limited number of factoid types.[9] The work was completed by 2000; publication online was an intention, but not yet a realistic possibility, so PBE I was published on a CD-ROM, which could, however, be read using a browser (Netscape 2.0). This allowed, among other things, for the presentation of ancient Greek, since Unicode for polytonic Greek was not yet available. The rich search facilities were enabled by the work which John had done (Martindale 2001).

In 1998 the national research landscape was transformed by the establishment of the new Arts and Humanities Research Board (AHRB), which took over funding for research projects from the British Academy (Conisbee n.d.). Its remit was to develop a 'broad strategic framework' for research, and the fundamental nature of large research databases to support humanities research fitted well into this. At KCL the Director of CCH, Harold Short, who himself had a background in database design and development, saw the important potential of John's work with the PBE, and worked closely with him in the planning of two further prosopographical projects. One of these was *The Clergy of the Church of England* (CCE), jointly nurtured by another KCL historian, Arthur Burns, with colleagues at Kent and Reading.[10] Over the same period, while Kruse (a Viking-Age archaeologist by training) and Nelson (a mainly Carolingian historian) had been teaching together, they had found that their interests overlapped in Anglo-Saxon England, and had begun planning a digital *Prosopography of Anglo Saxon England* (PASE). As with CCE, this project was developed with colleagues at other universities, principally Cambridge, where Simon Keynes became a co-director with Nelson; team researchers were Alex Burghart, David Pelteret and Francesca Tinti. Both of these projects were developed in partnership with Harold (as Technical Research Director) and John, and both were granted funding, for five years each, by the AHRB in 1999.

The year 2000 saw some important reflections on the nature of prosopography. An international conference was convened by Averil Cameron at the British Academy to mark 50 years since the announcement of the project on Late Roman Prosopography at the FIEC meeting of 1950 (Cameron 2003). It also marked the opening of the second phase of the *Prosopography of the Byzantine Empire* project, with AHRB funding. It had been agreed that the British team would leave the period 867–1024 to the scholars in Berlin and would start work on the period 1025–1204 (initially, to 1180). John Martindale retired once PBE I was published; it was the good fortune of the project that Michael Jeffreys, Professor of

Modern Greek at the University of Sydney, had moved to the UK some time after the appointment of his wife, Elizabeth Jeffreys, to the Bywater and Sotheby Chair at Oxford. He was appointed as the manager of the next phase of the project, assisted by Tassos Papacostas, together with Mary Whitby and Olga Karageorgiou; the digital management was undertaken by John Bradley, working increasingly with Elliott Hall. This undertaking was rapidly revealed to be very different in character from what had gone before. The Byzantine Empire of the first period had been a fairly clearly defined entity. By the eleventh century the fortunes of the empire were intertwined with those of a wider medieval world. The scope and nature of the project were encapsulated in a new name, *Prosopography of the Byzantine World* (PBW) and a PBW workshop was held at the British Academy in 2002 to explore some of these complexities, with experts on the history and prosopography of several adjacent cultures (Whitby 2007). It became increasingly clear that the contents would be not a total account of each actor involved, but instead an assembling of the materials from a clearly defined range of sources. For this the factoid approach was the perfect tool; as Jeffreys stated, the resource is 'a prosopographical reading of Byzantine sources, 1025–1180 . . . while PBW should be examined for what it contains, it should never be assumed that what it does not contain does not exist' (Jeffreys et al. 2016, home page).

All these projects reflected one of the crucial new aspects of working in a digital environment, which facilitates collaboration in a transformative way. Each of these projects drew on different kinds of source and presented different challenges. CCE traces the careers of clerics in the Church of England between 1540 and 1835, based on a very specific body of evidence: 'the Database draws on a core of four types of record maintained in diocesan collections: registers, subscription books, licensing books and *liber cleri* or call books' (Clergy Database 2013). The sources therefore provide the structure for the data.

For PASE, as for PBE and PBW, the sources were defined by period, the initial phase drawing on 'sources written during the period from 597 to 1042'.[11] These projects all demanded collaborative work on a large scale, across sources of very different kinds; in the case of PBW these were in several languages. For such collaboration to be productive, the intellectual structure had to be crystal clear to all contributors. John Bradley further defined the factoid concept and its deployment: 'No factoids (including Events) appear unless they are linked both to Persons and to Sources. This principle is rigorously applied so that users are in a position to follow the Person-to-Source "trail", and to make their own reference to the relevant Source at any stage' (PASE 2010). CCH had been looking for an alternative to the INGRES system for some time, and the development of the open-source MySQL system offered the opportunity to do this. It was John who was given the responsibility for undertaking and overseeing this transition. This then became the basis of all future projects that required database technology – mainly but not exclusively the prosopographies. For collaborators who were geographically dispersed or only had access to slow internet connections, he created 'data collection databases' (DCDs), where the information was recorded in basic factoid format, ready for uploading to the master database, where it could be linked into the wider network of factoids; this was to enable and empower real and increasing collaboration (Nelson 2012). Alongside members of the research team, postgraduate students at King's were given the opportunity to contribute to PBW. The outcome was several publications of remarkable consistency and clarity; while scholars may use the materials to reach varied conclusions, and while new sources may come to be examined, the basic assemblage of the data will not become obsolete.

PASE I was published online in 2005; in 2006 the first edition of PBW was published at the International Congress of Byzantine Studies. In 2005 the PBW team obtained funding from the Leverhulme Trust to add more materials from Arabic sources;[12] in 2006 the Leventis Foundation funded a three-year Research Fellowship, which allowed Dr Judith Ryder to undertake important new work on ecclesiastical sources. In 2005 the PASE team obtained a second Resource Enhancement grant from the AHRB to cover the shorter but highly complex period 1042–66, adding coverage of all English persons down to c.1100.[13] It also added information on landholders recorded in Domesday Book for 1066 (*Tempore regis Edwardi*) and from 1086 (*Tempore regis Wilhelmi*).[14] Its use of Domesday, in particular, was to have considerable impact on the wider public, not least because of the work of Stephen Baxter. This ambitious second edition, enhanced thanks to John and his team by a more user-friendly web interface and more powerful search functions, was launched in 2010, and subsequently enhanced. A new edition of PBW was launched in 2011,[15] and a third edition in 2016.[16]

Over this period the research environment had again changed. In 2005 the AHRB was converted into the Arts and Humanities Research Council, to provide full parity in status – if not in funding – with the other Research Councils. This brought Humanities Research into the remit of the Department for Trade and Industry, which later became the Department for Innovation, Universities and Skills. The new Council lost some of the independent input from other bodies (the Funding Council of the AHRB had included representatives from the Department for Education and Skills, the Department for Culture, Media and Sport and the Leverhulme Trust). It also lost the commitment to basic, facilitating projects, particularly long-term ones, and to data collection; research projects were now required to demonstrate that they were intended to deal with a 'research question', and they were encouraged to respond to research 'themes' proposed by the Council. Frustratingly, this has tended to overshadow the kind of enabling methodological research which John undertook in partnership with the other projects, and which was fundamental to the collaborative work of CCH. It also led to the design of a new kind of project; the assembling of essential data needed to be justified by a specific question. Further very important prosopography projects, conceived to meet these requirements, continued to use and develop the factoid structure; these are what John has described as third-generation Factoid Prosopographies.[17]

John was therefore involved over almost two decades in the development and delivery of several complex, similar but not identical, databases of people; among other important advances, this allowed him to develop and test the factoid model. This was primary research in its own right; it is set out in several articles (Bradley and Short 2005), and in particular in his 'What is Factoid Prosopography All About?' (Bradley n.d.). This creative work was extremely demanding; the demands were regularly underestimated by the researchers working on the sources – something which continues to be a problem in joint projects. The value-added amount of technical work over and above what had been estimated was calculated by John as 'more than 1.5 person years' (and what had not been estimated had not been funded). John's firm grip on such costings, his responsiveness to colleagues, and, again, to resultant synergies, were particularly important in ensuring the advance of both PBW and PASE.

The digital prosopographies at King's grew from a series of insights and interactions, which enabled the emergence of a profoundly new understanding of how to describe and record individuals in history. The creation of a Centre for such activities meant that a series of projects could be conceived not just within the boundaries of subject expertise, but as presenting a shared intellectual challenge (Bradley 2012). In a manner typical of digital humanities projects over this period, each undertaking could build on the experience of the others. John listened carefully to the demands, possibilities and problems of each project; he then explored the ways of responding, which were evolving as the technologies evolved. John's key role – with the support of the team that grew up around him – was to ensure this methodological clarity, and incremental growth in understanding, from which many more projects will benefit in future. Interdisciplinarity is always going to be difficult, and collaboration is hard to cost and administer; these groundbreaking projects were not easy, but they demonstrate what can be achieved when experts in a range of fields – from historical analysis to computer science – work together.

Notes

* Recent history is surprisingly hard to reconstruct. We are very grateful to colleagues who have helped us in clarifying this narrative, particularly Harold Short. Unless otherwise stated, all websites cited in the notes below were accessed and checked 6 September 2022.
1. fiecnet.org.
2. *Prosopographie chrétienne du Bas-Empire*. Four volumes have been published: A. Mandouze, *Prosopographie de l'Afrique chrétienne (303–533)* (1982); C. and L. Pietri, *Prosopographie de l'Italie chrétienne (313–604)* (2000); S. Destephen, *Prosopographie du Diocèse d'Asie (325–641)* (2008); L. Pietri and Marc Heijmans, *Prosopographie de la Gaule chrétienne (314–614)* (2013).
3. Michael Borgolte and Philippe Depreux were to become leading scholars of medieval European history, but not (to our knowledge) leaders in the field of digital humanities.
4. The first historian (who is one of the present authors) had been overly optimistic: Anglo-Saxon historical records have proved curiously resistant to inquiries for information about women. The wiser historian was Averil Cameron.
5. Established in 1998 by the British Academy, the Department of Education for Northern Ireland, and the English, Welsh and Scottish funding councils, the AHRB emerged after a long campaign by the arts and humanities community to create a British national arts and humanities funding body – a research council in all but name for research outside the sciences. On 23 April (St George's Day) 2005, in the last decade of the second millennium, the AHRC came into being.
6. Rathbone, personal communication.
7. *Digitalised Prosopography of Roman Egypt* (DPRE).
8. *PBE* I, introduction.
9. 'How to Publish PBE?', http://www.pbe.kcl.ac.uk/how-publish-pbe
10. *The Clergy of the Church of England Database 1540–1835*. http://theclergydatabase.org.uk
11. 'Introduction', http://pase.ac.uk/about. The proposal was to create 'a relational database aiming to provide structured information to all the recorded inhabitants of England between 597 and 1042, based on a systematic examination of the available written sources for the period, and intended to serve as a research tool suitable for a wide range of users with interests in the Anglo-Saxon period'.
12. *A Prosopography of Arabic Sources for Byzantines and Crusaders, 1025–1204*: the researchers were Letizia Osti and Bruna Soravia, both working from Italy.
13. The researchers were Alex Burghart (KCL), Andrew Bell (Cambridge), Natasha Hodgson (Cambridge), Juliana Dresvina (KCL) and Ben Snook (Cambridge).
14. http://domesday.pase.ac.uk/pde/about.jsp (consulted 1 February 2021).
15. http://db.pbw.kcl.ac.uk/jsp/index.jsp (consulted 1 February 2021).
16. 'Welcome to PBW 2016!', https://pbw2016.kdl.kcl.ac.uk
17. 'Factoid Prosopographies at CCH/DDH KCL', https://www.kcl.ac.uk/factoid-prosopography/projects

References

Bradley, J. n. d. 'What is Factoid Prosopography All About?'. Accessed 5 September 2022. https://www.kcl.ac.uk/factoid-prosopography/about
Bradley, J. 2012. 'No Job for Techies: Technical contributions to research in the digital humanities'. In *Collaborative Research in the Digital Humanities*, edited by Willard McCarty and Marilyn Deegan, 11–26. Abingdon: Routledge.

Bradley, J. and H. Short. 2005. 'Texts into Databases: The evolving field of new-style prosopography', *Literary and Linguistic Computing* 20 (Suppl.): 3–24.

Brunt, P.A. 2004. 'Jones, Arnold Hugh Martin (1904–1970), historian'. *Oxford Dictionary of National Biography*. Accessed 5 September 2022. https://www.oxforddnb.com/view/10.1093/ref:odnb/9780198614128.001.0001/odnb-9780198614128-e-34223

Bullough, D. 1985. '*Aula renovata*: The court before the Aachen palace', *PBA* 71: 267–301.

Cameron, Averil (ed.). 2003. *Fifty Years of Prosopography: The Later Roman Empire, Byzantium and beyond*. British Academy Scholarship Online. https://doi.org/10.5871/bacad/9780197262924.001.0001

Cannon, John. 2004. 'Namier, Sir Lewis Bernstein (1888–1960), Historian'. *Oxford Dictionary of National Biography*. Accessed 5 September 2022. https://www.oxforddnb.com/view/10.1093/ref:odnb/9780198614128.001.0001/odnb-9780198614128-e-35183

Conisbee, M. n.d. 'The History of the Arts and Humanities Research Council'. Accessed 5 September 2022. https://www.history.ac.uk/makinghistory/resources/articles/AHRC.html

Davies, C.S.L. 2004. 'Stone, Lawrence (1919–1999), Historian'. *Oxford Dictionary of National Biography*. Accessed 5 September 2022. https://www.oxforddnb.com/view/10.1093/ref:odnb/9780198614128.001.0001/odnb-9780198614128-e-72453

Eck, Werner. 2003. 'The Prosopographia Imperii Romani and Prosopographical Method'. In *Fifty Years of Prosopography: The Later Roman Empire, Byzantium and beyond*, edited by Averil Cameron. British Academy Scholarship Online. https://doi.org/10.5871/bacad/9780197262924.003.0002

Fiorillo, M. 2015. 'Il progetto "Digital Prosopography of Roman Egypt"', *Aegyptus* 95 (1): 135–56.

Gelzer, Matthias. 1912. *Die Nobilität der römischen Republik, von Matthias Gelzer*. Leipzig-Berlin: B.G. Teubner.

Jeffreys, M. et al. 2016. *Prosopography of the Byzantine World*. King's College London.

Jones, A.H.M., J.R. Martindale and John Morris. 1971–92. *The Prosopography of the Later Roman Empire*. Cambridge: Cambridge University Press.

Le Roy Ladurie, E. 1975. *Montaillou, village occitan de 1294 à 1324*. Paris: Gallimard.

Marriott, I. 1979. 'The Authorship of the Historia Augusta: Two computer studies', *Journal of Roman Studies* 69: 65–77.

Martindale, J.R. (ed.) 2001. *Prosopography of the Byzantine Empire*. Aldershot: Ashgate.

Martindale, J.R. 2003. 'The Prosopography of the Later Roman Empire, Volume I: A memoir of the era of A.H.M. Jones'. In *Fifty Years of Prosopography: The Later Roman Empire, Byzantium and beyond*, edited by Averil Cameron. British Academy Scholarship Online. https://doi.org/10.5871/bacad/9780197262924.003.0001

Mathisen, Ralph W. 2003. 'The Prosopography of the Later Roman Empire: Yesterday, today and tomorrow'. In *Fifty Years of Prosopography: The Later Roman Empire, Byzantium and beyond*, edited by Averil Cameron. British Academy Scholarship Online. https://doi.org/10.5871/bacad/9780197262924.003.0003

Münzer, Friedrich. 1920. *Römische Adelsparteien und Adelsfamilien*. Stuttgart: J.B. Metzler.

Nelson, Janet L. 2012. 'From Building Site to Building: The *Prosopography of Anglo-Saxon England* (*PASE*) project'. In *Collaborative Research in the Digital Humanities*, edited by M. Deegan and W. McCarty, 123–34. Farnham: Ashgate.

Nelson, Janet L., David A.E. Pelteret and Harold Short. 2003. 'Medieval Prosopographies and the Prosopography of Anglo-Saxon England'. In *Fifty Years of Prosopography: The Later Roman Empire, Byzantium and beyond*, edited by Averil Cameron. British Academy Scholarship Online. https://doi.org/10.5871/bacad/9780197262924.003.0011

Sansone, D. 1990. 'The Computer and the *Historia Augusta*: A note on Marriott', *Journal of Roman Studies* 80: 174–7.

Siemens, Raymond G., Susan Schreibman and John Unsworth. 2008. *A Companion to Digital Humanities*. Hoboken, NJ: Wiley.

Strassi, S. 2015. 'Premessa', *Aegyptus* 95 (1): 115–17.

Syme, Ronald. 1939. *The Roman Revolution*. Oxford: Clarendon Press.

Tomsin, A. 1966. 'Projet de prosopographie de l'Égypte romaine'. *Association Internationale de Papyrologues. XIe Congrès International de Papyrologie*, Milan, 195–208.

Trapp. E. (ed.) 1976–96. *Prosopographisches Lexikon der Palaiologenzeit*. Vienna: Veröffentlichungen der Kommission für Byzantinistik / Österreichische Akademie der Wissenschaften, 1.

Ullmann, W. 1979. *The Carolingian Renaissance and the Idea of Kingship*. Cambridge: Cambridge University Press.

Whitby, Mary (ed.) 2007. *Byzantines and Crusaders in Non-Greek Sources, 1025–1204*. British Academy Scholarship Online. https://doi.org/10.5871/bacad/9780197263785.001.0001

3
Braving the new world: REED at the digital crossroads

Sally-Beth MacLean

> . . . if eREED is built properly, it has the potential to support sig-
> nificant integration between REED itself and the research work of
> others around the world who share common interests with REED –
> placing REED solidly in the emerging global interconnected digital
> library. (Bradley 2011)

John Bradley has had a seminal influence on the evolution of the Records
of Early English Drama (REED) project, from print volumes to open
access digital editions. At a SSHRC-funded research workshop in April
2011 titled 'Envisioning REED Online', he presented an analysis of the
consistently structured data then locked in our print volumes, pointing
the way to a more dynamic future that would exploit the data in a linked
digital universe.[1] This essay will draw upon John's insights while reporting on the varied challenges of moving prosopographical data using a
long-established methodology for print production to a new digital platform. Thanks to his thoughtful guidance as our Senior Digital Humanities
Advisor, REED is moving in deliberate steps to increase access to our historical data for early modern theatre studies and to engage with Web 3.0
strategies in order to increase its potential for diverse applications.

Records of Early English Drama (REED) is a widely respected international humanities research collaboration based at the University of
Toronto, with partners in Canada, the United States and Britain. The
project was founded in 1976 to locate documentary evidence about
early entertainment practices and their connection to the cultural life of
Great Britain in the medieval and renaissance periods. The date range
for a systematic survey of surviving records of drama, secular music and

mimetic entertainment for England, Scotland and Wales by a collaborative team of editors would focus on the earliest date of record until 1642, when the public theatres in London were closed because of civil unrest. The goal of the multi-volume series envisaged was to publish transcriptions of the relevant portions of diverse historical documents, accompanied by a critical apparatus, including an introductory essay with detailed document descriptions; textual and endnotes; translations; English, Latin and Anglo-French glossaries; and an index anticipating varied interdisciplinary interests. The individual research projects of the team were to be organised along geographical boundaries: initially major cities such as York, Chester, Coventry, Newcastle upon Tyne and Norwich, but subsequently expanding to focus on historical counties and the even more formidable, biggest city of them all, London. Opening up the research survey to include county-wide performance records led to a wider range of documents to be explored, many never published previously and some difficult for all but the most determined to access, much less transcribe. Not only civic, guild and cathedral ordinances and accounts but also parish churchwardens' accounts and vestry minute books, civil and ecclesiastical court cases, monastic accounts, private household accounts, letters and journals, all became part of an editor's task, with richly rewarding results.

Beyond the research phase, there were foundational principles and guidelines for the series established during the early years of REED. Uniform guidelines for manuscript transcription were debated and agreed at the outset by members of the international Executive Board, in order to guarantee consistency and lasting quality of scholarship. A commitment to accuracy was to be another founding principle: all transcriptions submitted by an editor were to be checked by a qualified member of staff against manuscript reproductions, or in some cases, by an associate commissioned to check on site against the original. Organising a team of editors (currently 44 in total) soon identified the need for a standardised editorial methodology as well as common research guidelines for the series.[2] In 1980, the REED Handbook for Editors was published by the project, primarily for members of the editorial team, but it has also been used by others.[3] These principles have been followed, as much as humanly possible, by staff and editors ever since, thereby guaranteeing a stable body of cumulative research data reliable enough to be used by a wider community.

Between 1979 and 2015, 36 REED volumes were published in print and, with the exception of the seven London volumes, all are freely available in pdf format online on the Internet Archive (http://archive. org). In 1998 REED negotiated ownership of the electronic rights to all its publications with its publisher at the time, the University of Toronto Press, so the project has been unencumbered by copyright restrictions as the possibilities of contributing resources for the world wide web have opened up. Admittedly, it took many years to build capacity to produce the born-digital editions that were launched in 2017 with *Staffordshire*, edited by J. Alan B. Somerset.[4]

The steps taken during REED's digital transformation have been published elsewhere and the details need not be repeated here, but there were two factors that persuaded REED's Executive Board to move beyond their original vision of the project as a print-based series (MacLean 2014; MacLean with Somerset 2011). The first was ongoing frustration with ineffective dissemination of research discoveries that challenged entrenched orthodox accounts of the evolution and diversity of pre-modern English theatre practices. If the years of work by the collaborative team failed to reach most classrooms and if their publications were limited in availability to the major research libraries that could afford to purchase the increasingly expensive volumes, the outreach to wider audiences offered by the web held compelling advantages. The second factor was the increasing support – even preference – of grant funding agencies for digital development projects. REED has depended on public- and public-sector funding since its beginning, so following the money became another incentive. As a scholarly endeavour, open access dissemination of all REED's resources has therefore been a practical as well as a moral choice.

Although the complex three-volume set of *Civic London to 1558*, edited by Anne Lancashire with David J. Parkinson, was still published in print as recently as 2015, the foundations for *REED Online* had been laid during the previous decade. REED's *Patrons and Performances* research and educational website, launched in its first phase in 2003, was the cornerstone.[5] Developed in partnership with the University of Toronto Libraries and the GIS & Cartography Office in the Department of Geography, University of Toronto, the website has a schema for events relating to patronised touring performers culled from published REED records texts to date, linked with new research into patron biographies, provincial performance venues and historical touring routes and locations, interoperable with mapping.

A three-year grant in 2007 from the Arts and Humanities Research Council (AHRC) in Britain supported the collaboration with John J. McGavin (University of Southampton) and John Bradley (King's College London) for a second digital initiative, to develop a bibliographic research website titled *Early Modern London Theatres* (EMLoT), which launched in its first phase in February 2011.[6] EMLoT seeks to locate, assess and digest all transcriptions of pre-1642 documents relating to the London theatre that have been published from the mid-seventeenth century to the present (MacLean et al. 2014). At the time of writing the website includes data for eight Middlesex theatres north of the Thames, six Surrey theatres south of the river, and four within London's city walls.

The logical next step, funded by the Andrew W. Mellon Foundation, was to develop the framework for a prototype born-digital edition for delivery on the web in 2012, with our technical partners led by John Bradley at the Department of Digital Humanities, King's College London.[7] The pilot project took a small subset of REED records relating to the Fortune Theatre already collected by Jessica Freeman for the *Middlesex, including Westminster* edition but not yet in final production at the Toronto office. The Fortune records and some elements of the editorial apparatus were used to develop and explore new protocols, workflows, data formats and software, thereby paving the way for implementation of 'eREED' editions to come. The *Fortune Theatre Records: A prototype digital edition*, launched in 2013, successfully tested development of a new online production environment for REED editorial staff, experimentation with TEI markup of complex texts, digital indexing of persons and places, and linking with related data in REED's *Patrons and Performances* and EMLoT websites. The TEI-XML schema, open source Entity Authority Tool Set (http://eats.readthedocs.org) and Kiln platform framework (http://git hub.com/kcl-ddh/kiln) used for the Fortune were further customised for more sophisticated digital delivery of the eREED editions launching in 2017, not long after the final print volumes were published.[8]

Much has been accomplished, but REED remains at the crossroads, wanting always to maintain its solid foundations but ready to embrace deeper engagement with the affordances that Web 3.0 offers. The challenge of converting 36 legacy print volumes to TEI-encoded digital editions for interoperability with current and forthcoming digital editions is enormous and can only be managed with fresh funding and new partners willing to adopt some or even one of the print editions for new digital purposes. An initiative titled 'REED London Online', led by Diane Jakacki (Digital Scholarship Coordinator at Bucknell University), in partnership with REED and Susan Brown (Canada Research Chair in Collaborative Digital Scholarship, Guelph University), was funded by the Andrew W. Mellon Foundation in 2018 to explore, in greater depth, ways to bring REED's London legacy volumes into the new digital platform of Canadian Writing Research Collaboratory (CWRC/CSEC), while also adapting and connecting data in REED's other London-centric digital resource, EMLoT.

This partnership work continues, thanks to a generous three-year further grant from Mellon, as part of a broader Liberal Arts Based Digital Editions Publishing Cooperative project.[9] It is obvious that the full potential of cross-collection searching will not be realised until all collections are online as digital editions, but we have also pledged to develop interoperability with both EMLoT and *Patrons and Performances*.

Despite these immediate challenges we have to go beyond internal goals for *REED Online*. The founders of REED could not have conceptualised the series in this way but it can now be recognised as a massive, richly annotated dataset of dramatic, ceremonial and minstrel activity ripe for mining on the web. As Bradley pointed out in 2011:

> although the REED collections have quite bit of narrative text that is meant to be read through (acknowledgements, historical background, several of the appendices, description of editorial procedures, introduction to glossaries and index), most of each volume, both in terms of the number of sections and the number of pages, present significantly formal, structured materials: the records themselves and their translations, of course; documents, patrons and travelling companies (included in print in earlier volumes, now dealt with in REED's P&P online database); the actual glossaries and index; and the bibliography. Thus, REED volumes contain a large amount of formally structured material that one would not think of primarily as narratives. This confirms that the narrative-oriented e-book approach to their publication would be leading one in the wrong direction. (Bradley 2011, 14)

Editorial experience with structuring REED data for digital delivery really began with the *Patrons and Performances* project, initiated in 1999 but dating back to 1984 as an in-house database in BASIC, titled 'Pastime', and programmed on a Commodore 64 computer. The data subsequently migrated through d-Base II and IV, to Microsoft ACCESS, and finally to a more powerful open-source MySQL relational database.[10] The patrons data will now be the remaining focus for this essay, not only because the issues relating to identification of historical persons stimulated the move to adoption of database technology in the first place but also because these same patrons, whose performance troupes number over 1,600, will be our first step into the wider world of linked data.

Even before the Ur-database in BASIC, the complexities of developing scholarly standards for identification of individuals in the royal, noble, ecclesiastic and gentry classes had to be faced for indexing the first volumes in the series. The requirement was set early to index every individual named in REED records using consistent standards. Many names from local sources were parishioners and guild members in towns who appeared only once, or very sporadically, and whose surnames could only be represented by their spelling (sometimes with minor variants) in the original record. For those belonging to higher levels of society, standard reference works offered more reliable modernised spellings of recognised family names and titles that could be used to help users approaching REED volumes via the indexes (probably the most common strategy). For the purpose of establishing consistent series principles for identifying persons, R.F. Hunnisett's historically informed *Indexing for Editors* provided essential guidance. One of his opening statements still resonates as we contemplate our next moves towards sharing our prosopography and ontologies for the web:

> If all indexes could in future be compiled and set out uniformly, it would be a considerable aid to historical scholarship. It is the purpose of this work to discuss the principles on which indexes to record publications should be compiled, to suggest solutions to the practical difficulties which confront all indexers, and to recommend rules and practices which it is hoped will be generally approved and adopted for future publications. (Hunnisett 1972, 8)

The guidelines for indexing inspired by Hunnisett's useful manual have been the basis for subsequent representation of persons in REED indexes, but the key reference works recommended for identifying nobility and gentry, such as *The Complete Peerage* and the *Dictionary of National Biography*, have also served for the *Patrons and Performances* prosopography. Others, such as the *History of Parliament* series with up-to-date biographies of members of parliament, have been added since as new publications appeared; the availability of many such sources online now has accelerated the research task greatly.[11]

The impetus for REED's prosopographical work, now over three decades in progress, was inspired by some apparently simple payment records for provincial performances by touring medieval and renaissance entertainers kept by town, monastic and household accountants, such as this one: 1587–8: 'Given to my Lorde Stewardes players x s' (Exeter Receivers' Account Rolls, mb 5d) (Wasson 1986, 164). The following account entry for the queen's players was easy enough to index: many sources would verify that Elizabeth I ruled in 1587–8. However, what or who was the Lord Steward?

Dedicated research was needed both to index and identify this Lord Steward of the Household: Robert Dudley, Earl of Leicester, appointed in 1587 for a brief year before his death in September 1588. When the patrons research began in the 1980s, it was already apparent that Leicester's players appeared elsewhere across the country. Why and where did they travel, what connections political or regional did their patron have, and did these connections affect the troupe's choice of itinerary or the patron's motivation to lend his name to their activities? Did his other relationships, family background, marriages, and preferred residences reveal motivations for travel? The theory underlying the creation of the patrons database was that some of these questions might be answered through systematic research into the titles, political and locally held offices, lands and residences of each patron, as well as basic birth and death dates. Some years later, genealogical data was comprehensively collected, with fields added for parents, grandparents, siblings and offspring. For the queen's favourite, Robert Dudley alone, the database contains specific dated details for five titles, 75 offices, six major residences, lands in 19 counties and 155 events naming his performance troupes. Furthermore, the interactive GIS map helps to locate spheres of influence: all performance locations, those locally held offices that can be precisely located, and principal residences (whether they remain standing, have been reduced in size or are archaeological sites). Although reporting on cartographic work is not my purpose here, it should be noted that the same editorial standards have been followed systematically in this context: modernised names have been adopted from Eilert Ekwall's standard reference work, *The Concise Oxford Dictionary of English Place-Names*, 4th edn (1960). Geographical coordinates primarily derived from authoritative Ordnance Survey of Great Britain maps and Ordnance Survey Openmap online base mapping resources provide the foundation for the current updated version on *Patrons and Performances*.[12] Visualising research data through mapping is a fundamental and ongoing purpose for REED that began with this first website project.

Analysis of REED's patrons and performances data has stimulated research by others into specific performance troupes and the political implications of related patronage, but the accumulation of prosopographical detail could invite wider application. The data has been double-checked and builds on the solid foundations of standard reference works. Funding limitations have prohibited more ambitious archival research for individual patrons' biographies, but the reference works chosen, especially the online publications of the *History of Parliament* and the *Oxford Dictionary of National Biography*, are grounded in recent studies of archival sources. At this stage in REED's digital evolution, there has been recognition of the need to establish an ontology of terms for persons and troupe names consistent across the eREED collections, *Patrons and Performances* and EMLoT. As a first step towards engaging with more widely recognised formal ontologies, we plan to add VIAF and wikidata links to forthcoming REED editions.

Yet even establishing common terms for faceted browsing across REED's own resources is raising fundamental questions. It is readily apparent that maintaining some aspects of the REED *Patrons and Performances* work would involve unwelcome duplication of effort by staff already engaged in creating entity pages for patrons, places and events for digital editions. As we look at including more detailed patrons' biographical data using the EATS tool, should we ingest from the patrons database all the offices and lands collected for all patrons over the course of three decades? For example, the national and regional significance of Robert Dudley, Earl of Leicester, can be established by ingesting his titles, major offices and principal residences: is there still value in knowing that he held the local office of commissioner of *custos rotulorum* in Caernarvonshire, c.1579, at a time when he was also Chancellor and Chamberlain of the county?[13] The open access *History of Parliament* biography for Robert Dudley includes the same information. If we add links to the *History of Parliament* – as seems an obvious step that would eliminate the need for repeated annotation of references to him and other historical persons in the editorial apparatus – should that be sufficient? Even the addition of *ODNB* links could be considered, though the required subscription for access could render these links less useful for some. Another option could be to selectively add offices relevant to individual locations that have yielded evidence of performance. The staff labour required to create entities, for example, for every *custos rotulorum* appointment held in Welsh counties that have no patronised entertainers in their surviving performance records must be a practical, even a humane, concern.

Looking at the VIAF links for Dudley raises another question: one of the items on the VIAF list identifies him as 'Robert Dudley, 1st Earl of Leicester English nobleman and the favourite and close friend of Queen Elizabeth I'.[14] When REED's guidelines for indexing were established in 1980, the decision was made to follow *The Complete Peerage*'s style in using absolute succession numbers for the nobility, a practice followed consistently ever since for all REED publications. As a result, Robert Dudley is identified throughout as the 14th Earl of Leicester, seemingly in conflict with the VIAF reference. Is this a problem?

Despite present debates about the ingestion of *Patrons and Performances* prosopography data for dissemination in digital editions via *REED Online*, we are now looking ahead to its further evolution as a viable contribution to linked open data. As a first step into the world of RDF triple store and shared ontologies, the historical persons associated with medieval and renaissance theatrical patronage seem a less contentious aspect of REED's data than, for example, agreement on a common terminology for performance activities themselves, that vary widely in usage across our field: an internal debate has been raging recently around the variously named 'summer king', 'summer lord', 'May lord', Robin Hood, and 'summer, May or Whitsun game' events. The person entity structure customised by its developer, Jamie Norrish, for EATS, currently includes Existences (authority, with date(s)); type (nobility, male or female); Name type (Primary: family, given, major title); Relationship (with related entities of various types, including locations); Notes; and Subject Identifiers (URLs specifically about the entity, wikidata, *ODNB*). Ingesting the patrons data will require substantial expansion of relationship entities in particular: additional titles, offices (select or comprehensive), and genealogy. Yet the potential for linking to other datasets on the web where appropriate becomes feasible for the first time in REED's history: for each entity, the Published Subject Indicator (PSI) is the information resource (the webpage), and the PSID at the top of each entry screen is the URI for that resource. REED's performance patrons in particular represent a medieval and renaissance cultural heritage dataset that should offer a valuable resource for broader analysis of individuals of historical significance such as Robert Dudley, Earl of Leicester, whose social network, activities and relationships can be traced not only with his performers but also with royalty, other nobility, gentry, towns, counties and several levels of government. Even within eREED collections, dated events associated with Dudley extend beyond appearances of his entertainers (bearwards, players, musicians) at multiple locations to include other instances of him appearing in person on the road. Just to cite one example, he was appointed chamberlain of the county palatine of Chester in 1565 – a post that the Stanley earls of Derby had regarded as theirs by hereditary right. During Leicester's visit to Chester in June 1584, Stanley, the 13th Earl of Derby (or 4th, according to *ODNB*), was a prominent member of Leicester's entourage – perhaps too prominent, since the orator's assigned speech of welcome to 'the Cheefe mentayno < . . . >defendourr and patrone' of the city 'was not well liked of because he did direct it to *Earle* darby: & hauinge ended sayd God blesse the Earle of darby' (Manley and MacLean 2014, 32). When the legacy edition of

Cheshire including Chester (Baldwin et al. 2007) joins other editions on *REED Online*, tagging of the entity for Dudley will expand to include his relationship as chamberlain of the county palatine of Chester and to his cousin, Henry Stanley, earl of Derby, an important patron in his own right.

At REED we have been committed to using free, open-source software to build our web research and educational resources since the launch of the EMLoT project in partnership with John Bradley and King's College London. This has enabled the sharing of software tools and has saved on annual licence fee costs. The open content of the eREED digital editions is made available to the public under CC licenses. Yet both the *Patrons and Performances* and EMLoT relational databases are still locked into specific content management systems: Drupal, favoured by the University of Toronto Libraries when *Patrons and Performances* was upgraded in 2015, and Django, used by King's College London's digital development team when EMLoT was initiated and recently upgraded when the data was transferred to a UTL server in 2018. Obviously, we should be migrating all our research resources into a single repository, using the same TEI-XML format and entity-tagging system, and that is an immediate goal. But as we consider how best to integrate our own resources, we also recognise the need to begin untethering them for diverse uses and repurposing.

Several of the boxes of Tim Berners-Lee's 5-Star Open Data scheme[15] can be ticked already: the data is open on the web; *Patrons and Performances'* patrons, troupes and events, EMLoT and some of the eREED data is structured; and non-proprietary open source software tools are used. Not all the data has public URIs but the eREED's accumulating entities do and as patrons data is ingested from *Patrons and Performances,* that need will gradually be met for linking prosopographical data with other resources of global scholarship on the web. Some dedicated and immediate homework lies ahead to seek out existing ontologies dealing with related structured data from the historical period we are dealing with ourselves: for example, we have just learned about the Cambridge Group for the History of Population and Social Structure. The authoritative Campop website has datasets with controlled vocabulary for occupation terms used in historical records that we will be using for those entities going forward, looking also towards establishing links between REED and the Cambridge Group.[16] In the spirit of collaboration that has been a hallmark of REED's scholarship from its earliest days, we must also consider creating entities for offices and relationships that might not be considered fundamental to our purpose: for example, would other historians of our period welcome access to the cumulative data we have been collecting for patrons such as the lords chamberlain of the royal household or the justices of the peace, county by county?

As we look towards interoperability of controlled and authoritative data within and beyond REED's own framework, we have much of the infrastructure required to support linked open data in *REED Online*, via Kiln's built-in RDF triple store and processes for generating RDF and for populating and querying the triple store. With EATS used as our entity system at this time, all of the entities created to date have URIs suitable for use in a LOD context, and, with the addition of patrons' biographical data soon to be ingested from *Patrons and Performances*, even more will be added. Encounters with RDF, OWL ontologies and SPARKL lie ahead, across the digital crossroad that we have reached.[17] For now, we recognise the beckoning signpost but are still gathering resources and comrades for the journey.

Notes

1. The two-day workshop brought together an international group of junior, mid-career and senior scholars who were interested in REED's future and could provide expert guidance in planning the project's digital development. Bradley's paper (as yet unpublished) was titled 'What is This Thing called REED? Capturing and expressing REED's essence in a digital future'. All websites cited in the notes below were accessed and checked 6 September 2022.
2. Douglas and MacLean's *REED in Review* (2006) includes an initial chapter describing the origins of the project by REED's founder, Alexandra F. Johnston, as well as others by two of the first members of the Toronto editorial staff, outlining the development of methodology for the series: MacLean, 'Birthing the Concept: The first nine years', 39–51; and Abigail Ann Young, '"Practice Makes Perfect": Policies for a cross-disciplinary project', 52–62.
3. The *Handbook for Editors* was first compiled by Alexandra F. Johnston and Sally-Beth MacLean and subsequently revised by MacLean in 1990. It is freely available on REED's website in pdf format.
4. See *REED Online*, http://ereed.library.utoronto.ca. *Cambridgeshire*, edited by John Geck with Anne Brannen, was published in 2022.
5. http://library2.utm.utoronto.ca/otra/reed/
6. http://emlot.library.utoronto.ca. EMLoT has been migrated from its original host at King's College London to join other REED digital resources at the University of Toronto Libraries.
7. The third partner for the Fortune Theatre project was Jason Boyd as co-PI at Ryerson University, Toronto.
8. An SSHRC Connection grant for 'An open source digital publishing framework for theatre history' supported the engagement of James Cummings, our TEI-XML expert for the schema, and Jamie Norrish, developer and programmer of both EATS and Kiln.
9. https://cwrc.ca/reed
10. The MySQL database, with ColdFusion as the middleware, was maintained on a University of Toronto Library server, thanks to our partnership with Sian Meikle, now Director, Information Technology Services, University of Toronto Libraries.
11. http://www.history.ac.uk/projects/digital/history-parliament-online. To quote from the website, 'Since 1964, the History of Parliament Trust has been researching and publishing one of the most highly regarded works of historical reference . . . The History of Parliament Online contains the 21,420 biographies and the 2,831 constituency surveys published by the History of Parliament so far.'

12. For other historical sources used, see 'About the Maps', http://reed.library.utoronto.ca/content/about-maps
13. The *custos rotulorum* appointment was for the principal justice of the peace in a county and keeper of its court records.
14. http://viaf.org/viaf/52588603/#Leicester,_Robert_Dudley,_Earl_of,_1532?-1588
15. http://5stardata.info/en
16. http://www.campop.geog.cam.ac.uk. For example, the database of '1580–1830 Testamentary Occupational Data for England and Wales' provides 'data for the occupations and gender of decedents, collected from indexes to probate documents in England and Wales from county record offices and other sources covering the years between 1580 and 1830'.
17. Although I have not cited directly from these essays, both have had an influence on the direction ahead: John Bradley and his collaborator on EMLoT, Michele Pasin, co-authored a useful article, 'Factoid-based Prosopography and Computer Ontologies' (2015). Bradley also published a solo article, 'Silk Purses and Sow's Ears' (2014).

References

Baldwin, Elizabeth, Lawrence M. Clopper and David Mills (eds). 2007. *Cheshire including Chester*. Records of Early English Drama. Toronto: University of Toronto Press.

Bradley, John. 2011. 'What is This Thing Called REED? Capturing and expressing REED's essence in a digital future', University of Toronto symposium *Envisioning REED in the Digital Age*, Toronto, Canada.

Bradley, John. 2014. 'Silk Purses and Sow's Ears: Can structured data deal with historical sources?', *International Journal of Humanities and Arts Computing* 8(1): 13–27.

Bradley, John and Michele Pasin. 2015. 'Factoid-based Prosopography and Computer Ontologies: Towards an integrated approach', *Literary and Linguistic Computing* 30(1): 86–97.

Douglas, Audrey and Sally-Beth MacLean (eds). 2006. *REED in Review: Essays in celebration of the first twenty-five years*. Studies in Early English Drama. Toronto: University of Toronto Press.

Hunnisett, R.F. 1972. *Indexing for Editors*. Archives and the User, No. 2. London: British Records Association.

Lancashire, Anne with David J. Parkinson (eds). 2015. *Civic London to 1558*. Records of Early English Drama. 3 vols. Woodbridge: Boydell & Brewer.

MacLean, Sally-Beth. 2014. 'Records of Early English Drama: A retrospective', *Renaissance and Reformation* 37(4): 235–51.

MacLean, Sally-Beth, with Alan Somerset. 2011. 'From Patrons Web Site to REED Online', *Medieval and Renaissance Drama in England* 24: 25–37.

MacLean, Sally-Beth, Tanya Hagen and Michele Pasin. 2014. 'Moving Early Modern Theatre Online: The Records of Early English Drama introduces the Early Modern London Theatres Website'. In *New Technologies in the Renaissance*, vol. 2, edited by Tassie Gniady, Kristina McAbee and Jessica Murphy, 91–114. Medieval and Renaissance Texts and Studies Series. New York: Iter Academic Press.

Manley, Lawrence and Sally-Beth MacLean. 2014. *Lord Strange's Men and Their Plays*. New Haven, CT: Yale University Press.

Wasson, John M. (ed.). 1986. *Devon*. Records of Early English Drama. Toronto: University of Toronto Press.

4

Sustainability and modelling at King's Digital Lab: between tradition and innovation

Arianna Ciula and James Smithies

How to sustain a rich legacy

This chapter focuses on the development of technical approaches that support projects that John Bradley worked on during his career, but it is worth reflecting on another important legacy before we start: the development of career paths for King's Digital Lab (KDL) staff members, which are derived in large part from the work of previous generations of experts, like John, who helped define the career of Research Software Engineer (RSE). As generational change occurs and in line with reorientations across the digital humanities community (see Boyles et al. 2018), it has become increasingly clear that the surest way to sustainability is to ensure continuity of technical expertise, domain knowledge and tacit understanding. In the final analysis, John's enduring legacy, like those of so many of his colleagues, will be human as much as technical.

A career path for 'people like me'

John Bradley's career at King's College London spanned almost 20 years and paved the way for the RSE careers offered in KDL. The evolution of this professional identity occurred in subtle but inexorable ways over the course of his career. In the interview transcript by Nyhan and Flinn (2018, 209–26), Bradley frequently refers to 'people like me', a modest remark intended to emphasise an uncertain but also privileged institutional status. This repeated reference identifies a type of expert – consciously not a humanist, nor a technical support professional – who works closely with academics but retains a separate identity and an awareness that they inhabit different career paths. Characteristically, although this position has not always been optimal, Bradley (2012) takes care to note that it often brought rewards too, for example in the UK research assessment exercises.

KDL became operational in the year of Bradley's retirement (2015), creating a team of Research Software (RS) experts in an independent Digital Humanities (DH) Lab designed to support the Faculty of Arts & Humanities (FAH). The team (including John's colleagues along with some new recruits) evolved from the Department of Digital Humanities (DDH), itself an outgrowth of the Centre for Computing in the Humanities (CCH).[1] Before KDL was established in 2015, CCH/DDH delivered undergraduate and postgraduate teaching programmes, a PhD programme (DDH expanded further and delivers one undergraduate and five postgraduate programmes, as well as a PhD programme), and around 100 technical research projects.[2] Initially within the Centre, and later the Department, Bradley held non-academic posts (designated as 'analyst' roles) before moving to the academic role of Senior Lecturer in 2011. Building on his previous career at the University of Toronto, which he felt was enriched by inspirational colleagues and a pioneering environment, he moved to King's College London in 1997. After moving, he enjoyed a feeling of 'enormous liberation', based on a sense of intellectual freedom and possibility (Nyhan and Flinn 2018, 225).

Bradley occupied an interesting position between academia and research software development for most of his career, buttressed by a keen awareness of the North American system of tenured versus non-tenured faculty and its attendant issues (Bradley 2012), which he felt was replicated to a certain extent in the United Kingdom (Nyhan and Flinn 2018, 225). This experience led him to reflect on his role, the unsustainability of precarious labour and the lack of legitimacy and institutional status offered to people like him with considerable expertise and of unquestionable value to the research enterprise. Intriguingly, he often couched this in positive terms, noting the special relationships DDH staff developed with colleagues in academic departments – even as they had to accept the anomalous situation of being described in one way by the Human Resources department, while conducting quite different work:

> DDH exemplifies exactly this approach to collegiality between the digital humanities and established humanities disciplines, and promotes the view that the language that DDH 'supports' scholarship

for the rest of our school only tells a part of the story . . . Collegiality at DDH goes beyond interaction between full academic staff in our department and academics in other departments, but is also encouraged and supported for professional technical specialists, who are recognized as intellectual workers in their own right. Indeed, I like to think that I am an example of this kind of a role for professional staff within DDH. For years, much of my work within DDH/CCH has been closer to what in the computing world would be developer rather than academic, and was centred on project development work. (Bradley 2012, 22)

In his role in CCH/DDH Bradley paved the way for a third path, leading to the institutionalised RS careers at KDL. Indeed, there is a direct line from Bradley's experience and the professional orientation CCH/DDH staff brought to collaborative research projects (Bradley 2012, 17), to the KDL career model and its guiding assumptions:

The Lab sits in a boundary area of what we might term the 'RSE career continuum' between the research-intensive activity of full-time academics and post-docs, and technical roles supporting High Performance Computing and other resources. (Smithies 2019)

After undertaking a trial to define a career development model in 2018, KDL chose a relatively flexible model, reflecting the experience of people like John. Although the core staff (12 permanent employees) at KDL are hired under a Professional Service or PS contract, their career development document and RSE role definitions are flexible enough to be applied to other contractual models too, including academic or research contracts. Significantly, however, while the RS roles of Analyst, UI/UX Designer, Engineer, Project Manager and Systems Manager at KDL are defined in alignment with relevant emerging national and international approaches to RS careers (see Society of Research Software Engineering 2019), they are also mapped to the Software Skills for the Information Age Framework[3] and industry software development via the Agile DSDM® framework (Agile Business Consortium 2014).

The RS career development model used in KDL was designed to address the specific characteristics of DH at King's College London, building on an ethos of collegiality – making the model scalable across research traditions and related expertise building, and capable of interfacing with digital systems, data and infrastructures – and in collaboration with the Information Technology Services (ITS) and Human

Resources (HR) departments. Among other things, the model suggests that the productive intersections between the DH and RSE communities and networks (workforce, workflows and workplace culture) remain relatively unexplored.

Bradley's legacy is therefore intimately connected to the human dimension of KDL, comprising people like him – experts whose roles are inscribed in 'a research culture that recognizes the contribution of non-teaching staff to its research goals, and works to maintain some space for non-teaching staff to work on their own research' (Bradley 2012, 13). These are people capable of 'develop[ing] their own appropriate professional expertise . . . outside of the constraints of only a single project' (Bradley 2012, 23). Indeed, the establishment of KDL in 2015 provided an opportunity to review career models, to establish permanent roles beyond a single project lifecycle, and not only provide a legitimate RS label for the holistic approach outlined above but give it an operational spin as a career pathway that overlays and maps pragmatically onto the higher education context. While KDL's RS career model could have been developed in various disciplines, it is telling that it evolved in an Arts & Humanities research facility with a pressing need to retain a *continuum* of expertise and channel professional identities into sustainable career profiles. Recognition of expertise is not abstract; it is always anchored in the work of people like John who carve out professional identities over the course of long careers. A DH lab team inevitably operates in a multidimensional space (Smithies and Ciula 2020), inhabited not only by technical infrastructures but also by other social systems where, together with financial pressures and constraints, status and frameworks of career development and progression play a prominent part – not only to retain expertise but ideally to nurture talent and foster a diverse range of intellectual contributions to research.

Overview of archiving and sustainability effort

As the section above suggests, the socio-technical system informing the life of the lab is varied and inclusive; it encompasses human, financial, administrative and technical systems. Given the scale of DH at King's, people with specialist expertise and tacit knowledge represent the key to bridging continuity and innovation. The second dimension needed to sustain the DH tradition and fulfil KDL's mandate to increase digital capability across the Arts & Humanities is caring for the cluster of technical systems entangled with the lab team.[4] KDL's technical systems encompass multiple interacting layers: (1) the lab (micro) system of hardware and software (the first inner layer of technical system in Figure 4.1)

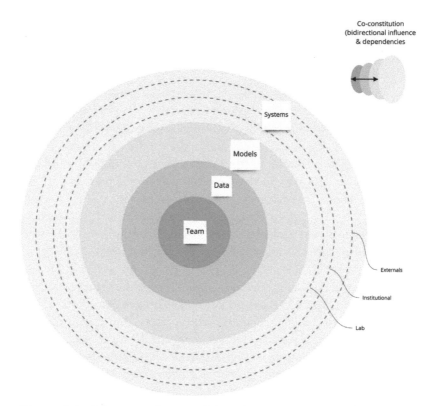

Co-constitution
(bidirectional influence
& dependencies

Systems

Models

Data

Team

Externals

Institutional

Lab

Figure 4.1 RSE team, data, models and systems are entangled with each other. Concentric circles denote co-constitution as opposite to exogenous relations. The socio-technical system is multilayered.

which also interacts with (2) the university technical systems (e.g. college network and daily backup system; high-performance computing facilities); and (3) external (national, such as the UK's national high-speed research network, and international) infrastructure and services more widely. KDL technical systems (1) are comprised of hardware and software, web servers, network infrastructure, application frameworks, programming languages, tools (for project, data and code management) and equipment.

It is important to recognise the ways in which the social and technical aspects of the lab co-constitute each other and have evolved into their current form over several decades. More pointedly, in the context of this chapter, the team's decisions and actions enable and constrain the process of model creation and manipulation (as discussed further below), which in turn is enabled and constrained by the technical systems in place operating at the three layers mentioned above. Coordinated by the lab Senior Systems Managers and Principal Research Software Engineer, the team's decisions and actions have a direct impact on lab systems. This is less direct yet still strong at an institutional level (via the University eResearch team) and on external systems (for instance, national network and cloud services).

We hinted above at the scale of web development activity and projects at King's College London, which intensified in the 1990s–2000s at CCH/DDH (in 2011 DDH also merged with the Centre for eResearch in the Humanities, CeRch). KDL 'inherited' these projects, along with a set of pressing challenges:

> A generation of legacy projects that need maintenance but are out of funding have reached critical stages of their lifecycles, an increasingly hostile security context has made DH projects potential attack vectors into institutional networks, heterogeneous and often delicate technologies have complicated the task of maintenance, and an increasing number of emerging formats have made archiving and preservation yet more difficult. (Smithies et al. 2019)

Prior to the establishment of KDL, and because of the scale of their DH footprint, CCH, DDH and CeRCH engaged with and reflected upon some of these challenges too; however, the establishment of KDL – with a clear mandate to develop RSE methods – created the opportunity for closure and subsequent transition towards a systematic yet holistic approach to technical systems and infrastructure management, alongside a mature project development lifecycle. In a recent overview of KDL's archiving and sustainability effort, Smithies et al. (2019) present an extended report on the issues at stake and the approach KDL took to dealing with c.100 legacy websites inherited from DDH. The projects were heterogeneous in disciplinary as well as technical terms, built using a wide range of technical systems. In terms of server operating systems alone:

> KDL projects were running: Windows 2003 (2 servers); Windows 2008 (9 servers); Debian 4 (13 servers); Debian 5 (32 servers); Debian 6 (33 servers); Debian 7 (10 servers). (Smithies et al. 2019)

At the time of transfer of ownership and responsibility to KDL, DDH infrastructure was already significant by DH standards; it included rack servers supporting 400GB RAM, over 180 virtual machines, 27TB of data,

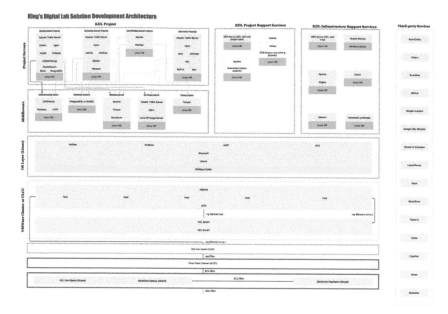

Figure 4.2   KDL solution development architecture by Brian Maher, Tiffany Ong, Miguel Vieira and Tim Watts.

and hosting of over 100 digital projects. The back-end and front-end of these projects used application frameworks comprising a mix of technologies: Java (with custom-based frameworks such as rdb2java and DJ Facet), Python (particularly the web framework Django), the bespoke XML-based publishing solutions XMod and Kiln, and PHP-based frameworks such as WordPress, Omeka and Typo3.

As explained in Smithies et al. (2019), the techniques used to manage these rich and heterogeneous projects matured into an ongoing process of archiving and sustainability tailored to KDL's historical, technical and business context. It is applied to new as well as legacy projects, in a manner which ensures that systems as well as data are maintained throughout defined lifecycles (King's Digital Lab 2019). To control this, open-ended Service Level Agreement (SLA) contracts are offered to Principal Investigators (PIs) of collaborative research projects to secure maintenance of legacy projects in their live state; however, other options for archiving are also possible and assessed as described below. To make the overall approach sustainable, it had to be integrated into the lab's Software Development Lifecycle (SDLC, briefly discussed in section 2) and, in so doing, align with KDL infrastructure architecture (Figure 4.2) and core technical stack (Figure 4.3), while at the same time informing practices of forward planning for new projects:

Dependencies	Languages	Frameworks	Building	Testing	Continuous Integration	(Continuous) Deployment
pip	Python	Django	Django Compressor	Pytest		
		Django REST Framework		Tox		
					Fabric	GitHub Actions	GitLab Pipelines	Travis	
npm	JavaScript	Vue	Vue CI	Jest		
	SCSS	Bootstrap	Gulp	Siteimprove		
PostgreSQL						
Elasticsearch / Kibana						
Fastly						Redis / nginx / Traefik / ATS
Docker / Docker Compose						

Figure 4.3 KDL core development stack by KDL solution development team.

> The experience of KDL suggests that the most effective strategy is to offer open ended contracts and then embed archiving and maintenance deep into the culture of technical development, from requirements definition and the identification of digital research tools and methods, through to infrastructure design, deployment and maintenance. This is based on a conception of 'infrastructure' that moves beyond material technical necessities, templates, and process documents (as essential as they are), towards one that acknowledges the centrality of people, funding, ethics, technology strategy, software engineering method, and data management to the long term health of our research infrastructures. (Smithies et al. 2019)

In practice, at the level of the lab's technical systems, as Figures 4.2 and 4.3 indicate, sustainable management of lab projects required the adoption of limited server and development environment stacks, in a move away from the more flexible but difficult to manage environment used in earlier eras.[5] KDL infrastructure underwent a major hardware upgrade in spring/summer 2018 with the installation of 5 Dell R640 servers, a solid SAN (44 x 960GB SSD disks, 6 x 6TB 7.2k spinning disks) comprising 35TB RAID6 and an 18TB slow archive. Over 200 virtual machines, running Debian and Ubuntu Linux, are hosted on this infrastructure (physical cabinets are located in the University of London Computing Centre), which supports a software stack primarily constituted by Django Python, Javascript and associated management tools (Solr / Elastic Search, Docker, Travis) but also including a range of legacy software (Java, PHP). Additional servers are used for centralised services such as image storage, mail and user authentication (Smithies and Ciula 2020; De Roure et al. 22–8). While the infrastructure is not used at its full capacity and will undergo expansion (for additional projects and corresponding virtual machines), a business model and cost recovery process to support its migration to King's College London's central eResearch platform and conversion to infrastructure-as-code in 2023 are in place.

The lab approach to its technical systems is not presented here as a model of best practice *ad absolutum* and in a vacuum, but as the reasoned result, hopefully useful to others, of a contingent process of assessment, maintenance and upgrading of technical systems undertaken by KDL from its establishment. It represents a process of rationalisation that built directly on the efforts of previous generations of digital humanists at King's College London, incorporating many of their approaches and resolving many of the issues they struggled with as systems and projects grew in scale and complexity. Inevitably, this approach to sustaining KDL's legacy in a renewed technical environment will undergo other phases of change, some regular and planned (for example, infrastructure upgrades occurring every five years, software framework upgrades recurring at pre-planned intervals), others less predictable in frequency and effect (such as alternative solutions to support projects dependent on discontinued applications, or external service providers and vendors; malware attacks).

A degree of change is of course implied by the entropy inherent in technical systems; we need to assume that Django and other components of KDL's development stack will be supplanted one day. It is, however, the responsibility of an RSE unit embedded in a research and education context to define boundaries and manage change, to control risk to project owners and institution alike. Rather than imposing a hermetic (closed) system, KDL's management of their technical systems aims to create and monitor a risk-resistant and sustainable technical environment. In another change from earlier iterations of DH at King's, this philosophy is supported by an increasingly close and transparent relationship with external university technical teams (eResearch, IT Services, library and archives teams as appropriate) and beyond (RSE networks, DH communities, national and international funders and policy makers). The team recognises the risks of this approach, given the tendency to standardise systems and infrastructure in large organisations, but feels that the benefits are outweighed by a sense of community and a growing sense that 'good citizenship' leads to mutual trust. The risks at stake are of course of a different magnitude from earlier generations, too, necessitating a more open approach: from issues of security and vulnerability to obsolescence and unwieldy heterogeneity of systems. In a DH laboratory like KDL, where dozens of projects are often developed simultaneously and dozens of others are maintained in the background, it is essential to create spaces capable of facilitating experimentation and change, but thoughtful constraints have to be applied to protect the core development stack and infrastructure.

Pragmatic diversity of approaches and some examples

The archiving and sustainability approach that KDL adopted is layered and holistic. Indeed, operating in a dynamic research context and dealing with a heterogenous legacy portfolio requires pragmatic and creative solutions cognisant of the technical systems that projects are built with or rely on for their access, functionalities and presentation. In practice, the legacy projects that Bradley worked on while employed at King's College London were subject to different maintenance and management approaches, described below. While not always ideal, they represent pragmatic solutions to often highly complex technical and financial issues.

As described in King's Digital Lab 2019, in alignment with the needs of partners and their research community, several options to sustain and/or archive a legacy project have been developed:

1. Maintenance under costed SLA (usually of 5-year duration).
2. Migration (to the College ITS microsite service until it ceased to be available or to an external host, often another higher education institution or commercial provider).
3. Static conversion whereby public access to legacy projects' websites and datasets is maintained but, more often than not, with reduced functionalities.[6]
4. Dataset deposit within the lab or institutional technical systems as well as external repositories.
5. Minimal archiving entailing minimal storage (for two years minimum) for a project website (virtual machine) and data on KDL infrastructure as well as web archives. A placeholder page is shown at a project URL with description, metadata, and links to snapshots as appropriate.[7]

Two cases are sufficient to illustrate how option 1 translated into practice for two of the projects Bradley had direct involvement with: *Clergy of the Church of England Database* (Burns et al. 2005) and *People of Medieval*

Scotland (Beam et al. 2010–19). Although now both under SLA, these two projects exemplify how, for complex DH legacy projects, hosting and maintenance usually has to be complemented by ad hoc costed Statements of Work (SoW) and associated 'repair' activities.

With three project directors – Arthur Burns (King's College London), Stephen Taylor (University of Durham) and Ken Fincham (University of Kent) – and in partnership with CCH from the start,[8] the *Clergy of the Church of England Database 1540–1835* (CCEd) began in 1999 and was funded by the UK Arts and Humanities Research Council (AHRC). It makes available and searchable the records of clerical careers from over 50 archives in England and Wales, and aims to provide coverage of as many clerical lives as possible, from the Reformation to the mid-nineteenth century. CCEd is an invaluable research tool for both national and local, academic and amateur historians, as well as genealogists. The expansion of the database (at the time of writing holding 161,251 people, 3,010 sources and over 2 million data points) has relied on three senior research officers and a sizeable community of volunteers (over 60 research assistants across England and Wales), who have provided additional archive entries on an ongoing basis.

In 2017, the SLA was supplemented by a modest SoW,[9] supported by the Department of History and the Faculty of Arts & Humanities at King's College London, for KDL to undertake urgent bug fixing and a minimal modernisation of the project architecture. Though pioneering at the time of its initial development by CCH in 2000, it had reached end of life by 2017 and, more importantly, posed substantial security risks to KDL infrastructure. Bradley's involvement in defining the complex CCEd architecture was of paramount importance in the process of assessing maintenance issues – testament to the value of tacit knowledge and interaction beyond written documentation (which in the case of CCEd was not all retrievable due to a change in documentation system that resulted in some loss of material). CCEd relies on a suite of software components, including rdb2java, designed by Bradley and other CCH/ DDH colleagues to facilitate the development of interfaces between web applications under J2EE servers such as Tomcat and relational databases. The admin web application interface was built entirely using Java. The front-end public site is mixed, as it also includes WordPress (built with a custom theme querying the MySQL database) and a content management system that KDL excluded from its core technical stack to lower maintenance overhead. As part of the SoW delivery, CCEd was 'transplanted' from a Tomcat server (running Suse Linux 9 dating back to 2003) into a new secure Debian virtual machine;[10] the deployment process was made more secure; bugs in the queries of the admin web application interface were diagnosed and fixed; and the live updates of the CCEd master (MySQL) database were transferred to the KDL team, thus bypassing individual dependencies on Bradley. Local databases that fed the master database via several architectural components, including sophisticated Perl scripts, were conceived to develop a pioneering solution architecture for co-editorial work of multiple remote volunteers in the early 2000s, but were built with software that had reached end of life (for instance, FileMaker Pro v. 5) and presented substantial issues for project sustainability. Given these complexities in the project dependencies and architecture, when KDL agreed to a short SLA and associated (now completed) SoW, they also recommended a full redevelopment, and are working with the team of PIs to assess its feasibility and seek external funding as needed. The CCEd example shows how project life-cycles are organic and evolving; KDL's SDLC is designed to support this process with a governance model intended to streamline often complex conversations within and outside the team.

People of Medieval Scotland (PoMS) is a database of all the known people of Scotland between 1093 and 1314 mentioned in over 8,600 contemporary documents, complemented by some Social Network Analysis tools. The PoMS website is an outcome of three projects: *The Paradox of Medieval Scotland* (2007–10), *The Breaking of Britain* (2010–13), also funded by the AHRC, and the *Transformation of Gaelic Scotland in the Twelfth and Thirteenth Centuries* (2013–16), funded by the Leverhulme Trust. The prosopography project was led by Dauvit Broun (University of Glasgow) as PI and completed in 2013, two years before the establishment of KDL (note that in 2016 some further work was undertaken to complement it with some Social Network Analysis tools).[11]

As with CCEd, widespread use of PoMS across the national and international research community provided a strong case for post-project support, which, in the case of PoMS, was also fuelled by some investment from a new project. *Community of the Realm of Scotland, 1249–1424: History, law and charters in a recreated kingdom* (CoTR, Caton et al. 2021), funded by the AHRC and led by PI Alice Taylor (King's College London),[12] started in 2017 with KDL involvement as technical partner. This project includes resource enhancement for PoMS, not only demonstrating the project's continued intellectual value but de facto supporting its maintenance. CoTR makes use of PoMS data and extends it with new records and information, therefore requiring the PoMS database to remain functional (if not necessarily publicly accessible) in its post-project phase until at least 2025 (recently renewed to 2028). It is an example of the sometimes inventive ways in which project maintenance and sustainability need to be managed, and the need to explore all angles before deciding to close down an important project.

As in the CCEd case, the PoMS SLA was complemented by a SoW,[13] detailing the work needed to upgrade the PoMS server, any out-of-support web application components, and how to rationalise the code base as needed. Newer than the CCEd infrastructure, the resources published as PoMS were hosted across Debian 5 and 6 servers (operating systems that were significantly out of date by the time KDL was established). The back-end of the project was built in Python 2.6 on Django 1.4.5, with Mezzanine and a MySQL database, venv 1.4.9, and DJ Facet. As well as needing to upgrade the server to a supported version, the faceting component (in particular) had to align with the new KDL architecture (Solr/Elasticsearch as per Figure 4.2). The SoW is now complete; requirements have been prioritised following the popular MoSCoW technique and are being managed in line with the lab's Agile methodology. While the refactoring of the PoMS front-end, in this case also partially relying on WordPress, and porting it into the Django web publication framework Wagtail were less of a priority, they were undertaken within budget. Other desirable features, such as migrating the visualisations of PoMS data or 'labs', were deemed impractical given the resources available and hence remained out of scope. Having noted that, however, Bradley was appointed honorary research fellow in KDL from 2019, presenting other opportunities for experimentation outside the funding available via CoTR. It was therefore possible for KDL to foster further collaborations and data re-use, with the aim of making PoMS prosopographical datasets (for instance, personal and location entities) available as bulk downloads and exposed Linked Open Data.[14] Originating as a cluster of multiple projects, and dynamically feeding other KDL legacy resources[15] – and then evolving via a more recent project – PoMS illustrates the opportunities and challenges of managing complex intersections across RSE expertise, scholarship, data, models and systems.

To conclude this section, we can note that, provided the relevant core research communities (historians of the Church in the case of CCEd; historians of medieval Scotland in the case of PoMS) engage with, support and value a legacy resource, and provided the project passes KDL technical feasibility assessment,[16] it is possible to extend the life of projects and slow the often-inevitable process of decline. Guided by supporting documentation and project management tools, projects can leave the limbo of their legacy state and enter a monitored post-project phase (such as undergoing targeted upgrades aligned with KDL's new infrastructure and core development stack, tailored conversions of data models and associated applications development). In many cases, these post-project phases de facto lay the foundations to scope and cost the requirements for a new project out of the legacy one. However, only when multiple factors (human, financial, political, ethical and technical) coincide can archiving and sustainability methods facilitate the transition from gentle sunsetting to repair (Nowviskie 2015) or even re-building.

Data cataloguing and exposure

Accessing data via dynamic web applications and sophisticated front-ends is not, however, the only option and surely not the most sustainable option in the long run. In the DH community and GLAM sector, a significant shift from systems to data is occurring – a process that can ease the maintenance burden of many long-running projects. When KDL projects are still functional or have been subject to repair via SoWs, they may also provide access to surrogates of project sources (be they philological, historical, geographical, musicological or archaeological), making it possible to query their metadata or textual versions and to link to interpretative outcomes. However, with some important exceptions, such as the cluster of epigraphical projects led by Charlotte Roueché (King's College London) and Gabriel Bodard (School of Advanced Study), project data often remain hidden behind web interfaces and inaccessible to users in their 'raw' formats.

It is important to consider the complexities of opening up hidden data. Smithies (2017, 220) has previously suggested that open access, when examined in the wider context of technical systems and processes, reveals an interlocking chain where open data represents only one bead (enabled by open standards and open-source code). While data exposure is therefore good per se, it is not enough to ensure access, and should not mask the need for attention to standards, workflows, systems and services. This is especially the case given the ever-widening audiences and communities of academics, students, cultural sector professionals and the general public, who demand access to data and expect to be able to engage with it programmatically, especially where project outputs have been supported by public funding. The success of initiatives providing humanities researchers and students with the skills and tools to manipulate data directly, such as *The Programming Historian*, reflect a parallel demand and a shift in data literacy;[17] the opportunities for exploiting public data to study and re-imagine social systems is echoed further in the digital social sciences and living laboratory platforms. Reflections on the performativity of data (Gray 2018) and initiatives such as The Public Data Lab claim the concept of 'digital infrastructure literacy' 'to include not just competencies in reading and working with datasets but also the ability to account for, intervene around and participate in the wider socio-technical infrastructures through which data is created, stored and analysed' (Gray et al. 2018, 1).[18] While arguably less relevant for the research domains that KDL legacy projects tend to occupy, DH research needs to embrace open approaches to technologies, including the unpacking of subjectivity in the creation of data and adoption of platforms, and the analysis of performative aspects of data and platforms. Exposing data to make explicit the context of its production and analysis, to credit the labour that produced it, but also to make data workflows verifiable and contestable is important work.

This has become a key element in KDL's approach to archiving and sustainability: option 4 (mentioned above) entails data deposit for those cases where access to project data is suitable and viable. In addition to external institutional or subject-specific data repositories identified on a case-by-case basis as appropriate, KDL currently uses two internal King's College London solutions to publish data from inherited and new projects. One is the College-wide University Research Data Management System (KORDS)[19] and the other is the KDL-DDH CKAN data catalogue and repository (Ciula 2020).[20] The former belongs to the institutional layer of technical systems and solutions, while the CKAN solution is hosted on lab infrastructure (Figure 4.1). This system was implemented in consultation with College colleagues involved in research data management (RDM) and its use has evolved in collaboration with colleagues in DDH (in particular Paul Spence), the College library data management team and other partners who, like Bradley, were invested in the production of legacy projects or in teaching activities making use of legacy resources. In addition to access and re-use, this data cataloguing and exposure work aims to enhance projects' data citability and improve or enable integration with external collections, while also safeguarding their data from the potential loss (through technical entropy) of their front-end systems.

The attention Bradley and colleagues at CCH/DDH paid to data structures and models when designing their projects (for example, by adopting standards amenable to cross-project interoperability) makes it possible to mitigate technical change that is so much more limiting when, as seen above, systems are taken into account. Data exposure and data publication open up a range of other opportunities too, from unearthing and distilling documentation and tacit knowledge about past projects to integration with teaching activities and student involvement; from responsible communication with partners regarding co-created data to identification of appropriate data licences encouraging re-use while guaranteeing attribution. Five datasets and associated metadata (for *The Gascon Rolls, Henry III Fine Rolls, The Inquisitions Post Mortem, Schenker Documents Online* and, as mentioned above, *People of Medieval Scotland* projects) have been made public on KDL's CKAN instance, as part of the 'KDL-DDH legacy data exposure' project.

Modelling activities between continuity and change

The sections above described the three main dimensions of the lab: its team, data and systems. We reflected on the continued DH expertise at King's and its renewed RSE identity as well as the portability of technical systems and associated data from legacy to new projects. Next, we will address an important gap in the discussion, namely the core activity of creating models as bridges across the three dimensions of team expertise, data and systems. It is worth foregrounding this discussion with some deeper epistemological context that speaks to the way modelling functions in KDL as integrative glue, tying together technical, business and methodological elements (Ciula et al. 2020 and forthcoming). Studies exploring distributed cognition have demonstrated that when computational tasks are socially distributed, as is the case in KDL, 'computational dependencies are also social dependencies' (Hutchins 1996, 224). While partially captured by governance and technical documentation, live interactions are lost but some 'operational residua' (Hutchins 1996, 373) of the team's interaction with the lab systems and data remain and propagate in the form of models of different kind and function. Research quality and sustainability depend on multiple factors, including their level of integration with the other three dimensions.

Notes on modelling and what it means

Modelling, defined as the translation of complex systems of knowledge into computationally processable models, is considered by many a core practice in DH research (McCarty 2005, 20-72; Buzzetti 2002; Beynon et al. 2006; Ciula and Marras 2019). A recent publication which contextualises modelling within the humanities and DH research traditions (Ciula et al. 2018b) offers some further reflections:

The high reliance on modelling in this discipline [DH] is due to the fact that explicit models are extensively required in DH in order to operationalise research questions. This operationalisation process includes representation of objects of study in the form of data to process, in order to make objects and observations computable, as well as to analyse, transform and visualise data.

In DH as in other scientific settings, modelling can be considered a creative process of reasoning in which meaning is made and negotiated through the creation and manipulation of external representations . . . In the DH context models . . . are created in a way so as to lend themselves to be used and manipulated in a computational setting. However, the form models take can vary extensively, from a formal schema, to the logics informing the running of code (programs or apps) as well as to digital objects such as maps or 3D models. Such frameworks can be local to one institution, one project, or even to one single researcher, but can also be generalisable and scalable, as we see in the development of common formalisms or standards such as the recommendations of the Text Encoding Initiative (TEI) guidelines to encode textual sources.

. . . [I]n the humanities and cultural heritage . . . the goal of the modelling is often to describe idiosyncratic phenomena or artefacts of human creation, acknowledging and valuing subjectivity as part of the modelling process. Often the objective is to express principles grounded to specific contexts rather than general laws. (Ciula et al. 2018a, 10–11)

Even if the production and use of models in DH is not and, arguably, ought not be limited to computational models, they play a crucial role 'as abstractions that allow data about the world to be stored in simplified structures (often relational databases) and acted upon by algorithmic processes that are models of logical or mathematical procedures themselves' (Smithies 2017, 172).

The DH tradition at King's College London contributed extensively both to the epistemology of modelling as well as its practical application through design and technical development. Willard McCarty, Professor of Digital Humanities at DDH, has reflected extensively on the ontology and epistemology of modelling, particularly in relation to historical styles of reasoning using digital machines (McCarty 2005; 2009; 2014; 2018). His main concern has been to shy away from a stagnant focus on models, in favour of a dynamic conceptualisation of modelling as knowing.

McCarty has called 'for a shift from models as static objects (e.g. what functionalities they enable) to the dynamic process of modelling (e.g. how were models built and used and for what purpose, what constraints they embed, what effect they have in refining research questions)' (Ciula et al. 2018a, 10).

McCarty's preoccupation with modelling is reflected in many of the DH projects developed at King's over the years, privileging explorations and practical demonstrations of how humanists can use computers to reason via modelling. That being said, the role modelling plays in a research and RSE context can vary and has not been systematically studied. If we accept Smithies' (2017) argument about the *continuum* of practices in DH research, in particular with respect to data analysis and algorithmic criticism, modelling can be at the core of empirical, exploratory and even deformative methodologies and need not be confined to the kinds of projects inherited by KDL (Smithies 2017, 168–79).

A detailed ethnographic analysis of the products of King's DH tradition would provide many examples of modelling activities, but it is possibly in the detailed reflections on the construction of data models (Bradley and Short 2005; Pasin and Bradley 2015; https://www.kcl.ac.uk/fact oid-prosopography) that the value of those efforts become most apparent. As discussed elsewhere, the factoid data model adopted in several projects that constitute part of the legacy estate of KDL is emblematic of limited yet 'adaptable' models able to 'grasp domain-specific concepts'. A factoid is an assertion made by an individual or a group of historians: a source 'S' at location 'L' states something 'F' about person 'P'. Coinage of the word 'factoid' evokes the 'historian's worry' (Bradley and Short 2005, 8) that records of assertions in historical sources are not the same as facts. The concept reflects a longstanding context-aware approach to historiography which, with adaptations and extensions, has been operationalised as a data model in several DH projects developed by CCH/DDH and elsewhere since 1995. Conceptually, as recognised by Pasin and Bradley (2015), the success of the model lies in its ability to grasp the relations of the components of very nuanced (multidimensional, complex, non-linear) narratives, not easily translatable to the unambiguous language of databases. Pragmatically, the model structures the projects that adopt it at the level of: data acquisition (acting as a conceptual metaphor for the underlying historiographical approach and as a guiding principle for data entry); data storage (factoid as a schema to inform the design of the projects databases); and data presentation (factoid as a core design concept to shape user interfaces). However, as Pasin and Bradley (2015) argue, factoid modelling is not a systematic application of formal structures to the prosopography of specific pre-modern societies, but rather a process of conceptualisation and formal structuring designed to accommodate a range of views on a certain society from the perspectives of different sources (Ciula and Marras 2019, 47–48).

Complementary to the foundational work on the theory of modelling by McCarty, the factoid example is pivotal in showcasing how, from an RSE perspective, data models have a cascading effect on storage solutions, interface design and data integration. With respect to the latter, Bradley's later research interests connecting to the Semantic Web and Linked Open Data principles[21] promise to widen the impact of these modelling practices beyond the single institutional context. The instantiations of these models (for example in relational databases) are in some cases already or will eventually be superseded; however, in the RSE context where they were designed and developed, they fulfilled the pragmatic function of bridging the tension between idiosyncratic objects of study, research questions, methods and datasets on one hand, and scalable and sustainable solutions on the other.

The key legacy of the pre-KDL generation is, therefore, epistemological in a rather praxis-oriented sense; while standards and technologies change, evolve and decay, efforts to achieve adaptable models continue. This epistemological legacy could well prove to be more significant for KDL and the DH community at large than its technical legacy.

KDL context

To understand what modelling is in the current KDL workflow it is necessary to take a closer look at its SDLC and at projects lifecycle, aligned to Agile DSDM methodologies. In Figure 4.4, the bold headings describe the lifecycle of a project idea for those cases when it can evolve from an initial contact with partners to the release process and maintenance phase. Key milestones in KDL projects can easily be mapped to Agile project phases, namely pre-project, foundations and feasibility assessment running from initial contact to kick-off meeting, followed by an evolutionary development phase with planned deployments and release process, followed in its turn by the post-project phase that is the subject of the earlier parts of this chapter. The interrupted-line boxes enclose overarching key high-level methods that shape those SDLC phases, namely design, build, maintain and monitor methods (Smithies and Ciula 2020).

While all data is 'taken and constructed' (Drucker 2011), depending on the project idea KDL is engaged with, data sometimes already exists at the pre-project phase (often in need of massaging or cleaning); in other

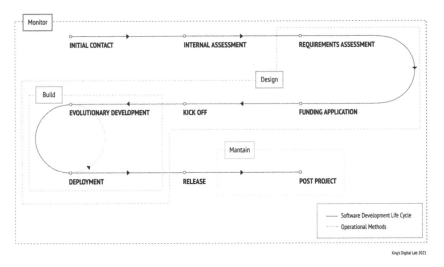

Figure 4.4 Integration of KDL SDLC with the lab operational methods by Tiffany Ong (based on Smithies and Ciula 2020, fig. 3).

cases, data is collected as part of a project activity. Either way, the team makes sense of project data and imports it into KDL systems (when not already present in some legacy format) by constructing and interpreting models. As discussed above, we define models in a relatively wide sense here, as artefacts of different kinds including but not limited to computational models. They can be produced during several phases of the SDLC (Figure 4.4). Thus, modelling can encompass, for example: negotiations around the meaning of the project units of analysis documented in diagrams and definitions which shape an agreed project language (during a design process that usually starts in the pre-project phase and evolves throughout the lifecycle); paper drawings used to draft the solution architecture for a project in its feasibility assessment (design method in feasibility or foundations phases); wireframes and static mock-ups of user journeys (design method in evolutionary development phase); and data models implementing the logical structure of a database (build method in evolutionary development phase). In the case of the legacy projects described above, when the team has to intervene to repair and rebuild, modelling requires an understanding of the units of analysis and mechanisms of legacy data models, along with the processing flows that act on them.

The creation of these models is – depending on the level of formalisation of the modelling process being considered – informed, guided and regulated by specific RSE expertise and processes, including research software analysis, UI/UX design and technical approaches

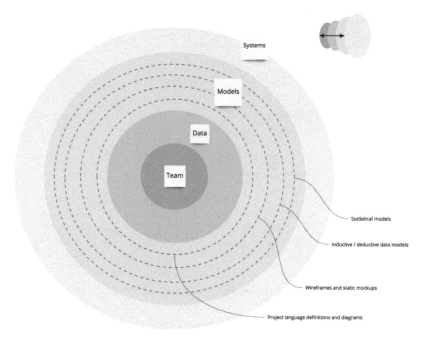

Figure 4.5   Models mediate and bridge team expertise, data and technical systems. Models are of different kinds and produced in different phases of the SDLC as part of the team's processes and methods.

to code development and systems management. Ideally, a 'cognitive ethnography' (Hutchins 1996, 371) exercise will be undertaken to pin down the range of interactions among the team (in line with its defined RSE roles discussed above), technical systems, processes and products of modelling at a given moment in time.[22] In lieu of that, and without the benefit of a systematic analysis to support it, our claim is that those interactions are guided by pragmatic alignment across technical innovations, standards, digital methods and relevant conceptual frameworks. Creativity and openness to diverse research domains, as well as the ability to identify patterns of similarity across heterogeneous projects, also play an important role and are integral to RSE expertise and processes.

In this respect, it is interesting to note that aspects of Bradley's background, education and life outside higher education influenced his academic and technical development work – especially his creative interest and knowledge in music (mentioned more than once in Nyhan and Flinn 2018). Not surprisingly, his acquaintance with music also influenced his thinking about the epistemology of DH tools, where the composer's workspace is used as a hook for a thought-provoking analogy:

> A performer might think of the piano as an instrument for making music. The music arises in the performer's head and is presented through the piano to the world. On the other hand, pianos also sit in composers' workplaces, where they can act as the tool to help make musical fragments that arise in the composer's mind more substantial so that they can be assessed better about how they might fit into a current composition. Here the piano is acting as a tool for thinking, in some ways, like what mathematics does for many scientists . . . Clearly, simple intent plays a role when a tool for exploring becomes a tool for making. However, the explanation for why a tool for making, such as the piano, can also act as a tool for thinking is not based solely on the user's intent to do so. What is it in the nature of the piano that makes it a tool that can function in these two quite different contexts: performance and composition? Do any of our DH-made tools operate in both these domains? (Bradley 2019, 6)

Without entering into the merits of the discussion about what constitutes a tool for thinking in a DH context, it is worth noting that the modelling efforts that underpin KDL's SDLC, carried out both across projects and on a project-by-project basis, serve multiple functions. As more general reflections on knowledge production from Science and Technology Studies demonstrate,[23] a model's primary function is to translate, reduce (Gooding 2003) and mediate (Bouiller 2018) the team's flow between representational states (for instance, from a verbal exchange with partners, to project governance documents, to whiteboard sketches, to a UML diagram) and performative functions across the SDLC (such as mapping across data models to process and integrate datasets). Positioned in the multidimensional context of the lab's team, data and systems, models are KDL's primary contribution to the epistemology of DH. It is through the production of models that software engineering processes guide the team in providing tailored and, as much as possible, adaptable and scalable technical solutions for data storage and infrastructure, as well as user interfaces for data entry and publication. However, depending on the project scope, modelling is organic not only to the team's SDLC but also to specific research project methods and discovery. While KDL's portfolio of projects is dependent on multiple factors (from legacy systems and expertise to evolving individual research interests; from funding opportunities to technical constraints; from institutional priorities to time allocation), the team has a great deal of agency in shaping it. Models are deeply entangled with tacit knowledge held across the team, as well as the lab's technical systems. Exploratory modelling is a risky but exciting avenue through which the team can challenge its technical stack, test new areas, and stretch lab capabilities. Setting aside the practical legacy provided by Bradley and his colleagues (represented in projects like CCEd and PoMS), it is reasonable to suggest that his most enduring legacy will be in the conceptual development and technical implementation of computational models designed for and in collaboration with researchers in the humanities.

If we accept Flanders' argument about the fundamental 'productive unease' of DH engagement with technology, we cannot but recognise that all models are inherently inadequate, or, in more positive terms, constrained by their purpose and improvable ad infinitum. In parallel to the discussion on open data, their sustainability depends on an interlocking chain of factors (of which, in the case of KDL, context, standards adoption and code integrity are paramount). In this chapter, we foregrounded their interdependence with core elements of the lab's socio-technical environment: namely expertise, systems and data. Following the start-up phase, where sustainability frameworks for expertise and systems are provided with solid foundations, lab efforts will most likely further refine its strategy with respect to data and models – the premise being that the core intellectual and technical challenges still lie in aligning all four dimensions.

Conclusions

The aim of this chapter was to examine issues of continuity as well as change in the practice of digital humanities with particular reference to the history of the field at King's College London. From the relatively long and unique tradition of DH at King's, KDL inherited an undoubtedly wonderful platform, but one which came with challenges and responsibilities. By reflecting on KDL team expertise, systems, data and modelling activities, the chapter has drawn a multi-layered picture of its socio-technical environment as it has evolved from this legacy and as it continues to identify and design practical approaches to sustain itself. Reflections on archiving and sustainability of legacy projects, along with modelling processes deeply integrated with the SDLC, are used to evoke a complex and multifaceted interplay between innovation and tradition, affected by the socio-technical settings within which KDL operates, and permeable to institutional changes as well as to individual and collective approaches. As for systems and data, the KDL team's language and practices around modelling have evolved and continue to change but remain at the core of its contribution to the epistemology of DH.

Notes

1. For a sketch of the earlier history of DH at King's see Short et al. 2012.
2. Around 100 projects, usually corresponding to public websites, are hosted in the KDL infrastructure. Some of these were inherited, as discussed in the following sections. Around 40 of them were referred to by Bradley (2012, 13) as multi-year collaborative research projects.
3. SFIA Foundation: https://sfia-online.org/. All websites cited in the notes below were accessed and checked 6 September 2022.
4. For reference concepts in the *social shaping of technologies* (SST) see in particular Russell and Williams 2002; on the relation of entanglement between humans and things see also Hodder 2014 and Preda 1999.
5. For more details of the tools used to support the stack see: https://stackshare.io/kings-digital-lab. For a more up to date overview on KDL infrastructure and technical stack see De Roure et al 2022, 22–8.
6. See e.g. http://pbe.dighum.kcl.ac.uk
7. See e.g. https://wip.cch.kcl.ac.uk
8. Technical staff who worked on the CCEd project from 1999 to 2013 include: Harold Short (technical supervision until retirement); John Bradley (Technical Consultant until retirement; construction of relational database and software, career modelling and search engines); Hafed Walda, Mark Stewart, Payman Labbaf, Paul Vetch, Arianna Ciula, Eleonora Litta Modignani Picozzi, Juan Garcés and Zaneta Au (Technical Project Officers); Elliott Hall (Software Developer); Paul Spence (Technical Consultant, publishing framework TEI XML); and Ginestra Ferraro (UX/UI Developer, implementation of new front-end in 2013, originally developed by Beatriz Caballero).
9. SLA and SoW documentation and associated work for CCEd were led by KDL team members Arianna Ciula, Elliott Hall, Brian Maher and Carina Westling.
10. Following the SoW completion, new upgrades were necessary and took place in 2019 and 2021, including the move of the VM to an Ubuntu machine. Updates of records and contextual content are on hold until funding is available for new development to take place.
11. Technical staff who worked on the PoMS website include John Bradley (Co-Investigator), and Michele Pasin, Charlotte Tupman, Beatriz Caballero and Miguel Vieira (technical support).
12. Alice Taylor was also Co-Investigator (Co-I) for PoMS. Not surprisingly, projects are linked to individual research careers and interests, revealing how much the KDL legacy portfolio intersects with colleagues' legacies at much more than the development level.
13. SLA and SoW for PoMS were led by KDL team members at the time: Paul Caton, Elliott Hall, Neil Jakeman, Brian Maher, Pam Mellen, Tiffany Ong, Miguel Vieira and Carina Westling.
14. See https://doi.org/10.18742/pszz-m429 and https://www.poms.ac.uk/rdf/doc/. With minimal support from KDL, Bradley had also worked on the RDF data conversion and exposure for the *Digital Prosopography of the Roman Republic* project (Mouritsen et al. 2017); see http://www.romanrepublic.ac.uk/rdf
15. In addition to the three projects out of which PoMS originated, the *Models of Authority: Scottish Charters and the Emergence of Government, 1100–1250* project (Broun et al. 2015–17) also imports data from PoMS for selected records.
16. See KDL's SDLC templates in our GitHub repository (King's Digital Lab 2018 onwards).
17. https://programminghistorian.org
18. https://www.publicdatalab.org
19. KORDS is an instance of Figshare which was purchased in 2020 to substitute the previous College Research Data Management System (https://librarysearch.kcl.ac.uk).
20. This approach to DDH legacy data cataloguing and exposure (2017–20: https://data.kdl.kcl.ac.uk) was undertaken by KDL with the involvement of Samantha Callaghan, Paul Caton,

Arianna Ciula, Neil Jakeman, Brian Maher, Pam Mellen, Miguel Vieira and Tim Watts in collaboration with colleagues and students at the Department of Digital Humanities (Paul Spence, Kristen Schuster, Minmin Yu). This work was a continuation of the wider archiving and sustainability effort described in Smithies et al. 2019 and was made possible through a seed fund grant offered by DDH (with Paul Spence as PI) and complemented by a student internship on the MA in Digital Humanities.

21. See http://romanrepublic.ac.uk/technical-overview/; Mouritsen et al. 2017.
22. A two-year Marie Curie fellowship was awarded to Urszula Pawlicka-Deger to conduct training and ethnographic research at KDL from October 2020 (see https://dhinfra.org). The project end has been postponed to September 2023 but several publications are out or in print.
23. See e.g. Latour and Woolgar 1979; Pickering 1995; Traweek 1992.

References

Agile Business Consortium. 2014. *The DSDM Agile Project Framework Handbook*. Accessed 5 September 2022. https://www.agilebusiness.org/resources/dsdm-handbooks

Beam, Amanda, Dauvit Broun, John Bradley, David Carpenter, John Reuben Davies, Kathryn Dutton, Nicholas Evans, Matthew Hammond, Roibeard Ó Maolalaigh, Michele Pasin and Andrew Smith. 2019. *People of Medieval Scotland 1093–1371* (1st edn *1093–1286*, 2010; 2nd edn *1093–1314* with Sophie Ambler, Alejandro Giacometti, Beth Hartland and Keith J. Stringer, 2012; 3rd edn including mapping and SNA functionality with Neil Jakeman and Cornell Jackson, 2016; 4th edn *1093–1371* with Ginestra Ferraro, Elliott Hall and Alice Taylor, 2019). King's College London. Accessed 5 September 2022.

Beynon, Meurig, Steve Russ and Willard McCarty. 2006. 'Human Computing: Modelling with meaning', *Literary and Linguistic Computing* 21(2): 141–57.

Boullier, Dominique. 2018. 'Medialab Stories: How to align actor network theory and digital methods', *Big Data & Society* July–December: 1–13. https://doi.org/10.1177%2F2053951718816722

Boyles, Christina, Carrie Johnston, Jim McGrath, Paige Morgan, Miriam Posner and Chelcie Rowell. 2018. 'Precarious Labor in the Digital Humanities: DH 2018'. In *Digital Humanities 2018: Book of abstracts / Libro de resúmenes*, edited by Élika Ortega, Glen Worthey, Isabel Galina and Ernesto Priani, 47–52. Mexico City: Red de Humanidades Digitales AC.

Bradley, John. 2012. 'No Job for Techies: Technical contributions to research in the digital humanities'. In *Collaborative Research in the Digital Humanities*, edited by Willard McCarty and Marilyn Deegan, 11–25. Abingdon: Routledge.

Bradley, John. 2019. 'Digital Tools in the Humanities: Some fundamental provocations?', *Digital Scholarship in the Humanities* 34: 13–20.

Bradley, John and Harold Short. 2005. 'Texts into Databases: The evolving field of new-style prosopography', *Literary and Linguistic Computing* 20 (Suppl.): 3–24.

Broun, Dauvit, Peter A. Stokes, Tessa Webber, Alice Taylor and John Reuben Davies. 2015–17. 'Models of Authority: Scottish charters and the emergence of government, 1100–1250'. Accessed 5 September 2022. https://www.modelsofauthority.ac.uk

Burns, Arthur, Kenneth Fincham and Stephen Taylor. 'The Clergy of the Church of England Database'. Accessed 5 September 2022. http://ccedb.org.uk

Buzzetti, Dino. 2002. 'Digital Representation and the Text Model', *New Literary History* 33(1): 61–88. https://doi.org/10.1353/nlh.2002.0003

Caton, Paul, Ginestra Ferraro, Geoffroy Noël, Miguel Vieira, Dauvit Broun, John Reuben Davies and Alice Taylor. 2021. 'The Prototype Dynamic Edition', *The Community of the Realm in Scotland, 1249–1424: History, law and charters in a recreated kingdom*. Accessed 5 September 2022. http://www.cotr.ac.uk/

Ciula, Arianna. 'Exposing Legacy Project Datasets in Digital Humanities: KDL experience'. King's Digital Lab blog, 7 July 2020. Accessed 5 September 2022. https://www.kdl.kcl.ac.uk/blog/legacy-project-datasets

Ciula, Arianna and Cristina Marras. 2019. 'Exploring a Semiotic Conceptualisation of Modelling in Digital Humanities Practices'. In *Meanings & Co: The interdisciplinarity of communication, semiotics and multimodality*, edited by Alin Olteanu, Andrew Stables and Dumitru Borțun, 33–52. Cham, Switzerland: Springer.

Ciula, Arianna, Øyvind Eide, Cristina Marras and Patrick Sahle. 2018a. 'Modelling: Thinking in practice. An introduction', *Historical Social Research* 31 (Suppl.): 7–29.

Ciula, Arianna, Øyvind Eide, Cristina Marras and Patrick Sahle (eds). 2018b. 'Models and Modelling between Digital & Humanities: A multidisciplinary perspective', *Historical Social Research* 31 (Suppl.).

Ciula, Arianna, Geoffroy Noël, Paul Caton, Ginestra Ferraro, Brian Maher and Miguel Vieira. 2020. 'The Place of Models and Modelling in Digital Humanities: Intersections with a Research Software Engineering perspective'. In *Book of Abstracts of Digital Humanities 2020*. Alliance of Digital Humanities Organizations. http://dx.doi.org/10.17613/789z-9p59

Ciula, Arianna, Geoffroy Noël, Paul Caton, Ginestra Ferraro, Tiffany Ong, James Smithies and Miguel Vieira. Forthcoming. 'The Place of Models and Modelling in Digital Humanities: Some reflections from a research software engineering perspective'. In *Elisabeth Burr Festschrift*, edited by Julia Burkhardt, Elena Arestau, Nastasia Herold, Rebecca Sierig and Marie Annisius. Leipzig: Universitätsbibliothek.

De Roure, David, John Moore, Kevin Page, Toby Burrows, David Beavan, Timothy Hobson, Giles Bergel, Abhishek Dutta, Andrew Zisserman, Aruna Bhaugeerutty, Samantha Blickhan, Alan Chamberlain, Arianna Ciula, Ian Cooke, Stella Wisdom, Graeme Hawley, Tim Crawford, Golnaz Badkobeh, David Lewis, Alistair Porter, Laurent Pugin, Rodolfo Zitellini, Nicholas Cronk, Birgit Mikus, Neil Jefferies, Peter Cornwell, Huw Jones, Cristopher Melen, Kieron Niven, Rachel Proudfoot, Gethin Rees, Pedro Máximo Rocha, Amy Sampson, Martin Wynne, Nicola Barnet, Masud Khokar and John Salter. 2022. *DigiSpec: Scoping future born-digital data services for the arts and humanities: case reports*, 22–8. Zenodo. https://doi.org/10.5281/zenodo.4716148

Drucker, Johanna. 2011. 'Humanities Approaches to Graphical Display', *Digital Humanities Quarterly* 5(1). Accessed 5 September 2022. http://www.digitalhumanities.org/dhq/vol/5/1/000091/000091.html

Gooding, David. 2003. 'Varying the Cognitive Span: Experimentation, visualization, and computation'. In *The Philosophy of Scientific Experimentation*, edited by Hans Radder, 255–84. Pittsburgh, PA: University of Pittsburgh Press.

Gray, Jonathan. 2018. 'Three Aspects of Data Worlds', *Krisis: Journal for contemporary philosophy* 1: 4–17.

Gray, Jonathan, Carolin Gerlitz and Liliana Bounegru. 2018. 'Data Infrastructure Literacy', *Big Data & Society* 5(2). https://doi.org/10.1177/2053951718786316

Hodder, Ian. 2014. 'The Entanglements of Humans and Things: A long-term view', *New Literary History* 45(1): 19–36.

Hutchins, Edwin. 1996. *Cognition in the Wild*. 2nd edn. Cambridge, MA: MIT Press.

King's Digital Lab. 2018–20. 'A Software Development Life Cycle for Research Software Engineering'. Accessed 5 September 2022. https://github.com/kingsdigitallab/sdlc-for-rse/wiki

King's Digital Lab. 2019. 'Archiving and Sustainability: KDL's pragmatic approach to managing 100 digital humanities projects, and more . . .'. Accessed 5 September 2022. https://www.kdl.kcl.ac.uk/our-work/archiving-sustainability

Latour, Bruno and Steve Woolgar. 1979. *Laboratory Life: The social construction of scientific facts*. Princeton, NJ: Princeton University Press.

McCarty, Willard. 2009. 'Being Reborn: The humanities, computing and styles of scientific reasoning'. In *New Technologies in Medieval and Renaissance Studies*, edited by William Roy Bowen and Raymond George Siemens, 1: 1–23. New York: Iter Press/Arizona Center for Medieval and Renaissance Studies.

McCarty, Willard. 2014. 'Getting There from Here. Remembering the future of digital humanities. Roberto Busa Award lecture 2013', *Literary and Linguistic Computing* 29(3): 283–306.

McCarty, Willard. 2005. *Humanities Computing*. Basingstoke: Palgrave Macmillan.

McCarty, Willard. 2018. 'Modelling What There Is: Ontologising in a multidimensional world', *Historical Social Research* 31 (Suppl.): 33–45. https://doi.org/10.12759/hsr.suppl.31.2018.33-45

Mouritsen, Henrik, Doninic Rathbone, Maggie Robb, Lee Moore and John Bradley. 2017. 'Digital Prosopography of the Roman Republic (DPRR)'. Accessed 5 September 2022. http://www.romanrepublic.ac.uk

Nowviskie, Bethany. 2015. 'Digital Humanities in the Anthropocene', *Digital Scholarship in the Humanities* 30 (Suppl. 1): i4–i5. https://doi.org/10.1093/llc/fqv015

Nyhan, Julianne and Andrew Flinn. 2018. *Computation and the Humanities: Towards an oral history of digital humanities*. Cham, Switzerland: Springer.

Pasin, Michele and John Bradley. 2015. 'Factoid-Based Prosopography and Computer Ontologies: Towards an integrated approach', *Literary and Linguistic Computing* 30(1): 86–97.

Pickering, Andrew. 1995. *The Mangle of Practice: Time, agency, and science*. Chicago, IL: University of Chicago Press.

Preda, Alex. 1999. 'The Turn to Things: Arguments for a Sociological Theory of Things', *Sociological Quarterly* 40(2): 347–66.

Russell, Stewart and Robin Williams. 2002. 'Social Shaping of Technology: Frameworks, findings and implications for policy with glossary of social shaping concepts'. In *Shaping Technology, Guiding Policy: Concepts, spaces and tools*, edited by Knut H. Sørensen and Robin Williams, 37–132. Cheltenham: Edward Elgar.

Short, Harold, Julianne Nyhan, Anne Welsh and Jessica Salmon. 2012. '"Collaboration Must be Fundamental or It's Not Going to Work": An oral history conversation between Harold Short and Julianne Nyhan', *Digital Humanities Quarterly* 6(3). Accessed 5 September 2022. http://www.digitalhumanities.org/dhq/vol/6/3/000133/000133.html

Smithies, James. 2017. *The Digital Humanities and the Digital Modern*. Basingstoke: Palgrave Macmillan.

Smithies, James. 2019. 'The Continuum Approach to Career Development: Research software careers in King's Digital Lab', *King's Digital Lab – Thoughts and Reflections from the Lab* (blog). Accessed 5 September 2022. https://www.kdl.kcl.ac.uk/blog/rse-career-development

Smithies, James and Arianna Ciula. 2020. 'Humans in the Loop: Epistemology & method in King's Digital Lab'. In *Routledge International Handbook of Research Methods in Digital Humanities*, edited by Kristen Schuster and Stuart Dunn, 155–72. Abingdon: Routledge.

Smithies, James, Anna Maria Sichani, Carina Westling, Pam Mellen and Arianna Ciula. 2019. 'Managing 100 Digital Humanities Projects: Digital scholarship & archiving in King's Digital Lab', *Digital Humanities Quarterly* 13(1). Accessed 5 September 2022. http://www.digitalhumanities.org/dhq/vol/13/1/000411/000411.html

Society of Research Software Engineering. 2019. 'The Global Skills and Competency Framework for the Digital World'. Accessed 5 September 2022. https://society-rse.org

Traweek, Sharon. 1992. *Beamtimes and Lifetimes: The world of high energy physicists*. Cambridge, MA: Harvard University Press.

5

The *People of Medieval Scotland* database as history[*]

Dauvit Broun and Joanna Tucker

Introduction

On a superficial level it may seem obvious that an open access database of people in the past such as *People of Medieval Scotland* (PoMS) can be regarded as a kind of historical publication. It is an example of 'factoid prosopography', a form that John Bradley has played an integral part in developing across a number of projects (Bradley n.d.; Bradley and Short 2005). A factoid is 'a spot in a source that says something about a person or persons', which is presented not as part of a 'story' about an individual (as in other prosopographies), but as a piece of data in a 'collection of factoid-assertions': Bradley has contrasted this with 'the vast preponderance of historical research products even now in the digital age [which] is expressed as writing' (Bradley n.d.). This raises deeper questions about the nature of history itself, which we discuss in this essay. What happens to our understanding of history and the role of historians if a database like PoMS is seen not only as a research tool but also as a mode of historiography in its own right? We argue that the result can be seen as an inversion of historiography as this is normally understood, and leads to a broader view of history than is currently embraced by historical theory.

Historical theory and databases

In his 2013 essay on PoMS, co-written with Michele Pasin, John Bradley drew attention to how its structure could 'accommodate contradiction and diversity' found in the source material. In this way, he continued, the database could reflect the inherently 'provisional' and 'fragmented' nature of our understanding of history, which has a capacity to 'simultaneously represent a number of different perspectives' (Bradley and Pasin 2013, 214). This is in tune with a widely held view that the writing of history is not the same as recreating the past. Since the 1970s there has been a gradually increasing recognition that the narrative or 'lineal' forms in which the past is presented (either as story, argument or other lineal expositions) are inescapably artefacts produced by historians.[1] There is no all-embracing objective reality which historians can hope to inch towards through 'better' research. Instead, they typically take some surviving sources – as 'traces' of the past – and engage with them to create material for others to read. This is not all: traces of the past are complex sources of information. The factoid model used for PoMS neatly captures the essentially uncertain nature of all data derived from historical texts. No piece of information can be accepted automatically as accurate; it is very helpful, therefore, to refer to this primary level of data as factoids rather than 'facts'. It is left to the historian (or user) to judge how best these can be deployed in creating their presentations of the past (Bradley n.d.).

These insights are generally referred to as postmodern or narrativist. They were developed by theorists who were chiefly concerned with challenging deeply embedded assumptions about history as primarily about recovering the 'truth' of what happened and how this can best be explained. This has led to calls for historians to 'develop an alternate set of understandings of what they do' (Munslow 2012, 190), or even that 'we can now live without histories of either a modernist or postmodernist kind' (Jenkins 2009, 15). In recent years, however, there has been an increasing concern to move beyond an emphasis on what history is *not* and to explore in more detail what it *is* or *could* become. This has led to a particular interest in understanding the nature of history as an experience in the present.[2] There is, at the same time, a growing engagement by theorists in the work of practising historians (Kuukkanen 2015; see also Froeyman 2017). A new term – 'postnarrativist' – has been coined.

All these theorists – postmodernists (or narrativists) and postnarrativists – share a common focus on the writing of history. For Alun Munslow, one of the leading proponents of postmodernism, 'history is a narrative' (Munslow 2012, 189).[3] A particularly stark statement is given by Frank Ankersmit, the first postmodernist to move towards a concern for understanding history as experience.[4] In the preface to his most recent book, he draws a contrast between '"historical writing" (*Geschichtsschreibung*)' and '"historical research" (*Geschichtsforschung*)', with his book focusing solely on the former (Ankersmit 2012, x).[5] In this context the experience of the past is essentially that of an historian-author, who then, through their prose, conveys this to readers. It is no surprise, therefore, that the most far-reaching recent discussion of history as experience – Anton Froeyman's *History, Ethics and the Recognition of the Other*, published in 2016 – is avowedly a study of history writing.[6]

The distinction between historical writing and research is more important for theorists than for practitioners. In the words of Chris Wickham, former Professor of Medieval History at the University of Oxford, 'most people are doing both at once' (Fairbrother and Wickham 2018, 537). The emphasis on historical writing by those who specialise in thinking about the nature of the relationship between the past and the present is striking, therefore.[7] The term 'postnarrativist' might seem more appropriate for an approach that explicitly eschews the primacy of writing – but this is not how it is used. It may be guessed that the reason databases as such have not featured so far in the work of the most prominent theorists is because they are regarded as a function of 'historical research'.[8] Equally, discussions of 'digital history' have not engaged explicitly with the work of postmodern or postnarrative historical thinkers.[9]

In this paper we consider how historical research might be considered as more than simply a prelude to writing in the case of freely available databases such as PoMS. When John Bradley concluded his essay on PoMS, written with Michele Pasin, with a brief discussion of 'structure and narrative', he provided a perceptive indication of how a database such as PoMS could offer opportunities to think of history in a non-narrative, non-lineal form (Bradley and Pasin 2014, 213). In what follows we will consider PoMS not as a means to an end – the end typically conceived as academic books and articles – but as an historical experience in its own right. Moreover, we will argue that putting databases like PoMS centre stage leads to a view of history as an activity as much as an experience, and that, as an activity, it is facilitated (rather than created) by historians, collaborating with others. First, we will outline PoMS and how it has been developed since it was first launched in 2010.

The genesis and development of PoMS, 2007–19

People of Medieval Scotland (www.poms.ac.uk; Beam et al. 2019) is one of many freely available online prosopographical databases whose structure was designed by John Bradley. It was initially created as the main outcome of the 'Paradox of Medieval Scotland' AHRC-funded project, which ran from 2007 to 2010.[10] At that stage it was a database of all individuals and institutions (such as abbeys and burghs) mentioned in the 6,014 'transactional' documents (broadly referred to as 'charters') that survive, either as original single sheets or as later copies, from the Scottish kingdom up to the death of Alexander III on 19 March 1286. The earliest charter is datable to sometime between 13 November 1093 and 12 November 1094 (probably later in that date range).[11] The database's territorial reach was defined by the kingdom's bounds on 19 March 1286, rather than by modern Scotland: as a result, Berwick and the Isle of Man were included (which are now within England), but not Orkney or Shetland (which were part of the Kingdom of Norway until 1469). If a document related to anywhere within these boundaries, or was likely to have been produced there, then it was included. The first step towards the database was Matthew Hammond's unpublished calendar of all these documents, assigning each a number (which came, not unnaturally, to be referred to as 'Hammond numbers'), and providing a date-range for undated documents (which is the great majority).[12] By the time the database was completed in 2010 it contained references to 15,221 individuals and institutions (Hammond 2013, 7).

The emphasis on transactional documents, to the exclusion of other mentions of individuals in sources relating to this period (such as chronicles), marks PoMS out from other prosopographical databases. This was not such a radical step as it might seem in the context of the Scottish Kingdom, however, because charters and similar texts are by far the main source of extant information on individuals and institutions in this period. The focus on transactional documents also had the benefit of giving the database a coherence it would not otherwise have had. Any document which recorded or represented an interaction between individuals and/ or institutions was included, such as a charter giving, granting or renewing property and/or privileges, or a document addressed by one or more people to named individuals (such as a brieve instructing them what to do or not do, or notifying them of something), or a record of an inquest into property or rights that had been in dispute between individuals. As a result, PoMS is a database not just of individuals and institutions, but also of their interactions (for example, as parties to a transaction, or witnesses, or as participants in an inquest), and of the various ways that individuals might be identified in the context of interactions between others (for example, as neighbouring or previous landholders, or as beneficiaries of the prayers that would be offered in return for a gift of land to a monastery). As such, it represents a different kind of prosopography from the traditional focus on individual careers. Instead, the emphasis is on relationships and how these were expressed and structured at the time through the medium of the documents themselves. Each individual and institution still has their 'person page', but this is a record not so much of their career but of how they appear in the context of interactions with others, or by others. The person page is but a small part of what PoMS has to offer the researcher. It is chiefly a prosopography of social interactions in a specific context, rather than of individuals on their own.

Great care was taken to ensure that the database reflected relationships as they were represented in the documents themselves, without any interpretation or elaboration. This led to a heightened awareness of the language and form of the documents (discussed also in Bradley et al. 2019). There was scope within the lifetime of the project to incorporate a new understanding of the dispositive language of charters into the database's structure (Davies 2011). Fresh insights into the nature of brieves, however, which suggested that the database's classification of brieves and brieve-charters was unsatisfactory, emerged after the core development of the database (Tucker 2013; see also Davies forthcoming). This research into brieves was initiated using PoMS, thereby highlighting a paradox: although an innovative research tool may be expected to lead to a transformation in how we use and understand a body of material, its design must be based on how this material was understood before the database existed – in this case, the category of documents known as brieves.[13] It might be said that an innovative digital research tool worth its salt will start to become obsolete as soon as researchers begin engaging with the new potentialities that it offers.

PoMS was extended to 6 November 1314 as part of another AHRC-funded project, 'The Breaking of Britain', which ran from 2010 to 2013.[14] The new end date marked the point when any landholder who had failed to recognise Robert I as king was to be disinherited: this in effect forced those with lands in Scotland and England to choose, for the first time, which kingdom their allegiance lay with (Brown 2008, 187–8.) The new PoMS included the addition of a new type of record, referred to generically as 'English Royal Administration' (ERA), for the period after 12 June 1291. These were for documents (such as instructions, memoranda and records of fealties) produced in Scotland, or relating to Scotland, by the King of England or those acting on his authority.[15] As a result the original coherence of the database, with its exclusive focus on Scottish transactional documents, began to be compromised. Only a limited amount of information was extracted from ERA documents.[16] The extended database was launched on 5 September 2012 (Beam et al. 2019). The project also included the creation of *People of Northern England* (PoNE) (www.pone.ac.uk; Ambler et al. 2013), a sister database of the appearance of individuals in the three northern counties of England – Cumberland, Northumberland and Westmorland – in two sets of English royal records (pipe rolls 1216–86, and plea rolls 1216–75).[17]

The next stage in the development of PoMS was a project funded by the Leverhulme Trust: 'Transformation of Gaelic Scotland in the Twelfth and Thirteenth Centuries', which ran from 2013 initially to 2016, extended to 2017.[18] This enabled a new mapping functionality to be added, based on the mapping of Domesday Book as part of the Leverhulme-funded 'Profile of a Doomed Elite' project (2010–12).[19] The most innovative aspect of the project was the use of PoMS as a tool for Social Network Analysis (SNA) (Hammond with Jackson 2017), a particular interest of John Bradley's. As a result, PoMS gained a new feature: visualisations of the networks which every individual in the database is identified with through the documents. It is now possible, at a glance, to begin to appreciate the vibrant, messy and cross-cutting relationships represented by medieval Scottish society itself in its surviving transactional documents. We can enter into this web of relationships and move from one individual to the next, or stand back from it and view the fuzzy ball of inter-threading connections that represents the totality of interactions in a particular period.[20]

The most recent stage in the development of PoMS was as part of an AHRC-funded project, 'The Community of the Realm in Medieval Scotland, 1249–1424', running from 2017 initially to 2020, extended to 2021.[21] A new interface was developed (launched in September 2018) and all royal charters up to 1371 added to the database, a task completed by Matthew Hammond in April 2019.

Users of PoMS

In all these projects, PoMS has ostensibly been developed primarily as a research tool to enable the project team to investigate the specific core question that has served in each case to define the project. There was also an aspiration that, because PoMS was freely available on the internet, it could be used by any scholar to pursue their own research questions. A notable example is the work of Valeria Di Clemente, of the University of Catania in Sicily, who has studied the names in the Ragman Roll using PoMS (Di Clemente 2012; Di Clemente 2019). The database has, however, been used much more widely. According to

Google Analytics, there were 74,516 users between 5 September 2012 and 21 August 2017: 26% were from Scotland, 24% from the USA and 23% from England. Edinburgh, Glasgow and London accounted for 23% of users. There were users in every country in Europe, Australasia, the Middle East, and North, Central and South America (except Paraguay), in nearly every country in Asia (apart from North Korea and some former Soviet republics), in 22 countries in Africa and three in the Caribbean.[22] There is no way of telling in any detail how the database has been used by all these people across the world: overall, there were nearly twice as many sessions (123,098) as users in this period, and nearly 10 times as many page views (727,208). This could suggest that, in most cases, the database has been dipped into only once or twice, with few if any users availing themselves of its range of functions. Within this overall figure, however, there are some hot spots of relatively intense activity: the 'hottest' is Szczecin in Poland, whose 19 users had 1,117 sessions, an impressive average of 58.8 sessions per user. It might be suspected that this may, in turn, conceal sustained activity by a very small number of researchers, perhaps associated with the university.

Some effort has been made to encourage a deeper engagement with PoMS by non-specialists. In the initial project senior students from Williamwood High School were involved in testing the effectiveness of its interface; in July 2016 a workshop for postgraduates was held at the Institute for Historical Research in London; and a public event was held in September 2018 at Newbattle Abbey College. There are other ways in which PoMS has had a wider impact. The inclusion of the Wars of Independence in PoMS 2012 made it relevant for Scottish schools, where there was a demand for fresh material on this popular topic. There was potential to use the database to produce resources not only for the early years of secondary schools, but across the range of primary education. This was achieved by teachers and researchers working together in an AHRC 'Follow-On' project, in collaboration with Education Scotland, which ran from September 2013 to April 2014.[23] This particular project caused us to think more deeply about the nature of history as a discipline in ways that we have developed in this paper.[24]

PoMS and new interactions with the past

There is very little information on how PoMS is actually being used, not only by scholars but more widely.[25] There is a strong suspicion that PoMS is generally treated, like any website, as a source of immediate information rather than sustained enquiry; the web, after all, routinely provides an experience of instant knowledge. The PoMS interface, indeed, integrates the experiences of googling (through the search box) and online shopping (through the predetermined 'facet' categories which allow users to browse the category options). In the absence of specific evidence on how PoMS is used, it is possible to consider in a more general way how PoMS has the potential to change the nature of research in the field. Our emphasis here is not on the results of the research leading to publications, but on how far PoMS can offer new interactions with the material in the database as traces of the past, leading to fresh awareness and experiences.

The most obvious change offered by PoMS is the ability to find information immeasurably more quickly than before, and to do so knowing that you are searching the entire corpus of extant transactional documents. It is tempting to think of PoMS as a motorway system enabling researchers to travel more efficiently to their destination. This would, however, conceal the extent to which PoMS represents a significantly different mode of moving through the material. The researcher is no longer working methodically from one edition or calendar of texts to another, refining their method and approach as they go, but covers the entirety of the available material all at once. The results are limited in new ways, too, not by the researcher's endurance for reading the texts and notetaking but by the way the data is structured, searched and presented in the database. The speed of results and structure of the information can also change the dynamic of research. Instead of pursuing a predetermined question, PoMS makes it possible to create connections and generate questions rapidly and unpredictably through interacting with historical material, as mediated by the database.

Another key difference is that, whereas before PoMS a researcher would have to engage with the entire document (very often in its original Latin) in order to find the information they desired, the factoid structure of PoMS now allows for researchers to home in on specific aspects (such as particular clauses, roles, people, transaction types, and so on) or combine different searches (such as searching for 'agreements' with 'a fraction of knight's service'). At the same time, however, PoMS has the effect of decontextualising the factoids from their original textual environment. It always bears restating to users that PoMS is not a database of texts; it is a database of statements (or factoids) extracted from the source texts. The art of close reading and an awareness of context are therefore still necessary for a deep and full understanding of the results generated by the database.[26] This can readily be appreciated by researchers who have experience of reading transactional documents, or who are already aware of different kinds of documentary contexts. Presumably this cannot be assumed of users who lack such experience or awareness.

It should also be acknowledged that using PoMS can itself require a particular level of experience and understanding. For example, searching for a place-name will mean something different if the search is made by 'people and institutions' or by 'sources': this will only make sense if it is realised that it was sometimes stated in a charter that the document was produced (literally 'given') at a particular place (a statement known as a 'place date'). A search for a place-name by 'people and institutions' will give all instances where that place-name occurs in the name or title of an individual or a monastery (or other major church), whereas a search by 'sources' will only give instances when the place-name appears as a 'place date'. Searches can also be made in much the same way using the mapping function, embracing every context in which places are mentioned. The current interface makes the database much easier to navigate than before, but there are pitfalls for the unwary user. Using PoMS for any analytical research therefore requires specialist knowledge and experience. Without this, and without an awareness of when close reading or context might be required, the results are one-dimensional.

There is, on the other hand, the possibility of increased awareness of some essential aspects of the material. None of this is new; the database simply heightens our appreciation of these aspects and offers the opportunity to explore them from another angle. For example, the capacity to search the entire corpus throws into sharp relief the issue of how representative it is. The corpus is, of course, only what exists today, not every transactional document that was ever produced, and there are variable patterns of survival. PoMS allows us to begin to investigate these patterns against the backdrop of the totality of surviving texts. The experience of having everything that survives at our fingertips makes it even more urgent to think about what does not survive and to begin to integrate this realisation into the way we think about the material.[27] This can lead, for instance, to a more vivid appreciation of how the corpus has been shaped not only by chance but also by decisions that have been made about what to keep and how to keep it. This began soon after the documents were produced, when each was first placed in an archive.

Another way of reflecting on the material could be prompted by an awareness of the database as an abstraction of the documents. The factoids in the database are, in fact, nearly always derived from edited texts – the only exception being a few unpublished documents. These edited texts are themselves abstracted from the manuscripts and yet as historians we are accustomed to using them as though they are the source itself. In doing so, we are unaware of their handwriting and placement in the manuscript, or (in the case of original single sheets) their size or the seals hanging from the document that might still be seen on a tongue or strip of parchment. Once we hold it in mind that the texts also have physical aspects, we are better able to appreciate them more fully as a trace of the past. For example, a document's physical aspects can provide information about how it was intended to be seen, read and stored (in the case of original single sheets), or how, why and when it was copied (as exemplified in the methodology developed in Tucker 2020). Perhaps an awareness of the database as giving access to only a selective view of a document will prompt a keener appreciation of what is hidden from view when encountering documents as edited texts.

The most obvious change afforded by PoMS is that it is, at least ostensibly, much more accessible to the non-specialist user than other resources, such as original medieval manuscripts or printed scholarly editions. It allows the user to search for anything across the corpus of surviving documents in the comfort of their home, without being limited to whatever books they can find in a library or on the internet. The user does not need to be able to read medieval languages or handwriting in order to begin to make any sense of it. Every document is summarised in English and the search menus are, of course, in English. This only goes so far, however. Much of the terminology is not in everyday language, but refers to the particularities of medieval society as represented in the documents (for example, 'in feu and heritage', 'forinsec service', 'sicut clauses' and 'pro anima clauses'). This is an inescapable consequence of the database's fundamental commitment to reflecting statements as they are presented in the documents, without adding any interpretation beyond what is strictly necessary in translating terms into English. On the face of it, then, PoMS allows non-specialist users to have access to an immense body of source material much more openly than was hitherto possible – albeit in a structured way. Almost immediately, however, the inexperienced user is confronted with terminology and prose that is unfamiliar and obscure. What they lose in comprehension, however, they gain by a keener sense of the past in its own terms.

Perhaps the most fundamental way in which PoMS represents a new kind of interaction with the past is by providing an inherently 'non-narrative' experience of this material. The closest a PoMS user gets to any basic sense of a narrative is when results are given in a list format, which can then be ordered by date (either on the main search page or in an individual's or institution's profile page). This is not as straightforward as plotting dates on a timeline, however, since the majority of document texts in this period do not have a single 'date' (such as 23 April 1124) but can only be assigned a date range (such as 23 April 1124 × 24 May 1153). Even if an exact date of a text is known, charters only capture a moment in a story that is usually otherwise unknown.

PoMS as a non-lineal and personal experience of history

It could be said that PoMS provides a 'non-lineal' experience of the past that goes deeper than simply a poverty of narrative. For example, whenever a researcher picks up a book, they are instinctively aware that it has a beginning and an end. This is even the case for books which have no narrative aim, such as dictionaries. Even an article on the web has an intuitive lineal flow, even though its start or finish may not be visible. PoMS, by contrast, is like a pool without a discernible bottom. It is possible to scan the surface by looking at the different facets, but not to see its extent or depth. Dipping into this pool is a thoroughly different experience from reading an historian's discussion of the key people or themes relating to this period. In PoMS, researchers are confronted with a mass of information which has no innate starting point or final destination. Search results are presented as lists, or maps, or network visualisations. As John Bradley and Michele Pasin have pointed out, tools like PoMS encourage their users to make sense of the material through finding patterns rather than constructing narratives (Bradley and Pasin 2013, 205–6). This represents a different experience from reading history in an article or book, where a sense of a single narrative flow is inherent, even if that is not how the reader is interacting with it.

There is a second way in which databases like PoMS represent an experience different from reading a piece of written history. As a decentred collection of information, research can follow an unlimited number of directions. These can be pursued by any researcher on their own terms and can respond immediately to that individual researcher's curiosity. The researcher might begin, for example, by tracing a particular person, family or institution through the database, or surveying the participants in sales, quitclaims or inquests, or examining an individual's connections through the SNA 'gephi visualisations', or identifying all of the factoids associated with a particular place. This fundamentally personal, self-guided engagement with the material is reminiscent of the experience of a researcher in an archive gathering information from their perusal of documents. Unlike being in an archive, however, this can be achieved any-where and anytime where there is access to the internet – and by anyone.

Putting both the inherently non-lineal and personal aspects together, tools like PoMS can be understood as not only an experience but also an activity. In order to make the material in PoMS come to life, the user has to actively weave their own path through it. This active engagement is, in a sense, in contrast to the experience of reading his-tory. Reading is not, of course, a 'passive' activity, but the road and direc-tion of travel are laid out in a way that for databases they are not. Instead, the database's interface offers a plethora of pathways for the user to con-sciously select or accidentally stumble upon.

This is not to say that PoMS replaces, or ought to replace, traditional historical practices such as writing books and articles. Instead, it could be recognised as a different kind of activity in its own right, not simply preparatory to a piece of written work. Such a broad and ideal view of his-tory returns us, however, to the issue of accessibility. It could be said that, for many, especially those with limited or no primary experience of the documents themselves, this decentred experience of the material and its raw presentation is not liberating but rather disorientating, and that the urge to have the material presented within a wider framework (such as that provided by a grand narrative) is too strong to resist. As John Bradley and Michel Pasin observed, the database 'expects a significant degree of interpretation from its users' (Bradley and Pasin 2013, 214). Within the family of historical activity, therefore, working with analytical research tools is not any less demanding. Its relationship to lineal forms of history is wider than simply as a research tool for writing books and articles. Readers who are users of the database might turn to published prose for a narrative framework. If they do, however, they might no longer be quite so dependent on what they read as they might have been before experi-encing PoMS. The possibility of checking a historian's statements or sup-plementing what is published by dipping into the database could lead to a new dynamic between historical books and their readers.

Nearly all these issues – particularly the possibility of a decentred, non-lineal approach to history and a more open and fluid relationship between historians and their audiences – have been explored and thought about in the realm of digital history (Barker 2012, Rigney 2010). There are significantly different points of emphasis and opportunity, however, when thinking about a factoid database like PoMS compared with what may loosely be described as the mainstream of digital history. The most important is that PoMS is not a database of texts, structured (for exam-ple) using the Text Encoding Initiative. Most of the discussions of digital history, however, relate either to digitised texts or the process of history writing (such as crowd-sourcing, or collaborations between historians and their audience). PoMS shares much the same spirit, but is different in practice. This also has an impact on how we think about the digital world. When, for example, it is suggested by Chiel Van Den Akker that 'the dialogue is the underlying concept of information technology' (Van Den Akker 2013, 107), this does not apply so readily to PoMS. When, on the other hand, Sherman Dorn observes that the digital age allows the public to see history writing at a 'preargument' stage, this brings us closer to the experience of PoMS (Dorn 2013, 27). Indeed, we have argued that PoMS goes further by making the raw material for history writing a destination in its own right – something that the interested public might be more ready to accept than professional historians.

PoMS is not intrinsically better or worse than written forms of history: we have discussed some of the ways in which it is problematic and challenging as well as liberating and potentially transformative. It is simply different. As such, we have argued that it offers a particular experience of digital history, emphasising the myriad personal engagements with the past that it makes possible. Above all, it opens the possibility of thinking of history in a more pluralistic way as an activity, rather than only as history writing or text.

PoMS and theories of history

This essay began by referring to insights about the nature of history that have been developed by theorists and observing that these focus on history writing rather than research, despite the difficulty of disentangling them in practice. The focus on history writing makes intuitive sense when the main form of publication is the finished texts of historians. Publications of primary sources are seen simply as preparatory to history writing and only accessible to scholars with the training and expertise to make sense of them. We have argued that PoMS – more so than in text-based forms of digital history – represents a fundamentally different kind of published history. We have suggested that this prompts a broader understanding of history as an *activity*. How does PoMS, therefore, relate to fully developed ideas of history, particularly the more recent postnarrativist theories that envisage history as an *experience*?

A particularly useful point of reference is provided by Anton Froeyman's work. This has been heralded by Frank Ankersmit as a 'wholly new approach' that announces a new 'existentialist' phase in the philosophy of history (Ankersmit 2016).[28] At one level Froeyman's proposition is simple: 'in writing about the past, we deal not with things, but with human beings, people from another time, but people nonetheless' (Froeyman 2016, 209). He takes this deeper, however, by highlighting not only that people from the past are different from us (the reader or user today), but also that it is impossible for us to meet or see them face-to-face.[29] He regards the historian's key skill as being about developing a 'sensitivity for the contingent nature of the other from the past' (Froeyman 2016, 208).

Because PoMS is primarily a database of individual people, it seems at least minimally to be aligned with Froeyman's approach to history. It would appear at first sight that PoMS, as an assemblage of data in a non-lineal structure, is incapable of providing anything akin to the awareness of a contemporary person's 'lived experience' that Froeyman regards as an essential component of his philosophy.[30] A fully developed lineal narrative, by contrast, can achieve this much more compellingly. PoMS, however, is not merely a collection of data; its factoids are fragments of information taken directly from how people at that time were described in a social context they participated in themselves. The user therefore engages with people in the past as these individuals were represented in their own lives – their identity, status, roles and relationships – free from our interpretations. The unfamiliarity of some of the terminology could enhance this as an experience of the past, particularly for those who lack specialist knowledge of medieval Scottish charters and society. It is left to users to construct micro-narratives and provide their own interpretation (as pointed out in Bradley n.d.). For at least one non-academic user of PoMS, the result is an unmistakeable sense of engagement with other people from the past. In answering the question 'Has using the *People of Medieval Scotland* database changed your understanding of medieval Scotland or your own family or locality?', they replied: 'It has helped to make the period feel more realistic. Discovering individual stories, you begin to feel you know some of the people.'[31] This might, however, be expecting too much for most users: it might seem more natural to make sense of PoMS by seeking patterns rather than by creating accounts of individuals in the past. As John Bradley and Michele Pasin noted, pattern is 'an essential idea of any database such as the one we created for PoMS' (Bradley and Pasin 2013, 205). In comparison to narratives, it is difficult to see such patterns as anything other than a depersonalising of the material in the database, rather than heightening our experience of people as individuals in the past.

There is one way, however, in which PoMS could be recognised as offering a particular dimension to Froeyman's approach in a new way, counterbalancing the database's limitations in providing a vivid lived experience of the past. What matters, Froeyman argues, is 'not the concrete way in which we approach or represent the other, but rather the intention itself, the genuine feeling of interest in and concern for the other, which drives us to try and encounter or represent her in the first place' (Froeyman 2016, 102, where this statement is part of his summary of Levinas's ethics). Froeyman's emphasis on historical writing seems – from the perspective of the reader – to be more passive than active. A database, by contrast, has *users* rather than readers, and requires a more active interaction with the 'traces' of the past. As such, PoMS is a platform for people in the here and now to take a direct and personal interest in the people of medieval Scotland. PoMS itself may be extremely limited as a way of developing what Froeyman refers to as a 'genuine feeling of interest in and concern' for people in the past, but it at least provides a basic experience of independent active engagement.

Perhaps, therefore, seeing history as an activity would not only allow other forms of interaction with the past apart from writing (and reading) to be embraced more fully as forms of historical experience in their own right. It could also make it possible to embrace a wide range of forms of engagement with the past as opportunities to develop a greater 'sensitivity for the contingent nature of the other from the past' (Froeyman 2016, 208). As a 'discipline', history could be defined by the use of traces of the past to encourage and nurture such sensitivity for individuals who we can never encounter in person. Froeyman emphasises that there is no general method for achieving this (see for example Froeyman 2016, 188–91).[32] This mix of connection and remoteness, intimacy and distance, between people today and in the past might, nevertheless, be recognised as a particular essence of history. As an activity, history's effectiveness could be gauged by how far it provides this sense of connection and distance with a defined group of people or individuals in the past. PoMS may only offer a tiny opportunity to achieve this. By allowing history to be seen as an *activity*, however, it could trigger much more personally involved and meaningful experiences of the past to be devised, not only digitally, but in other ways.

PoMS as history

It has been observed that, 'despite the innumerable possibilities suggested by media and information technologies, history remains largely a matter of rewriting the already written traces of the past' (Tredinnick

2013, 41). It has also been remarked specifically of digital history that its tools might be imagined potentially as 'constituting a new historiographical mode in their own right', but that this is 'a challenge to which it has so far largely failed to rise' (Anderson 2019, 293; Winters 2019b, 295). It could be said that the challenge is beginning to be met by developing more interactive and collaborative modes of researching and writing history. Another is by expanding historiography into other ways of communicating experiences of the past, for example through digitised images and visualisations (Theibault 2013; see also Tredinnick 2013). There are also ways of using 'spatial technologies' to present historical information on interactive maps (Bodenhamer 2013). PoMS can be seen in this context as an example of another mode of digital history – derived from texts, but not itself a database of texts; making research material widely accessible, but without any intention to provide a framework for collaboration between historians and the interested public. It also offers a variety of digital capabilities, such as its visualisations of social networks and the facility to interact with the database's factoids though maps, as well as the word search and faceted browser that are presented to the user on first arriving at its interface.

Is PoMS a form of historiography at all, however? It can, of course, function as a preliminary to writing standard modes of historiography. But it can also be regarded as a fully fledged historical publication in its own right. All its users engage with people in the past, however minimally that might be for some; only a few will develop this into forms of extended prose. It could even be argued that, by involving users directly in the way individuals in the past were represented within their own society, it potentially offers a more personal historical experience than is often the case for readers of standard academic writing – especially when users of the database are making their own decisions and reacting to the results of their own queries. It is therefore possible to characterise PoMS as an inversion of historiography as this is normally understood. Unlike historical writing, PoMS has no particular meaning or message to convey. There is no author-historian, but instead the potential for each user to find their own experience of the past. Instead of perpetuating a hierarchy of knowledge and understanding, PoMS enables anyone with access to the internet to interact, however minimally, with people in the past both as individuals and in relation to one another. As such, it could be said to offer a more radical example of postnarrativist history than has hitherto been envisaged, moving decisively beyond the idea of history primarily as writing.

This, in turn, changes the role of the historian or scholar. They are primarily facilitators rather than writers. In this context the scholar's main role may no longer be to craft a narrative that can convey a compelling experience of the past. They are in this instance devoted to creating, through the database, an opportunity for the interested public to interact immediately with traces of the past. When PoMS is regarded in this way, it is the digital humanists, technicians, interface designers, charter scholars and prosopographers who take centre stage, working collaboratively, rather than the 'historian' as traditionally conceived of, researching and writing their sole-authored publications.

There are many other contexts in which scholars can work collaboratively with others to provide the means for history to be experienced through activity, especially in ways which encourage a 'sensitivity for the contingent nature of the other from the past' (Froeyman 2016, 208). What this entails is a diversification of what is understood to be 'the destination' of the activity (not simply history writing) and a diversification of the practitioners of history (not just those who write history but also those who engage with it in all its forms). For example, historians might work with teachers to provide materials appropriate to all levels of school education. This is not a matter of school-learners being given simplified versions of what historians have discovered through their research and written about; neither is it chiefly about learning to understand arguments about what happened and why. If history can be seen as an activity that engenders an awareness of the past as something both immediate and remote, then all forms of engaging with people in the past can be valued.

It is possible to recognise PoMS and other databases as expanding the practice of history in a way that is compatible with the standard emphasis on historical writing (by using them as research tools for books and articles), and which also inverts this and the role of the historian (because the database is widely accessible as an experience of the past in its own right). Much of this is consistent with postmodern and particularly existentialist understandings of history, even if PoMS might for many be only a meagre medium for developing a sensitivity to people in the past. In the end, however, it could be said that imagining the tools of digital history as constituting only a new historiographical mode is to miss the radical potential of PoMS (and similar digital resources). Its most significant contribution is in showing how history can be conceptualised as an *activity*. This has the potential to go far beyond databases by making it easier to recognise the diversity of historical modes that are available, or could be developed, within an existentialist understanding of history as a discipline.

Notes

*   The ideas developed in this paper first took shape as part of our work in the AHRC-funded project AH/E008348/1, 'School Curriculum Reform and the Scottish War of Independence', which was a follow-on to the AHRC-funded project AH/H040110/1, 'The Breaking of Britain: Cross-border society and Scottish independence 1216–1314', and ran 2013–14. We are very grateful to the Arts and Humanities Research Council for their support. We are also grateful to Matthew Hammond for reading this in draft and for his comments. All websites cited in the notes below were accessed and checked 6 September 2022.

1. The theorists most often referred to are Hayden White (1928–2018) and Frank Ankersmit (b.1945) (White 1973; White 1987; Ankersmit 1983; Ankersmit 1994). For Hayden White's development from a historian of the twelfth-century papacy to a 'narrativist' see Paul 2011. For a critical discussion of early and late Ankersmit, see Domanska 2009. White's and (early) Ankersmit's focus is on 'narrative' rather than argument; Chris Lorenz (b.1950), by contrast, sees argument as the 'fuel' of history's 'motor' (Lorenz 1998, esp. 326–7). The potential of 'nonlinearity' is given more prominence in the broader field of postmodern thinking about culture and history (Poster 1997, esp. 68–71), where digital modes of engaging with text are highlighted as an example.

2. See in particular Froeyman 2016, chapter 5, which provides an analysis of how experience of the past has been approached in different disciplines, from Johan Huizinga (1872–1945) to the most recent theorists (to which could be added Carr 2014).

3. The quotation is from the conclusion of Munslow's discussion of the nature of history, where he explains that 'because history is a narrative, it makes sense to me that historians should start with the form of their history rather than its content' (Munslow 2012, 189). Note also his argument that 'it is the historian who creates the-past-*as*-history', and therefore, 'as I have argued at some length, for me engaging with the past is first, last and always a narrative-making process' (Munslow 2012, 171–2).

4. For Domanska, 'narrativism entered its late phase' in Ankersmit's 'gradual shift of interest . . . to historical experience' (Domanska 2009, 190), which 'can be viewed as a regression' (Domanska 2009, 175) to more traditional Romantic and Enlightenment ideas of history. For negative responses by narrativists see Munslow 2012, 148–52, 157–69 and Jenkins 2009, 295–314: at 312 he regards Ankersmit as 'bewitched by the crazy notion of accessing "historically" some or other aspect of the past direct'.

5. Ankersmit added that 'what is not discussed in the book I consider of no relevance for a proper understanding of historical writing. In this way the book is also an implicit comment on what is not in it' (Ankersmit 2012, x). The omission of historical research by Ankersmit and White has been noted in Lorenz 1998, 317.

6. Froeyman explains that his perspective on experiencing the past and its 'virtue-based methodology' is equally applicable to 'other, more public forms of historical representation' (Froeyman 2016, 195), and discusses historical performance practice in classical music as an example (Froeyman 2016, 195–202). Here, however, the musician is regarded as fulfilling a similar role to that of the author-historian. Although Froeyman does not, therefore, see his perspective as exclusively about history writing, in his work it only extends to contexts that are analogous to the practice of history writing. Moreover, he distinguishes his perspective on experiencing the past from memory or commemoration, which can take other forms apart from historical writing (Froeyman 2016, 93); see, for example, his discussion of textual 'fragments', as proposed by the literary theorist Hans-Ulrich Gumbrecht (b.1948), or everyday objects from the past, as expounded by Huzinga (Froeyman 2016, 86–87, 93–95), which he distinguishes from his own approach (Froeyman 2016, 108).

7. An exception is Chris Lorenz: see, for example, Lorenz and Tamm (2014, 505): 'I regard the interconnections between historical writing and historical research of constitutive importance for history as a cognitive enterprise.'

8. Although occasional reference is made to the 'digital turn', historical theorists have almost exclusively been concerned with the range of 'born digital' historical writing that is accessible on the web: see, for example, Rigney 2010. An exception is Barker (2012, chapter 8); his concern is with databases and theatre, however, not the theory and practice of historical writing and research. Barker's comments on the distinction between 'narrative time' and 'archival time' (where 'we are not presented with history as a readable sequence of events') (Barker 2012, 181) could, however, be applied equally to history if a database like PoMS is regarded as history.

9. For example, their work does not feature in Weller 2013, Doughert and Nawrotzki 2013 or Zaagsma 2013, or most recently in Winters 2019a. This could be seen as part of a wider lack of engagement between historical practitioners and theorists. Alternatively, given that digital historians tend generally to be particularly open to developing new ideas and practices, it may be more likely that the most fundamental insights of historical theorists have become so assimilated into their thinking that specific reference is no longer called for: it has been commented that 'a history of forgetting about the history of history might be in order here' (Tanaka 2013, 39).

10. Award ref. AH/E008348/1. The main research team was Amanda Beam as Research Associate, John Bradley as Co-Investigator, Dauvit Broun as Principal Investigator, David Carpenter as Co-Investigator, John Reuben Davies as Research Associate, Matthew Hammond as Lead Researcher and then Co-Investigator, Roibeard Ó Maolalaigh as Co-Investigator, and Michele Pasin as Research Associate responsible for designing the interface.

11. https://www.poms.ac.uk/record/source/775

12. The numbering system is explained at https://www.poms.ac.uk/information/numbering-system-for-documents

13. The understanding of brieves prior to 2012 was based on the seminal work of Geoffrey Barrow (1924–2013), in particular in his introductions to his editions of royal charters (broadly defined): Barrow 1960, 62–68; Barrow with Scott 1971, 70–75.

14. Award ref. AH/H040110/1. The research team was Sophie Ambler and Amanda Beam as Research Associates, John Bradley as Co-Investigator, Dauvit Broun as Principal Investigator, David Carpenter as Co-Investigator, John Reuben Davies as Research Associate, Matthew Hammond as Co-Investigator, Beth Hartland as Research Associate, Michele Pasin as Research Associate responsible for designing the interface (with Alejandro Giacometti taking over this role when Michele Pasin moved to a new job towards the end of the project), and Keith J. Stringer as Co-Investigator.

15. In the absence of a king following the death of Alexander III, Scotland was governed initially by guardians elected by parliament in April 1286, and then by Edward I of England from 12 June 1291; Edward I later conquered Scotland in 1296 and 1304, and for much of the period up to 1314 significant parts of the Scottish kingdom were under English royal control (Brown 2004, 157–209; Duncan 2002, 249, for Edward I's governing Scotland from 12 June 1291).

16. As explained in https://www.poms.ac.uk/information/numbering-system-for-documents/volume-5; fealties and homages were treated separately from other ERA: https://www.poms.ac.uk/information/numbering-system-for-documents/volume-6. Information found only in Macpherson et al. 1814–19 was not included.

17. www.pone.ac.uk: the members of the 'Breaking of Britain' team with particular responsibility for PoNE were Sophie Ambler and Amanda Beam (working on the plea rolls), John Bradley (Co-Investigator leading on the database) and David Carpenter (Co-Investigator leading on the pipe rolls), Beth Hartland (working on the pipe rolls), Michele Pasin (working on the database and its interface) and Keith Stringer (Co-Investigator leading on the plea rolls). The interface is no longer available. The data has been archived in raw SQL format by the University of Glasgow: *People of Northern England (1216–1286) Database Archive*: https://researchdata.gla.ac.uk/1126/

18. Project RPG-2012-805. The research team was John Bradley as Co-Investigator, Dauvit Broun as Principal Investigator, Matthew Hammond as Lead Researcher, Cornell Jackson as Research Associate with responsibility for Social Network Analysis, and Neil Jakeman creating the mapping and SNA visualisations.

19. The Principal Investigator was Stephen Baxter, with Christopher Lewis and Duncan Probert as Research Associates, and Neil Jakeman creating the mapping.

20. Other visualisations are also used in Hammond with Jackson 2017.

21. Award ref. AH/P013759/1. The academic project team, led by Alice Taylor (Principal Investigator), was Steve Boardman and Dauvit Broun (Co-Investigators), John Reuben Davies (Research Fellow) and Matthew Hammond (Research Associate), with interface development of PoMS by Elliott Hall and design by Ginestra Ferraro.

22. There is only information for users while they were at a location, which could include travellers as well as residents.

23. Award ref. AH/E008348/1. The project team was Dauvit Broun as Co-Director, John Reuben Davies as Research Associate, Lynne Robertson as Co-Director, and Joanna Tucker as Lead Project Officer. The resources produced by the project can currently be found at https://education.gov.scot/improvement/learning-resources/People%20of%20Medieval%20Scotland

24. When the resources were first published in 2014, the website included a 650-word piece we wrote on 'History as a Discipline: Academia and schools'; this was lost when the resources were transferred to the current website.
25. An online questionnaire was initiated in 2019.
26. For example, Broun 2017, 45–6 and nn. 73, 74, on the use of PoMS to identify charters where 'the kingdom of Scotland/Scots' was given as a point of reference for holding property; the exact Latin statements given in the texts had to be checked, and all instances datable to before 1200 were given in an appendix, along with the 'Hammond number' for each text, allowing readers to follow up the charters in the database (Broun 2017, 75–83).
27. This is discussed further in Tucker (2022).
28. Froeyman's book is briefly set in Ankersmit 2016 within the development of the philosophy of history in the last 90 years, and regarded as the first fully developed theoretical work on historical experience: an 'absolute must' for understanding 'the recent "existentialist turn in contemporary philosophy of history"' (Ankersmit 2016, xi).
29. This applies also to those living today who witnessed events in the past (for example, the upheavals of 1968), insofar as it is impossible to meet them face-to-face in that moment in the past in 1968.
30. See Froeyman 2016, 81, where he contrasts 'the empirical kind of experience' such as 'sensorial input' or 'the gathering of data' (in German *Erfahrung*) with 'a concrete, lived experience' (German *Erlebnis*) that makes an impression on us as 'sensitive human beings, rather than as perceptory machines'.
31. This is in an answer, given on 9 April 2019, to the online questionnaire initiated by Alice Taylor on 8 April 2019 as part of the 'Community of the Realm in Scotland' project (https://www.surveymonkey.co.uk/r/Y8NC7HV).
32. In this section of his work, for example, Froeyman emphasises the personal character of the historian: 'moral education is not a matter of teaching rules, but rather of shaping character', and 'The historiographical equivalent, then, would not be that explicitly learning particular skills and methods can never be the essence of an education as a historian. The central part of such education should be the slow creation and shaping of a kind of historical sensitivity that allows the historian to strike the right balance between all kinds of different methods, techniques and traditions' (Froeyman 2016, 191).

References

Ambler, Sophie, Amanda Beam, Dauvit Broun, John Bradley, David Carpenter, Alejandro Giacometti, Beth Hartland, Michele Pasin and Keith J. Stringer. 2013. *The People of Northern England 1216–1286*. King's College London. Accessed 5 September 2022. http://www.pone.ac.uk/

Anderson, Steve F. 2019. 'Comment' [on Winters 2019a]. In *Debating New Approaches to History*, edited by Marek Tamm and Peter Burke, 289–93. London: Bloomsbury.

Ankersmit, Frank. 1983. *Narrative Logic: A semantic analysis of the historian's language*. The Hague: Martinus Nijhoff.

Ankersmit, Frank. 1994. *History and Tropology: The rise and fall of metaphor*. Berkeley, CA: University of California Press.

Ankersmit, Frank. 2012. *Meaning, Truth, and Reference in Historical Representation*. Ithaca, NY: Cornell University Press.

Ankersmit, Frank. 2016. 'Foreword'. In *History, Ethics, and the Recognition of the Other: A Levinasian view on the writing of history* by Anton Froeyman. Abingdon: Routledge.

Barker, T.S. 2012. *Time and the Digital: Connecting technology, aesthetics, and a process philosophy of time*. Hanover, NH: Dartmouth College Press.

Barrow, G.W.S. (ed.). 1960. *Regesta Regum Scottorum*, vol. i: *The Acts of Malcolm IV, 1153–65*. Edinburgh: Edinburgh University Press.

Barrow, G.W.S. with W.W. Scott (eds). 1971. *Regesta Regum Scottorum*, vol. ii: *The Acts of William I, 1165–1214*. Edinburgh: Edinburgh University Press.

Beam, Amanda, Dauvit Broun, John Bradley, David Carpenter, John Reuben Davies, Kathryn Dutton, Nicholas Evans, Matthew Hammond, Roibeard Ó Maolalaigh, Michele Pasin and

Andrew Smith. 2019. *The People of Medieval Scotland 1093–1371* (1st edn *1093–1286*, 2010; 2nd edn *1093–1314* with Sophie Ambler, Alejandro Giacometti, Beth Hartland and Keith J. Stringer, 2012; 3rd edn including mapping and SNA functionality with Neil Jakeman and Cornell Jackson, 2016; 4th edn *1093–1371* with Ginestra Ferraro, Elliott Hall and Alice Taylor, 2019). King's College London. Accessed 5 September 2022. http://www.poms.ac.uk/

Bodenhamer, David J. 2013. 'The Spatial Humanities: Space, time and place in the new digital age'. In *History in the Digital Age*, edited by Toni Weller. 23–38. Abingdon: Routledge.

Bradley, John. n.d. 'What is Factoid Prosopography All About?'. Accessed 5 September 2022. https://www.kcl.ac.uk/factoid-prosopography/about

Bradley, John and Michele Pasin. 2013. 'Structuring that which Cannot be Structured: A role for formal models in representing aspects of medieval Scotland'. In *New Perspectives on Medieval Scotland, 1093–1286*, edited by Matthew Hammond, 203–14. Woodbridge: Boydell & Brewer.

Bradley, John, Dauvit Broun, Alice Rio and Matthew Hammond. 2019. 'Exploring a Model for the Semantics of Medieval Charters', *International Journal of Humanities and Arts Computing* 13: 136–54.

Broun, Dauvit. 2017. 'Kingdom and Identity. A Scottish perspective'. In *Northern England and Southern Scotland in the Central Middle Ages*, edited by Keith J. Stringer and Angus Winchester, 31–85. Woodbridge: Boydell and Brewer.

Brown, Michael. 2004. *The Wars of Scotland 1214–1371*. Edinburgh: Edinburgh University Press.

Brown, Michael. 2008. *Bannockburn. The Scottish War and the British Isles, 1307–1323*. Edinburgh: Edinburgh University Press.

Carr, David. 2014. *Experience and History: Phenomenological perspectives on the historical world*. Oxford: Oxford University Press.

Davies, John Reuben. 2011. 'The Donor and the Duty of Warrandice: Giving and granting in Scottish charters'. In *The Reality behind Charter Diplomatic in Anglo-Norman Britain*, edited by Dauvit Broun, 120–65. Centre for Scottish and Celtic Studies, University of Glasgow.

Davies, John Reuben. Forthcoming. 'Royal Government in Scotland and the Development of Diplomatic Forms, 1094–1249'. In *Identifying Governmental Forms in Europe, c.1100–c.1300: Palaeography, diplomatics and history*, edited by Alice Taylor.

Di Clemente, Valeria. 2012. 'Antroponimia femminile nella Scozia del xiii secolo: la testimonianza del *Ragman Roll* (1296)', *Reti Medievali* 13: 301–31. (We are very grateful to Matthew Hammond for this reference.)

Di Clemente, Valeria. 2019. 'Masculine Given Names of Germanic Origin in the Ragman Roll'. In *Personal Names and Naming Practices in Medieval Scotland*, edited by Matthew Hammond, 148–65. Woodbridge: Boydell and Brewer.

Domanska, Ewa. 2009. 'Frank Ankersmit: From narrative to experience', *Rethinking History* 13: 175–95.

Dorn, Sherman. 2013. 'Is (Digital) History More Than an Argument about the Past?'. In *Writing History in the Digital Age*, edited by Jack Doughert and Kristen Nawrotzki, 21–34. Ann Arbor, MI: University of Michigan Press.

Doughert, Jack and Kristen Nawrotzki (eds). 2013. *Writing History in the Digital Age*. Ann Arbor, MI: University of Michigan Press.

Duncan, A.A.M. 2002. *The Kingship of the Scots, 842–1292: Succession and independence*. Edinburgh: Edinburgh University Press.

Fairbrother, Daniel and Chris Wickham. 2018. 'Medieval History and Theory: A conversation', *Rethinking History* 22: 525–45.

Froeyman, Anton. 2016. *History, Ethics, and the Recognition of the Other: A Levinasian view on the writing of history*. Abingdon: Routledge.

Froeyman, Anton. 2017. 'Review of Kuukkanen 2015', *Journal of the Philosophy of History* 11: 33–37.

Hammond, Matthew. 2013. 'Introduction: The paradox of medieval Scotland, 1093–1286'. In *New Perspectives on Medieval Scotland, 1093–1286*, edited by Matthew Hammond, 1–52. Woodbridge: Boydell & Brewer.

Hammond, Matthew, with contributions by Cornell Jackson. 2017. *Social Network Analysis and the People of Medieval Scotland 1093–1286 Database*. Centre for Scottish and Celtic Studies, University of Glasgow. Accessed 5 September 2022. https://www.poms.ac.uk/information/e-books/social-network-analysis-and-the-people-of-medieval-scotland-1093-1286-poms-database

Jenkins, Keith. 2009. *At the Limits of History: Essays in theory and practice*. Abingdon: Routledge.

Kuukkanen, Jouni-Matti. 2015. *Postnarratavist Philosophy of Historiography*. Basingstoke: Palgrave Macmillan.

Lorenz, Chris. 1998. 'Can Histories be True? Narrativism, positivism, and the "metaphysical turn"', *History and Theory* 37: 309–29.

Lorenz, Chris and Marek Tamm. 2014. 'Who Knows Where the Time Goes?', *Rethinking History* 18: 499–521.

Macpherson, David, John Caley and William Illingworth (eds). 1814–19. *Rotuli Scotiae*, 2 vols. London: Record Commission.

Munslow, Alun. 2012. *A History of History*. Abingdon: Routledge.

Paul, Herman. 2011. *Hayden White: The making of a philosopher of history*. London: Polity Press.

Poster, Mark. 1997. *Cultural History and Postmodernity: Disciplinary readings and challenges*. New York: Columbia University Press.

Rigney, Ann. 2010. 'When the Monograph is no Longer the Medium: Historical narratives in the online age', *History and Theory, Theme Issue* 49: 100–17.

Tanaka, Stefan. 2013. 'Pasts in the Digital Age'. In *Writing History in the Digital Age*, edited by Jack Doughert and Kristen Nawrotzki, 35–46. Ann Arbor, MI: University of Michigan Press.

Theibault, John. 2013, 'Visualizations and Historical Arguments'. In *Writing History in the Digital Age*, edited by Jack Doughert and Kristen Nawrotzki, 173–85. Ann Arbor, MI: University of Michigan Press.

Tredinnick, Luke. 2013. 'The Making of History: Remediating historicized experience'. In *History in the Digital Age*, edited by Toni Weller, 39–60. Abingdon: Routledge.

Tucker, Joanna. 2013. 'The Development of Brieves, 1124–1249'. Unpublished MLitt dissertation, University of Glasgow.

Tucker, Joanna. 2020. *Reading and Shaping Medieval Cartularies: Multi-scribe manuscripts and their patterns of growth*. Woodbridge: Boydell and Brewer.

Tucker, Joanna. 2022. 'Survival and Loss: Working with documents from medieval Scotland', Dark Archives, vol. i: Voyages into the Medieval Unread and Unreadable, 2019–2021, edited by Stephen A. Pink and Anthony J. Lappin, 61–96. Oxford: The Society for the Study of Medieval Languages and Literature.

Van Den Akker, Chiel. 2013. 'History as Dialogue: On online narrativity', *Low Countries Historical Review* 128(4): 103–17.

Weller, Toni (ed.). 2013. *History in the Digital Age*. Abingdon: Routledge.

White, Hayden V. 1973. *Metahistory: The historical imagination in nineteenth-century Europe*. Baltimore, VA: Johns Hopkins University Press.

White, Hayden V. 1987. *The Content of Form: Narrative discourse and historical representation*. Baltimore, VA: Johns Hopkins University Press.

Winters, Jane. 2019a. 'Digital History'. In *Debating New Approaches to History*, edited by Marek Tam and Peter Burke, 277–89. London: Bloomsbury.

Winters, Jane. 2019b. 'Response'. In *Debating New Approaches to History*, edited by Marek Tam and Peter Burke, 294–6. London: Bloomsbury.

Zaagsma, Gerben (ed.). 2013. *Low Countries Historical Review* 128(4), *Digital History*.

Part II:
People Making

6
The history of the 'techie' in the history of digital humanities

Julianne Nyhan

Introduction

> [M]ost institutions view the kind of technical contributions which [the Department of Digital Humanities, King's College London] makes as a kind of support work – perhaps, in extreme cases, as similar to what is done to the academic's car by his garage mechanics. From this position arises, I believe, the application of the diminutive term 'techie' by some to describe those individuals doing this kind of work. (Bradley 2011, 11)

Digital humanities (DH) often categorises itself as an interdisciplinary and collaborative field that has been built by a wide range of actors, including technical experts, information professionals, curators, members of the general public and academics (Siemens 2009; Siemens et al. 2010; Deegan and McCarty 2011; Hunter 2014). Nevertheless, the contributions of some individuals, like the technical experts referred to in the quote from Bradley above, have tended to be overlooked and have generally been held in lower esteem than the contributions of academics (e.g. Griffin and Hayler 2018). Perhaps unsurprisingly, then, histories of DH have often foregrounded successful academics, techniques and technologies, while neglecting the contributions of many other categories of DH collaborator or co-worker.

Mahoney has argued that:

> Whatever one wants to say about such abstractions as the Turing machine, it is hard to know how physical computers and the systems

running on them could be anything other than socially constructed. Computing has no nature. It is what it is because people have made it so. (Mahoney 2011, 109)

Here I argue that the writing of inclusive studies of the history of DH should be a priority for those who wish to understand how DH 'people', across the *piste*, have helped to make computing, and in turn the Digital Humanities, 'so'. The recent work of Kaltenbrunner has demonstrated the wealth of insight that a social-epistemological study of DH can deliver. His study of a trans-European, digitally mediated literary studies project which involved the collaborative production of a database interrogated how 'specific ways of organising scholarly labour make possible certain forms of knowledge, and [reveal] the obstacles scholars face when trying to adapt established organisational models' (Kaltenbrunner 2015, 207). This chapter argues that much could be gained by taking such an approach to the history of DH too, by asking how historical models of organising collaborative labour have enabled and constrained certain forms of DH knowledge. A prerequisite of this, I argue, is a shifting of our collective gaze from the contributions of 'great scholars' to the broader 'peoplescapes' (Nyhart 2016) of collaborative teams who have contributed much to DH over the longer term.

In this chapter, I present the example of the technical developer (including the individual now often called a research software engineer) as a microcosm through which to explore this argument. In particular, I argue that histories of the origins and development of the role of the technical developer are crucial for developing better understandings of knowledge production in DH. In proposing this, I do not argue that the contributions of technical staff are necessarily 'scholarly'; neither do I imply that their contributions must be portrayed as such to merit their acknowledgement. Rather, my point is that in digital humanities, as elsewhere, definitions of expertise are subjective and socially constructed (Abbate 2012, 4). The esteem in which a role is held may bear little correspondence to the relative importance of that role in the context of a given project. Appreciating this, and analysing and historicising the contributions of actors other than the 'great scholars', is necessary in order to build richer understandings of how DH has been executed by many people.

I begin with a short overview of the history of DH, looking at some of the main themes and interests of recent scholarship. From there I turn to scholarship from the history of science and cognate areas that has shown that an overemphasis on accounting for the contributions of prominent researchers and scientists can result in fractured and incomplete understandings of how research happens. I then reflect on the work that is done by technical collaborators in DH projects, and draw on publicly conduced social media conversations and formal literature to discuss how technical work is sometimes devalued or overlooked in scholarly publications. Drawing the preceding sections together, I then present a case study of my research on the little-known contributions that were made to the *Index Thomisticus* by the female keypunchers who worked with Roberto Busa. I offer this as an example of the more inclusive historicisation of DH that I call for in this chapter.

A brief historiography of the history of DH

The origins of the field of humanities computing are often traced back to around 1949 and the work of Fr Roberto Busa S.J. on the *Index Thomisticus* (e.g. Unsworth 2006). Until around 2004, when the field's name changed to 'digital humanities', studies of its history appeared but occasionally. Those studies tended to be article-length surveys of the history of the application of computing to particular fields of the humanities, like classics and musicology (Hewlett and Selfridge-Field 1991; Brunner 1993); histories of the development of indexes and concordances, humanities computing's canonical tools (Burton 1981a; Burton 1981b; Burton 1981c; Burton 1982); articles on acclaimed scholars like Busa (Winter 1999); and bibliographies (Adamo 1994). Since around 2003, a more sustained interest in the history of DH can be noticed. There has been a steady stream of publications, presentations at major conferences (e.g. Earhart et al. 2017), blog posts (e.g. Scheinfeldt 2014), symposia (e.g. Nyhan n.d.) and digital projects (e.g. Jones 2018) which all address aspects of the history of DH. In the following, I examine some of the main themes that can be noticed in the formal literature.

Survey articles that presented bird's eye syntheses of the outlines of humanities computing or its subfields were published in the early 2000s. In one, an outline of the development of the field centred major individuals, centres, organisations and journals along with some moments of 'crisis and change' (McCarty 2003, 1226). The *Companion to Digital Humanities* included a 'History' section of articles which gave an overview of the take-up of computational technology in fields like archaeology and lexicography (Eiteljorg II 2004; Thomas III 2004). Hockey's chapter in that volume, which has become one of the most often cited articles of its kind according to Google Scholar, presents a

> chronological account which traces the development of humanities computing. Within this, the emphasis is on highlighting landmarks where significant intellectual progress has been made or where work done within humanities computing has been adopted, developed or drawn on substantially within other disciplines. (Hockey 2004, 3)

Other synoptic studies also appeared – for example Unsworth surveyed the move 'from digitizing to analysing, from artefacts to aggregates, and from representation to abstraction', again foregrounding the contributions of major players (Unsworth 2006). By 2008, McCarty was arguing for 'computing to be *of* the humanities as well as *in* them[;] we must get beyond catalogues, chronologies, and heroic firsts to a genuine history. There are none yet' (McCarty 2008, 255).

More recent scholarship on the history of DH has tended to problematise, sometimes implicitly, sometimes explicitly, the whiggish portrayals of the field's history that underpin many of the synoptic articles mentioned above, and, perhaps, the suggestion that DH has 'a history' rather than histories. I set up the 'Hidden Histories: Computing and the Humanities c.1949–1980' project around 2013. The project seeks to build a deeper understanding of the social, cultural and institutional contexts that shaped the emergence and development of humanities computing and, in turn, DH. Through archival research and oral history interviews with well- and lesser-known individuals, the project seeks to focalise a myriad of contributions to the field and understand more about the experiences of those who have helped to develop it. It has also demonstrated that oral history can open robust ways of responding to problems that can attend the writing of inclusive histories that seek to centre the contributions of non-hegemonic actors to digital humanities (and other knowledge domains). The oral history interviewing undertaken during the project has opened ways of mitigating the paucity of extant sources on the contributions of women and lesser-known actors in archives that contain an abundance of documentation on dominant actors (Chaudhuri et al. 2010). Below I will present a case study of research that has been undertaken as part of this project on the hidden, feminised labour that was contributed to the *Index Thomisticus* project of Fr Roberto Busa S.J.

The methods and analytical frameworks of media archaeology and platform studies have also proved influential in and for the body of literature on the history of digital humanities that is under discussion. Media archaeology problematises dominant theories of media development – often rooted in social, political and intellectual orthodoxies – that can hinder understandings of the deep structure, age, process and definition of media history. By looking at 'technologies that are not in canonical histories as precursors to "successful" technologies . . . [a] study of forgotten technologies can help us understand opportunities and challenges as they were perceived at the time and on their own terms rather than imposing our prejudices' (Sinclair and Rockwell 2014, 357). Exemplifying this, Rockwell and Sinclair published media archaeology-inflected studies of forgotten text analysis technologies (see also Nyhan and Flinn 2022). Studies have also incorporated the methods of humanistic fabrication to recover, or perhaps reimagine, otherwise poorly understood or lost details of the methodology of the *Index Thomisticus* (Sinclair 2016; Rockwell and Sinclair 2020). Jones's book on the first 10 years of Busa's work, from 1949 to 1959, also draws on media archaeology, platform studies and archival research to explore how 'the specific technologies of the punchedcard data-processing era afforded and constrained the academic research agenda of humanities computing at the moment of its emergence' (Jones 2016). This chapter's call to rebalance what might be seen as an overemphasis on dominant figures like Busa does not amount to a call to turn away from histories of canonical figures. Rather it is a call to approach those histories with the critical lenses offered by approaches like oral history, media archaeology, humanistic fabrication and others, so as to position canonical figures in a wider landscape of endeavour rather than mistaking them for the landscape itself.

Next to this work, scholars have been pushing forward our understandings of other, less-examined aspects of the history of DH (writ large) too. These include discipline-specific studies of the early years of digital literary scholarship (Earhart 2015) and digital history (Crymble 2021); studies of scholars who made largely overlooked contributions to DH (Buurma and Heffernan 2018); studies of the emergence of scholarly associations, for example in Canada (Gouglas et al. 2013); studies of the field's central platforms for information and knowledge dissemination and creation, like *Humanist* (Nyhan 2016); outlines of the field's attitudes to the establishment of processes like peer review (Nyhan 2020); and studies of the portrayal of computing during the early phase of the field of humanities computing in the major Canadian newspaper *Globe and Mail* (Rockwell et al. 2011).

Thus, as partially outlined above, a wealth of publications on the history of DH have either recently appeared or are in train, and they are notable not only for their pluralisation of the topics that are now being historicised but also for the wealth of the methodological approaches and theoretical framings that are being brought to the study of the history of digital humanities. This chapter argues that an important next step for this scholarship is to turn its attention to those lesser-known individuals whose contributions may not have been 'innovative' or 'scholarly', according to conventional definitions of those terms. As will now be set out, answers to the question 'why should those actors be studied?' are found in important work that has emerged from fields like the history of science, the history of computing and feminist technology studies. Those fields have shown the important insights that can be derived from social constructionist approaches to the understanding of knowledge production and the history of disciplinarity. I will now reflect on some of the key findings of this scholarship before moving to consider the perspectives that such scholarship may open for scholarship on the history of DH.

Beyond the scholar

Despite emphasising its radical and collaborative credentials (Presner et al. 2009), DH often draws on a 'great narrative' about a 'great man' (such as Fr Roberto Busa S.J.) to explain its origins. Accounts of 'great men', 'grand narratives' and revolutionary breakthroughs have, of course, sustained many histories of science, technology and computing (Basalla 1988, 21).[1] This focus on the role of a pre-eminent individual has resulted in the contributions made to science by the large teams who worked for them often being overlooked (Russell et al. 2000). The contributions made to research by individuals and teams who supported 'the great man' were not usually deemed 'original', 'creative' or 'innovative' and so were often overlooked as merely supplementary. As various studies have shown, definitions of expertise are socially and culturally situated, and influenced by factors like gender, class and race (McNeil 1987). With regard to archaeological fieldwork, for example, it has been shown that the work of the famous archaeologist Flinders Petrie could sometimes overlap with the work of his 'hidden hands', or assistants hired locally in Egypt. As such, the borderlines that demarcated aspects of the work of Petrie from the work of his hired helpers were hewn by colonial power dynamics, actively perpetuated (however intentionally or unintentionally) by researchers like Petrie rather than naturally and objectively occurring (Quirke 2010). The categorisation of work as ancillary, or merely mechanical, is not necessarily any more objective than the categorisation of work as innovative or creative, however. As Carroll has argued in relation to the term 'originality' and associated terms like 'innovation' and creativity':

> The concept of 'originality', though essentially empty of substantive meaning, is used today to justify and rationalize a class system based upon claims of property in ideas. The system assigns most men and almost all women to positions in the lower classes and preserves for a small group of self-recruiting males both hegemony over received knowledge and control of a variety of rewards and privileges. Among the various techniques of depreciation and dismissal of the work of women as intellectuals and scholars, one of the most prevalent has been the denial of its 'originality'. (Carroll 1990, 136)

Furthermore, as feminist technology studies scholarship has shown, technology and gender are fundamentally interconnected. Gender stereotypes can influence what is and is not identified as 'technology' (Cockburn and Ormrod 1993) and technology can replicate or mobilise gender inequality, also intersectionally (Noble 2018). With regard to the history of computing in the UK, for example, this can be detected in the gendered labour segregation that confined many women to the lowest-ranking posts and resulted in the devaluing and overlooking of their work (Hicks 2017). In early computing projects, the work assigned to women typically covered computer operation and programming (Hicks 2017), which was seen as lower in status, less difficult and less technical than the hardware-oriented work done by men (Light 1999). In other words, technology is not neutral but has been created 'in the interests of particular social groups, and against the interests of others' (Wajcman 1996, 135). Computing in particular is 'an explicitly hegemonic project built on labour categories designed to perpetuate particular forms of class status' (Hicks 2017, 6). Thus, judgements as to what counts as 'skilled' versus 'unskilled' or 'original' and 'innovative' versus 'support work' do not necessarily reflect the actual content of the work and must be approached with eyes wide open.

Shapin's study of the 'invisible' workers of Robert Boyle's experimental laboratory in early modern England argued that these devalued workers made important, if usually quotidian, contributions to the early-modern scientific project (Shapin 1989, 554–63). Yet few references acknowledging the agency of such individuals occur in corresponding publications. In his work on Boyle, Shapin argued that this is partly due to the low regard in which their work was held for various reasons, including its manual nature and the remuneration they received for it (Shapin 1989, 554–5). Since the 1970s, the 'social constructionist' turn in fields like the history of science has questioned individualistic models of scientific progress. This turn views the 'development of scientific knowledge as depending heavily on particulars of local circumstances, people, epistemes, and politics . . . that doesn't necessarily drive ever closer toward a single truth' (Nyhart 2016, 7). Accordingly, numerous studies have been undertaken in recent years to plumb those factors (e.g. Russell et al. 2000; Baird 2004; Dascal 1998). While scholars acknowledge a plurality of genealogies and that 'twentieth-century scientists are not gentlemen of independent means and do not employ . . . junior laboratory staff themselves, to an extent their authority still derives from claims made on this historical basis. This may partly explain why modern laboratory support staff are sometimes as invisible as Boyle's assistants' (Russell et al. 2000, 240). In the history of computing literature, attention has likewise been given to otherwise individual or overlooked individuals, instruments and circumstances. The field has 'increasingly situated seemingly internal developments in electronic computing within their larger social, technological and political context. The result has been more rigorous, convincing, relevant explanations of how the computer shapes, and is shaped by, modern society' (Ensmenger 2004, 96).

From the perspective of the history of DH, following Russell, we might similarly inquire as to the historical basis from which the authority of the DH scholar derives, and about the historical basis that contributed to the devaluing of the work of the DH technician. As I will now argue, I believe that there is much in this literature that can help us to examine how DH has been shaped by the contributions of the technical worker and of how judgements as to the nature of their contributions have ultimately helped to set boundaries between the scholars of DH teams and the techies who contribute to them.

Like the invisible workers of Shapin's laboratory, in many cases DH relied on the contributions of the technical developers on DH project teams. This is brought out by Bradley's discussion of the collaborative nature of computational modelling, where he describes how the 'digital humanities specialist' (which I read as being synonymous with 'technical developer') and 'discipline expert' (which I read as being synonymous with 'academic') work together to build a digital model of an object of study – a rather classic activity in the field of DH. Bradley writes that the technical developer and academic both significantly enrich the results that come from the shared endeavour . . . [by] combining the [academic's] insights and experience of the materials of study . . . with the [technical developer's] ability to express these things in the formal language of digital modelling. (Bradley 2011, 12, 16)

Notwithstanding this intellectual and procedural union, a hierarchically incommensurate relationship has often existed between the technical developers and academics who work on DH projects.[2] To a large extent, DH projects pursued in universities have a two-tier workforce, where a sharp division exists between faculty, or those whose primary role is to do research and teach, and technical staff, whose primary role is to code, programme and do other technical and infrastructural work (Nyhan and Flinn 2016). The work of technical developers is not necessarily accorded parity of esteem with the work of scholars. Their work can be overlooked, devalued and silenced by the wider academy. References to the ambiguity that can exist towards technical and collaborative DH can be found in the formal literature of the field (Edmond 2020) and in digital humanities' social media discussions. Discussions have been carried out on Twitter about how some receive little or no acknowledgement from scholars for the technical artefacts they build – artefacts that allow scholars to do their very research. In a public post, Victoria Van Hyning asked: 'Hey #twitterstorians and humanities folks, how/do you acknowledge the intellectual contributions to your work of project collaborators or connectors who aren't co-authors? I'm bummed out by # of times my work/ideas and those of others are unacknowledged. STEM offers alt. models.'[3]

The work of digital humanities technical staff can be devalued in this way because it is often not categorised as research and thus is not 'innovative' and 'original'. Rather, it is sometimes held to be the support work that allows the 'real' research of the scholar to take place. Yet, exemplifying how assessments of what does, or does not, count as expert work can remain detached from the actual content of the work, Bradley has convincingly argued that the contributions of technical developers to such collaborations show many of the hallmarks of research. External validation of this claim is provided by, for example, the submission of the Department of Digital Humanities at King's College London to the Research Evaluation Framework 2014:

[O]ur results compared favourably with the RAE results from across the entire School of Humanities at KCL, which was ranked, overall, as among the very best in the UK. This result, I should reiterate, was from a submission that contained many contributions from people not elsewhere normally recognised as scholar. (Bradley 2011, 21)

Leaving aside what are ultimately rather circular questions about what is or is not scholarly, the more pertinent question in the context of this chapter concerns what a dh-specific historical basis can be drawn on to devalue the work of the technical developer and valorise the work of the scholar in this way? This question is, of course, one that requires a detailed and long-form response, which is beyond the limits of this chapter. The question that will instead be opened here is: given that DH was only recently institutionalised as a field and has rather recently entered the academic mainstream (Kirschenbaum 2010), does the devaluing of technical contributions have a historical basis? Might it be a turn that has instead been imposed on the field by the wider Academy? My work on the devalued and largely hidden contributions that were made to the *Index Thomisticus* project by the young women who keypunched it (c.1955–67) suggests not. The following section draws on a much more substantial discussion of this in Nyhan (2022).

Hidden contributions to the *Index Thomisticus*

Roberto Busa S.J. is often portrayed as the progenitor of DH. His renown is based on many achievements, most of all his research on the automation of concordance production. This resulted in the first instalment of the *Index Thomisticus* in 1974, whose publication would continue over 56 volumes until 1980. In 1992, the *Index Thomisticus* was published on CD-ROM and in 2005 it was published as hypertext on the world wide web. For the most part, Busa portrayed himself, and has subsequently been portrayed, as a lone scholar in the sense that he was responsible for the ideation and execution of the *Index Thomisticus* project. For example, Busa himself wrote that he 'had to solve problems which no longer exist today. Without assistance and in addition to finding financial support, I had to develop and test a method which had no predecessor and had to use a technology which developed progressively' (Busa 1980, 87). This portrayal is often reflected in secondary discussions of his work. For example, Raben emphasised Busa's lone scholar status when he stated: 'Through his perseverance and intellectual application, Roberto Busa has demonstrated the efficacy of utilizing the newest technology to comprehend the thought of a master synthesizer of 700 years ago' (Raben 1987, 227).

Nevertheless, as Busa himself sometimes made clear, he did not work alone: his team comprised 60 individuals at its zenith (Busa 1965). Among them were the young women who were recruited as trainees to Busa's Literary Data Processing Centre (CAAL) in Gallarate from around 1954 onwards. These young keypunch operators made crucial but undervalued contributions to the *Index Thomisticus* project, and some other projects that CAAL took on, during the period 1954–67. Without their work, Busa could not have processed and analysed the texts of Thomas Aquinas and related authors that formed the basis of the *Index Thomisticus*. Their work resulted in an archive of millions of punched cards. They inputted 'natural texts containing 12,000,000 words in 9 different languages in the Latin, Hebrew, Greek, and Cyrillic alphabets, which deal with different, subjects, periods, and cultures: such as the Qumran manuscripts, the works of St Thomas Aquinas, and abstracts of nuclear physics' (Busa 2019d [1968], 120). From contemporaneous discussions of keypunching we can infer that the keypunching they did would have been considered most challenging (Van Ness 1963). The particular kind of keypunching that they did required intense concentration and skill, and it required them to know complex key combinations so as to encode the many special characters and symbols used in the texts they were transcribing (Busa 2019d [1968]). They worked with Busa until 1967, when, as he wrote, '*I* completed the punching of all my texts' (Busa 1980, 85, emphasis mine).

During his lifetime Busa published around 400 texts (Nyhan and Passarotti 2020). Acknowledgement of keypunch labour does not routinely occur in those texts. The few references to this work that can be found tend either to obscure or to diminish it. This happens in various ways, for example when the use of the passive voice hides keypunching labour: 'The Centre at Gallarate is still today the one in the whole world that has put the greatest number of words on cards: there are to date about four million, and the number is increasing' (Busa 2019b, 79 [1962]). Or when keypunch operators' identities are subsumed by Busa's so that we find various examples in his writing of the claim that 'I have now completed the punching of the 220,000 cards that represent all the lines of the Summa Theologiae of St Thomas' (Busa 2019a, 66 [1958]). Even the few ostensibly positive and comparatively detailed extant discussions of their contributions seem to diminish their agency:

> I started a training school for keypunch operators. For all those admitted, the requirement was that it was their first job. After a

month of testing, only one out of five was accepted for a program of four semesters, eight hours per day. The success was excellent: industries wanted to hire them before they had finished the program. (Busa 1980, 85)

This discussion is, entirely from Busa's perspective. The mentions of selective admission and hiring by industries all describe actions that were done *to* the operators. We have no sense of them as individuals who made their own decisions. Even the success that is mentioned is not theirs; rather it is implicitly that of Busa's training programme.

Oral history interviewing with nine of the keypunchers whose work with Busa collectively spanned the years 1954–65 and archival work has allowed me to rediscover some aspects of the work that they did and their experiences of working in an early digital humanities project. The post of keypunch operator was actively framed by Busa as a rather dead-end role. Busa sought to hire young girls for the role (most of those we interviewed recalled that they were around 14 years of age when hired) who had completed the minimum legally allowable level of education. Despite the skills that they learned and the importance of the work that they did, they do not seem to have been understood as anything other than sources of low-cost and low-skilled labour. In contrast with the young men who were admitted to the slightly more esteemed role of machine operator, the young women were not eligible to progress in their roles. In the oral history interviews, it was recalled that a young woman who had been performing the role of manager was blocked from formally taking up this role on grounds of gender. Instead, a man with less knowledge and experience of keypunching was appointed. The individual who recounted this incident felt that this was because 'Father Busa would have preferred a man in charge'.

Busa was not necessarily unusual in this. Such treatment of female employees and trainees to some extent echoes how many women who used electromechanical accounting machinery in government, the academy and industry were treated. This silencing of the work and contributions of the operatives, and their longer-term invisibility, was symptomatic of Busa's times and was informed by the wider cultural and social realities of women's positions as clerical workers in the office, and their treatment in statistical computing bureaus and the burgeoning computing industry. Moreover, the treatment of Index Thomisticus keypunch operators corresponds to a marked degree with the treatment of amanuenses over the longer history of concordance making. Busa's predecessors also tended to make their amanuenses invisible in the public-facing scholarship that resulted from such projects. Yet my argument is that

Busa was not a passive recipient of these traditions, for he drew on the historical basis that devalued the work of amanuenses and female information worker such as keypunch operators.

I argue that we can see this by comparing and contrasting Busa's discussions of the keypunch operators with his discussions of the 'scholars' who also worked on the *Index Thomisticus* project. The scholars, who were male and usually clerics, also made an important contribution to Busa's project. Their main task was to 'pre-edit': they marked up the project's texts in various ways so that they could be encoded onto punched cards by the keypunch operators. The scholars also lemmatised headwords. Their names may not be routinely given in Busa's publications, but they have a distinct presence and their personal agency is acknowledged. Busa does not silence or devalue their work, rather he claims that 'To put data into elementary information units is an exquisitely philosophical work of classification' (Busa 2019c [1966], 107). Busa's discussions of the work of the scholars show that it must have involved the need to make subjective and interpretative decisions that would have been open to contestation by others who might have interpreted the material differently. Despite this, I have not been able to find any published discussions of errors detected in the scholars' work, or disagreements about the decisions they reached. Most tellingly, indications of such concerns on Busa's part are only, in fact, to be found in archival materials.

Busa's public portrayal of the scholars stands in stark contrast to his portrayal of the female keypunch operators. In one of the few sustained discussions of their work that is currently known to be extant, Busa complains bitterly about the mistakes that they made and calls for 'Centres of Psychology and Communication' to create 'programs to train such people, [and to discover] the rules of human behaviour regarding mistakes in the preparation of computer input' (Busa 2019d [1968], 124). In the meantime, he would require technical workers to prepare a punched card 'for half a day's work, or less. This contains their own identity, the quantity and references of the material used, the mistakes they made while working, and those each one found while checking their own work or that of another' (Busa 2019d [1968], 122). His portrayal of the work of the keypunch operators as error-prone and requiring constant supervision, partly as a result of their 'bio-type' (Busa 2019d [1968], 124), thus stands in stark contrast to that of the scholars. Indeed, his portrayal might almost be read to justify the limited opportunities that were given to the keypunch operators and to reinforce Busa's portrayal of himself as a de facto lone scholar.

I interpret the cumulative import of these discussions as an early insight into how the boundaries between the scholar and the technical worker were drawn in a major, early project that is usually seen as being at the source of the humanities computing and, subsequently, digital humanities fields that would follow. The Index Thomisticus project actively perpetuated gendered, class-based (for instance between scholar and technical assistant) and techno-determinative divisions in its set-up and running, and in the reporting of its outcomes. Thus, the role of the scholar was privileged – Busa's most especially – to the exclusion of others, who were portrayed as carrying out less important work with electromechanical accounting machines, and later, computers. It may come as little surprise, then, that the work of the keypunch operators is mostly absent from the academic literature on the *Index Thomisticus* project; it was likewise mostly forgotten by the DH community until the research reported on here was carried out.

For me, what is most startling about this is not only the realisation that what was deemed scholarly or not in one of the earliest DH projects appears to have been decided with regard to the identity and gender of those who undertook the work, rather than the nature of the work itself. It is also the realisation that, at least in the context of the *Index Thomisticus*, the devaluing of technical labour came not from the wider academy but rather from the context of the *Index Thomisticus* itself. To what extent, then, did the example that was set by the *Index Thomisticus* influence subsequent decisions about whose contributions to DH projects have and have not tended to be acknowledged? How have attitudes to this changed over time? To what extent might a history of the technical developer in DH extend to revising our histories of large-scale projects in the field, to acknowledge and understand the previously undocumented contributions of those who were overlooked by founding father narratives? These questions remain to be answered and are, I argue, important next steps for the history of DH.

Conclusion

By drawing on scholarship from areas like the history of science and feminist technology studies I have argued that there is much to be gained from interrogating the power structures and dynamics that have been at play in historic DH projects and that arguably continue to manifest in the labour organisation of the field of DH. One productive way of approaching this is, I argue, through the histories of hidden, undervalued or lesser-known contributions that were made, for example, by those now known as research software engineers, or technical DH workers more broadly, whose work is rarely given parity of esteem with scholars and has thus often been overlooked. I have exemplified this through a case study of the hidden, feminised contributions that were made to the *Index Thomisticus* project.

This reading of the history of DH seeks to reveal the everyday contributions of those individuals who did not receive praise or even individual acknowledgement for their DH work, yet without whose contributions the work of Busa and others would have been impossible. As Morus has put it:

> Paying close attention [to hidden workers] offers historians ways, therefore, of looking more closely at how scientific authority is constructed and how . . . [g]oing behind the individual focus provides a way of re-emphasising the role of the collective instead. It gives historians an opportunity to demonstrate that the notion of science as the product of individual genius is itself a construct. (Morus 2016, 108–9)

In *Histories of Egyptology*, Carruthers asks: 'What, in the second decade of the twenty-first century, constitutes the history (or histories) of Egyptology? What does this history consist of, and what (or who) should it be for?' (Carruthers 2014, 1). He goes on to consider some beliefs about this that are implicit in the literature on the history of Egyptology. Among others, he discusses the problematic 'desire to improve Egyptological research and remove it from unnecessary biases through a process of historical reflection' (Carruthers 2014, 3). He observes:

> [O]ne way of thinking about these discussions is as a number of more or less powerful claims to authority. Here, Gieryn's conception of boundary work is useful. Through this process . . . a set of knowledge practices is defined that constitute the proper object of a field of inquiry, practices that contain the source of that field's continued reproduction and relevance while also setting the rules of who can and cannot partake in it and defining the worlds in which the field can be said to be connected. Histories of Egyptology have been a useful way of setting such boundaries. (Carruthers 2014, 7)

Indeed, decisions about who and what is written in and out of disciplinary histories can have far-reaching implications for present and future understandings of what constitutes legitimate and non-legitimate research topics. Attention to the role of the 'techie', and other workers who have been portrayed as subaltern, whether intentionally or not, can foreground this for us as the detailed work of writing the histories of DH proceeds in earnest.

Notes

1. Of course, the 'great man' explanation of progress and innovation has been evoked to explain developments in any number of areas, covering contexts like scholarly, technical and computing innovation, the formation of major museum collections, architectural heritage and colonial wealth.
2. Those examples notwithstanding, it is not universally the case that the work of the technical developer is devalued either by digital humanities colleagues or by the wider academy. Some recent scholarship has argued that 'there have tended to be hierarchies in the digital humanities, ranking programming as secondary to humanities. However, this study has demonstrated a more complex relationship, with the humanities largely being regarded as the driving force behind the digital humanities yet with the impetus to use digital technologies to explore the boundaries being seen are equally important' (Hunter 2014, 29). The issue of fair and appropriate acknowledgement of co-workers' contributions is an issue that is explored in many digital humanities project charters and value statements. Linked to this is the work that has been done on the evaluation of digital scholarship, which has broadened definitions of scholarship.
3. https://twitter.com/VanHyningV/status/1110685273984299008 (accessed 5 September 2022). As of 2022, Van Hyning's twitter profile states that she is '[Assistant] Prof of Library Innovation [University of Maryland College of Information Studies]. Formerly By the People/ Library of Congress; Zooniverse Humanities PI' (https://twitter.com/VanHyningV).

References

Abbate, J. 2012. *Recoding Gender: Women's changing participation in computing*. Cambridge, MA: MIT Press.

Adamo, G. 1994. *Bibliografia di Informatica umanistica*. Rome: Bulzoni.

Baird, D. 2004. *Thing Knowledge: A philosophy of scientific instruments*. Berkeley, CA: University of California Press.

Basalla, G. 1988. *The Evolution of Technology*. Cambridge: Cambridge University Press.

Bradley, J. 2011. 'No Job for Techies: Technical contributions to research in the digital humanities'. In *Collaborative Research in the Digital Humanities*, edited by Marilyn Deegan and Willard McCarty, 11–26. Farnham: Ashgate.

Brunner, T.F. 1993. 'Classics and the Computer: The history of a relationship'. In *Accessing Antiquity: The computerization of classical studies*, edited by J. Solomon, 10–33. Tucson, AZ: University of Arizona Press.

Burton, D.M. 1981a. 'Automated Concordances and Word Indexes: The fifties', *Computers and the Humanities* 15: 1–14. https://doi.org/10.1007/BF02404370

Burton, D.M. 1981b. 'Automated Concordances and Word Indexes: The early sixties and the early centers', *Computers and the Humanities* 15: 83–100. https://doi.org/10.1007/BF02404202

Burton, D.M. 1981c. 'Automated Concordances and Word Indexes: The process, the programs, and the products', *Computers and the Humanities* 15: 139–54. https://doi.org/10.1007/BF02404180

Burton, D.M. 1982. 'Automated Concordances and Word Indexes: Machine decisions and editorial revisions', *Computers and the Humanities* 16: 195–218. https://doi.org/10.1007/BF02263544

Busa, R. 1964. 'An Inventory of Fifteen Million Words'. In *Literary Data Processing Conference Proceedings September 9, 10, 11 1964*, edited by Jess B. Bessinger, Stephen M. Parrish and Harry F. Arader, 64–78. Armonk: NY: IBM Corporation.

Busa, R. 1980. 'The Annals of Humanities Computing: The Index Thomisticus', *Computers and the Humanities* 14: 83–90. https://doi.org/10.1007/BF02403798

Busa, R. 2019a [1958]. 'The Main Problems of the Automation of Written Language'. In *One Origin of Digital Humanities: Fr Roberto Busa in His Own Words*, edited by J. Nyhan and M. Passarotti, 59–68. Cham, Switzerland: Springer International.

Busa, R. 2019b [1962]. 'Linguistic Analysis in the Global Evolution of Information'. In *One Origin of Digital Humanities: Fr Roberto Busa in his own words*, edited by J. Nyhan and M. Passarotti, 75–86. Cham, Switzerland: Springer International.

Busa, R. 2019c [1966]. 'Experienced-Based Results with Preparations for the Use of Automatic Calculation in Biology'. In *One Origin of Digital Humanities: Fr Roberto Busa in his own words*, edited by J. Nyhan and M. Passarotti, 105–10. Cham, Switzerland: Springer International.

Busa, R. 2019d [1968]. 'Human Errors in the Preparation of Input for Computers'. In *One Origin of Digital Humanities: Fr Roberto Busa in his own words*, edited by J. Nyhan and M. Passarotti, 119–24. Cham, Switzerland: Springer International.

Buurma, R.S. and L. Heffernan. 2018. 'Search and Replace: Josephine Miles and the origins of distant reading', *Modernism/Modernity* 3:1. Accessed 5 September 2022. https://modernismmodernity.org/forums/posts/search-and-replace

Carroll, B.A. 1990. 'The Politics of "Originality": Women and the class system of the intellect', *Journal of Women's History* 2: 136–63. https://doi.org/10.1353/jowh.2010.0060

Carruthers, W. 2014. 'Thinking about Histories of Egyptology'. In *Histories of Egyptology: Interdisciplinary measures*, edited by William Carruthers, 1–18. New York: Routledge, Taylor & Francis.

Chaudhuri, N., S.J. Katz and E.M. Perry (eds). 2010. *Contesting Archives: Finding women in the sources*. Urbana-Champaign, IL: University of Illinois Press.

Cockburn, C. and S. Ormrod. 1993. *Gender and Technology in the Making*. London: SAGE.

Crymble, Adam. 2021. *Technology and the Historian: Transformations in the digital age*. Urbana-Champaign, IL: University of Illinois Press.

Dascal, M. 1998. 'The Study of Controversies and the Theory and History of Science', *Science in Context* 11(2): 147–54. https://doi.org/10.1017/S0269889700002957

Deegan, M. and W. McCarty. 2011. *Collaborative Research in the Digital Humanities: A volume in honour of Harold Short, on the occasion of his 65th birthday and his retirement, September 2010*. Farnham: Ashgate.

Earhart, Amy E. 2015. *Traces of the Old, Uses of the New: The emergence of digital literary studies*. Ann Arbor, MI: University of Michigan Press.

Earhart, Amy E., S.E. Jones, T. McPherson, P.R. Murray and R. Whitson. 2017. 'Alternate Histories of the Digital Humanities'. Conference paper, ADHO-2017, McGill University, Université de Montréal, Canada, 8–11 August. https://dh-abstracts.library.cmu.edu/works/3836

Edmond, J. 2020. 'Introduction: Power, practices, and the gatekeepers of humanistic research in the digital age'. In *Digital Technology and the Practices of Humanities Research*, edited by Jennifer Redmond, 1–20. Cambridge: Open Book.

Eiteljorg II, H. 2004. 'Computing for Archaeologists'. In *A Companion to Digital Humanities*, edited by Susan Schreibman, Raymond George Siemens and John Unsworth, 20–30. Malden, MA: Blackwell.

Ensmenger, N. 2004. 'Power to the People: Toward a social history of computing', *IEEE Annals of the History of Computing* 26: 96. https://doi.org/10.1109/MAHC.2004.1278876

Gouglas, S., G. Rockwell, V. Smith, S. Hoosein and H. Quamen. 2013. 'Before the Beginning: The formation of humanities computing as a discipline in Canada', *Digital Studies/Le champ numérique* 3.

Griffin, G. and M.S. Hayler. 2018. 'Collaboration in Digital Humanities Research – Persisting silences', *Digital Humanities Quarterly* 12(1) (online).

Haigh, T. 2014. 'The Tears of Donald Knuth', *Communications of the ACM* 58: 40–44. https://doi.org/10.1145/2688497

Hewlett, W.B. and E. Selfridge-Field. 1991. 'Computing in Musicology, 1966–91', *Computers and the Humanities* 25: 381–92.

Hicks, M. 2017. *Programmed Inequality: How Britain discarded women technologists and lost its edge in computing*. Cambridge, MA: MIT Press.

Hockey, S.M. 2004. 'The History of Humanities Computing'. In *Companion to Digital Humanities*, edited by Susan Schreibman, Ray Siemens and John Unsworth. Oxford: Blackwell.

Hunter, A. 2014. 'Digital Humanities as Third Culture', *MedieKultur: Journal of media and communication research* 30: 16. https://doi.org/10.7146/mediekultur.v30i57.16318

Jones, S.E. 2016. *Roberto Busa, S.J., and the Emergence of Humanities Computing: The priest and the punched cards*. Abingdon: Routledge.

Jones, S.E. 2018. 'Reverse Engineering the First Humanities Computing Center', *Digital Humanities Quarterly* 12.

Kaltenbrunner, W. 2015. 'Scholarly Labour and Digital Collaboration in Literary Studies', *Social Epistemology* 29: 207–33. https://doi.org/10.1080/02691728.2014.907834

Kirschenbaum, M.G. 2010. 'What is Digital Humanities and What's it Doing in English Departments?', *ADE Bulletin*: 55–61. https://doi.org/10.1632/ade.150.55

Light, J.S. 1999. 'When Computers Were Women', *Technology and Culture* 40: 455–83.

McCarty, W. 2003. 'Humanities Computing', *Encyclopedia of Library and Information Sciences* 1224–1235. New York: Marcel Dekker.

McCarty, W. 2008. 'What's Going On?', *Literary and Linguistic Computing* 23: 253–61. https://doi.org/10.1093/llc/fqn014

McNeil, M. 1987. *Gender and Expertise*. London: Free Association Books.

Mahoney, Michael Sean. 2011. *Histories of Computing*, edited by Thomas Haigh. Cambridge, MA: Harvard University Press.

Morus, I.R. 2016. 'Invisible Technicians, Instrument Makers, and Artisans'. In *A Companion to the History of Science*, edited by Bernard Lightman, 97–110. London: John Wiley & Sons.

Noble, S.U. 2018. *Algorithms of Oppression: How search engines reinforce racism*. New York: New York University Press.

Nyhan, J. 2016. 'In Search of Identities in the Digital Humanities: The early history of HUMANIST'. In *Social Media Archaeology and Poetics*, edited by Judy Malloy. Cambridge, MA: MIT Press.

Nyhan, J. 2020. 'The Evaluation and Peer Review of Digital Scholarship in the Humanities: Experiences, discussions and histories'. In *Digital Technology and the Practices of Humanities Research,* edited by J. Edmond, 163–79. Open Book Publisher. Accessed 5 September 2022. http://library.oapen.org/handle/20.500.12657/22813

Nyhan, J. 2022. *Hidden and Devalued Feminized Labour in the Digital Humanities: On the Index Thomisticus project 1965–67*. Digital Research in the Arts and Humanities. New York: Routledge.

Nyhan, J. n.d. *Meetings*. 'Hidden Histories: Digital humanities 1949–present'. https://hiddenhistories.omeka.net/meetings

Nyhan, J. and A. Flinn. 2016. *Computation and the Humanities: Towards an oral history of digital humanities*. Cham, Switzerland: Springer International.

Nyhan, J. and A. Flinn. 2022. 'Oral History and the (Digital) Humanities'. In *Writing the History of the Humanities. 153–170.* London: Bloomsbury.

Nyhan, J. and M. Passarotti (eds). 2019. *One Origin of Digital Humanities: Fr Roberto Busa in his own words*. Cham, Switzerland: Springer Nature.

Nyhart, L.K. 2016. 'Historiography of the History of Science'. In *A Companion to the History of Science*, edited by Bernard Lightman, 7–22. Oxford: Blackwell.

Presner, T. et al. 2009. 'The Digital Humanities Manifesto 2.0'. UCLA Mellon Seminar in Digital Humanities.

Quirke, S. 2010. *Hidden Hands: Egyptian workforces in Petrie excavation archives, 1880–1924*. London: Bristol Classical Press.

Raben, J. 1987. In *Studies in Honour of Roberto Busa S.J.*, edited by Antonio Zampolli, A. Cappelli, L. Cignoni and C. Peters. Pisa: Giardini.

Rockwell, G. and S. Sinclair. 2020. 'Tremendous Mechanical Labor: Father Busa's algorithm', *Digital Humanities Quarterly* 14.

Rockwell, G., V. Smith, S. Hoosein, S. Gouglas and H. Quamen. 2011. 'Computing in Canada: A history of the incunabular years'. In *Digital Humanities Book of Abstracts*, 207–10. Stanford, CA: Stanford University Library.

Russell, N.C., E.M. Tansey and P.V. Lear. 2000. 'Missing Links in the History and Practice of Science: Teams, technicians and technical work', *History of Science* 38: 237–41. https://doi.org/10.1177/007327530003800205

Scheinfeldt, T. 2014. 'The Dividends of Difference: Recognizing digital humanities' diverse family tree/s', *Found History*. Accessed 5 September 2022. https://foundhistory.org/2014/04/the-dividends-of-difference-recognizing-digital-humanities-diverse-family-trees

Shapin, S. 1989. 'The Invisible Technician', *American Scientist* 77: 554–63.

Siemens, L. 2009. 'It's a Team if You Use "Reply All": An exploration of research teams in digital humanities environments', *Literary and Linguistics Computing* 24: 225–33.c

Siemens, L., R. Cunningham, W. Duff and C. Warwick. 2010. '"More Minds are Brought to Bear on a Problem": Methods of interaction and collaboration within digital humanities research teams', *Digital Studies/Le champ numérique* 2. https://doi.org/10.16995/dscn.80

Sinclair, S. 2016. 'Experiments with Punch Cards'. Accessed 5 September 2022. https://stefansinclair.name/punchcard

Sinclair, S. and G. Rockwell. 2014. 'Towards an Archaeology of Text Analysis Tools'. Paper presented at the Digital Humanities Conference, Lausanne, Switzerland. http://dh2014.org/

Thomas II, W.G. 2004. 'Computing and the Historical Imagination'. In *A Companion to Digital Humanities*, edited by Susan Schreibman, Raymond George Siemens and John Unsworth, 56–68. Malden, MA: Blackwell.

Unsworth, J. 2006. 'Digital Humanities Beyond Representation'. University of Central Florida, Orlando, 13 November. Accessed 1 December 2022. https://people.brandeis.edu/~unsworth/UCF

Van Ness, R.G. 1963. *Principles of Punched Card Data Processing*. USA: OA Business Publications.

Wajcman J. 1996, *Feminism Confronts Technology*. University Park, PA: Pennsylvania State University.

Winter, T.N. 1999. 'Roberto Busa S.J. and the Invention of the Machine-Generated Concordance', *The Classical Bulletin* 75: 3–20.

7
Jobs, roles and tools in digital humanities

Julia Flanders

One major impact of the field of digital humanities upon the humanities academy is to create self-consciousness about professional roles. Over the past 30–40 years, the frameworks of professional identity and expertise in which digital humanities jobs are situated have been continually changing and even now remain contested and liminal. Formations such as digital humanities centres and projects have the dual effect of bringing new kinds of jobs and roles into visibility (the programmer-analyst, the data engineer, the user interface designer) and putting familiar jobs into unfamiliar working relationships (faculty working with developers; librarians working with project managers). Furthermore, the tendency towards contingent and short-term funding, combined with the small size of such units, means that people tend to 'wear many hats', and those who make their long-term career in digital humanities often find themselves adapting to take on radically new roles and forms of expertise during their professional lifecycles.

The resulting scrutiny of digital humanities jobs has significance for the design of professional training (in particular, graduate study in the humanities as well as in library science) but it also has an even more urgent significance for our understanding of how digital projects and organisations can achieve more than a short-term vitality. Two major reports on the state of the field within the past decade or so have identified sustainability as a pre-eminent challenge, with staffing called out as a core problem. Diane Zorich's 2008 survey of digital humanities centres flagged staffing instability as one of three major threats to sustainability (Zorich 2008, 32), and the concluding recommendations in Nancy Maron and Sarah Pickle's *Sustaining the Digital Humanities* (Maron and

Pickle 2014) include a section headed 'Invest in people', which notes the vulnerability of digital humanities centres and projects to staff turnover, and the difficulties of finding and retaining staff. However, as familiar and even unremarkable as these points are to those familiar with the field, they are also perplexing. Staff in other areas of the university advance and change jobs all the time, without posing a threat to the fundamental sustainability of the enterprise. While resource scarcity is certainly a problem – particularly in competing with industry for developers – no part of the academy is especially well resourced. Why is digital humanities distinctly vulnerable to these shifts?

I would like to argue in what follows that in order to understand the vulnerability – and hence also the potential vitality – of digital humanities organisations, we need to look in more detail at how jobs in the field are imagined and designed. Because digital humanities organisations are in many ways profoundly new kinds of workplaces (at least as far as the academy is concerned), the framing of jobs (as specific alignments of effort and responsibility) tends to lag behind the emergence of roles necessary for the effective conduct of these workplaces. Traditionally framed jobs exert force as models even though we may be aware that they do not apply completely or directly. For example, the position of 'librarian' possesses relevant subject expertise (and in many cases technical expertise) but is not typically accorded the agency to participate in project leadership (including external funding proposals). The 'programmer' position is designed around technical expertise but has no provision for subject expertise. The 'faculty' job has subject knowledge but typically little or no project management expertise. While it is easy to speak of the importance of collaboration as a way of putting these jobs into complementary relationships, in practice such accommodation also requires subtle but crucial adjustments of work habits and professional identity. And people in these jobs may play many different roles while at the same time facing difficulties explaining those roles (and the different professional paradigms, training/professional development needs, forms of credit, and working relationships they need) to colleagues, collaborators, supervisors, potential employers.

To complicate the situation further: the scarcity and ephemerality of resources often means that available funding must be concentrated in a single individual or a very small team. Maron and Pickle (2014) note the difficulty that arises when a centre is organised around a single charismatic figure and ask what happens when that person moves on. But a more fundamental problem is the attempt to staff and operate such a centre with a single person, even if that person stays put. A case in point, mentioned in Maron and Pickle: the 'digital humanities coordinator' role (Maron and Pickle 2014, 25), which as they note is quite often a recent humanities PhD tasked with performing as a developer, administrator, researcher, advocate, fundraiser, consultant and teacher.

To better understand this terrain, I have found it helpful to tease apart several overlapping conceptual spaces. The first of these is jobs: as described above, specific alignments of individuals with quantised effort and specific spheres of responsibility and reporting. The second is roles: vectors of participation in the workplace that accomplish some specific kind of task. A single job may entail many roles; a single role may be shared across many jobs. The third is skills: the competencies needed to perform a role effectively. And finally, because the varying relationships between people and tools is a defining characteristic of digital humanities professional spaces and identities, I urge that we look at those as well. To illustrate the complexity of the landscape we are attempting to parse here, consider the following set of questions from Maron and Pickle's report:

> Are project managers in an IT unit able to support the technical needs of a digital humanities research project when it comes to metadata and other elements close to the scholarly aims of the project? Do library technical staff have the time and training to deliver user-interface design geared to drive user engagement on a crowdsourcing site? While many units could fill certain roles, should they be doing so?' (Maron and Pickle 2014, 22)

The alignment of jobs, roles and skills is precisely at issue here.

From jobs to roles

> Is humanities computing merely a hobby for tenured faculty? I am beginning to think so. I have just finished looking through the October MLA job list along with the computer science equivalent. As in past years, I see no jobs relating to humanities computing. At best, there are 1 or 2 positions where experience in computer aided instruction might be helpful . . . I started out as a German professor here at Yale and then was, in effect, booted out when I consorted with the CS people. Now I am a full-time lecturer in computer science, teaching a curriculum of humanities computing along with regular CS courses . . . But I am also painfully aware of the fact that

I have this job because I MADE this job, and it took 5 years of continuous drudge-work and diplomacy to get to this point . . . I can tell you this: if humanities computing is to be more than a gentleman's sport, somebody has got to start creating jobs for this field. How many more Goethe specialists do we need? Give it a rest. Hire someone who will rock the status quo . . . 20 years from now there will be departments of humanities computing. No doubt someone will write a doctoral thesis on the history of the field and my name will appear in a footnote: 'wrote some interesting early works, "German Tutor", "MacConcordance", "Etaoin Shrdlu", and then disappeared from the field'. I don't want to be a footnote. I want to be the head of the department. Make a job in humanities computing this year. (Clausing 1992)

Jobs are a good starting point here because they are unambiguously visible. This quotation is curiously telling: even while calling for 'a department of humanities computing' (that is, more faculty jobs representing a hybridisation of humanities and CS expertise), it subtly registers the fact that the very 'gentlemanliness' of the faculty jobs (and the way they would tend to position the more practical aspects of building, teaching, and using technological systems) might not in fact serve humanities computing very well in the long run. With hindsight, we can also note that in fact the jobs in humanities computing that first proliferated were not in fact faculty positions. There were plenty of faculty involved in the early period of humanities computing (as evidenced for instance in the membership of the Humanist discussion list), but they tended to have fairly normal faculty jobs and their 'computing' dimension was acknowledged as odd. The distinctively 'humanities computing' (or, later 'digital humanities') jobs were in other institutional spaces: in libraries, particularly within library-led digitisation efforts like the University of Virginia's EText Center but also in some cases as an outgrowth of library support for digital publications and projects (for instance, IATH and MITH); in information technology organisations dedicated to supporting faculty research (such as Brown University's Scholarly Technology Group, Oxford University Computing Services and the Centre for Computing in the Humanities at King's College London; in instructional technology groups, for instance at Northwestern University, the University of Virginia and NYU); and finally in independent research projects (such as ARTFL, the Women Writers Project and Perseus).

Jobs represent an institutional understanding of what people do, and an institutional way of framing that work so that it can be accomplished within 40-hour work weeks, year-round, by people who actually exist and can be hired and retained within a specific organisational niche for purposes of management, assessment and professional advancement. There exist established training pipelines that produce candidates for jobs like faculty member, librarian, programmer, administrative staff, graduate student research assistant, and likewise well-established organisational spaces within which the work of each of these jobs can take place. But in many digital humanities organisations and projects (particularly when in the early stages), there are tasks to be performed and roles to be played that are not explicitly staffed, because of limitations on funding. For example, a small digital humanities project like the Early Caribbean Digital Archive at Northeastern University might have a small team of faculty and graduate students, but no administrative staff or programmers. In addition, there are tasks and roles that initially may not even be defined within the normal institutional rubrics. For instance, in the early decades of humanities computing, people in a variety of different jobs (library staff, IT staff, graduate students) found themselves taking on – improvisationally – what later became the recognisable and essential role of data and project analyst: someone with subject expertise in a humanities field, paired with sufficient technical proficiency and analytical skills to identify the distinctive set of data modelling standards, workflows and digital tools needed to undertake a specific digital project. Whether for reasons of scarcity or novelty, jobs in digital humanities thus often involve taking on varied tasks and roles that lie outside the conventional scope of a particular job. For instance, a faculty member might also perform some of the work normally allocated to a manager or administrative staff member (such as overseeing student payroll); library staff might find themselves writing external funding proposals, doing project management or undertaking technical development.

So to understand the real categories that are emerging here, it is helpful to bring into visibility the actual working roles people are playing, regardless of their job title. I would like to propose the following rubric for characterising the most common and essential roles around which digital humanities scholarship and project development are organised.

- Information management: creating effective information ecologies for the project and institution
- Scholarship: research and teaching in a disciplinary subject area
- Analysis: needs assessment, design, documentation

- Technical development: programming, integration of systems at the technical level
- Project management: oversight of working groups and work systems
- Administration: oversight of resources, fiscal and legal arrangements
- Data creation: digitisation, encoding, metadata creation, georeferencing of maps, etc.

These characterisations help us see the functions these jobs play in the larger ecology, and also understand what people actually do, regardless of their institutional location. It is important to remember that an individual 'job' might entail more than one 'role' as I am describing them here.

We can probe even further into these roles by asking what kinds of skills and expertise distinctively belong to each one. It is important to note that skills and expertise here are not simply 'the things people know how to do'. I (in my 'analyst' role) know how to write a TEI customisation, and my colleague Syd Bauman (in his 'developer' role) knows how to write a TEI customisation, but that skill operates very differently for the two of us because of the different kinds of metaknowledge we each have. By 'metaknowledge' I mean domains in which we possess a comparative perspective, an understanding of why things are the way they are. As a developer, his metaknowledge concerns the design of schema languages and the systems that process them; as an analyst, my metaknowledge concerns discipline-specific approaches to textual analysis. So it may also be useful to consider the distinctive skills and metaknowledge each of these roles characteristically possesses. Table 7.1 offers a preliminary analysis.

Tools

> Personally, I think Digital Humanities is about building things . . .
> If you are not making anything, you are not . . . a digital humanist.
> (Ramsay, 2013)

What's a tool? We use the term as if we know them when we see them: things we use to do tasks. In digital humanities, terms like 'build' and 'tool' are necessarily a bit metaphorical: you can't break your toe by dropping these things on your foot.

In early discussions on the Humanist discussion list (for example in the late 1980s and early 1990s), the term 'tool' often carried a pejorative tone, with the implication of considering something as 'merely

Table 7.1 Roles and their characteristic metaknowledge and skills.

Role	Metaknowledge	Skills
Developer	Software architecture, code design	Efficient and elegant system design, knowledge and integration of disparate systems
dministrator	Varieties of resources (staff, funding, in-kind support), bureaucratic processes	Fiscal management, personnel management, project management
Manager	Organisational systems	Prioritisation towards strategic goals; identifying and removing obstacles; creating effective working conditions
Scholar	Research methods, disciplinarity and discipline-specific theorisation	Reading and interpretation, reasoning with content; originating and developing research arguments
Analyst	Disciplinarity and information modelling	Decision-making about approaches, translation between discourses, representing processes and decisions
Data creator	Content representation	Creation of data, consistent application of procedures, decision-making about exceptional cases
Information manager	Data management and data representation systems	Efficient translation of information into usable and sustainable forms, at scale

a tool'. More precisely, through discussions of how and whether a tool determines our relations with the world (the 'if all you have is a hammer, everything looks like a nail' analogy), we can see concerns about the effect that the *use* of computational tools would have on humanistic research: a loss of nuance in our methods, a tendency to reduce complexity in the interests of computational tractability, and, conversely, expectations about the usefulness of the computer as a 'fast and accurate tool', an 'analytical tool'. Tools also figure prominently in definitional discussions of digital humanities as a domain and as a profession: for instance, the ACLS Cyberinfrastructure Report (ACLS 2006) lists five things 'digital scholarship has meant', of which four mention tools and three of these items are 'creating tools':

In recent practice, 'digital scholarship' has meant several related things:

a) Building a digital collection of information for further study and analysis
b) Creating appropriate tools for collection-building
c) Creating appropriate tools for the analysis and study of collections
d) Using digital collections and analytical tools to generate new intellectual products
e) Creating authoring tools for these new intellectual products, either in traditional forms or in digital form. (ACLS 2006, 7)

Alongside these discussions is another visible strand, concerning the question of whether the computer is more like a 'tool' or a 'method': essentially, a set of questions about how these systems sit in relation to our own thought processes and theories. The hammer/nail metaphor imposes a strict thingness on the tool: its shape determines our use of it, and this metaphor also suggests a certain self-evidence about the tool (we all know about hammers) and a desire for transparency. The hammer works, unproblematically, as a hammer: its purpose is to drive the nail, not to open up a discussion about the process. But if something that looks like a tool could also be a method, then the concept of the tool starts to seem more plastic, more responsive to and engaged with our own thought processes. Stephen Ramsay observed at the Modern Language Association conference in 2011 that 'If you're not making anything, you're not a digital humanist', but far from offering this kind of 'making' or 'building' as a pure, bone-headed space of theory-free praxis, he proposes making as 'a new kind of hermeneutic'. As he and Geoffrey Rockwell argue in 'Developing Things', under the right conditions tools can even be theories:

> For tools to be theories in the way digital humanists want – in a way that makes them accessible to, for example, peer review – opacity becomes an almost insuperable problem. The only way to have any purchase on the theoretical assumptions that underlie a tool would be to use that tool. Yet it is the purpose of the tool (and this is particularly the case with digital tools) to abstract the user away from the mechanisms that would facilitate that process. In a sense, the tools most likely to fare well in that process are not tools,

per se, but prototypes – perhaps especially those that are buggy, unstable, and make few concessions toward usability. (Ramsay and Rockwell 2011)

In particular, tools can be theories if they operate to draw attention to themselves, especially by functioning in frictional ways.

We can start to see here that there is a reason why digital humanists are so preoccupied with tools, and it is not because tools are important in themselves: it is because they are an irritant. They catalyse something complex and difficult concerning professional identity, scholarly methods and practices, and specific types of expertise. The questions of 'who is digital humanities?' and 'how is digital humanities?' can evidently be reframed as questions like 'what are the design goals of our tools?', 'when should a tool "just work"?', and 'are we tool users, tool builders, or tool theorists?'

So we can now come back to think about how each of these digital humanities roles understands the category of the 'tool' – bearing in mind that we are talking here about 'roles' rather than 'people', so a given person might occupy more than one role and hence have a more complex positioning. The 'scholar' role tends to use tools in the spirit of experimentation and theorisation, delegating their use (for instance, to a data creator or developer) in cases where systematic production-grade use at scale is required. The metaphor of 'getting our hands dirty' characteristically expresses this somewhat distanced orientation towards tools. In practical terms, the scholar role also has a tendency to regard tools abstractly, as a category or set of fungible surface functions rather than as a set of specificities ('we need a tool that can . . .' rather than 'we need an open-source content management system with the following specifications . . .'). From this perspective, for instance, a car and a tricycle would appear more similar (as tools for carrying humans over the ground) than a tricycle and a wheelbarrow (non-motorised wheeled devices with a single axle and no gearing).

The 'developer' builds tools, and uses tools in ways that do not preserve their surface integrity: for instance, by modifying them or configuring them in expert ways. There are many tools that are visible to the developer and not to the scholar: version control tools, tools for editing code, environmental tools (operating systems, virtual server software, integrated development environments, diagnostic systems). The developer also often has an under-the-hood or architectural view of tools whose conventionalised surfaces are also visible to the scholar. For example, 'publication tools' are visible to the developer as database programs, content management systems and rendering engines; 'search tools' are visible as search engines and indexing systems; 'visualisation tools' are visible as data analysis and interface management tools such as JavaScript libraries and data pipelines. Developers are less likely than scholars to be interested in a frictional relationship with tools, although they are likely to have a much greater awareness (metaknowledge) of the kinds of design and implementation issues that could inform an understanding of their theoretical implications. This makes sense: these jobs are typically the ones that involve building things that 'actually work', and they are likely to have close working relationships with colleagues elsewhere in the institution (such as the central information technology unit or library systems group) who are operating under an extremely practical set of metrics for success: Did my beeper go off at midnight? Is the server down? Did I have to fix bad code someone else wrote five years ago who apparently didn't know what they were doing? People in these jobs often have impolite words for tools that are 'buggy, unstable, and make few concessions towards usability': they are not in a position to benefit professionally from (nor do they have the professional space to interact meaningfully with) the forms of theoretical provocation such tools might offer.

The 'analyst' chooses tools, specifies tools, documents tools, and typically is aware of the tools that the developer uses directly, but in a manner both less expert and more contextualised with respect to questions of disciplinary theorisation. The analyst can participate in decision-making that concerns these genres of tools, but does not participate directly in or have responsibility for their creation or management. It is worth noting that analysts probably have the strongest interest of all these roles in theorising tools; they understand them well enough to do so and their interest is not purely practical. They are aware (like the developer) of how much of a difference the choice of tools makes, but by the nature of their job they can afford to be less pragmatic about it; in the analyst we see an almost anthropological or ethnographic perspective. The analyst also has tools native to their position. These include design and prototyping tools (such as tools for wireframing), documentation tools (wikis, content management systems, literate programming, code commenting), standards and reference systems, ontologies and authority systems. It is worth noting that the 'tool' aspect of these systems with respect to the analyst's role lies largely in the expertise with which the analyst uses the capabilities of these systems to ensure that the information they contain can be used effectively within the project context. In other words, these systems become tools through the work of information design and organisation, ergonomic optimisation within a specific workflow, ease of use (training, reference), and effectiveness in preserving records of decisions and actions.

The 'administrator' stands aside from the specifically digital humanities 'tool' ecology, but of course this role has its own tools: payroll systems, grant management systems, budgeting tools, record-keeping tools. These tools are assumed to be theoretically neutral with respect to the research enterprise, but it is interesting to contemplate the effect they have on the ecology, for instance by defining professional roles, differentiating spheres of expertise and authority, and limiting access to information. Indirectly, by supporting or hindering specific roles in participating in managerial processes, such tools have a powerful impact in determining what professional roles can be combined in a single job. In a similar way, the 'manager' has an indirect relationship to the tools of digital humanities, focused on benchmarking and assessing tools in relation to the role they need to play in workflows. This work requires a comparative understanding of tools that is akin to that of the analyst role, but oriented more specifically towards their usage by data creators.

The 'data creator' uses tools, often with somewhat more critical perspective than the scholar (although of course these roles may be combined): the data creator operates as an expert tool user who is familiar not only with the tool's documented functions but also with its ergonomics, its efficiencies and its inefficiencies. Tools natural to this role include authoring tools (particularly those that offer specific forms of data constraint such as XML editors or content management systems), simple data conversion and cleaning tools (such as OpenRefine), and digitisation tools for tasks like scanning, optical character recognition, colour correction and video captioning. Expert data creators who have used multiple different tools for the same kind of task develop a kind of parallax or metaknowledge about these tools. Inexpert data creators – understandably – fetishise and personify the tool as a kind of totalising context for their work ('Oxygen didn't like my code') and may also not fully understand the data apart from the tool through which they encounter it. For instance, it is common to find that someone who has deep familiarity with spreadsheet data through a tool like Excel may nonetheless not know that the same data can be exported as comma-separated values, and viewed in a database tool such as FileMaker.

The 'information manager' is very similar to the analyst in choosing, specifying and documenting tools, but these tools tend to be infrastructural (or serve as portals to infrastructure) rather than user-oriented. The characteristic tools of the information manager include data management tools (such as repository systems, or tools for integrity checking, data migration and data conversion) and tools for data dissemination and discovery (such as online library catalogues, and application programming interfaces that expose data and metadata for automated discovery).

So what does a healthy ecology for digital humanities look like, taking all of this into account? How can we build organisations in which digital scholarship in the humanities can thrive and where practitioners in a variety of roles can work together effectively?

First, the 'analyst' role is clearly an important one, and also one that interestingly seems to inhabit a number of different possible institutional locations and job identities: the library, IT, research centres; postdoctoral fellows, data curation and DH librarians, instructional technologists, research support specialists, programmer/analysts. Furthermore, because the analyst is so often an infrastructural position rather than a project-specific one, that role brings with it an inherent attention to longevity and sustainability. The analyst is likely to know about things like data standards, institutional repositories, data curation and reuse. The analyst's skill profile also includes knowing how to identify and assess relevant work by peer institutions, to avoid reinventing the wheel (or worse, repeating common mistakes).

Second, the developer role is also crucial, but it is not easy to make good use of a single human developer working in isolation. The expertise the developer role possesses is directly translatable into good architectural decisions and the skill to write program code that is efficient, effective, well documented and intelligible to others, easy to maintain and extend, and not subject to obscure breakage. If the project is building prototypes for purposes of theorisation (which is entirely legitimate), then these may not be concerns, but if the goal is to build a tool or system that will work in the future, then it is a mistake to substitute non-developers for developers. Data creators and analysts are often mistaken for developers (especially by scholars to whom the difference is not always visible). Furthermore, because there are many different kinds of developer expertise, a developer who has deep expertise with XML tools may not know anything about customising Drupal or building web applications in JavaScript, let alone building digital repository systems. Scholars are not necessarily aware of these differences and there is a tendency to say 'we need to hire a developer' without specifying what kind and what skills. Often, one needs pieces of several different developers to build an entire system. In an ecology that lacks an analyst, translating between scholars (or data creators) and developers is not always easy, which is why a developer who is also an analyst is a huge asset.

Third, it is important not to overload junior *jobs* (such as graduate student, postdoctoral fellow or entry-level developer) with *roles* that are outside the scope of their capacity: for instance, administrator (with responsibility for financial administration or grant oversight) or sole developer (with responsibility for larger architectural decisions and integration of systems as well as code execution). If this kind of early seniority is unavoidable, it should be approached with care for the incumbent and added oversight for their work. Such jobs may offer exceptional learning opportunities and professional value in the long term, but they place tremendous pressure on the incumbent and may result in fragilities elsewhere in the project ecology. If you are going to overload a junior position, make sure you have strong mentoring and training in place, and make sure you have infrastructural roles somewhere else in the system (analysts, developers) who can provide additional support when needed.

This leads to a larger point. It is important not to use short-term *jobs* as a way of filling long-term *roles*. In situations of scarcity and constraint, it is tempting to make technically gifted graduate students or postdocs serve as solo developers or managers, but this is a risky approach: not because they are not capable of doing this work, but rather because those roles need greater continuity. Turnover in those positions results in loss of organisational memory, poor or incomplete implementation of systems, lack of documentation, and long-term difficulties both for the project and for those who stay behind: scholars, analyst roles in the library or IT organisation who will have to pick up the pieces, and administrators who have to make sense of financial and HR situations.

Finally, it is important to be aware of the different professional trajectories and accompanying reward systems that are in play for these different roles, again bearing in mind that the same person may occupy different roles (and may have multiple professional trajectories in play). This is an area where significant discussion has taken place in recent years, particularly in venues like the University of Maryland's 'Off the Tracks' workshop (Clement et al. 2011) and of course in the discussions of '#alt-ac', citation practices, and related issues. It is important to think about the forms of professional development each role needs: additional degrees, opportunities to attend conferences, opportunities for practical training or internships. It is also important to think about the forms of professional visibility each role needs, such as opportunities to publish, opportunities to participate in open-source software development and standards bodies, opportunities to mentor others and participate in professional associations. And it is very important to think about the next job each role is likely to be seeking – whether that is a tenure-track faculty position, a more senior analyst or developer position, a post-doc, a position in an MA or PhD program – and to think about whether that role will be in your organisation (and if not, why not?).

The strongest digital humanities centres have succeeded in creating generational systems: viable succession plans in which students trained as data creators grow into developer, analyst or manager roles while also maturing as scholars. But they also have invested in creating permanent jobs for the infrastructural roles (developers, analysts, administrators, managers) that give the ecology its stability and continuity.

References

American Council of Learned Societies (ACLS). 2006. *Our Cultural Commonwealth: The report of the American Council of Learned Societies Commission on Cyberinfrastructure for the Humanities and Social Sciences.* Accessed 6 September 2022. https://www.acls.org/wp-content/uploads/2021/11/Our-Cultural-Commonwealth.pdf

Clausing, Stephen. 1992. 'Humanities Computing: A gentleman's sport?', *Humanist* 6(357), 15 November.

Clement, Tanya and Doug Reside. 2011. *Off the Tracks: Laying new lines for digital humanities scholars.* White Paper. Maryland Institute for Technology in the Humanities. Accessed 6 September 2022. http://hdl.handle.net/1903/14731

Maron, Nancy L. and Sarah Pickle. 2014. *Sustaining the Digital Humanities: Host institution support beyond the start-up phase.* Ithaka S+R blog. Accessed 6 September 2022. https://sr.ith aka.org/blog/new-report-sustaining-the-digital-humanities-host-institution-support-bey ond-the-start-up-phase

Ramsay, Stephen. 2013. 'Who's In and Who's Out?' In *Defining Digital Humanities: A reader*, edited by Melissa Terras, Julianne Nyhan and Edward Vanhoutte, 239–42. Abingdon: Routledge.

Ramsay, Stephen and Geoffrey Rockwell. 2011. 'Developing Things: Notes towards an epistemology of building in the digital humanities'. In *Debates in the Digital Humanities*, edited by Matthew K. Gold. Accessed 6 September 2022. https://dhdebates.gc.cuny.edu/projects/deba tes-in-the-digital-humanities

Zorich, Diane. 2008. A Survey of Digital Humanities Centers in the United States. CLIR Publication No. 143. Alexandria, VA: Council on Library and Information Resources.

8

The politics of digital repatriation and its relationship to Rongowhakaata cultural data sovereignty

Arapata Hakiwai, Karl Johnstone and Brinker Ferguson

Introduction

On 31 July 2012, the government of New Zealand passed the *Rongowhakaata Claims Settlement Act*, which returned ownership of the meetinghouse, Te Hau-ki-Tūranga, from the Museum of New Zealand Te Papa Tongarewa (the National Museum of New Zealand, 'Te Papa' for short) back to the indigenous *iwi* (tribe) Rongowhakaata (New Zealand Legislation, 2012). During the related parliamentary hearings, representatives of the *iwi* described the meetinghouse as integral to their identity and heritage. To those representatives, Te Hau-ki-Tūranga embodied the *iwi*'s *whakapapa* (genealogical history) and served as a physical and symbolic reminder of their integrity as an *iwi* (Whiting 2013, 17). The outcome of these legal actions represented the first time in over 150 years that the Rongowhakaata *iwi* had full rights to Te Hau-ki-Tūranga, including all decision-making power over the presentation, conservation, and interpretation of the meetinghouse. These decisions also helped to set the stage for important developments at Te Papa, and by extension the New Zealand government, and policies concerning the redress of Māori grievances. The *iwi*'s decisions about Te Hau-ki-Tūranga thus serve as an important case study regarding the politics of indigenous agency and cultural heritage memory at the local, national and international levels.

However, this return of ownership did not extend to *all* of Te Hau-ki-Tūranga. Since the 1860s, when the meetinghouse was first confiscated (New Zealand Legislation, 2012) by British troops during the

New Zealand Wars (1845–72), a number of its carvings disappeared, believed to have been sold off during the meetinghouse's voyage from the Tūranga area on the North East coast of New Zealand to what was at the time known as the Colonial Museum in Wellington, Te Papa's predecessor, on the southernmost tip of the North Island. Rongowhakaata scholars have since been able to identify many of the missing pieces of Te Hau-ki-Tūranga, which ultimately ended up in collections abroad, including the National Gallery of Australia and the British Museum. However, due to the legal frameworks in these other countries, it appears unlikely, at least for now, that these carvings will be returned to the *iwi* alongside the rest of Te Hau-ki-Tūranga. For the *iwi*, this is an issue; as *iwi* representative Te Aturangi Nepia-Clamp pointed out in an interview in 2017, 'Each carving represents a specific ancestor, and without them all being together and in the right order, it is like the pages of our *iwi*'s encyclopedia have been jumbled around. We want to put it right again.' These ancestral carvings have thus become central to an ongoing dialogue about ownership, representation and stewardship between the Rongowhakaata *iwi*, Te Papa, and those international museums presently holding the carvings in their care. Over the course of several conversations, a compromise has arisen in the form of a 'digital repatriation' initiative. In this instance, 'digital' refers specifically to 3D digital capture of the meetinghouse and its carvings through photogrammetric or stereo-imaging techniques, and 'repatriation' refers to the ownership of this imaging data, along with the return of the object's museum records, exclusively for the *iwi*'s archives.

For many museums around the world, repatriation is a controversial and politically sensitive issue that is nevertheless central to the process of reconciliation between indigenous communities and cultural heritage institutions. The concept of 'digital repatriation', however, raises its own questions about its relationship to restitution. After all, how can one truly 'return' something that in itself implies a potentially infinite number of (digital) copies? Does digital repatriation actually shift any real power to the *iwi*, or does it instead perpetuate an asymmetrical hierarchy that privileges the physical ownership of the objects over the cultural claims of the Rongowhakaata *iwi*? On its surface, digital repatriation projects cannot and should not replace claims for the physical repatriation of cultural patrimony, but the issues brought to the fore are more complex than a debate about the physical object versus its digital surrogate (Cameron 2010). This case study will demonstrate how the more common approach to 'digital repatriation' projects in the museum field are not working and will offer an alternative model through the physical/digital repatriation project of Te Hau-ki-Tūranga as led by the Rongowhakaata *iwi*.

Re/connect: the politics of cultural heritage access versus control

There are more than 18,000 Māori *taonga* (cultural treasures) held in over 160 museum collections over the world, often with locations unknown to their source communities (Sully 2007, 46). This loss of connection is largely due to the fact that the museum institution, as we know it today, evolved out of an eighteenth-century European 'enlightenment' model designed to sustain a particular cultural hegemony and display 'other' cultures in an evolving trajectory of curiosities, specimens, crafts and art/history. Within these tightly controlled and guarded narratives of world history resided a small and elite circle of 'experts', with positions often funded by the respective governments. These museum professionals upheld a conviction that cultural objects had to be organised and categorised through research, and that there was an inherent (fixed and immutable) value to the object itself that needed only to be uncovered by these 'experts', rather than inscribed by the source community (West 2010, 130). The museums' presentation efforts further introduced a literal and figurative separation between the cultural objects on display, usually in a glass box or segregated area, and their viewing audience (Ames 1992, 23). This divide, coupled with the one-way dissemination of information about the objects, granted most of the agency to the museum professionals and their particular interpretations. As a result of the professionalisation and bureaucratisation of such heritage practices over the course of the twentieth century, laypeople and their communities were increasingly locked out of decisions about what heritage was collected and how to both conserve and interpret it (Harrison 2013, 223). Heritage scholars such as LauraJane Smith have since examined the ways in which this dynamic arises and self-perpetuates (Smith 2006). When a privileged group in power arrives at generally unchallenged decisions about what is important, a very specific type of history becomes presented to the public as fact. These 'facts', often displayed in civic institutions, then become part of the history of the nation, propagating and maintaining the viewpoints of those groups in power, often for political advantage.

In the wake of global civil rights movements came a push in the 1980s and 1990s toward a more open and audience-driven museology. Places such as the British Museum, Smithsonian and Te Papa,[1] to name only a few, came under scrutiny from domestic and international indigenous communities who sought more access to their cultural patrimony. These communities wanted to know, among other things, where their cultural objects lived, how they were cared for, and what information was freely accessible to the public. Included in these communities was the Rongowhakaata *iwi*, whose members, for over a decade, had been researching and visiting collections all over the world to find out where their *taonga* settled and how it is preserved and presented today. Currently there are thought to be more than 20 institutions that hold Rongowhakaata *taonga*, including at least eight ancestral carvings from Te Hau-ki-Tūranga itself (Johnstone 2017).

During this push towards more open and accessible cultural institutions, museums underwent radical changes as they strove for greater recognition of community perspectives and approaches – an effort that led to a critical reassessment of some of the most fundamental concepts underpinning the interpretation, conservation and representation of objects in museums. The balance of power in the collection, preservation and representation of cultural objects seemingly began to shift away from the singular museum voice and toward a plurality of voices involving the museum's communities as well. Cultural anthropologist James Clifford has described this change as a conscious 'shift from a "colonial" to a "cooperative" museology' (Clifford 1991, 212–54). This new museology was neoliberal in the sense that it focused more on visitor learning and education and took for granted the open access to information (Boast 2011, 64).

As a result of this demand for a more open and accessible museum, the past 20 years have seen a major push toward the digitising of collections to be accessed on the internet for all to experience. Indeed, today, anyone with an internet connection can access hundreds of millions of digitised cultural objects, with cultural institutions adding thousands of new works to the digital sphere every day. What is, at first glance, a 'simple' act of digitisation (that is, the transformation of an object into open sets of data through images and text) becomes, on closer examination, a complex process teeming with diverse political, legal and cultural investments and controversies. The practices of the mass digitisation of objects and their subsequent dissemination through online platforms are forming new nexuses of knowledge transmission and introducing different ways of engaging with that knowledge onsite at the museum as well as online from anywhere. Out of this proliferation of museum cultural heritage data online came many museum initiatives on 'digital repatriation'[2] projects that sought to re/connect the museums' holdings with their source communities. A problematic theme that quickly became apparent was, in a sense, a re-witnessing of the colonial project through the museum's online archives, revealing legacies of colonial categorisation systems and taxonomies.[3] Often, museum analogue cataloguing systems were converted verbatim into digital database systems either by in-house staff or by larger content management system companies such as Gallery Systems and Past Perfect. These online results from searching the collection are presented as an 'unbiased' account of historical information.[4] Scholars Lisa Gitelman and Lev Manovich warn us, however, that data is never actually unbiased but instead collected, compiled and interpreted by fallible individuals with their own sets of assumptions and predispositions.[5] Both Gitelman and Manovich write about the often hidden or unacknowledged human intervention in computer software development, such as the online database, and its manipulation of information. Often, what most of us simply take for granted – for example, the ways in which software works to aggregate and visualise line-item data from analogue archiving systems – is actually the product of a series of decisions by the people and companies designing and developing the software. Understanding how these digital analogue systems convert to digital databases to then be pushed out onto online platforms requires understanding the conditions under which creation, archiving and dissemination has occurred and continues to occur within the museum walls.

This is not to say that all museum digital database technologies are inherently colonial. Instead, this situation highlights questions of power, directionality, design and economic privileging of particular systems and infrastructures of knowledge that serve the legitimacy of the system in charge. The careful investigation of the impacts of various digital systems involves, among other things, articulating the boundaries of these systems, including their limitations, affordances, requirements, social context and outcomes of use. One must begin to acknowledge that the processes of making collections and their related archival material available online continues to be shaped by a museum staff structured and trained in ways that historically reinforce the authority of the Eurocentric academy. As it was for the nineteenth-century anthropologist or twentieth-century photographer, so it remains today: the person in control frames the process and product of the recording, collecting and interpretation of information or data.

So while it remains a challenge for Rongowhakaata *iwi* to work inside numerous international legal systems, especially given that the repatriation claims involving indigenous cultural heritage can mean vastly different things in different nations, the Rongowhakaata digital repatriation project can be viewed as a first strategic step toward building relationships for physical repatriation. Put another way, rather than seeing 'digital repatriation' as a failed endgame in the effort to physically reconnect and return ancestors to their *iwi*, we might instead see it as only the first step in helping to place *taonga* on the map and activating existing museum resources to make data accessible to the *iwi*. Where relevant national legal systems do not yet exist, this could be a means of circumnavigating authorised procedures and pointing to programs such as long-term loans, through which the *iwi* would gain dual-ownership rights to their *taonga*, restore the union of ancestors and descendants, and work with the museums to establish contracts on use, care and possession of the objects. This approach is echoed in the essay 'After the Return: Digital repatriation and the circulation of indigenous knowledge,' by Haidy Geismar, who emphasises that the digital 'is a process rather than a fixed materiality' (Geismar 2014). However, it remains to be seen whether or not national museums could or would have the resources to scale case-by-case projects in relation to their larger indigenous collections. Still, one thing is clear: the digital repatriation or digital return of *taonga* information to its *iwi* opens up a larger dialogue not just on 'access' to the collection, but on the rights of tangible and intangible care, interpretation and proprietorship of cultural data sovereignty.

To this end, many communities[6] have begun to question the lasting effects of the more common museum 'digital repatriation' or 'digital reciprocation' project including Rongowhakaata *iwi*. Through their Te Hau-ki-Tūranga digital repatriation project, Rongowhakaata *iwi* members offer an alternative approach to more common 'digital repatriation' projects, namely as the re/connection of museum holdings to their source communities as just the first step in the much larger process of restitution. Rongowhakaata leaders also see this first step as an obligation of the museum, as a civic institution, to connect its current holders with source communities (Hakiwai 2019). Rongowhakaata's 'digital repatriation' project around the protection and ownership of Te Hau-ki-Tūranga's cultural data can be seen as a case study that is pushing the boundaries of indigenous agency and the legal protection of community cultural heritage property rights.

Re/calibrate: revising power dynamics in the museum contact zone

Within this emerging open and audience-centric museology of the 1980s and 1990s many museum staff and board members around the world began to revisit the use of and access to their collections (and, by extension, archives and histories). One important aspect of this 'new' museum was its *dialogical* orientation to the relationships among people, objects, places and practices. In terms of agency, the dialogical model often took place within the museum's 'contact zone', and it had radical implications not only for the study of heritage but also for the viability of the official divide between the 'layperson' and the 'expert' (Harrison 2013, 4). For a time, it took the form of consultations to correct or fill in missing cultural information for the archives. Still, questions remained. Who has the final say on what the national narratives are, to whom they speak, and for whom they speak? Can these multiple narratives complement indigenous histories, or do they blur or dilute them? What hierarchies remain in the dialogical 'consultation' model? Does it, in fact, only obscure rather than eliminate asymmetrical relationships?

In her 1991 article 'The Arts of the Contact Zone', Mary Louise Pratt associates this zone concept with 'social spaces where cultures meet, clash, and grapple with each other, often in contexts of highly asymmetrical relations of power, such as colonialism, slavery, or their aftermaths as they are lived out in many parts of the world today' (Pratt 1991, 33). The contact zones that Pratt went on to describe, expand upon and discuss in her 1992 book *Imperial Eyes: Travel writing and transculturation* were indeed deeply asymmetrical spaces where a dominant culture (in this case, European imperialism) would provide a 'negotiated' space for the kinds of cultural exchanges and transactions that were necessary to sustain an imperialistic program. These highly selective and reciprocal but unequal exchanges create a two-way dialogue that both 'defines the colonial other and redefines the metropole' (Boast 2011, 57). Museum studies and anthropology have since appropriated the contact zone, thanks in particular to the work of James Clifford, including his 1997 essay 'Museums as Contact Zones'. These dialogical spaces often struggle to negotiate a pluralistic approach to interpretation and presentation, and it remains true, even to this day, that the intellectual oversight, care and representation of cultural heritage largely continue to reside with those in control.

These contact zones – or 'spaces of friction' (Karp 2006) or 'zones of awkward engagement' (Tsing 2005) – are spaces that facilitate the relationships or mediations among different stakeholders inside the museum. Though museum staff and *iwi* share the dialogical space through the interpretation of Māori *taonga*, for example, anthropologist Robin Boast calls attention to the 'inherent asymmetry' within the contact zone as well:

> The key problem lies deeper, deep in the assumptions and practices that constitute the museum in the past and today . . . the new museum, the museum as contact zone, is and continues to be used instrumentally as a means of masking far more fundamental

asymmetries, appropriations, and biases. The museum as a site of accumulation, as a gatekeeper of authority and expert accounts, as the ultimate caretaker of the object . . . as its documenter and even as the educator has to be completely redrafted. Where the new museology saw the museum being transformed from a site of determined edification to one of educational engagement, museums of the twenty-first century must confront this deeper neocolonial legacy. This is not only possible but, I would argue, could renovate the museum into an institution that supported enrichment, rather than authorization or collection. To do this, however, requires museums to learn to let go of their resources, even at times of the objects, for the benefit and use of communities and agendas far beyond their knowledge and control. (Lonetree 2012, 24)

Scholars who look at these relationships in the museum (Robin Boast, Amy Lonetree, Bernadette Lynch, Conal McCarthy and James Clifford) have noted that the overwhelming experience of these object stakeholders has taken the form of 'token consultations without authentic decision-making power' (Lynch 2017, 14). Much of the debate and criticism centres around what scholars Andrea Cornwall and Vera Schatten Coelho call 'empowerment-lite' (Lynch 2017, 13). Despite good intentions, the participation enabled through museum institutions is not always the democratic process it claims to be, and token consultations without authentic decision-making power, as well as relationships that disempower and control people, remain widespread within the museum arena. Even the most 'progressive, well-meaning, inclusive, and engaged museum thus inadvertently continues to rely upon a center-periphery model' (Clifford 1988, 85). Many of the recent 'digital repatriation' projects built upon this current model of access and control of cultural heritage information have thus been found to be fundamentally flawed.

An honest lens on the current 'contact zone' and its related power hierarchies within the museum institution has thus pushed Rongowhakaata *iwi* representative Karl Johnstone to 'recalibrate our *iwi*'s power relationship to museum' (Johnstone 2017). Johnstone characterises this effort as activating *Mātauranga* Māori, a desire to 'speak back' to colonisation, reassert the *iwi*'s identity, and restore its fluency with its distinct culture, language and heritage. As stated by the Waitangi Tribunal in the Wānanga Capital Establishment Report of 1999, *Mātauranga* Māori is 'a way [of] studying the universe from a Māori perspective' (Waitangi Tribunal 1999, 21). Today, the notion has been expanded to include contemporary, historical, local and traditional knowledge. In attempting to practise *Mātauranga* Māori through the Te Hau-ki-Tūranga projects, instead of trying to navigate the pre-existing power hierarchy of the museum's 'contact zone', it was better to try to completely 'recalibrate Rongowhakaata's position within the institution' (Johnstone 2017). The Rongowhakaata digital repatriation project does this by reframing what was owned and thus controlled by the *iwi*, rather than simply 'accessible' to the *iwi*. For example, before agreeing to work with the *iwi*, Rongowhakaata leaders made sure that they had legal control over any of the data generated or aggregated in the 'digital repatriation' project. This cultural data was archived by *iwi* community members within their own internal archiving system for their exclusive use. Decisions are now being made as to whether and what cultural information to 'gift' back to the museums. By reframing the data generated and aggregated about Te Hau-ki-Tūranga in terms of the *iwi*'s data sovereignty, Rongowhakaata leaders shift the focus from the Western preconception of what 'open access' actually means to the *iwi*'s interest in reviving its heritage knowledge and relinking its ancestors to their descendants.

Rongowhakaata leaders articulate the importance of *iwi* control over both the physical and digital archive regarding Te Hau-ki-Tūranga, especially as it is tied to intellectual property rights *and* privacy rights. For many *iwi*, *taonga*, or Māori, cultural treasures are living entities with personalities, lineages and spirits. These objects are active and present mediators between the past and the present, and between the dead and the living. In terms of their agency, these objects are bound up in a personalised relationship with the *iwi*, so that the Māori take care of their *taonga*, and the *taonga* take care of them. *Taonga* are vital links to the past that serve as guides for their *iwi* descendants. Māori scholar Moko Mead describes Māori *taonga* and their *mauri* (life force): 'For the living relatives the *taonga* is more than a representation of their ancestors: the figure is their ancestor and woe betide anyone who acts indifferently to their *tipuna* [ancestor]' (Mead 1990, 166). An understanding of these Māori carving data not as inanimate objects but as ancestors of specific *iwi* opens up the possibility of incorporation the views of Te Hau-ki-Tūranga's living cultural stakeholders. A crucial part of the Rongowhakaata 'digital repatriation' project, then, is to 'give the ancestors their history, and reconnect them to their *iwi* through identifying them by name and [virtually] realigning them with their kin' (Whaitiri 2017). Built into all new data aggregation processes involving Te Hau-ki-Tūranga was the essential step of having a Rongowhakaata *iwi* member onsite at the British Museum and National Gallery of Australia, to physically awaken or reconnect with ancestors in an opening and closing ceremony. After the 3D imaging was complete, all data was collected and archived in the *iwi*'s digital repository for their exclusive use. The repatriation of these datasets is seen as the return of a specific and unique knowledge base for learning from and reconnecting with intangible *taonga* made by the ancestors. The question of value tied to the digital database on Te Hau-ki-Tūranga then becomes whether the inherent and essential qualities that give a *taonga* its meaning and significance are transferred to its digital information. If Rongowhakaata *iwi* deem this to be the case, then these technologies offer immense opportunities for other communities to recover their cultural heritage.

Currently, Rongowhakaata *iwi* members are working both inside and outside the museum institutions to achieve their goals. National museums like Te Papa, the British Museum and the National Gallery of Australia are on the threshold of a major period of change, and *iwi* such as Rongowhakaata are wondering whether the only way to finally disrupt colonial legacies is to go outside the museum institution and find venues and strategies that allow *iwi* to have full control of the care and interpretation of their cultural heritage. The Rongowhakaata 'digital repatriation' project serves as an experiment in alternative models for reconnecting *taonga* with their descendants, as well as getting Rongowhakaata stories about Te Hau-ki-Tūranga out into the public on their own terms. Māori scholar Aroha Harris articulates the history of *rangatirantanga*, the encompassing Māori notion of self-determination, indigenous authority and autonomy in her book *Hīkoi: Forty years of Māori protest*. In it, she writes about the long line of indigenous movements in the nineteenth and twentieth centuries – movements that form the legacy of Māori activism to recover and reassert *rangatirantanga* today. This decision by Rongowhakaata leaders to 'speak back' around the history of Te Hau-ki-Tūranga helps to realign, or recalibrate, stakeholders' thinking from the Eurocentric view of what constitutes an object record, open access and different types of knowledge dissemination, so that they might begin to recognise alternative approaches and convictions and support the effort to 'transfer control of our heritage fully back to the *iwi*'. In this context, indigenous agency can come to be defined as heritage work done with, for and by indigenous peoples, altering standard museum practice to suit their needs.

Re/make: new rangatirantanga systems for cultural patrimony data

As part of Te Hau-ki-Tūranga's long history of interpretation and conservation within the various national museums, both domestically, as in the case of Te Papa, and internationally, as in the cases of the British Museum and the National Gallery of Australia, a large amount of data has been recorded and archived. Included in this trove is a full 3D data set of the interior and exterior surface geometry of the meetinghouse, as it stood inside Te Papa in 2017, compiled through photogrammetry and laser-scanning technologies. This databank is an invaluable resource for an understanding of the meetinghouse's current and previous histories of stewardship. The importance of cultural or personal community data for indigenous self-determination and development has been emphasised by indigenous NGOs, communities and tribes around the world. The United Nations Permanent Forum on Indigenous Issues (UNPFII), for example, held a number of meetings and conferences to discuss data collection in 2004, 2006 and 2010 (Kukutai and Taylor 2016, 3). At these gatherings, observers have written, 'indigenous representatives have raised concerns about the relevance of existing statistical frameworks for reflecting their worldviews and have highlighted their lack of participation in data collection processes and governance' (Kukutai and Taylor 2016, 3). Despite these conferences, the collection of data on indigenous peoples is still viewed by nations as primarily in the service of government census information rather than indigenous peoples' data property. These ideas have been written about extensively in the seminal book *Indigenous Data Sovereignty: Toward an agenda* edited by Tahu Kukutai and John Taylor, but focus on national censorship and health data. The case study of Rongowhakaata's leadership in Te Hau-ki-Tūranga's 'digital repatriation' project hopes to push these concepts further by aligning cultural heritage data with other forms of information protection on communities, especially information that has had a legacy of manipulation and coercion.

For Rongowhakaata, sovereignty over Te Hau-ki-Tūranga implies the ability to continue to manage information in ways that are consistent with the *iwi*'s collective decisions on access, control and representation of that information. Much like the protocol or permissions for outsiders to enter a *Marae* (*iwi* communal precinct), effective data management of community cultural heritage assets requires the development of indigenous expertise as well as permissions oversight. Many of these larger issues have been explored by scholar Linda Tuhiwai-Smith in *Decolonizing Methodologies: Research and indigenous peoples* (2012), and by Maggie Walter and Chris Andersen in *Indigenous Statistics: A quantitative research methodology* (2013). Out of these conversations, the Māori data sovereignty network Te Mana Raraunga (TMR) has developed a charter that provides the most complete expression to date of the basis for indigenous data sovereignty in New Zealand:

> The network recognizes that data form a living *taonga* and identifies six key means of advancing Māori data sovereignty:
>
> 1. Asserting Māori rights and interests in relation to data.
> 2. Ensuring data for and about the Māori can be safeguarded and protected.
> 3. Requiring the quality and integrity of Māori data and its collection.
> 4. Advocating for Māori involvement in the governance of data repositories.
> 5. Supporting the development of Māori data infrastructure and security systems.
> 6. Supporting the development of sustainable Māori digital businesses and innovations. (Kukutai and Taylor 2016, 15–16)

These ideals were then reinforced by the UN Declaration on the Rights of Indigenous Peoples (UNDRIP), which collects historical indigenous grievances, indigenous contemporary challenges, and indigenous sociopolitical, economic and cultural aspirations. Article 31 of the declaration speaks directly to intellectual property and indigenous control over data and information:

> Article 31: Indigenous peoples have the right to maintain, control, protect, and develop their cultural heritage, traditional knowledge, and traditional cultural expressions, as well as the manifestations of their sciences, technologies, and cultures, including human and genetic resources, seeds, medicines, knowledge of the properties of fauna and flora, oral traditions, literatures, designs, sports, and traditional games and visual and performing arts. They also have the right to maintain, control, protect, and develop their intellectual property over such cultural heritage, traditional knowledge, and traditional cultural expressions. (United Nations 2007)

This article reaffirms the Māori rights to self-determination, recognising the Māori as exclusive owners of their cultural and intellectual property, and emphasising the importance of ensuring that the *iwi* is the first beneficiary of indigenous knowledge and indigenous cultural and intellectual property rights. The Te Hau-ki-Tūranga 'digital repatriation' project led by Rongowhakaata *iwi* members serves as an example of indigenous-centric cultural revitalisation efforts. Enforcing the *iwi*'s sovereignty over the databank of information means building systems with which to archive knowledge for future generations of Rongowhakaata *iwi* members. As the *iwi* positions itself to control the digital repository of Te Hau-ki-Tūranga data for many more generations to come, it seeks to ensure its access not only to utilise the new data networks and infrastructures but also to disseminate and control the content for the benefit of their community. Rongowhakaata are now developing their own views about the culturally appropriate management and use of this data, and they are establishing appropriate boundaries in relation to their own indigenous knowledge.[7]

Conclusion

The physical/digital repatriation and reinterpretation of Te Hau-ki-Tūranga represent an embodied performance of community heritage memory that allows the meetinghouse's *iwi* to retake control of its cultural meaning-making, while re-inscribing the identity of the *iwi* and the *iwi*'s connection to its past. The digital repatriation project contributes to a political stance for the *iwi* in relation to the way in which they want to control the memory and ultimate fate of the meetinghouse's tangible and intangible information to be accessed, disseminated and archived or remembered. While indigenous peoples have long claimed sovereign status over their lands and territories, debates around 'data sovereignty' and especially 'cultural data sovereignty' have largely been missing, especially as it relates to the collection, ownership and dissemination of data about their peoples and lifeways. Achieving data sovereignty is more than just a technical problem, as the legacy of colonialism has marginalised or even eradicated indigenous epistemologies. As various indigenous communities attempt to re/locate or re/connect with cultural patrimony objects from around the world, they face the potential of re-witnessing the colonial project through 'open access' online portals of cultural patrimony information. The Te Hau-ki-Tūranga digital repatriation project helps to articulate how other cultural heritage databases might intersect with theories of indigenous sovereignty rights for ongoing self-determination efforts. Rongowhakaata leaders raise important questions for other communities interested in leveraging information and technology to subvert the legacies and processes of colonialisation as they manifest in the present. Indigenous cultural data sovereignty calls into question the multifaceted legal and ethical dimensions of data storage, ownership, access and consent to intellectual property rights and practical considerations regarding how data are used in the context of research, policy and practice.

Notes

1. Prior to becoming the Museum of New Zealand Te Papa Tongarewa, the museum was known as the 'National Museum' until 1992.
2. Also known as 'digital reciprocation' projects.
3. In her book *Decolonizing Museums* (2012), Amy Lonetree writes about such re-witnessing of historical trauma and the importance of truth-telling in these spaces.
4. Also known as 'tombstone' information, search results often produce such lines as creator or community (if known), title (given by either creator or curator), date of creation (century sometimes used), physical dimensions, materials, acquisition number, date of acquisition, who the object was gifted by, etc.
5. See Gitelman 2013 and Manovich 2013.
6. Another example of an indigenous-centred CMS project was the Mukurtu project by Warumungu community members and Professor Kim Christen from Washington State University. *Mukurtu* is a Warumungu word meaning 'dilly bag' and is used to remind users that the archive 'is a safekeeping place where Warumungu people can share stories, knowledge, and cultural materials properly using their own protocols' (https://mukurtu.org/about, accessed 6 September 2022).
7. Out of respect for the Rongowhakaata *iwi* and their ownership of Te Hau-ki-Tūranga, this article does not include any photos or datasets of the meetinghouse.

References

Ames, Michael. 1992. *Cannibal Tours and Glass Boxes*. Vancouver: UBC Press.
Boast, Robin. 2011. 'Neocolonial Collaboration: Museum as contact zone revisited', *Museum Anthropology* 34.
Cameron, Fiona. 2010. *Theorizing Digital Cultural Heritage: A critical discourse*. Cambridge, MA: MIT Press.
Clifford, James. 1988. *The Predicament of Culture, Twentieth-Century Ethnography, Literature, and Art*. Cambridge, MA: Harvard University Press.
Clifford, James. 1991. 'Four Northwest Coast Museums: Travel reflections'. In *Exhibiting Cultures: The poetics and politics of museum display*, edited by Steven Lavine. Washington DC: Smithsonian Institution Press.
Geismar, Haidy. 2014. 'After the Return: Digital repatriation and the circulation of indigenous knowledge'. *Material World: A global hub for thinking about things* (blog), 10 October 2014. Accessed 6 September 2022. http://www.materialworldblog.com/2014/10/review-essay-after-the-return-digital-repatriation-and-the-circulation-of-indigenous-knowledge
Gitelman, Lisa. 2013. *'Raw Data' is an Oxymoron*. Cambridge, MA: MIT Press.
Hakiwai, Arapata. 2019. Interview, 24 September.

Harrison, Rodney. 2013. *Heritage Critical Approaches*. New York: Routledge.

Johnstone, Karl. 2017. Interview, 10 February.

Karp, Ivan. 2006. *Museum Frictions: Public cultures/global transformation*. Durham, NC: Duke University Press.

Kukutai, Tahu and John Taylor. 2016. *Indigenous Data Sovereignty: Towards an agenda*. Canberra: Australian National University Press.

Lonetree, Amy. 2012. *Decolonizing Museums: Representing Native America in national and tribal museums*. Chapel Hill, NC: University of North Carolina Press.

Lynch, Bernadette. 2017. 'The Gate in the Wall: Beyond happiness-making in museums'. In *Engaging Heritage, Engaging Communities*, edited by Bryony Onciul and Michelle Stefano, 11–29. Woodbridge: Boydell Press.

Manovich, Lev. 2013. *Software Takes Command*. London: Bloomsbury.

Mead, S. 1990. 'The Nature of Taonga'. In *Taonga Māori Conference Papers*, Wellington: Cultural Conservation Advisory Council, Department of Internal Affairs.

New Zealand Legislation. 2012. 'The Crown's Apology to Rongowhakaata'. Rongowhakaata Claims Settlement Act 2012, section 8. Accessed 6 September 2022. http://www.legislation.govt.nz/act/public/2012/0054/latest/DLM4321628.html?search=sw_096be8ed819f2497_confiscated_25_se&p=1&sr=1

Pratt, Mary Louise. 1991. 'Arts of the Contact Zone', *Profession*, 33–40. Accessed 6 September 2022. http://www.jstor.org/stable/25595469

Smith, LauraJane. 2006. *Uses of Heritage*. New York: Routledge.

Sully, Dean. 2007. *Decolonizing Conservation: Caring for Māori meeting houses outside New Zealand*. Walnut Creek: Left Coast Press.

Tsing, Anna. 2005. *Friction: An ethnography of global connection*. Princeton, NJ: Princeton University Press.

United Nations. 2007. UN Declaration to the Rights of Indigenous Peoples, UNESCO. Accessed 6 September 2022. http://www.un.org/development/desa/indigenouspeoples/wp-content/uploads/sites/19/2018/11/UNDRIP_E_web.pdf

Waitangi Tribunal. 1999. Wananga Capital Establishment Report. Wellington: Waitangi Tribunal.

West, Susie. 2010. *Understanding Heritage in Practice*. Manchester: Manchester University Press.

Whaitiri, Lewis. 2017. Interview, 13 September.

Whiting, Dean. 2013. 'Conservation Plan – A Living Document, Te Hau-Ki-Turanga Wharenui', *New Zealand Historic Places Trust*. Wellington: Museum of New Zealand Te Papa Tongarewa.

Part III:
Making Praxis

9
Towards an operational approach to computational text analysis

Dino Buzzetti

Big data and theory

In a keynote speech at the DH 2009 conference at College Park (Boston University 2009), Christine Borgman voiced Chris Anderson's acclaimed thesis of the 'end of theory' (Anderson 2008) and the inception of the 'fourth paradigm' (Bell et al. 2009, 1297) in the new era of 'data scholarship' (Borgman 2015, *passim*), defined as 'a concept that transcends theory, practice, and policy' (Borgman 2015, 38). Big data is now an indisputable fact, but theory doesn't seem to have disappeared at all and what we actually have is indeed a new kind of theory. Theory has emerged in the form of a new epistemological paradigm that takes into account self-organising models and operations:

> The failure of classical programming to match the flexibility and efficiency of human cognition is by their lights a symptom of the need for a new paradigm in cognitive science. So radical connectionists would eliminate symbolic processing from cognitive science forever. (Buckner and Garson 2019)

The overturning of the Good Old-Fashioned Artificial Intelligence (GOFAI) paradigm was essentially due to an operational shift. What was fostering this new emerging paradigm was not anything thoroughly new, it was just sound computational practice.

The connectionist turn

What kind of theory is required by big data analysis? The state of the art points to the heuristic approach based on abductive reasoning that has been provided by the algorithmic model of the new connectionist procedures that have imposed themselves in Artificial Intelligence and led to the development of *reflecting machines*.

Computational practice is indeed one essential element of the digital humanities, a domain that can be thought of as a metadiscipline comprising an operational component, consisting in the application of computational methods, and a theoretical component, resulting from an epistemological reflection on the adequacy of the methods applied in a given context to achieve relevant results. The operational dimension assigns a crucial role to the very *making* of the computational practice. An almost 'legendary episode' concerning the effectiveness of neural networks (Cardon et al. 2018, iii) can be mentioned to support this contention. In natural language processing, neural networks are usually credited with good results, but reservations have been raised about their formal adequacy[1] and an epistemological reconsideration of the current opinion is therefore much needed. In this regard that episode turns out to be quite instructive. As reported in an interview quoted in the same paper by Cardon et al., Geoffrey Hinton, 'the "father" of the neural networks revival', decided to engage in the 2012 ImageNet Large Scale Visual Recognition Challenge. He took two of his graduate students and 'locked up one of them in a room, telling him: "You can't come out until it works!"' (Cardon et al. 2018, iii). And it did work. The resulting deep convolutional neural network architecture (Krizhevsky et al. 2012) was submitted and 'beat the field by a whopping 10.8 percentage point margin, which was 41% better than the next best' (Gershgorn 2017). Performance was decisive to overcome theoretical resistance.

An actual performance and its making is the direct outcome of computational practice, whose operational dimension shows itself also at a theoretical level. Hinton and his students' achievement has radically changed the landscape of Artificial Intelligence. Their connectionist approach – stemming from cybernetic studies and the 'formal treatment' of the activity of the nervous system conceived of as 'a net of neurons' by McCulloch and Pitts (1943, 117, 115) – had long been opposed and marginalised by the prevailing symbolic orientation of the GOFAI and 'is now in a position to very profoundly redefine the field from which it had been excluded' (Cardon et al. 2018, vi). This episode, then, 'bears witness to the effects that the sudden success of a long-marginalized heterodox paradigm has on a scientific community' (Cardon et al. 2018, iv). Artificial Intelligence has changed and is facing an emerging paradigm shift, that moves away from the previous symbolic, representational approach and conforms to the newly revived connectionist approach.

Before turning to other cases of this new emerging operational trend, some epistemological observations are in order. In a recent post on *Humanist*, Willard McCarty (2019) directed our attention to the importance of heuristics. He points out that according to the psychologist Gerd Gigerenzer (2004) 'Einstein used the term *heuristic* to indicate an idea that he considered incomplete, due to the limits of our knowledge, but useful (Holton 1988)'. However, in this respect, we may add some remarks concerning the reconsideration by Cardon et al. (2018) of the 'revanche of neurons' on the so-called symbolic AI, based as it was on a 'hypothetical-deductive' (Cardon et al. 2018, v) model of reasoning. In the concluding section of their paper, they trace the 'successive configurations' of the 'profound transformation' undergone by the operational 'architecture' of much sought-after 'intelligent machines'. Their architecture was 'profoundly reorganized' and Cardon et al. see the chief result of such a process in the 'invention of inductive machines', as mentioned in the very title of their essay.

In this view, the introduction of inductive machines led to 'different definitions of intelligence, reasoning, and prediction' (Cardon et al. 2018, xxxvi). But from a heuristic point of view this conclusion may be questioned. The inferential procedure of the 'neural-network-inspired paradigms for cognition' has been described in these terms: 'neural networks just use big activity vectors, big weight matrices and scalar nonlinearities to perform the type of fast "intuitive" inference that underpins effortless commonsense reasoning' (LeCun et al. 2015, 441).

Now, this kind of inference is not simply an inductive one, and is more properly characterised as a form of *abduction*. In what is presented as 'knowledge engineering' (Tecuci et al. 2016a, xvii), abduction has been recognised as a type of inference 'to link evidence to hypotheses' (Tecuci et al. 2016b, xiv) and, in fact, supervised learning obtained through the employment of machines based on 'neural network architectures' (LeCun et al. 2015, 438) aims at validating that some given observed data conform to a certain hypothesis. According to Peirce, an inference of this kind concludes that a given *case* under scrutiny follows from a certain *hypothesis* and previous *results*, that in a supervised connectionist computation process are assumed as labelled examples.[2] This is how a certain prediction is obtained, endowed as it is with a constitutive degree of uncertainty that cannot absolutely be disposed of. Such uncertainty is ineliminable, for it is to be ascribed not to 'the limits of our knowledge', deemed as 'incomplete' according to the classical Laplacian understanding of probability, that Einstein seems to share, but rather to a nondeterministic model describing 'a purely virtual disposition or propensity', a 'second-order potentiality, as it were', that 'is no longer the measure of an ignorance', but 'is physical' and 'describes nature' (Vuillemin 1996, 265). Such a model that conforms to quantum indeterminacy – continually targeted, as is well known, by Einstein's scepticism – admits the possibility of different explanations and ways of modelling the available data, as long as they are all compatible with the experimental results. What departs from the symbolic approach of the GOFAI is the notion of a model that does not conform any more to an *a priori* assumption, but is the result of the analysis and the resulting organisation of the observed data. According to Cardon et al., 'in the connectionist model the calculation target' is no more 'the goal of the rational expectations of logic' that 'the intelligent machines devised by symbolic AI assigned themselves'; on the contrary, in this model, the calculation target 'belongs not to the calculator, but rather to the world that has given it "labelled" examples' (Cardon et al. 2018, xl), so as to validate the observed data as a *case* of a given hypothesis. However 'neural networks by no means eliminate "theory"'. Instead, they locate it 'within an increasingly broader space of hypotheses' by 'giving the word "theory" a less "symbolizable" meaning' (Cardon et al. 2018, xxxix).

It is also worth noticing that one crucial aspect of abductive inference implies control over the inferential process it consists in and is therefore endowed with self-referring import. According to Peirce, any inference involves a 'conscious control of the operation' (Peirce 1931–58, 2.442) and, as we shall see in more detail, the intrinsic self-referential metalinguistic relation between a logical consequence and its rule, or 'leading principle' (Peirce 1880), cannot be overlooked in any accurate account of the application of connectionist models to text analysis processing. It is precisely this theoretical self-referring aspect of the inferential process that the connectionist approach takes into account, and it does so by 'basing the performance of prediction on the world itself, renewing the adaptive promises of the *reflection machines* of cybernetics: to form a system with the environment to calculate, in order to implement a new type of feedback loop' (Cardon et al. 2018, xl). Like biological evolutionary systems, reflection machines operate by interacting with the environment they belong to.

Self-organising adaptive systems

The new reflecting machines are based on the principles of Joichi Ito's *Resisting Reduction* manifesto, inspired by Wiener's cybernetic theory. Similarly the *Agile Manifesto* introduces principles based on adaptation and self-organisation in the operational practice of software development, an approach now common to new research trends regarding IT ecosystems and in the new area of Organic Computing.

We have other examples of 'the strategic intentions of programmers' that 'were constantly seeking to eliminate all traces of prior "human" intervention (knowledge free) in the calculator's operations' (Cardon et al. 2018, xl), and of scholars endorsing their position. In his manifesto for *Resisting Reduction* (Ito 2019a) Ito argues against the prevailing attitude to get over complexity by treating it in terms of simpler and more basic phenomena, and firmly advocates, with higher epistemological awareness, for a radical 'paradigm shift in theories and methods of change' (Ito 2018, 6). From his point of view, intelligent machines operate on 'environmental inputs' like 'biological', 'evolutionary', and 'highly complex self-regulating systems' (Ito 2019a, 1, 4, 2). In his 'manifesto against the growing singularity movement, which posits that artificial intelligence, or AI, will supersede and eventually displace us humans' (Ito 2019b),[3] Ito refers back to 'Norbert Wiener's ground-breaking book (1950) on cybernetics theory' (Ito 2019a, 1), which 'has served as a model' for his 'Research Statement' as Professor of the *Practice*[4] in Media Arts and Science at the Massachusetts Institute of Technology (Ito 2018, 231), and whose insights were at the origins of the connectionist approach devised by McCulloch and Pitts. From this point of view, we should consider a 'system that integrates humans and machines', which is not 'artificial intelligence' in the GOFAI sense, but in the sense of an 'extended intelligence' which envisages 'many interconnected, complex, self-adaptive systems across scales and dimensions that cannot be fully known by or separated from observer and designer' (Ito 2019b). An epistemological stance of this kind fully supports an operational approach such as the connectionist one that overturned the dominance of Good Old-Fashioned Artificial Intelligence.

A more direct operational approach is to be found in yet another manifesto, the *Agile Manifesto* for software development. The *Agile Manifesto* advocates for a radically new stance, according to which the practice of software engineering should be based on adaptive and self-organising principles: 'The best architectures, requirements, and designs emerge from self-organizing teams' (see Beck et al. 2991a; 2001b).

Again, the Agile operational attitude is readily mistaken for a deliberate move away from theory and methodology, but indeed, in its own words, 'the Agile movement is not anti-methodology' (Highsmith 2001). Simply, its operational methodology refuses to abide by 'traditional project management', a principle for practice that has received the severe label of 'Newtonian neurosis'[5] – a description that, in this context, 'means attacking complex, nonlinear problems with simplistic, linear processes' (Cockburn and Highsmith 2001, 133). Traditional management procedure prescribes that one says 'in advance exactly what [one] intend[s] to do, and then do exactly that', or 'in CMM terms'[6] to 'plan the work and work the plan' (DeMarco 2002, xv), so that it does not take into account the fact that software development operates in highly 'volatile environments' (Highsmith 2002b). Agile software development practice interacts with its environment conceived of as an operational 'ecosystem', a word that

> conjures up a vision of living things and their interactions with each other. Within an organizational context, an ecosystem can then be thought of as a dynamic, ever-changing environment in which people and organizations constantly initiate actions and respond to each other's actions. (Highsmith 2002a, xxiv)

As 'proponents of ASDEs' (Agile Software Development Ecosystems), the Agilists themselves say (Highsmith 2002b), 'we plan, but recognize the limits of planning in a turbulent environment' (Highsmith 2001). However, 'although ASDEs involve careful planning, the fundamental assumption remains that plans, in a turbulent environment, are not predictable', which means that 'plans are hypotheses to be tested rather than predictions to be realized'. This is in fact what happens in connectionist abductive testing, and what gives 'the primary reason for using the word *ecosystem* rather than methodology'. For, 'to describe a holistic environment', the word *methodology* does not 'fit with the focal points of Agile development'. By merely using the word *Agile*, 'practices are instantly compared to traditional software development methodologies'. In a software development context, the word *methodology* does not convey a vision of responsive 'living things', it rather 'conjures up a vision of' predefined 'things – activities, processes, tools', that are assumed as fixed and invariable (Highsmith 2002a, xxiii, xxiv). On the other hand, by seeing themselves as 'part of a larger ecosystem', Agile project teams 'practice self-organization' and use 'an adaptive approach' (Shore and Warden 2008, 4, 367, 216). As a result, 'adaptive release planning' is understood as a radical 'alternative' to 'predictive release planning, in which the entire plan is created in advance' (Shore and Warden 2008, 220). Adaptive planning's 'emphasis on learning' implies 'iterative design' and puts 'the most valuable features of the code under continual review' (Shore and Warden 2008, 206, 369). To sum up, Agile software development ecosystems work in an adaptive, self-organising way.

Since its first appearance, the Agile development model has been amply discussed. In a paper on the Agile approach, Nerur et al. (2010) have pointed out that Agile Development Methodology (ADM) recognises that change is inevitable and advocates a 'sense-making process' (Berger and Luckmann 1967 as cited in Hirschheim and Klein 1989) that involves 'adaptive planning, frequent iterations informed by feedback from stakeholders, and reflective learning' (Hirschheim and Klein 1989, 24–5). Accordingly, 'this recently "emerged" paradigm can be interpreted as a re-combination of earlier viewpoints' (Hirschheim and Klein 1989, 25). In fact, long before the publication of the *Agile Manifesto*, Hirschheim and Klein had described such an approach in the following terms: 'The mechanism of prototyping or evolutionary learning from interaction with partial implementations is the way technology becomes embedded in the social perception and sense-making process' (Hirschheim and Klein 1989, 1205). Despite the fact that 'ADM has been proffered, in one form or another, for years', a generally accepted recognition of its significance as a kind of 'Kuhnian revolution' with regard to software development is still controversial (Nerur et al. 2010, 25). It has been lamented, for instance, that notwithstanding the 'widespread application of agile methods . . . there is still no clear agreement of what are the focal aspects' of the Agile approach (Abrahamsson et al. 2010, 32). A likely reason for these reservations may reside in a relative underestimation of the theoretical significance of a primarily operational approach, for although 'agile software development methods have caught the attention of software engineers' and 'software engineering practices', Abrahamsson et al. maintain, on the face of it, that 'scientific research' on these methods 'still remains quite scarce' (Abrahamsson et al. 2010, 31, 34, 31).

Emphasis on adaptation and self-organisation has nonetheless gained increasing attention. The 'concept of IT ecosystems' has been assumed 'as a new approach' for research 'from the perspective of software engineering' and as 'a step in the direction' of enabling a new 'paradigm shift' (Rausch et al. 2012, 31). More recently, 'the continuously growing complexity of software intensive systems' has led to 'biologically inspired ecosystems research' (Rausch et al. 2012, 31, 36) and to the pursuit of 'a paradigm shift for complex systems' (Müller-Schloer et al. 2011).

Thus, 'bio-inspired concepts' have been exploited 'for the design of a new generation of technical application systems', bringing forth 'a new area of research' which has been called 'Organic Computing' and which refers specifically to 'self-organising adaptive systems' (Rausch et al. 2012, v, 626) and 'emergence as self-organised order' (Mnif and Müller-Schloer 2006, 78). As we shall see, a central idea relevant to our argument was that of 'highlighting ways of transferring behavioural patterns of biological systems into Organic Computing systems' (Rausch et al. 2012, vii). This new research field, then, was 'emerging around the conviction that problems of organization in complex systems', in computer science, biology and several other disciplines, 'can be tackled scientifically in a unified way' (Würtz 2008, v). And this assumption applies not so surprisingly at this point to computational text analysis too.

Adaptive systems and natural language

Recently, the analogy between artificial adaptive systems, on the one hand, and between natural language and textuality as forms of autopoietic coding, on the other, has been emphasised not only in computer science applications, but also in literary studies, as in Jerome McGann's writings.

If, then, organisational problems across the disciplines can be treated in a unified way, the transfer of operational models from one discipline to another can also be done in reverse – namely not from biological systems to computing systems, but from artificial computer systems to natural systems – and can therefore be applied to natural language processing and computational text analysis. From this point of view, it has recently been maintained that the 'parallels' between 'the philosophy of artificial adaptive systems' and 'natural language' should not seem so 'striking' as is commonly assumed (Buscema 2014, 84). In actual fact, as Jerome McGann had already so perspicuously reminded us, we should recognise that, 'like biological forms and all living systems, not least of all language itself, textuality is a condition that codes (or simulates) what are known as autopoietic systems' (McGann 2003, 7). McGann points out that, in his 'key book' *La technique et le temps*[7] – which was actually 'anticipated' by McLuhan's 'studies of the extensions of man' (McLuhan 1964) – Bernard Stiegler maintains that a genuine operational point of view, which is 'the regular concern of instrumental reason', is to be achieved only 'by rethinking the status of established forms of knowledge'. These forms consist in 'the technical and systematic facticities by which knowledge gets materially implemented' and it is precisely by placing it 'among those "technics" of knowledge' that 'Stiegler focuses on written language' (McGann 2013, 335).

Moving from these assumptions, the rationale of the 'analogy' between the theory of adaptive systems, or 'artificial science', and 'natural language' becomes utterly clear: 'the computer is to the artificial sciences as writing is to natural language' (Buscema 2014, 53). The text and the computing machine memory are the material extensions of operational systems such as computational algebras and natural language: 'digital tools and archival repositories' (McGann 2007, 1590) are tangible 'prosthetic devices' that 'help to release the resources of the human mind' (McGann 2007, 1591), just as the 'text provides an interpreter with a sort of prosthetic device to perform autopoietic operations of sense communication and exchange' (Buzzetti and McGann 2006, 68). Thus, 'the artificial science' uses the rules of 'a formal algebra' – that is, a mathematical system consisting of 'a set of objects together with some operations for combining them' (Herstein 1975, 2) – 'for the generation of artificial models which are composed of structures and processes', just as 'the natural languages' use the rules of 'semantics, syntax, and pragmatics for the generation of texts' (Buscema 2013, 17). But more to the point, what matters for our argument is that in both cases a computational model is based on adaptive self-organising principles of the same kind and works in the same way. Adaptive models are learning systems that try 'to construct automatic models of natural and cultural processes' (Buscema 2011, 19). They do not proceed from pre-established rules to analyse the facts; they try instead to create, 'dinamically', a set of 'rules', fittingly 'contingent' and 'local', that are 'capable of change with the process itself' (Buscema 2011, 20). The observed connections that 'enable models to generate rules dynamically are similar to the Kantian transcendental rules': they are 'rules that establish the conditions of possibility of other rules', previously assumed within the system itself (Buscema 2011, 20). Adaptive systems are, then, reflexive systems and through the learning process they succeed in modelling the emergence of self-organising structures.

Computational text analysis: an outdated attempt

The first attempts towards computational text analysis were based on the now superseded GOFAI notion of *expert systems*, based on a hypothetico-deductive inference model – a clearly unsatisfactory approach for an efficient computational analysis of self-organising systems such as natural language.

An adaptive operational approach is apparently the leading principle for the computational analysis of texts. One of the earliest scientific projects on computational text analysis was conducted by Jean-Claude Gardin at the Centre de recherches archéologiques (CRA) of the Centre national de la recherche scientifique (CNRS), in his role as *directeur d'études* at the École pratique des hautes études. Gardin 'put forward the idea that the use of the computer would lead to a representation of the reasonings' of archaeologists (Plutniak 2018, 26), and to a reliable 'validation' of their hypotheses (Gardin 1980, 112), 'through an analysis of the mental operations in archaeological constructions of all sorts, from the collecting of data to the writing of an article or book in published form' (Gardin 1980, xi). In this kind of analysis, or 'logicism', as it was defined by Gardin (1980, 125), 'the description of the facts in natural language implies a dependence on the logical system that constitutes the grammar of that language' (Plutniak 2017, § 52). However, Gardin sees the limits of a thorough formalisation. In his opinion 'the "formalization" of interpretive constructions' is 'quite foreign' to 'the higher ambitions' of 'artificial intelligence'; therefore, he rather avows to 'agree with the opinion of J.-B. Grize' (Gardin 1980, 125) concerning

> the necessity of a distinction between *formalizations* in the strict sense, in which the proposed models are truly formal systems, relying in one way or another on the theorems of mathematical logic, and on the other hand, *schematizations*, defined as 'models generated through a discourse in natural language (Grize 1974, 204)'. (Gardin 1980, 125)

So, 'the goal of logicism' is 'to produce schematizations rather than formalizations of archaeological reasoning' (Gardin 1980, 125). In Gardin's approach, the word 'formalization' 'doesn't designate anything more than a formal rephrasing (*mise en forme*) of the archaeological reasonings in a calculation mode, as understood in computer science, with no connections to logical or mathematical formalization' (Gardin 1999, 119), and the term 'logicist analysis' alike designates 'a method of rewriting that consists in expressing interpretive constructions in the form of chains of propositions that link up archaeological observations to the enunciation of theories or "points of view" regarding ancient societies' (or 'vice versa'), arranged 'in a calculation mode' (Gardin 1993, 11, 12).

This methodological self-restraint, however, as appropriate as it is, depended on the state of the art of its time. Adaptive systems were yet to come, and Gardin could only rely on the expert systems available at that moment,[8] based as they were on the 'hypothetico-deductive method' (Gardin 1993, 131) proceeding 'from top to bottom' (Gardin 1993, 117) for the validation of predefined hypotheses, or vice versa, in the inductive process of their positing. Accordingly, the setting up of an 'archaeological construct' was conceived of as a process consisting of the following steps: (a) the use of a specialised *'language of representation'* for the passage 'from observation to theory'; (b) the acknowledgement of 'the *logico-semantic organizations*' (Gardin 1993, 172) – that is, 'the logical and semantic operations that account for the transition from the initial material data (the *explanandum*) to the final conceptual propositions (the *explanans*), or vice versa, depending on whether we proceed through induction or deduction' (Gardin 1980, 102) – as 'instrumental in interpretation processes'; and 'lastly' (c) the 'rationalization of existing constructions' in 'the *quasi-algorithmic forms* given to logicist reconstructions'; all this makes it 'easy to guess' the reasons for the 'convergence' (Gardin 1980, 172) of Gardin's 'logicism' and 'the principles of *systems analysis*' (Gardin 1980, 171): 'in giving an algorithmic structure to the reasoning which leads to a given theory, we can verify step by step the basis of the proposed schematization' (Gardin 1980, 172). But 'expert systems', built as inference engines for specialised knowledge bases, 'produced only very limited results', in comparison with the new connectionist, 'heterodox and deviant schools of thought', and brought symbolic Artificial Intelligence to a standstill:

> creating infinite repositories of explicit rules to convey the thousands of subtleties of perception, language, and human reasoning was increasingly seen as an impossible, unreasonable, and inefficient task. (Cardon et al. 2018, xxiii)

The formal models that expert systems were proposing, as Gardin's reservations about radical formalisation had already sensed, were unfit for the computational analysis of an autonomous self-organising system such as natural language, and for the text too, as its 'prosthetic' material extension.

Text as a system

Literary textual phenomena such as variability and polysemic instability can be explained as the result of the internal dynamics of self-regulating autopoietic systems, as analysed by Maturana and more formally by George Spencer Brown.

Text is indeed, in its working, isomorphic to natural language and shares all its properties as a self-regulating 'autopoietic' system, 'in the terms of Humberto Maturana and Francesco Varela [1980]' (McGann 2001, xiv). Let us quote once again Jerome McGann, the scholar who, in his groundbreaking book, *The Textual Condition*:

> considers texts as autopoietic mechanisms operating as self-generating feedback systems that cannot be separated from those who manipulate and use them. Their autopoiesis functions through a pair of interrelated textual embodiments we can study as systems of linguistic and bibliographical codings. (McGann 1991, 15)

The essential autopoietic nature of the text brings with it the ubiquitous and seemingly 'paradoxical' indication of its 'extreme variability' (McGann 1991, 185). Material, social, historical and semantic 'instability' is a persistent characteristic of any text: 'variation, in other words, is the invariant rule of the textual condition' (McGann 1991, 182, 185). Hence, according to McGann, 'no text is self-identical' and none of its units 'can be assumed to be self-identical', so that the underlying 'logic' of 'autopoietic forms' 'is only frameable in some kind of paradoxical articulation such as: "*a* equals *a* if and only if *a* does not equal *a*"' (McGann 2001, 145, 184, 189). This is 'especially clear in poetical texts', for 'no poem can exist without systems of "overlapping structure", and the more developed the poetical text, the more complex are those systems of recursion' (McGann 2001, 149, 175). However:

> whereas everyone knows this about poetical texts, we are less clear about how and why this network of recursions unfolds. Yet clarity on the matter is particularly important in a digital horizon if we are to have any hope of building adequate electronic re-presentations of our received textual archive. (McGann 2001, 204)

This observation gets to the core of the matter and sets the most decisive challenge for computational text analysis.

As a 'remarkable' (McGann 2001, 193) attempt to unfold the 'mysterious' structures of the 'polysemous' dimensions of – especially poetic – language (cf. Della Volpe 1960), McGann refers to George Spencer Brown's book *Laws of Form* (1969), which 'takes as its point of departure and central subject "self-referential paradoxes"', such as 'the famous one Spencer Brown cites in the preface to the American edition of his book: "This statement is false"' (McGann 2001, 193). Just as in poetical works, where 'ambiguities are often deliberately set in "controlled" play', Spencer Brown's logico-mathematical view also 'yields the axiom: a equals a if and only if a does not equal a' (McGann 2001, 254 n2). From the outset, Spencer Brown's mathematical argument is directed to 'produce the realization' (McGann 2001, 203) that 'the world we know is constructed in order (and thus in such a way as to be able) to see itself' (Spencer Brown 1969, 105). His formal system contains 'reflexive functions' (McGann 2001, 200) and is a calculus for 'self-aware reflection' (McGann 2001, xii). Self-reference, then, is not as dangerous and paradoxical as it is commonly thought to be; rather it turns up as the possible clue to unfold the riddle of the pervasive semantic instability of the textual condition.

Textual ambiguity

The textual phenomenon of ambiguity is also recognised by logicians and mathematicians. The operational understanding of one and the same ambiguous textual expression requires a heuristic approach based on an abductive inference model.

In actual fact, an 'adequate analysis' of the 'famous Liar paradox' that has just been mentioned has shown that the Liar sentence, 'This proposition is not true' (Barwise and Etchemendy 1987, 3, 12), 'is a sentence that can be used in many different ways to say many different things'. The Liar sentence 'gives rise to no genuine paradox' and 'what once appeared as paradox now looks like pervasive ambiguity' (Barwise and Etchemendy 1987, 177). In greater detail:

> let's distinguish between the meaning of a sentence and the propositional content of a statement made with it. Intuitively, the former should be a propositional function, something that gives us a proposition when supplied with the situation the proposition is about, while the latter would be such a proposition. Thus a sentence can be ambiguous in terms of propositional content without having two separate meanings, without expressing two distinct propositional functions. (Barwise and Etchemendy 1987, 138)

Ambiguity is not paradox, *pace* the 'logicians' who 'abhor ambiguity but love paradox' (Barwise and Etchemendy 1987, 177). The meaning of a Liar-like sentence, understood as a propositional function, is that of an operational rule; understood as propositional content, it is the statement made by applying that rule, that is the value of the propositional function. As a rule it has metalinguistic import; as propositional content it is an object-language assertion. In natural language, which is a language that contains its own metalanguage, a sentence whose meaning is operational is clearly self-referential.

This double import, operational and assertive, is not entirely foreign to formal languages either. As David Hestenes observes regarding the algebras that are named after him:

> Clifford may have been the first person to find significance in the fact that two different interpretations of number can be distinguished, the *quantitative* and the *operational*. On the first interpretation, number is a measure of 'how much' or 'how many' of something. On the second, number describes a relation between different quantities. (Hestenes 1999, 60)

Namely, it describes the operation that connects them together. The same ambivalence is to be found in Spencer Brown's calculus, which admits of a 'partial identity of operand and operator' (Spencer Brown 1969, 88). Its 'primary algebra provides immediate access to the nature of the relationship between operators and operands', for 'an operand in the algebra is merely a conjectured presence or absence of an operator' (Spencer Brown 1969, 87–8). This is an absolutely crucial point for our argument. The metalinguistic as opposed to the linguistic ambivalent reading, or the operational as opposed to the assertive reading of a textual sentence, is the real root of its 'interpretive differentials' (McGann 1991, 185). How, then, can this ambivalence be analysed, to provide a formal model for computational text analysis?

From an epistemological point of view we can say, again with McGann, that 'properly understood . . . every text is unique and original to itself when we consider it not as an object but as an action' (McGann 1991, 183). Likewise, regarding the comprehension of a text, we can say that 'interpretation is an act which gets carried out only as a response to a given textual condition', in which 'two interpreters of a particular text "read" it differently because they are not seeing the same "text", because they have imagined their interpretive object differently'. The root of 'these interpretive differentials' (McGann 1991, 184) is to be seen precisely in the operational understanding of the same textual expression, which is always read and understood in an ever-changing condition. To clarify this notion the following quotation[9] is very instructive, for it points out that each of three distinguishable 'functions of metaphor' enables the understanding of historical texts 'on a different epistemic level':

> Heuristic imagery advances deliberative, analytic understanding and falls within the domain of explanatory discourse. Depictive imagery presentationally facilitates the (phenomenological) apprehension of meanings and occurrences; it is a component of narrative, which includes sequential, discourse. Finally, cognitive imagery, operative on the meta-historical plane, orchestrates interpretive discourse and thereby governs the way that events (or actions) may be known in and of themselves. (Stambovsky 1988, 134)

The second, narrative, understanding can be seen as the assertive reading of a text, whereas the third can be construed as the operational one, which – as we shall see in more detail – is properly expressed on a metalinguistic discursive plane. As for the first understanding, the heuristic one, its structure can indeed be expounded in the following way, as proposed by Maurice Mandelbaum:

> What I shall term an explanatory structure is present only when a person – in this case a historian – already knows (or believes that he knows) what has in fact happened, and seeks an explanation of why it happened. (Mandelbaum 1977, 26)

It is not difficult to recognise, in this explanatory reading of a given expression, the heuristic structure of an abductive inference, for in this case 'the direction of inquiry' starts 'from a given outcome' and 'moves back from what is known' to 'its antecedents' (Mandelbaum 1977, 26). The abductive argument, which leads to the confirmation of an outcome as a *case* complying with a certain *rule* in accordance with previous *results*, originates the interpretive move that assumes that rule as an operational instruction for the understanding of the text.

Logical foundations

From a logical point of view, the operational reading of a sentence amounts to assuming it as a rule of inference with metalinguistic import comprised within the object language itself. The ambivalence between the referential and the operational understanding of one and the same sentence is formally expressed by the so-called deduction theorem. This principle is assumed by the contemporary theory known as 'inference-ticket' theory, and was also fundamental in medieval topical logic, which distinguished between *formal* and *material consequences*, which are respectively based on tautological versus empirical rule statements. Accordingly, the inference-ticket theory can be seen as a justification of the deduction theorem for material consequences. Likewise, Barwise and Etchemendy's, as well as Leśniewski's, formal treatment of operational object-language statements with metalinguistic import can be compared to Anselm of Canterbury's position, which regards them as *de re* statements – that is, referring to how things are, inferentially equivalent to *de voce* statements on the meaning of the words they are composed of.

From a more strictly logical point of view, an assertive reading of a textual expression sees it as a descriptive referential statement, whereas an operational reading of the same expression assigns it a metalinguistic import. Accordingly, one and the same sentence can be understood as a metalinguistic rule of inference or as an object-language asserted premise of the reasoning that assumes it as its leading principle. The clue to this kind of ambiguity is to be found in the so-called *deduction theorem*, which may be described in the following way:

> If an argument contains one or more premises, then it is valid if and only if the conditional statement, whose antecedent is the conjunction of the premises and whose consequent is the conclusion of the argument, is logically true. (Lambert and van Fraassen 1972, 28)

In other words, 'an argument is valid only if its corresponding conditional is true. That is to say, the argument "A_1, A_2, ..., A_n: therefore B" is valid only if the conditional assertible "If A_1 and A_2 and ... and A_n), then B" is true' (Barnes 2012, 42). But it should never be overlooked that the sentences acting as antecedents in the conditional are to be understood in a different way from the same sentences asserted as premises in the argument, for they 'differ from the premises in the sense' that they consist in 'already accepted rules, called rules of inference' (Lambert and van Fraassen 1972, 29).

This kind of ambiguity is responsible for what, in his careful analysis of ordinary language, Gilbert Ryle describes as 'category-mistakes' (Ryle 1949, 17). A category-mistake is made by people who treat the content of certain expressions 'as if they belonged to one logical type or category (or range of types or categories), when they actually belong to another' (Ryle 1949, 16). What is most relevant in our case is Ryle's observation that a statement expressing a general law, or a rule of inference, 'is used as, so to speak, an *inference-ticket* (a season ticket) which licenses its possessors to move from asserting factual statements to asserting other factual statements'. Laws can be stated in hypothetical sentences, but 'we do not call a hypothetical sentence a "law", unless it is a "variable" or "open" hypothetical statement, i.e. one of which the protasis can embody at least one expression like "any" or "whenever"' (Ryle 1949, 120).

And 'it is in virtue of this feature that a law applies to instances, though its statement does not mention them'. First and foremost, though, 'law-statements belong to a different and more sophisticated level of discourse from that, or those, to which belong the statements of the facts that satisfy them', just as 'algebraical statements are in a similar way on a different level of discourse from the arithmetical statements which satisfy them'. Law-statements are, then, higher-order and operational statements: they are 'rules' to be used 'in concrete operations', such as those 'of grammar, multiplication, chess or etiquette' (Ryle 1949, 120–1).

Due to the significant role they play in the formal reconstruction of textual processes – as we shall see – it is worth dwelling further on the logical features of these statements, which were later called 'inference-licences' and systematically dealt with in *The Uses of Argument* – a book first published in 1958 – by Stephen Toulmin (Toulmin 2003, 91), who openly admits that here he 'owes much' to Ryle's ideas, which he had also 'applied to the physical sciences' in his earlier book *Philosophy of Science*, issued in 1953 (Toulmin 2003, 239). These historical details are not included casually. In fact, in a brief note published in *Mind* in 1961, Otto Bird shows that the inference theory proposed by Ryle and Toulmin, commonly known as 'inference-ticket' or 'inference-licence' theory, 'has many similarities with the analysis of the Topics in medieval logic' (Bird 1961, 534).

The analysis proposed by Toulmin of 'the pattern of an argument' (Toulmin 2003, 89ff.) can be summarised as follows: the 'conclusion' is granted by a 'warrant' and a 'backing'; a warrant is a conditional statement, that may be written 'in the form "If D [data], then C [conclusion]"' (Toulmin 2003, 91), assumed as a 'general' rule of inference 'we argue *in accordance with*', and a backing is a 'special' (viii) rule, that is the 'proper' (Toulmin 2003, 63) specification of the general rule, one of its instances so to speak, to suit the 'data' or premises 'we argue *from*' (Toulmin 2003, 119). One important thing to note is that whereas the statements of warrants are 'hypothetical', the backing for warrants can be expressed 'in the form of categorical statements of fact quite as well as can the data appealed to in direct support of our conclusions' (Toulmin 2003, 98). In other words, the same expression can be understood as a backing or rule, which is operational, and as a premise or datum, which is just assertive. And that is precisely the kind of ambiguity we are trying to specify for the sake of our argument.

Bird clearly points out the similarity between Toulmin's analysis and the medieval analysis of topical logic: briefly, in what the medieval authors called 'the Topical Maxim and Difference we have the traditional logical counterparts of Toulmin's Warrants and Backing' (Bird 1961, 537). As defined by Albert of Saxony, in the Topics, a Maxim is 'a confirmatory rule that proves a consequence' or inference (Albert of Saxony 1522, f. 33ra), and so it 'performs the same function as a warrant', just as the Topical Difference performs the same function as a backing. From our point of view the function of the Difference is particularly important. The Difference 'indicates that diverse Maxims rest on different relations' between the terms of the argument, 'or the "matter" from which the Maxim is composed' (Bird 1961, 537) and, as we have seen, it can be expressed by a categorical statement occurring as an asserted premise in an argument. In the Topics, if the confirmatory rule of a valid inference is a Maxim – a logical law true by necessity – the inference is called 'formal' (*consequentia formalis*), but if the topical principle is a Difference – a factual statement only contingently true due to the nature of its terms – the inference is called 'material' (*consequentia materialis*). Without a confirmatory Maxim a material consequence is commonly described as an incomplete or enthymematic argument, which 'can be reduced to a formal consequence through the assumption of a necessary proposition' that can just be taken apart as a confirmatory rule or added to the argument as a further 'asserted' premise (Bird 1961, 538). Clearly, this is again a case of textual ambiguity, for the same sentence can be understood both as an operational rule (the topical maxim) and as a referential statement (the asserted premise), which is precisely what this lengthy digression intended to show. Moreover, we can discern in a connectionist text-mining procedure, or deep learning application, a fruitful heuristic approach to the discovery of hidden connections among the available data, aiming at the establishment of new and diverse interpretive perspectives.

The double, ambivalent understanding of textual statements is also openly recognised from the point of view of contemporary logic. In his review of Toulmin's *Philosophy of Science*, Ernest Nagel expressly observes that, owing to the deduction theorem, 'a rule of inference can in general be replaced by a premise' (Nagel 1954, 406) stated by the same sentence, and that this principle, like the 'distinction between premises *from which* one reasons and rules *in accordance with which* inferences are drawn', is 'canonical in modern logical theory'. Nagel also points out that Peirce, clearly referring to medieval logic, had already 'noted long ago' an important fact concerning rules, namely that 'while every argument has its tacit "leading principle" which prescribes what conclusion is to be drawn from the premises, some leading principles may be purely *formal*' whereas 'others may be *material*'. Moreover,

> Peirce also saw that one or more material premises can be eliminated from an argument without destroying its validity, provided that this elimination is compensated by the introduction of appropriate material leading principles which permit the derivation of the original conclusion from the remaining premises. (Nagel 1954, 405)

And since a rule – as we have already seen – can generally be replaced by a premise, 'the above manoeuvre can be introduced in reverse' as well, and 'in the case of material rules of inference this can apparently always be done' (Nagel 1954, 406).

In sum, the inference-ticket theory amounts to a deduction theorem for material consequences. Both points of view draw attention to the same decisive issue, namely the different functions performed by a premise and a rule of inference. For this distinction implies the ambivalent understanding of syntactically identical sentences, respectively used to express an asserted premise or a rule of inference: in the former case any such sentence is understood as an object-language statement referring to a factual state of affairs, whereas in the latter it is understood as being endowed with a metalinguistic import. But, in a language that contains its own metalanguage, as a natural language text, we find ourselves in a seemingly paradoxical condition, for the conclusions of 'metalevel' argumentations are assumed to be 'a feature of the world' and we would be forced to admit that 'the object language/metalanguage distinction is inappropriate' (Barwise and Etchemendy 1987, 175; 88). However, that difficulty is only apparent, for in a language containing its own metalanguage a higher-order statement, as we have recalled already, does not refer to a first-order statement that describes the word, but itself 'describes nature' or the world (Vuillemin 1996, 265). And 'this is an extremely important point', for 'if the object language contained the predicate *True*' (Barwise and Etchemendy 1987, 89), that is, its own metalanguage, we would be dealing with operational 'propositions' rather than 'sentences' (Barwise and Etchemendy 1987, 88). And here again a parallel with medieval logic comes appropriately into play.

According to Anselm of Canterbury, for instance, 'statements on the meaning of words', which he 'tickets as *de voce*', are 'obviously inferentially equivalent for him' to 'statements as to how things are', which he calls '*de re* statements' (Henry 1963, 183–4). So, as Barwise and Etchemendy maintain, the same natural language sentence can be used in two different ways: *de voce* and *de re*, or as a rule of inference and as an asserted descriptive statement, and can express different propositional contents, that have to be formally represented by different formulas. Accordingly, operational *de re* statements endowed with metalinguistic import do not necessarily require 'a metalanguage' severed from the object language, but 'can be adequately and even advantageously expressed using the means of Leśniewski's Ontology' (Simons 2016, 200). To sum up, object-language higher-order statements 'expressed in a *de re*, or thing-centred, fashion' (Henry 1974, 27), in other words as 'statements as to how things are', are in practice to be considered 'inferentially equivalent' (Henry 1963, 183–4) to first-order metalinguistic statements 'expressed in a *de voce*, or word-centred, fashion' (Henry 1974, 27), which are 'statements on the meaning of words', sentences, or other textual expressions (Henry 1963, 183).

A tentative model

A computational model of the interpretive process may be based on the assumption of the ambivalent diacritic dimension of the markup. Embedded and standoff markup perform the same diacritic function respectively for the expression and the content of the text. Their operational functionalities can be mapped onto a cyclical diagram, which represents the self-referential working of all diacritical textual expressions.

But do all our previous observations really have a bearing on computational text analysis? That's actually what is argued for here. Textual interpretation is a complex process that cannot easily be accounted for and what has been exposed so far is a tentative move towards finding an acceptable answer. To proceed further, we shall start from the following illuminating contention about embedded markup:

> To describe the meaning of the markup in a document, it suffices to generate the set of inferences about the document which are licensed by the markup. In some ways, we can regard the meaning of the markup as being constituted, not only described, by that set of inferences. (Sperberg-McQueen et al. 2000, 231)

On the basis of this operational definition, markup can be treated as an 'inference-licence'. However, as Allen Renear lucidly noted, 'the recognition that markup' is operational, or more specifically also 'performative', poses very 'difficult and consequential problems' as to 'what markup really is, and in particular, when it is *about* a text and when it is *part* of a text' or, above all, 'when, and how, it may sometimes be both' (Renear 2001, 419). Ambiguity, then, is an essential trait of embedded markup, as it is of punctuation.

A comma, which may change the meaning of a sentence or of a single word, can be regarded, like any other diacritical textual sign, as an element of the text, in that it is part of our writing system, and as an instruction or a metalinguistic rule, for it prescribes the way in which the text must be interpreted. Thus, it can be maintained that 'punctuation is not simply part of our writing system', but rather that 'it is a type of document markup' (Coombs et al. 1987, 935). Along the same lines, the condition of embedded markup, in its general understanding, can be likened to that of a diacritical sign which, as such, plays a double function: when it is used 'to describe a document's structure' (Raymond et al. 1992, 1) it performs a metalinguistic function, but since it is expressed with 'assigned tokens' which denote 'specific positions in a text' (Raymond et al. 1992, 3) it constitutes that structure. Markup, therefore, *denotes* structure and *is* itself structure, so that it can be characterised by its *diacritical ambiguity*. Therefore, embedded markup and all diacritical textual expressions just as well are all self-referential, for they are both part of the text and at the same time about the text. Their ambiguity is occasioned by self-reference as, in its turn, self-reference is due to that essential feature of natural language that enables it to comprise its own metalanguage. Because of its ambivalent nature, markup – and for that matter every form of diacritical expression – generates a cyclic process (a markup or diacritical loop) that is essentially inherent in textual dynamics:

> [W]e may say that an act of composition is a sense-constituting operation that brings about the formulation of a text. The resulting expression can be considered as the self-identical value of a sense-enacting operation. By fixing it, we allow for the indetermination of its content. To define the content, we assume the expression as a rule for an interpreting operation. An act of interpretation brings about a content, and we can assume it as its self-identical value. A defined content provides a model for the expression of the text and can be viewed as a rule for its restructuring. A newly added structure mark can in turn be seen as a reformulation of the expression, and so on,

in a permanent cycle of compensating actions between determina-
tion and indetermination of the expression and the content of the
text. (Buzzetti and McGann 2006, 68)

All this can conveniently be represented by a diagram (Figure 9.1) and it
is worth pointing out some of its formal aspects in more detail.

Figure 9.1 refers specifically to the markup tags that improve the
digital representation of the text and which can respectively be embedded in it or be made up of external pointers that refer to specific positions
in the string of characters forming the text. Since there is no direct one-
to-one correspondence between the elements that compose the syntactic
structure of the text and the components of its semantic structure, the
internal or *embedded* markup – inasmuch as it is that part of the string
of characters that constitutes its structure – describes diacritically the
syntactic properties of the expression of the text. On the other hand, the
external or *standoff* markup – since it is not bound to the linear structure of the string of characters that forms the expression of the text –
can freely express structural aspects of the content of the text that are
not necessarily linear. In our multidimensional diagram, which outlines
the self-referential cyclic dynamics of the text, there is therefore a correspondence between the two dimensions of the expression and the internal markup of the text, as well as between the two respective dimensions
of the external markup and the content of the text.

The dual linguistic and metalinguistic function of the markup,
which is due to its diacritical nature, implies that the same marker
serves both as a self-identical element of the expression and as a rule
that assigns a structure to the content of the text, by defining its specific

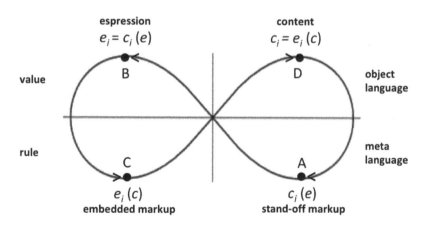

Figure 9.1   The markup loop (cf. Buzzetti and McGann 2006, 68).

elements. In their turn, the elements of the content serve on the one hand as self-identical content components and on the other as rules that assign a structure to the expression. Thus, the diacritic structural components of the expression and content of the text can be considered both the result of a restructuring operation and the very operations themselves, which alternately assign a structure to the expression and to the content of the text. Formally, all diacritic expressions can be understood as values of a function, or as those very functions, which constitute the rules that assign a given structure to the text.

Accordingly, in natural language, self-referential diacritic object-language expressions perform a double function: understood as first-order statements, they are used as structural markers of both the expression and the content of the text; understood as second-order statements, they constitute a rule of inference and are used in turn as a function of the expression that assigns a structure to the content, or conversely as a function of the content that assigns a structure to the expression of the text.

Generalising the model

The diagram exposed in Figure 9.1, which represents the operation of all diacritic textual expressions, corresponds remarkably to the diagram that represents the conversational cycle discussed by Frederick Parker-Rhodes, who appropriately observes that the process is not generally a closed, cyclic one, but is predominantly an open one which can more conveniently be mapped onto a spiral, such as the helicoidal process described by Jean-Claude Gardin.

Still on a formal level, we can observe that the structure of the markup cycle, represented above – which can however be generalised for all forms of diacritical expression – corresponds exactly to the 'conversational cycle', which according to Frederick Parker-Rhodes represents the actual 'speech process' between a speaker and a listener (Parker-Rhodes 1978, 16) or, dealing with texts, between the writing and the reading of a text (Figure 9.2).

In this cycle, the 'expression' (A) is an operation performed by the speaker 'which takes a "thought" as input (which we must think as formalised in some manner)' and produces a 'text' (B). One should note, incidentally, that by 'expression' here we mean an operation, which is a function of the content, and not its result, a fact that proves the ambivalence of the diacritic content component, assumed here in its operational

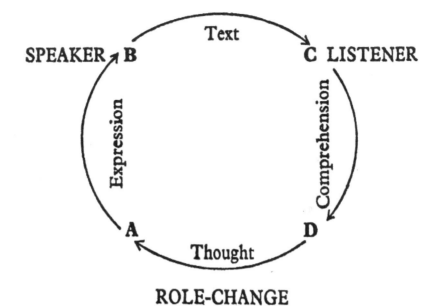

ROLE-CHANGE

Figure 9.2 The conversational cycle (see Parker-Rhodes 1978, 16). Used with permission of the author's estate.

sense. In turn, 'comprehension' (C), or the interpretive act, is an operation performed by the listener, which takes the text as an 'input containing all the information imparted to it by the speaker' and completes the cycle by producing 'a thought' (D) as its 'output' (17). It is clear, in spite of the use of different terminology, that the structure of this cycle corresponds exactly to that of the markup cycle examined earlier (Figure 9.1).

However, in this regard, an important observation made by Parker-Rhodes should not be overlooked. He explicitly refers to the indecisiveness of the interpretive process: the 'thought that the speaker had intended to convey', once received and interpreted in the mind of the listener, 'could produce the elaboration of a new thought' as a possible 'result' (Parker-Rhodes 1978, 17). In this case the diagram could take the form of an open spiral, which would provide a more appropriate representation of possible 'interpretive differentials' (Figure 9.3). For such a cycle could close itself at some point, returning to the starting position, or proceed indefinitely, depending on a different textual condition and the context in which a given expression is received. Jean-Claude Gardin recognises as 'self-evident' too the 'cyclical nature' of the process of scientific construction. However, he thinks, like Parker-Rhodes, that the cycle does not necessarily close itself and that it is therefore best represented by a 'helicoidal curve', more suited to retracing 'the successive steps of

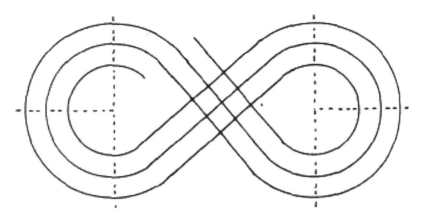

Figure 9.3 The helicoidal cycle (cf. Gardin 1980, 45). From *Graphic Representations of the Periodic System During One Hundred Years* by Edward G. Mazurs. Used with permission of University of Alabama Press.

its formation', produced as they are by a series of choices that depend not only on the data and their organisation but also and above all on the 'logico-semantic rules of interpretation' and the different 'interpretative models' that are equally possible (Gardin 1980, 145). This process can also be visualised by projecting the helicoidal curve on a plane shaped as an open 'plane lemniscate' (Mazurs 1974, 16), altogether similar to Figure 9.1 except that it is an open, non-closed, cyclic curve.

Epistemological implications

From an epistemological point of view, the self-referential cycle of the discursive and interpretive process implies an interaction between subjective and objective points of view which excludes their absolute separation, as maintained by Maurice Merleau-Ponty and Heinz von Foerster in his theory of second-order cybernetics. Our suggested diagram can, then, be considered as expressing both the subjective and the objective aspects of the linguistic and textual processes. Their self-referential character prevents the continual recursion of their separate status and the diagram can then be seen as a representation of their self-referential mutual relation and interconnection.

The cyclic and self-referential nature of the discursive process – which in the natural language form of expression jointly includes both the representation of its own object and the representation of the way in which the subject represents it – tends to incline towards an answer that excludes the absolute separation of subject and object, or in other words of the observer and the observed. This is the position embraced, for example, by theorists of autopoiesis (Varela et al. 1991), inspired by Maurice Merleau-Ponty's epistemology and his notion of the 'chiasm'. In one of his most incisive descriptions, Merleau-Ponty presents the chiasm as

> an exchange between me and the world, between the phenomenal body and the 'objective' body, between the perceiving and the perceived: what begins as a thing ends as consciousness of the thing, what begins as a 'state of consciousness' ends as a thing. (Merleau-Ponty 1968, 215)

In his essay *La Structure du comportement*, in order to clarify the connection between subject and object, Merleau-Ponty quotes (1942, 11) physiologist Viktor von Weizsäcker, who describes that relation in the following terms: 'the properties of the subject and the intentions of the subject . . . not only mix with each other, but also constitute a new whole' (Weizsäcker 1927, 45). This means that the subject and the object must be conceived not as separate, but as constantly connected in a continuous process of 'overlapping or encroachment (*empiétement*)' (Merleau-Ponty 1968, 123), as though one might continually take the place of the other. A chiastic interlacement thus consists of a relationship of 'activity and passivity coupled', in other words a representing and being represented of the subject and the object, in both language and perception. Thus, the understanding of the 'chiasm', as described by Merleau-Ponty, leads to the conclusion that language, understood as natural language, 'is the same' thing that simultaneously represents and is represented; not the same 'in the sense of real identity', but rather 'the same in the structural sense', that is, in the sense of a unique and self-identical semiosis, which also includes the semiosis that represents it (Merleau-Ponty 1968, 261).

The same relationship between the subject that represents and the object being represented, when conceived of as 'the same thing' – that is, as the 'new whole' that they constitute – is found in the notion of the subject assumed by cybernetics 'of the second order', the cybernetics of 'observing systems', in which 'the observer enters the system by stipulating *his own* purpose', as opposed to the cybernetics of 'observed systems', or 'first-order' cybernetics, in which 'the observer enters the system by stipulating *the system's* purpose' (von Foerster 2003, 285–6). Thus, in this context, one can find the following enlightening definition of the subject: 'I am the observed relation between myself and observing myself' (von Foerster 2003, 257). Here the subject is defined as one and the same thing: a new whole, constituted by the representation of the relationship between the self observing itself and the self observed by itself.

It is clearly not by chance that this reference to cybernetics brings us back to the starting point of our argument, which began by mentioning the idea of a 'net of neurons', stemming from cybernetics, as the origin of the connectionist, operational and adaptive approach.

At this point, our diagram of the self-referential cycle of the discursive process can be reconsidered, taking into account the reflexive character of the relationship between the subject and the object. Language, inasmuch as it is seen as *expression*, is *subjective*, because it is the representation of the form of our act of representing; however, inasmuch as it is seen as *content*, language is *objective*, because it is the representation of the form of what it represents. In turn, a form of diacritical expression of the text, *subjective* in itself, can be considered both from an *objective* point of view, as an element of the expression identical to itself, and from a *subjective* point of view, as a function that defines a structural element of textual content (Figure 9.4). The same can be said of an element of textual content, *objective* in itself, which can be considered both from an *objective* point of view as an element identical to itself, and from a *subjective* point of view as a function that defines a structural element of the expression.

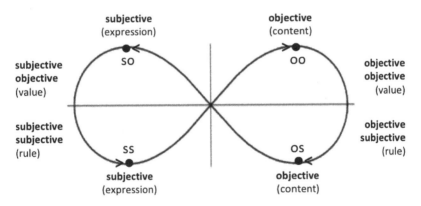

Figure 9.4 Subjectivity and objectivity in the speech process (cf. Parker-Rhodes 1978, 16).

The distinction between something that is subjective and something that is objective is therefore a recursive distinction that could continue indefinitely (Figure 9.5).

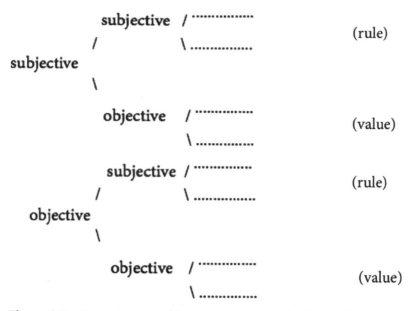

Figure 9.5 Recursiveness of the subjective/objective distinction.

But this does not happen, for the very reason that natural language is self-referential, as one can clearly infer from Figure 9.6.

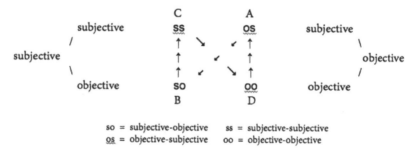

so = subjective-objective   ss = subjective-subjective
os = objective-subjective   oo = objective-objective

Figure 9.6 Chiastic self-referentiality of the subjective/objective distinction.

Towards a possible implementation

The diagram of the discursive process here illustrated may be assumed as the basis of an algorithmic model implemented by a corresponding artificial adaptive system.

Granted that a rigorous formalisation of such a model is possible, as I have tried to show, it can be surmised that its computational implementation could be obtained by developing a suitable adaptive system. If the adaptive artificial systems that I have described are built on the basis of a recognised analogy with the operation of natural language –that is, foreseeing the presence of rules capable of modifying other rules of the system – the same analogy allows us to suppose that a formal model of the discursive processes of natural language could be implemented precisely using an adaptive computational system of the same type.

As a matter of fact, the ambivalence of precise mathematical concepts strictly defined (operation and operand, function and value) can constitute the formal expression of the relationship between rules and values, subject and object, which I described by invoking the notion of the 'chiasm'. Moreover, it is precisely the undetermined character of the relation between syntax and semantics in natural language that originates the self-referential cycle of higher-order 'rules' that 'establish the conditions of possibility of other rules' within an adaptive system (Buscema 2013, 20). These conditions should make it possible to implement a computational model of the discursive processes that characterise scientific constructions in the humanities, through the development of an adequate self-organising adaptive system.

Conclusion

The theoretical recognition of the self-referential character of essential linguistic and textual processes provides a sound foundation for the implementation of an algorithmic model suitable to their appropriate computational analysis.

What has been proposed here is the tentative formal reconstruction of the dynamic discursive processes depending on the constant variation of the textual condition. The new forms of theory fostered by the availability of big data have brought to the fore operational and adaptive approaches to the analysis of natural and cultural processes based on the interaction between self-organising systems and their environment. A basic introductory survey of the formal and epistemological foundations of the self-referring processes that characterise the working of self-regulating systems has made us aware of the proposed solutions to their seemingly paradoxical implications. On that account, it has been possible to analyse specific natural language self-referring functions such as those performed by diacritical expressions.

This result has proved to be crucial in providing the decisive clue to the reconstruction of the interaction, mediated by natural language, between speaker and listener, writer and reader, and a possible approach to the exposition of the interpretive process. A tentative formal model for the functioning of textual variation and polysemic ambivalence has thus been suggested and it has been shown that a possible implementation of that model could be tested on the basis of a structural analogy between the role of operational directions in natural language and of dynamically generated rules in self-regulating adaptive systems. Should these conclusions prove to be tenable, we will have reaffirmed the essential role of both theory and epistemological awareness as the primary foundations of a sound research practice in the vast field of digital humanities.

Notes

1. For instance, Goldberg and Levy say – in a paper on the 'word-embedding method' of the word-2vec package based on neural networks (Goldberg and Levy 2014, 1) – that they would expect 'to see something more formal'. However, despite the 'very hand-wavy' character of its predictive assumption (5) they avow that it still 'remains superior' to linear count-based models and, in a later assessment, Goldberg admits that 'nonlinear neural network models solve some of the shortcomings of traditional language models' (Levy and Goldberg 2014, 2177).
2. According to Peirce, induction, which infers a general 'rule' from a 'case' and a 'result' that has been repeated a number of times, 'is not the only case of inverting a deductive syllogism' (which infers a 'result' from a 'rule' and a 'case'), for we may get 'the inference of a *case* from a *rule* and *result*', and 'this sort of inference is called *making an hypothesis*' (Peirce 1878, 471–2), or an 'abduction', which is the kind of inference that 'by its very definition leads to a hypothesis' (Peirce 1901).
3. Cf. Vinge 1993 and Kurzweil 2005.
4. My emphasis.
5. The phrase is ascribed to 'Doug DeCarlo' (Cockburn and Highsmith 2001, 133).
6. The Capability Maturity Model (CMM) is a software development model.
7. Cf. Stiegler 1994; Stiegler 1998.
8. 'The possible contributions of expert systems in archeology are discussed in Gardin *et al.* 1987' (Gardin 1993, 12 n1).
9. This quotation has been taken from an as yet unpublished paper by Manfred Thaller, accessed by courtesy of its author.

References

Abrahamsson, Pekka, Nilay Oza and Mikko T. Siponen. 2010. 'Agile Software Development Methods: A comparative review'. In *Agile Software Development*, edited by T. Dingsøyr, T. Dybå and N. Moe, 31–59. Berlin: Springer.
Albertus of Saxony. 1522. *Perutilis Logica*. Venetiis: Heredes Octaviani Scoti.
Anderson, Chris. 2008. 'The End of Theory: The data deluge makes the scientific method obsolete', *Wired*, 23 June. Accessed 6 September 2022. http://www.wired.com/science/discoveries/magazine/16-07/pb_theory
Barnes, Jonathan. 2012. 'Logical Form and Logical Matter'. In *Logical Matters: Essays in Ancient Philosophy II*, edited by Maddalena Bonelli, 43–146. Oxford: Clarendon Press.

Barwise, Jon and John Etchemendy. 1987. *The Liar: An essay on truth and circularity*. New York: Oxford University Press.

Beck, Kent et al. 2001a. *Manifesto for Agile Software Development*. Accessed 6 September 2022. http://agilemanifesto.org/

Beck, Kent et al. 2001b. *Principles behind the Agile Manifesto*. Accessed 6 September 2022. http://agilemanifesto.org/principles.html

Bell, Gordon, Tony Hey and Alex Szalay. 2009. 'Beyond the Data Deluge', *Science* 323: 1297–8.

Berger, Peter L. and Thomas Luckmann. 1967. *The Social Construction of Reality: A treatise in the sociology of knowledge*. New York: Doubleday Anchor.

Bird, Otto. 1961. 'The Re-Discovery of the Topics', *Mind* N.S. 70 (280): 534–9.

Borgman, Christine L. 2015. *Big Data, Little Data, No Data: Scholarship in the networked world*. Cambridge, MA: MIT Press.

Boston University. 2009. 'DH09 Tuesday: Christine Borgman keynote'. *DigiLib Blog*, 23 June.

Buckner, Cameron and James Garson. 2019. 'Connectionism'. In *The Stanford Encyclopedia of Philosophy*, edited by Edward N. Zalta. Fall 2019 edition. Accessed 6 September 2022. https://plato.stanford.edu/archives/fall2019/entries/connectionism/

Buscema, Massimo. 2011. 'Artificial Adaptive Systems: Philosophy, mathematics and applications'. In *Advanced Networks, Algorithms and Modeling for Earthquake Prediction*, edited by Massimo Buscema and Marina Ruggieri, 17–37. Denmark: Aalborg University Press.

Buscema, Massimo. 2013. 'The General Philosophy of Artificial Adaptive Systems'. In *Intelligent Data Mining in Law Enforcement Analytics: New neural networks applied to real problems*, edited by Massimo Buscema and William J. Tastle, 17–30. Dordrecht: Springer.

Buscema, Massimo. 2014. 'The General Philosophy of Artificial Adaptive Systems (AAS)', *Archeologia e calcolatori*, Supplemento 6.

Buzzetti, Dino and Jerome McGann. 2006. 'Critical Editing in a Digital Horizon'. In *Electronic Textual Editing*, edited by Lou Burnard, Katherine O'Brien O'Keeffe and John Unsworth, 53–73. New York: Modern Language Association of America.

Cardon, Dominique, Jean-Philippe Cointet and Antoine Mazières. 2018. 'La Revanche des neurones: l'invention des machines inductives et la controverse de l'intelligence artificielle', *Réseaux* 211(5): 173–220. https://doi.org/10.3917/res.211.0173

Cockburn, Alistair and James A. Highsmith. 2001. 'Agile Software Development: The people factor', *Computer* 34(11): 131–3.

Coombs, James H., Allen H. Renear and Steven J. DeRose. 1987. 'Markup Systems and the Future of Scholarly Text Processing'. *Communications of the ACM* 30(11): 933–47.

Della Volpe, Galvano. 1960. *Critica del gusto*. Milan: Feltrinelli.

DeMarco, Tom. 2002. 'Foreword'. In *Agile Software Development Ecosystems*, edited by James Highsmith, xv–xvi. Boston, MA: Addison-Wesley.

Gardin, Jean-Claude. 1980. *Archaeological Constructs: An aspect of theoretical archaeology*. Cambridge, Paris: Cambridge University Press, Maison des Sciences de l'Homme.

Gardin, Jean-Claude. 1993. 'Points de vue logicistes sur les méthodologies en sciences sociales', *Sociologie et sociétés* 25(2): 11–22. https://doi.org/10.7202/001281ar

Gardin, Jean-Claude. 1999. 'Archéologie, formalisation et sciences sociales', *Sociologie et sociétés* 31(1): 119–27.

Gardin, Jean-Claude, Olivier Guillaume, Peter-Q. Herman, Antoinette Hesnard, Marie-Salomé Lagrange, Monique Renaud and Élisabeth Zadora-Rio. 1987. *Systèmes experts et sciences humaines: le cas de l'archéologie*. Paris: Eyrolles. English translation: *Artificial Intelligence and Expert Systems: Case studies in the knowledge domain of archaeology*. Chichester: Ellis Horwood, 1988.

Gershgorn, Dave. 2017. 'The Data that Transformed AI Research – and Possibly the World'. *Quartz*, 26 July. Accessed 6 September 2022. https://qz.com/1034972/the-data-that-changed-the-direction-of-ai-research-and-possibly-the-world/

Gigerenzer, Gerd. 2004. 'Fast and Frugal Heuristics: The tools of bounded rationality'. In *Blackwell Handbook of Judgment and Decision Making*, edited by Derek J. Koehler and Nigel Harvey, 62–88. Oxford: Blackwell.

Goldberg, Yoav and Omer Levy. 2014. 'word2vec Explained: Deriving Mikolov et al's negative-sampling word-embedding method', arXiv:1402.3722.

Grize, Jean-Blaise. 1974. 'Logique mathématique, logique naturelle et modèles', *Jahresbericht der Schweizerischen Geisteswissenschaftlichen Gesellschaft*: 201–7.

Henry, Desmond Paul. 1963. 'Was Saint Anselm Really a Realist?', *Ratio* 5(2): 181–9.

Henry, Desmond Paul. 1974. *Commentary on De Grammatico: The historical-logical dimensions of a dialogue of St. Anselm's*. Dordrecht: Reidel.

Herstein, Israel Nathan. 1975. *Topics in Algebra*. 2nd edn. New York: Wiley.

Hestenes, David. 1999. *New Foundations for Classical Mechanics*. 2nd edn. Dordrecht: Kluwer Academic.

Highsmith, James A. 2001. *History: The Agile Manifesto*. Accessed 6 September 2022. http://agilemanifesto.org/history.html

Highsmith, James A. 2002a. *Agile Software Development Ecosystems*. Boston, MA: Addison-Wesley.

Highsmith, James A. 2002b. 'Agile Software Development: Why it's hot!', *Informit*, 15 March. Accessed 6 September 2022. http://www.informit.com/articles/article.aspx?p=25930&seqNum=4

Hirschheim, Rudy and Heinz K. Klein. 1989. 'Four Paradigms of Information Systems Development', *Communications of the ACM* 32(10): 1,199–216.

Holton, Gerald James. 1988. *Thematic Origins of Scientific Thought: Kepler to Einstein*. Revised edn. Cambridge, MA: Harvard University Press.

Ito, Joichi. 2018. *The Practice of Change*. Keio University, Tokyo.

Ito, Joichi. 2019a. 'Resisting Reduction: A manifesto'. Version 1.2. *Journal of Design and Science* 3 (20 February). https://doi.org/10.21428/8f7503e4

Ito, Joichi. 2019b. 'Forget about Artificial Intelligence, Extended Intelligence is the Future', *Wired*, 24 April. Accessed 6 September 2022. https://www.wired.co.uk/article/artificial-intelligence-extended-intelligence

Krizhevsky, Alex, Ilya Sutskever and Geoffrey E. Hinton. 2012. 'ImageNet Classification with Deep Convolutional Neural Networks'. In *Proceedings of the 25th International Conference on Neural Information Processing Systems*, edited by Pereira Fernando, Christopher J.C. Burges, Léon Bottou and Kilian Q. Weinberger, vol. 1, 1097–105. Red Hook, NY: Curran Associates, Inc.

Kurzweil, Raymond. 2005. *The Singularity is Near: When humans transcend biology*. New York: Viking.

Lambert, Karel and Bas C. van Fraassen. 1972. *Derivation and Counterexample: An introduction to philosophical logic*. Belmont, CA: Dickenson.

LeCun, Yann, Yoshua Bengio and Geoffrey Hinton. 2015. 'Deep Learning', *Nature* 521(7553): 436–44.

Levy, Omer and Yoav Goldberg. 2014. 'Neural Word Embedding as Implicit Matrix Factorization'. In *Advances in Neural Information Processing Systems 27* (NIPS 2014), edited by Zoubin Ghahramani, Max Welling, Corinna Cortes, Neil D. Lawrence and Kilian Q. Weinberger, 2177–85. Red Hook, NY: Curran Associates, Inc. Accessed 6 September 2022. http://papers.nips.cc/paper/5477-neural-word-embedding-as-implicit-matrix-factorization.pdf

McCarty, Willard. 2019. 'Being Heuristical', *Humanist Discussion Group* 33(317) (15 October).

McCulloch, Warren S. and Walter Pitts. 1943. 'A Logical Calculus of the Ideas Immanent in Nervous Activity', *Bulletin of Mathematical Biophysics* 5: 115–33.

McGann, Jerome J. 1991. *The Textual Condition*. Princeton, NJ: Princeton University Press.

McGann, Jerome J. 2001. *Radiant Textuality: Literature after the world wide web*. New York: Palgrave.

McGann, Jerome J. 2003. 'Texts in N-Dimensions and Interpretation in a New Key (Discourse and Interpretation in N-Dimensions)', *Text Technology* 2: 1–18.

McGann, Jerome J. 2007. 'Database, Interface and Archival Fever', *Profession* (*PMLA*) 122(5): 1588–92.

McGann, Jerome J. 2013. 'Philology in a New Key', *Critical Inquiry* 39(2): 327–46.

McLuhan, Marshall. 1964. *Understanding Media: The extensions of man*. New York: McGraw-Hill.

Mandelbaum, Maurice. 1977. *The Anatomy of Historical Knowledge*. Baltimore, MD: Johns Hopkins University Press.

Maturana, Humberto R. and Francisco J. Varela. 1980. *Autopoiesis and Cognition: The realization of the living*. Dordrecht: Reidel.

Mazurs, Edward G. 1974. *Graphic Representations of the Periodic System During One Hundred Years*. Tuscaloosa, AL: University of Alabama Press.

Merleau-Ponty, Maurice. 1968. *The Visible and the Invisible*, trans. Alphonso Lingis. Evanston, IL: Northwestern University Press.

Mnif, Moez and Christian Müller-Schloer. 2006. 'Quantitative Emergence'. In *SMCals/ 06: Proceedings of the 2006 IEEE Mountain Workshop on Adaptive and Learning Systems*, edited by Yuichi Motai and Bernard Sick, 78–84. Piscataway, NJ: IEEE.

Müller-Schloer, Christian, Hartmut Schmeck and Theo Ungerer (eds). 2011. *Organic Computing – A paradigm shift for complex systems*. Basel: Springer/Birkhäuser.

Nagel, Ernest. 1954. Review of *The Philosophy of Science* by Stephen Toulmin. *Mind* N.S. 63(251): 4034.

Nerur, Sridhar, Alan Cannon, VenuGopal Balijepally and Philip Bond. 2010. 'Towards an Understanding of the Conceptual Underpinnings of Agile Development Methodologies'. In *Agile Software Development: Current research and future directions*, edited by Torgeir Dingsøyr, Tore Dybå and Nils Brede Moe Dingsøyr, 15–29. Berlin: Springer.

Parker-Rhodes, Arthur Frederick. 1978. *Inferential Semantics*. Hassocks: Harvester Press.

Peirce, Charles Sanders. 1878. 'Deduction, Induction, and Hypothesis', *Popular Science Monthly* 13: 470–82.

Peirce, Charles Sanders. 1880. 'On the Algebra of Logic', *American Journal of Mathematics* 3(1): 15–57.

Peirce, Charles Sanders. 1901. *The Proper Treatment of Hypotheses: A preliminary chapter, toward an examination of Hume's Argument against Miracles, in its logic and in its history*. MS [R] 692.

Peirce, Charles Sanders. 1931–58. *Collected Papers*, vols I–VIII, edited by Charles Hartshorne, Paul Weiss and Arthur W. Burks. Cambridge, MA: Harvard University Press.

Plutniak, Sébastien. 2017. 'L'innovation méthodologique, entre bifurcation personnelle et formation des disciplines: les entrées en archéologie de Georges Laplace et de Jean-Claude Gardin', *Revue d'histoire des sciences humaines* 31.

Plutniak, Sébastien. 2018. 'Aux prémices des humanités numériques? La première analyse automatisée d'un réseau économique ancien (Gardin & Garelli, 1961). Réalisation, conceptualisation, réception'. *ARCS: Analyse de réseaux pour les sciences sociales*. Accessed 6 September 2022. https://hal.archives-ouvertes.fr/hal-01870945/document

Rausch, Andreas, Jörg Müller, Ursula Goltz and Dirk Niebuhr. 2012. 'IT Ecosystems: A new paradigm for engineering complex adaptive software systems'. In *Complex Environment Engineering: Proceedings of the 2012 6th IEEE International Conference on Digital Ecosystems and Technologies (DEST 2012)*, 31–6. Piscataway, NJ: IEEE. Accessed 6 September 2022. https://ieeexplore.ieee.org/xpl/conhome/6222390/proceeding

Raymond, Darrell Ronald, Frank William Tompa and Derick Wood. 1992. 'Markup Reconsidered', paper presented at the First International Workshop on Principles of Document Processing, Washington, DC (21–23 October). Accessed 6 September 2022. http://citeseerx.ist.psu.edu/viewdoc/download?doi=10.1.1.73.2348&rep=rep1&type=pdf

Renear, Allen H. 2001. 'The Descriptive/Procedural Distinction is Flawed', *Markup Languages: Theory & Practice* 2(4): 411–20.

Ryle, Gilbert. 1949. *The Concept of Mind*. London: Hutchinson.

Shore, James and Shane Warden. 2008. *The Art of Agile Development*. Sebastopol, CA: O'Reilly.

Simons, Peter. 2016. 'Who's Afraid of Higher-Order Logic?' In *The Limits of Logic: Higher-order logic and the Löwenheim-Skolem theorem*, edited by Stuart Shapiro, 197–204. Abingdon: Routledge.

Spencer Brown, George. 1969. *Laws of Form*. London: George Allen and Unwin.

Sperberg-McQueen, C. Michael, Claus Huitfeldt and Allen Renear. 2000. 'Meaning and Interpretation of Markup', *Markup Languages: Theory & practice* 2(3): 215–34.

Stambovsky, Phillip. 1988. 'Metaphor and Historical Understanding', *History and Theory* 27(2): 125–34.

Stiegler, Bernard. 1994. *La Technique et le temps*, vol. 1, *La faute d'Épiméthée*. Paris: Galilée, Cité des Sciences et de l'industrie.

Stiegler, Bernard. 1998. *Technics and Time*, vol. 1, *The Fault of Epimetheus*, trans. Richard Beardsworth and George Collins. Stanford, CA: Stanford University Press.

Tecuci, Gheorghe, Dorin Marcu, Mihai Boicu and David A. Schum. 2016a. *Knowledge Engineering: Building cognitive assistants for evidence-based reasoning*. New York: Cambridge University Press.

Tecuci, Gheorghe, David A. Schum, Dorin Marcu and Mihai Boicu. 2016b. *Intelligence Analysis as Discovery of Evidence, Hypotheses, and Arguments: Connecting the dots*. New York: Cambridge University Press.

Toulmin, Stephen Edelston. 1953. *The Philosophy of Science: An introduction*. London: Hutchinson.

Toulmin, Stephen Edelston. 2003. *The Uses of Argument*. Updated edn. Cambridge: Cambridge University Press.

Varela, Francisco J., Eleanor Rosch and Evan Thompson. 1991. *The Embodied Mind: Cognitive science and human experience*. Cambridge, MA: MIT Press.

Vinge, Vernor. 1993. 'The Coming Technological Singularity: How to survive in the post-human era'. *NASA. Lewis Research Center, Vision 21: Interdisciplinary Science and Engineering in the Era of Cyberspace* 21: 11–22. Accessed 6 September 2022. https://ntrs.nasa.gov/search.jsp?R=19940022856

von Foerster, Heinz. 2003. *Understanding Understanding: Essays on cybernetics and cognition.* New York: Springer.

Vuillemin, Jules. 1996. *Necessity or Contingency: The master argument.* Stanford, CA: Center for the Study of Language and Information.

Weizsäcker, Viktor von. 1927. 'Reflexgesetze'. In *Handbuch der normalen und pathologischen Physiologie*, Bd. 10, *Spezielle Physiologie des Zentralnervensystem der Wirbeltiere*, 35–102. Berlin: Springer.

Wiener, Norbert. 1950. *The Human Use of Human Beings: Cybernetics and society.* Boston, MA: Houghton Mifflin.

Würtz, Rolf P. (ed.). 2008. *Organic Computing.* Berlin: Springer.

10
From TACT to CATMA; or, a mindful approach to text annotation and analysis

Jan Christoph Meister

Thinking about interpretation

In his 2008 'Thinking about interpretation: *Pliny* and scholarship in the humanities', John Bradley set out with the sobering observation that irrespective of some 50 years of research into humanities computing,

> our effect on how most scholars work has been very small. Although tremendously innovative techniques have been developed by members of our community, few, if any, scholars from outside the DH community have taken them up. (Bradley 2008, 263)

One-and-a-half decades later this assessment, unfortunately, still holds. The digital humanities may well have turned out the most successful *institutional* venture in the humanities since the millennium – alas, no other recent methodological 'turn' in the humanities has resulted in a comparable number of dedicated funding lines, the founding of institutional entities such as departments and schools, the establishing of BA, MA and PhD curricula and degrees, and a significant demand for qualified junior academics.[1] But this metric is biased: for DH's *conceptual* role in and for the humanities at large, seen from the perspective of the traditional disciplines, is at best still that of a *Hilfsdisziplin* (ancillary science) and at worst that of a *parvenu* competitor who managed to nail a flimsy humanistic flag to the post of digitisation.[2] Indeed, if one settles for the modest former role the question becomes even more perplexing: why is there so little interest in DH's digital tools and methods among traditionalists? One methodological lacuna which might contribute to the lack of DH uptake was already identified by Bradley (2008),[3] who found existing DH tools to be conceptually at odds with many traditional humanists' reliance on associative, at times unstructured and recursive routines of exploring, comparing and mapping source documents, secondary documents and external references in a cumulative fashion – in other words, on a *modus operandi* that defies computational formalisation in terms of linear workflows. Bradley's own development *Pliny* was therefore a conscious attempt to prototype a working environment that would respect and support such exploratory practices.

More recent developments in DH methods have taken a different tack. Computational literary studies (CLS) in particular has spearheaded a trend toward quantitative modelling and analysis of literary data, be it primary (actual literary texts) or secondary (reception data, bibliometric data). The new approach has sparked considerable criticism, much of it polemical and ill-informed, yet some also voicing noteworthy concerns about a lack of rigour and transparency in how the respective quantitative methods are being selected and applied, as well as about the tendency of practitioners to present speculative, analogy-based rather than evidence-based justifications for having chosen a quantitative approach toward an object domain which in and by itself is phenomenologically extremely complex, yet at the same time not really a numeric 'big data' phenomenon per se. Or as Da puts it: 'The thing about literature is that there isn't a lot of it, comparatively speaking' (Da 2019).

The sparsity of raw digital data can however be compensated for by casting one's net beyond primary texts and other cultural objects and following the example of the social sciences, namely: shift DH's interest from the phenomenology of the object itself to the empirical traces of the social practices around it, and from the unique expression manifested in the form of an individual symbolic artefact to the multitude of manifestations of historical practices motivated by, and at the same time shaping, entire classes and genres of artefacts, such as texts, paintings and performances. This reorientation was proclaimed a future necessity already some 40 years ago, long before Moretti coined the term *distant reading*. However, this initial call was motivated not by pragmatic but by conceptual considerations. In 1978 Susan Wittig found the (then) field of humanities computing to be methodologically constrained by its unconscious allegiance to American New Criticism, which elevated the artistic object to a self-contained sign system. Influenced by contemporary reader response theory, Wittig argued that one would have to re-think the notion of 'text' as such in order for humanities computing to become more relevant to textual studies. She concluded:

> I am suggesting that we turn from our analyses of the signal system of the text to a new study of how, and why, and under what conditions, the text is fulfilled with meaning by its readers. (Wittig 1977, 214)

Against this backdrop, Bradley's 2008 'Thinking about Interpretation' was published just as DH approached their next crossroads – the one where data science and statistics would intersect with declarative and taxonomy driven methods of computational literary studies. The express aim of *Pliny* was to serve as a proof of concept, namely that a computational approach is not necessarily deductive, or as Bradley states: 'Pliny is meant to support scholarship when it is still "pre-ontological" – before concepts and their relationships to evidence from sources have solidified' (Bradley 2008, 19).[4]

Today's statistical and probabilistic approach towards humanistic objects is by comparison 'post-ontological': it is data-driven, no longer theory- or taxonomy-driven. Or so it seems. Consider for example the modelling of a semantic theme in terms of a statistical TOPIC: the approach is based on the principal assumption that this aspect of human language use, whatever the intentional motives transparent to the speakers, can be adequately modelled by way of a context-blind genetic algorithm. In the specific case of the LDA algorithm of Blei, Ng and Jordan (Blei et al. 2003) this assumption leads to the idea of *latent* expression of TOPICS through words. A word is thus not conceptualised as a pre-determined or intentionally selected Saussurean surface-level vector from a *signifiant* to a *signifié*, but rather as a node from which a multitude of stronger and weaker links reach out across the document's network. As a humanist one could argue that LDA thus implicitly acknowledges polysemy – but this is of course pointing out a conceptual 'family resemblance' rather than a logical connection. After all, the algorithm models collocation probability, not semantics, for it is conceptually an import from gene analysis (cf. Pritchard et al. 2000).

Similar conceptual premises do of course also abound in the seemingly 'pre-ontological' practices exercised by the traditional humanities scholars who *Pliny* aimed to support. Yet the hermeneutic circle, when travelled individually, does not necessarily need to be modelled or formalised in order to function. However, if we want to further our critical discourse, we will aim for a clearer understanding of how the traditional

humanities progress from the unstructured to the structured: exploratory, recursively, in trial and error mode and most of all, by way of critical
discourse, variation and continuous approximation. Developing a system
like *Pliny* is therefore not just a matter of providing a handy tool; it is at
the same time an exercise in modelling and making more explicit established pre-digital research practices in the humanities.

The digital turn has presented the humanities with a unique opportunity to reconceptualise their objects, and their practices, in terms of a
double take on structuring the unstructured. Reconceptualising our traditional objects of study – texts, paintings, music – has been made easier
by technology; we can nowadays almost effortlessly transform the fleet-
ing and continuous sensual phenomena that are presented to us in various modalities into the abstract lingua franca of digital data: into discrete,
computable points of observation. Reconceptualising and explicating in
terms of their complex logic and workflows the humanistic practices by
which we operate on these objects, whether presented in digital or in
'analogue' form, is a more complicated thing. Indeed, to formalise and
model an epistemology as well as an epistemic field of practice – that is,
the implicit assumptions, explicit theorems and exploratory, analytical
and synthetic methods which a domain specific discipline has developed
over time – from the perspective of measurability and computability is a
formidable task. Moretti's 'Conjectures on World Literature' presented an
attempt to showcase the potential of such an undertaking for one such
discipline, namely comparative literature (Moretti 2000). For humanities computing as it relates to the humanities in general this prospect had
however already been pointed out some 10 years prior by McCarty, who
observed that tools, such as the new digital tools:

> are perceptual agents. A new tool is not just a bigger lever and more
> secure fulcrum, rather a new way of conceptualizing the world, e.g.
> as something that can be levered. (McCarty 1996)

The digital tool whose conceptual affordances motivated McCarty's
reflection in this instance was TACT, a suite of text analytical computing
tools developed at the University of Toronto.[5] TACT's principal designer
was, again, John Bradley, and it is fascinating to re-read his concise
description of the program's functionality some 30 years later as an
implicit anticipation of its epistemological leveraging potential. Bradley
found three functional aspects of TACT to be particularly relevant: interactivity, index-based text analysis, and the ability to process text with
dense structural markup that may be organised in multiple, parallel

hierarchies. Among contemporary readers familiar with the then nascent OHCO debate,[6] the latter feature would indeed have deserved particular attention – but it seems that Bradley was simply too modest. Mentioning this particular aspect only in passing he wrote:

> *TACT* is interactive. It specializes in quickly answering questions related to a work's vocabulary. *TACT* achieves this relatively quick response time by working with a textual database, which contains not only the text, but a complete index of all the word forms in the text, with pointers to their position in the text ... *TACT* was designed to support texts with a rich structural Markup. Within *TACT* you can code such things as page numbers, speakers in a play, or other types of structural divisions . . . Furthermore, the different tags do not need to fit into a single hierarchical structure. Indeed, multiple hierarchical structures can be represented in parallel. (Bradley 1996)

Modelling the cyclical knowledge generation process

In the late 1970s many of the humanities disciplines began to refocus from the investigation of canonised aesthetic artefacts to the analysis and critique of norms and preferences that manifest themselves in how a society defines its canons and how it engages with them in cultural practice. If indeed contemporary DH has begun to follow the same post-structuralist trajectory, then ours is nevertheless a somewhat differently motivated *cultural turn*. For its ideological motivation, the enlightened historical-critical interest in the 'slaughterhouse' of the extra-canonical goes uncannily hand-in-hand with the methodological exigencies of big data-centred research.

We should therefore take care not to fall for the empiricist 'data science' narrative and rather consider the range of methodological options in more abstract terms. In dealing with symbolic artefacts and practices computationally DH can:

- investigate such symbolic artefacts and practices directly, but restrict the analytical procedures to interpretation free surface level phenomena, objective structural properties and taxonomically robust metadata; or
- re-define the object domain as such and focus on data-intense second-order phenomena of 'signs in practice' which manifest themselves around defined types of symbolic objects and practices; or

- attempt to model the traditional hermeneutic approach to symbolic artefacts and practices using computational means, and then methodically scale up from scarce data and exemplary exploration to more extensive and robust experimental configurations.

These options are neither mutually exclusive nor prescriptive: they constitute ideal types that may help us to identify better the nature of our own approach. The one which I will present in the following falls into the third category. Its strategy is to push the limits of the qualitative approach against the backdrop of a more complex, hermeneutic text and text annotation model. This vision is the underpinning of CATMA (https://catma.de), an open source software and web application for collaborative text annotation and analysis.[7] Its development began in 2008 and, thanks to project grants awarded by various funding agencies and bodies (including the Universität Hamburg, the German Academic Exchange Service DAAD, Google Inc., the German Ministry for Science and Education BMBF and the German Research Foundation DFG), has been ongoing since. CATMA is related to Bradley's TACT not only acronymically (*Computer Assisted Text Markup and Annotation* vs *Textual Analysis Computing Tools*), but indeed conceptually.[8] And this conceptual affinity can be precisely defined as:

$$Ix = i \, (Ix{-}\alpha, \, s(Ix{-}\beta, \, t(x{-}\,\beta)), \, t(x{-}\,\alpha))$$

This formula is not my invention; it is the brainchild of Manfred Thaller, who uses it to pin down his core concern with the way in which computer science thinks about 'information' (Thaller 2018). Thaller explains it as follows.

> To be read as: The information available at time x is the result of an interpretative process i() which has interpreted the information available at an earlier point of time x–α over the time span t between x and α, in the context of a knowledge generating process s(). This knowledge generating process in turn has been running over the time span t between x and β, using the available information at the point of the time preceding x by β. (Thaller 2018)

Thaller concludes that the 'implication of the ideas above is, that no such thing as static information exists; "representing it" just captures a snapshot of a continuously running algorithm' (Thaller 2018). In the annotation model presented below I will build on this observation and refer to the *axis of process*. However, this functional model will be extended further by an *axis of discourse* and an *axis of context*. All three axes need to be taken into consideration in order to conceptualise annotation as an interpretive (rather than merely declarative) activity that contributes to *meaning-making*, albeit on an elementary level.

From meaning-making to hermeneutics

Meaning-making as a defining desire and activity in humans was brought to particular attention by the psychiatrist and Holocaust survivor Viktor Frankl in his book *Man's Search for Meaning* (Frankl 1946). Of course, the subjective interpretation of life events and experiences in existential terms is one thing; the interpretation of symbolic phenomena, such as texts, which is motivated by a defined (pragmatic or aesthetic) interest is quite another – and even more so when the latter activity is undertaken in a disciplinary context which stipulates a theoretical and methodological framework. Yet in a structural perspective both are variants of the same semiotic activity: the activation of referential vectors from *signifiant* to *signifié*.

Against this backdrop, highly context dependent, unstructured interpretation practices constitute a particular methodological challenge for DH formalisation. The more *meaning-making* like, that is, the more subjective, historically contingent and idiosyncratic someone's interpretation of a given text, the less likely we are to capture all the variables and factors that have gone into producing the interpretive output. But this boundary is not incontestable, provided we gain a clearer understanding of what interpretation itself actually *is* or, rather, has developed into as a scholarly practice over time.

Today's practice of philological text interpretation is indebted, among others, to the development of the method of explication of textual meaning known as *hermeneutics*. Its theoretical and philosophical reflection as a scholarly method begins with Schleiermacher and others in the late eighteenth century.[9] As such it is based on two conceptual tenets: one, the interdependency of analytic and synthetic approaches to text which Friedrich Ast, the inventor of the term *hermeneutics*, stipulated as follows: 'The foundational law of all understanding and knowledge is to find the spirit of the whole through the individual, and through the whole to grasp the individual' (Ast 1808, 178, my translation). Two, the subjectivity, context dependency and hence historicity of interpretation which therefore cannot be conceptualised as a simple, unilinear transformation of 'text' into 'meaning', but which must rather be understood as an open-ended, recursive process of approximation. These two characteristics contribute to an epistemological condition later to become known as the 'hermeneutic circle'.

Acknowledgement vs refutation of the historicity of textual meaning, the *leitmotif* of nineteenth-century Western thought, as well as opposing views on whether it is the author's or the reader's prerogative to determine textual meaning, have continued to shape theories and methods of text interpretation from Hegel to Nietzsche. This debate continued well into the twentieth century, from Russian Formalism to Structuralism, Post Structuralism and Deconstruction. But the main *methodological* innovation introduced by eighteenth-century hermeneutics into the practice of textual interpretation has remained uncontested: our exegetic practices are based on the premise that the meaning of a text cannot be fixed dogmatically, but should rather be the product of rational discourse which takes into account textual (linguistic and structural) as well as contextual (historical) evidence. Or to put it differently, hermeneutics has introduced us to the idea that the interpretation of textual meaning is necessarily *parameterised* and *dynamic*.

What, then, is the *methodological* constraint that has to date precluded the hermeneutic activity of parameterised, dynamic interpretation from being successfully modelled and supported by twenty-first-century DH?

Reading vs interpreting

At the core of this problem lies the distinction between first order '*Bedeutung*' (pragmatic *meaning* as the referential denotation regularly assigned to a given lexical term) and second-order '*Sinn*' (*sense*, the value and subjective importance *for us* that we assign to a word or a phrase as encountered in a given context that is both textual and existential) which the mathematician, logician and philosopher Frege has pointed out (Frege 1892). First order *meaning* or denotation is relatively easy to look up and deduce; this is the activity which we normally call *reading*. Humans can do it, and machines can do it equally well (if not better and faster) provided the text is grammatical, and the correct grammar and lexicon are available. Of course, for a text to become 'machine readable' in a technical sense, some preceding operations will have to be performed, such as the translation of pixels into letters and other typographical information in ASCII or Unicode encoding and then further into a Text Encoding Initiative (TEI) notation. But the principle remains the same: *reading*, whether performed by a machine or by a human being, relies on rule-based transformation, look-up and combination procedures. In other words, it is driven by and can be modelled via formulae.

What clearly sets the human reader apart from the computational is their response to an irregular, non-grammatical or innovative case of language use. Unless provided with a choice of grammars and rule sets the machine reader will cease operating and return an error message. As human readers we tend to react differently – we will try to naturalise, to 'make sense' of, the apparent 'error'. The first strategy for doing so is to try and correct the text in order to make it grammatical again. If that attempt fails a second strategy comes into play: we can switch from first order exploration of domain-specific denotational meaning to a less formalised, more flexible kind of grammar that enables us to evaluate the statement in terms of Frege's definition of *sense*, of *meaning in existential context*. This seemingly redundant hermeneutic iteration is triggered as soon as we are not satisfied with a mere 'reading' of the passage in question. In such an instance the mere denotational *reading* does not *make sense* – that is to say, it fails to explain the motivational context and backdrop of the utterance. Indeed, very often human readers are not satisfied with finding out *what* has been said anyhow – they also want to know *why* it has been said and what the *relevance* of the utterance is.

Once we find ourselves at the threshold of *meaning-making* in this emphatic sense, things become significantly more complicated as suddenly a multitude of perspectives appear – for example, *relevance* as perceived by the speaker (narrator), or by the author, or by the reader themself. *Making sense* of statements that cannot simply be 'read' and taken at face (and even less so: at linguistic surface) value is essentially what hermeneutics enables us to do in a controlled fashion. First order grammar, like any formalism, tries to capture the *logic* of the phenomenon (in this case: language use) in an abstract, de-contextualised and generalisable manner. Hermeneutics however adds contingency to logic by considering the criterion of *relevance*. It does so by re-introducing the notion of context dependency into the conceptual model of the linguistic or symbolic phenomena that we encounter. Scholarly hermeneutics in the tradition of Schleiermacher and Gadamer focuses on this second-order functional dimension and stipulates criteria such as plausibility, discursiveness, rationality and salience which one might consider as regulative filters in its processing formalism. Hermeneutics is thus neither 'ungrammatical' nor in principle impossible to support by computational means – rather, it employs multi-level operating principles of interpretation which are more complex and challenging to express in a well-formed mathematical or logical formalism.

Modelling the hermeneutic circle: markup as annotation[10]

How can we tackle this problem in developing an annotation tool? By conceptualising digital text markup as one specific implementation of a more general, fundamental and richer practice that plays a crucial role in the hermeneutic approach to text as described above: that of text annotation. For in a cultural as well as a methodological perspective, text annotation is not only markup's historical forerunner, but also constitutes a significantly richer and more varied metatextual practice. One of the most prominent examples in this regard is the technique of interlinear annotation used by monastic scribes. It demonstrates how long before the digital turn different text types and their pragmatic function – such as religious and juridic exegesis of scripture and law – triggered the development of conventions for annotating and referencing source texts. These conventions are the antecedents of today's formal referencing schemata, and markup as a technique of adding declarative metadata to digital source documents is thus merely a recent, technology-driven derivate that employs a new set of media-specific conventions.

Markup itself is of course also varied. Coombs et al. (1987) were among the first to propose a systematic, functional differentiation of these variants by distinguishing between *punctuational, presentational, procedural, descriptive, referential* and *meta-markup*. At the same time, the authors already highlighted descriptive markup as the variant of particular relevance to the human reader.[11] Twenty-five years later Nyhan makes a similar point. She observes that descriptive markup 'can be applied to any kind or genre of text; indeed, any information that can be consistently represented using a symbol of some kind and then digitized can be marked up' (Nyhan 2012, 123).

However, the descriptive markup which Coombs et al. as well as Nyhan refer to is in practice declarative rather than interpretive. The descriptive schema, its categories and the type as well as the range of possible values which can be assigned to a selected character string – a morpheme, word, sentence, paragraph – are in most instances predefined and cannot be extended or modified ad hoc. In other words, the 'description' is again a declaration (note Nyhan's qualification 'consistently' in the above quote); it is constrained by a defined ontology and metric, both of which remain agnostic to the specific research question and text under investigation. To 'describe' a text document in TEI or to parse it and apply automatic POS tagging are thus operations based on the same deductive approach: in either case the referenced character string – be it a single word, be it an entire document – is conceptually sorted into an abstract table and assigned one or more values therein. This operation proceeds top down, not bottom up, as the table itself remains non-negotiable.

To date only few DH scholars have reacted to the methodological reductionism inherent in all types of digital markup listed by Coombs et al. – declarative, procedural, representational – by explicitly calling for the development of a completely different, namely an interpretive or hermeneutic, markup concept. Piez, for example, demands a 'markup that is deliberately interpretive' (Piez 2010); such a type of markup would 'not [be] limited to describing aspects or features of a text that can be formally defined and objectively verified. Instead, it is devoted to recording a scholar's or analyst's observations and conjectures in an open-ended way' (Piez 2010). But as rightly emphasised by Caton (2001), it is in fact not the choice of markup schema that counts in this hermeneutic perspective; rather it is the underlying concept of text as such. He comments:

> When OHCO encourages encoders to see a written text as a thing, they stay above the content and only drop down to engage with the text as message to identify the occasional editorial object whose nature is not obvious from its appearance. But when encoders see the written text as a communicative act, they must participate in the act: take on the role of hearer, attend to what the text says, and identify the speaker's intentions not just from the words' semantics but also from the attitudes conveyed. Metaphorically, encoders must be down at what would be the lowest level of an OHCO tree . . . As its practitioners well know, all encoding interprets, all encoding mediates. There is no 'pure' reading experience to sully. We don't carry messages, we reproduce them – a very different kind of involvement. We are not neutral; by encoding a written text we become part of the communicative act it represents. (Caton 2001)

This is the model of 'interactional encoding' – and to implement it in a digital tool we will have to relativise (but not necessarily discard: disagreement on certain textual features expressed via markup can only become productive against the backdrop of conventional 'ground truths') the ideal of reaching perfect inter-annotator agreement. At the same time, it would be naïve to ignore that the declaration of absolute, objective norms tends to serve a methodological as much as an ideological purpose. In DH the rationale for declaring inter-annotator agreement as a normative goal is equally programmatic as it is pragmatic: for example, machine learning, which holds substantial promises for the automation of aspects of humanities research practice, benefits substantially if the machine can be trained on unambiguous 'gold standard' annotation data.

Current introductions to DH nevertheless tend to present the ideal of non-ambiguous text markup as an undisputed norm.[12] This technological pragmatism is indicative of a methodological problem which van Zundert has termed the *Computationality of Hermeneutics* (van Zundert 2016). Van Zundert postulates that hermeneutic considerations should no longer be addressed merely 'after the algorithmic fact', but rather upfront. In other words, hermeneutic desiderata should already inform the computer science aided development of the concepts, codes and models which form the basis for any digital representation and analysis of life world phenomena and aesthetic artefacts.

As far as annotation is concerned, the main question to be considered 'before the algorithmic fact' is of a pragmatic order: why do readers actually bother to comment on a text in the first place? All variants of metalingual utterances, I would hold, have in common the same rhetorical motivation: to make explicit, document and share one or more observations and understandings of a source text, or of a part thereof. Annotation is thus always a type of communication with the next reader, whether it is expressed in the marginal form of a <b> tag or as eloquently as a commentary in an editorial footnote makes no difference. In other words, hermeneutics calls on us to conceptualise annotation (and thus in principle terms also markup) from the point of discourse pragmatics. In this perspective two boundary conditions of annotation become apparent: one, annotation is necessarily a form of metatext relating to an object text. Once annotation loses this nexus and becomes autonomous it turns into an object text itself.[13] Two, annotation is ideally a communication directed at someone other than merely the annotator himself or herself. Where it turns into an auto-communication it attains the quality of a *Privatsprache* (Wittgenstein) which may of course still have an aesthetic or mnemonic function, but no longer a discursive one.[14]

A hermeneutically inspired DH practice therefore requires a compatible model of markup which is conceptualised primarily in a discourse pragmatic rather than in a technological perspective. Such a model must be able to capture and represent the logic and workflow of practices that go beyond the base level encoding and declarative explication of object data, in particular the philological and critical practices not yet (or perhaps even not necessarily at all) oriented towards enabling a computer to perform algorithmic DH operations on the source text. *Horribile dictu*: putting this model into practice will also require us to not only tolerate, but in fact *facilitate* via a digital tool the communication, to the 'next reader', of inter-annotator disagreement, ambiguity and polyvalence, and the provenance and evolution (or 'versioning') of annotations across annotators and annotation iterations. But we can only strive for these goals if we accept the premise that non-contradiction and consistency are not intrinsic requirements of either annotation or markup. Indeed, both criteria constitute pragmatically and technologically defined constraints which in most instances are 'algorithmic facts' rather than phenomenological essentials. Depending on their pragmatic purpose, different types of markup will thus require different types of specification; however, all types of markup must share the fundamental discursive ethos of annotation.

But what exactly do we mean when we refer to 'annotation'? Unsworth (2000) lists *annotating* as one of seven 'scholarly primitives'–*discovering, annotating, comparing, referring, sampling, illustrating, representing* – which represent the fundamental and widely shared epistemic practices of humanistic research at large. In traditional literary studies, for example, this fundamental practice is encountered at three levels of complexity.

1. Base-level markup of linguistic, formal and structural features of text (layout, typography, grammar, and structural entities such as verse, paragraph, chapter) that in and by themselves are semantically neutral – that is, they do not carry an inherent or conventionalised meaning.
2. Explication of local semantic phenomena – this variant requires the annotator to process and interpret the semantic content of a larger section of text, in other words one that can be read as a particular statement or proposition about the text's reference domain, or about the text and its functions itself. This is the medium level of complexity which Piez refers to as 'hermeneutic annotation' (Piez 2010). While annotators tend to make use of disciplinary terminology in order to explicate semantics at this medium level, they will generally not have recourse to a specified taxonomy.
3. Relevance- and *meaning*-oriented text commentary, which explains, contextualises and cross-references specific features, statements and propositions of a text against the backdrop of a holistic interpretation of the entire document, and with a view to linking it to larger

entities – such as an author's work, an epoch, a genre, a critical discourse, a socio-historical trend, an aesthetic program, etc. Ideally, this type of philological text commentary should operate within the confines of a fully developed interpretive theory; in reality, however, such theoretical premises are often communicated only implicitly. Because of their complexity, their contextual reach and their exploratory, highly contingent nature, text commentaries cannot be modelled and produced digitally.

This three-level distinction differentiates annotation types along the axis of increasing semantic and thus hermeneutic complexity. With regard to technological complexity one might complement this with a second systematic which distinguishes annotation types in terms of the medial distance between an annotation and its reference domain – the annotated string – in the source text. In the print medium certain types of elementary annotation were inscribed directly into the source string, for example by using bold characters. By contrast, all SGML-based digital texts conceptually 'unflatten' the layers of source text and annotation right from the start.[15] At the same time the preference for inline tags in many markup schemes nevertheless conceptually emulate as closely as possible the spatial proximity between text and text markup which makes the traditional print medium so comfortable to process (and which is then fully emulated on-screen anyhow). More importantly, the pre-digital traditional practice of text studies had already developed a conventionalised, implicit semantics of spatial proximity between source document and annotation: the greater the distance between an object text and the metatextual annotation, the more likely a competent reader is to regard it, in the terminology of Boot (2009), as an interpretive *mesotext* which is destined to contribute to the eventual formulation of an independent secondary *metatext*. In traditional manuscripts and print this process of spatial as well as conceptual distancing begins with the progression from underlining to interlinear annotation and continues via the gloss, the margin commentary, the footnote, the endnote and the apparatus. Spatial proximity and distance between source document and annotation have thus attained a discourse pragmatic and rhetoric function – they are indicators for the status and ambit of the communicated 'reading'.

In the digital medium this valuable processing information can easily get lost when on-screen output conveniently hides all markup and 'flattens' the layers. But there are of course ample technological means (hover effects, pop-ups, integrated interactive data visualisations) that enable us to preserve and express this functional richness as well. Indeed, the

digital modelling of this particular aspect – the semantics of spatial proximity – in the relation between a source text and its annotations serves a
fundamental conceptual need that goes far beyond the emulation of traditional practices. This is where the controversy about inline vs standoff
markup becomes conceptual, rather than merely a quibble about technological constraints.[16] One of the main arguments pro standoff markup has
been the critique of inline markup's implicit OHCO (Ordered Hierarchy
of Content Objects) text model. Simply put, SGML inline markup with
closing tags cannot handle hierarchical overlaps in texts, such as that of
enjambement and verse in a poem, whereas standoff markup can. Yet it
is not just the source text whose internal organisation defies hierarchical
modelling and renders inline markup notoriously problematic: overlapping hierarchies, discontinuity and complex multidimensional layering
are also characteristics of readerly and scholarly practices and operations
performed on a text, as Buzzetti (2002) has pointed out.

Philological encounters with texts that are of this double 'overlapping' nature can in fact significantly benefit from giving the 'digital turn'
another, more ambitious spin. Before the advent of post-structuralism
many scholarly practices could still be adequately modelled on the basis of
an essentialist-hierarchical concept of text (primary objects and secondary
information resources), libraries (institutions for source object and knowledge management) and a clear-cut distinction between the roles of authors
(intentionally acting producers of texts), readers (lay recipients and interpreters of texts) and scholars and critics (authoritative instances). Twenty-
first-century textual practices, however, are by contrast characterised by
interconnectivity, flexibility of roles and competing conceptualisations of
text. A practice of 'literary annotation in the digital age' (Bauer and Zirker
2015) should accordingly no longer be modelled as one which is oriented
towards text objects in an essentialist sense and defined in terms of static
roles, but rather as one comprising a range of processes and events of reading, annotating, interpreting, evaluating, arguing; in short: as a discourse.

The practice of digital annotation therefore requires tools that allow
us to conceptualise the source text as well as its annotations alternatively
as nodes, or as edges in an *n*-dimensional, dynamically reconfigurable
network of textually encoded information. One of the agents in this
network is the reader, who, depending on their interest and method of
choice, will define, systematise and explore edges, nodes and clusters for
hermeneutic purposes. Digital models and technology make it far easier
for this agent to recombine, aggregate, reconfigure source and metadata
and capture as well as analyse and feedback processing information. For
a digital text hermeneutics this high-level model has some fundamental

consequences – most importantly, we are no longer required to conceptualise a text's interpretation as a finite whole. Rather, we can think of it as something dynamic, as one instance of 'output' that was generated from n-possible configurations of interpretive and declarative decisions made by one or more readers.

Against this backdrop standoff markup proves particularly suitable, in that it follows not a document, but a database-centred approach, as Schloen and Schloen point out:

> standoff markup deviates so much from the original markup metaphor that it no longer belongs within the document paradigm at all and is best implemented within the database paradigm. Standoff markup involves the digital representation of multiple readings of a text by means of separate data objects, one for each reading, with a system of pointers that explicitly connect the various readings to the text's components. But this amounts to a database solution to the problem. The best way to implement this solution is to abandon the use of a single long character sequence to represent a scholarly text – the document approach – in order to take advantage of the atomized data models and querying languages characteristic of database systems. (Schloen and Schloen 2014)

Yet if we want to employ standoff markup from the perspective of the database paradigm we must obviously also consider annotation itself as a type of data (meta-)modelling. With regard to data modelling practice in general, Flanders and Jannidis (2016) have suggested to distinguish *conceptual vs logical model* and *curation-driven vs research-driven modellers*. Building on their proposal, I would like to propose a matrix of four prototypical variants of digital annotation in which an annotator might 'datamodel' a given source text:

	conceptual model	logical model
interpretive digital annotating	hermeneutic 'bottom-up' annotation	explorative reading
declarative digital annotating	taxonomic 'top-down' annotation	formal categorisation

Figure 10.1 Prototypical variants of digital annotation as data modelling.

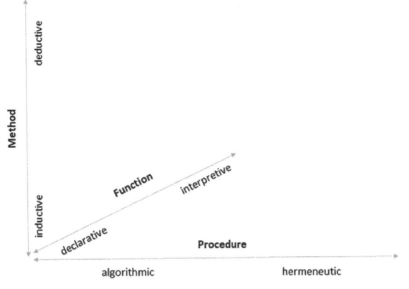

Figure 10.2 The three axes of digital text annotation.

In this matrix the qualifier *descriptive* has been re-labelled as *interpretive* because the latter fits the suggested discourse pragmatic model of annotation. Whereas declarative 'annotation as data modelling' approaches can already in many instances be performed automatically, exploratory bottom-up annotation can only be formalised via iterative approximation, be it 'manually' – that is, intellectually by human annotators who can abstract from concrete unstructured annotations by drawing on contextual knowledge and discussion among one another – or by machine learning.[17]

Importantly, though, the annotation variants which the above matrix juxtaposes categorically do in fact form a continuum: it makes no sense to distinguish dogmatically between inductive and deductive, between declarative and interpretive, and between 'manual' and automatic modes of annotation. One of the core features of a digital tool claiming to support annotation as a discursive practice of knowledge generation must be the ability to facilitate the gradual progression from structured to unstructured annotation and vice versa along the three axes of *Method*, *Function* and *Procedure*. In other words, such a tool needs to conceptualise 'annotation' as a vector within a multidimensional space which integrates a pragmatic, an epistemological and a technological dimension (see Figure 10.2).

Building CATMA, a web application for collaborative text annotation and analysis

When we set out to build CATMA (*Computer Assisted Text Markup and Analysis*) in 2008 the mission seemed straightforward: re-implement Bradley's DOS-based TACT (*Textual Analysis Computing Tools*) as a desktop application for Windows. After consulting TACT's original code, which John Bradley supplied, CATMA's system architecture was developed and then partially implemented by Malte Meister. He tried to emulate the leanness and transparency of TACT's modular architecture and UI in the new architecture and then implemented (in C#) its core function in what later became known as CATMA's *analyzer module*. This is how CATMA's customised, very powerful query language originated; it is still in use today. By mid-2008 Marco Petris had come on board as lead developer, bringing both his expertise as a commercial systems developer and his keen interest as a scholar of Italian literature and language to the table.

Petris first augmented the analytic function with a separate (written in Java) but integrated *annotator module*. The two modules combined were launched as CATMA 1.0 in 2009. Petris then gradually migrated the analyzer module to Java as well. We launched CATMA 2.0 soon after, and instantly a flow of feature requests by users started changing the scope of our project dramatically. Non-DH scholars in particular found our markup tool helpful and intuitive but they wanted more and different features than we had anticipated. Simply put, they were not content with just *marking up* texts; they also wanted to *annotate* them, discuss the annotated phenomena, interpret these, annotate them again or differently, try new tags, share their various resources – from work in progress to entire tag sets, from source texts to analytical results and visualisations. It turned out that our straightforward software development project had been sucked into the vortex of what is generally referred to as the hermeneutic circle. And so, after 10 years of continuous development, the 2019 version, CATMA 6, is a far cry from a mere re-implementation of TACT, not just technologically but, more importantly, conceptually: from a standalone desktop tool for single users that focused on text annotation and basic analytical functionality inspired by TACT's USEBASE module it has grown into a web application which:

- supports single user as well as collaborative text annotation and analysis undertaken by teams;

- works with any UTF 8 encoded text format in almost any language, including right-to-left written ones like Hebrew;
- allows for the import and/or on-the-fly creation of tagsets, and for the specification of tags via structured and unstructured properties;
- organises all workflows around the core concept of a 'project' and facilitates the sharing of tagsets, source texts and corpora, and of course, annotations and meta-annotations themselves;
- generates XML/TEI compatible external standoff markup using the TEI feature structure module and allows users to export results in Excel and comma-separated value (CSV) formats, as well as via an application programming interface (API);
- can ingest documents with e.g. TEI inline markup, which will be converted into (so-called *intrinsic*) standoff markup;
- supports overlapping and discontinuous annotating and is technologically 'undogmatic', i.e. non-prescriptive with regard to the markup schemata and annotation conventions that users might want to specify;
- allows for the interactive analysis of any combination of source text or source corpora and their respective annotation, up to highly complex and deeply nested queries (which can be formulated either directly in CATMA's query language or via a widget-like natural-language query builder);
- integrates base level automatic annotation functionality like POS tagging, as well as two use-case specific high-level automatic markup options for temporal expressions;[18]
- contains a set of basic 'off-the-shelf' visualisations for CATMA query output as well as a code 'sandbox' to build highly customisable VEGA visualisations that comply with the standards for *hermeneutic visualisations* developed in the 3DH project;[19]
- uses graph database technology and an integrated Gitlab-based user, team, project and versioning management functionality.

CATMA's system architecture and functional concepts for version 6 are detailed in the Appendix.[20]

Overall, CATMA builds on the foundations established by TACT, resulting in a uniquely 'mindful' markup and text analysis tool – that is, a tool whose development continues to be inspired and is driven primarily by desiderata of humanities research practice. This overall commitment to an approach that considers hermeneutic desiderata 'before the algorithmic fact' is encapsulated in CATMA's hermeneutic data model, which serves as a high-level conceptual scheme (Figure 10.3).

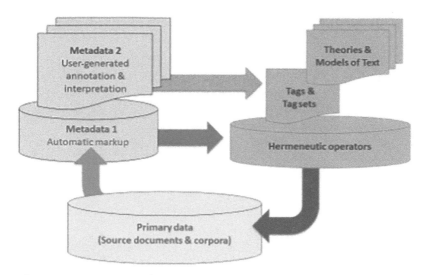

Figure 10.3 CATMA's hermeneutic data model.

Beyond emulation: strengths and weaknesses of standoff markup

A succinct appraisal of the epistemological and cultural relevance of adding meta information to text was formulated by Lou Burnard, who stated: 'Text markup is currently the best tool at our disposal for ensuring that the hermeneutic circle continues to turn, that our cultural tradition endures' (Burnard 2001).Thinking about annotation from the database perspective and utilising the unique flexibility of standoff markup has enabled us to develop CATMA as a digital tool and a working environment for scholars of text and language which does not just emulate the traditional disciplines' way of 'keeping the hermeneutic circle turning', as Burnard called on us to do. In addition, CATMA integrates functionalities which were previously not part of the hermeneutic workflow: automatic markup routines, versioning control and management, computational analysis of text and markup, data as well as process visualisation, and meta-annotation.

Like annotation itself, meta-annotation in CATMA comes in two variants: structured and unstructured. The structured variety enables the user to qualify a selected tag instance in terms of predefined attributes and value ranges by assigning a 'property value' to a particular text annotation. The unstructured variant comes in the form of a free-text commentary field into which a user may enter notes, observations and explanations. Both variants of meta-annotation can of course be analysed using CATMA's query language, allowing for complex searches such as (formulated here in semi-natural language, not in CATMA's query language):

Show me all instances in the corpus where:

- a source text string contains a word ending on the string 'shire' **and**
- where the word ending on this string has been automatically POS-tagged as SUBJECT **and**
- where the same string was manually annotated by annotator (1) by assigning the tag PROTAGONIST **and**
- where the same annotator (1) instantly qualified this tag instance in terms of the property CERTAINTY **and**
- where the value of this property was set at = 5 **and**
- where two or more annotators **subsequently** added a free-text comment containing one or more strings that possess a SIMILARITY OF >=75% with
- one or more of the phrases {DOUBT, QUESTION, EDITION, CON-TEXT} **while**
- DISREGARDING CASE SENSITIVITY in the similarity check.[21]

The basis for these complex and combined searches across *source text, annotation, meta-annotation* and *annotation timestamp* in CATMA is an implementation of the TEI feature structure tag concept. In the following example I have annotated the phrase 'he felt better than he had for many weeks, a fact' in Fitzpatrick's *Afternoon of an Author* as a 'claim' in terms of a predefined rhetorical tropes tagset. I then added two types of tag instance property information: a structured 'plausibility' property whose value I set at 'medium', and a free-text commentary intended to remind whoever might want to build on these annotations that this particular qualification needs to be discussed in more general terms because such opening statements in literary narratives typically aim to condition the reader (the so-called 'priming effect').

In an XML export file the relevant section of standoff markup extracted from CATMA's database takes on this form:[22]

<encodingDesc>

<fsdDecl xml:id="CATMA_08E831DC–EA5F–4367–932E–3A8F2C6D7DA8" n="Rhetorical Tags 2017–08–08T19:08:12.000+0200">

```
<fsDecl xml:id="CATMA_2965A186–18DD–4C47–9C7B–
D5061889D7CC" n="2019–06–24T11:16:33.000+0200"
type="CATMA_2965A186–18DD–4C47–9C7B–
D5061889D7CC">
    <fsDescr>claim</fsDescr>
    <fDecl xml:id="CATMA_EF8C7681–D140–469F–884A–
F4F2905FB79C" name="catma_displaycolor">
        <vRange>
          <vColl>
            <string>–8837951</string>
          </vColl>
        </vRange>
    </fDecl>

    <fDecl xml:id="CATMA_22612A10–E70F–400F–94F1–
4D7BB2B6BB12" name="catma_markupauthor">
        <vRange>
          <vColl>
            <string>mail@jcmeister.de</string>
          </vColl>
        </vRange>
    </fDecl>

    <fDecl xml:id="CATMA_32F02054–1031–41DE–B27A–
994C1CBA2E4F" name="Plausibility">
        <vRange>
          <vColl>
            <string>low</string>
            <string>medium</string>
            <string>high</string>
          </vColl>
        </vRange>
    </fDecl>
</fsDecl>
```

and the code section with my two property declarations is

```
<fs xml:id="CATMA_93B49892–DCAB–4785–B1CC–
C6CD304E9A4B" type="CATMA_2965A186–18DD–4C47–
9C7B–D5061889D7CC">
    <f name="catma_displaycolor">
      <string>–8837951</string>
    </f>
```

```
<f name="catma_markupauthor">
  <string>mail@jcmeister.de</string>
</f>
<f name="Plausibility">
  <vRange>
    <vColl>
      <string>medium</string>
      <string>to be revisited: priming effect</string>
    </vColl>
  </vRange>
</f>
</fs>
```

In reality a CATMA user will of course find it much easier to inspect tags and their properties via the UI, by making use of the hover function and/ or by inspecting the detailed description of the selected tag instance (Figure 10.4).

Figure 10.4   Instance of a rhetorical 'claim' tag with 'Plausibility' property set to 'medium' and a free-text comment by the annotator ('to be revisited: priming effect').

The JSON markup in the CATMA database contains a lot of information, including a unique tag ID, the character standoffs, the definition of tagsets, the assigned tags and properties, and their value ranges as well as display features such as colour. Every entry is also time-stamped, and references its annotator as owner as well as the annotation collection to which it belongs.

However, external standoff markup does come with one significant limitation: the annotated source document may not be changed as this would compromise the offsets which reference the character strings. This limitation should not be taken lightly; one of the most prominent feature requests from CATMA users is in fact to facilitate the direct editing of source documents during the annotation and analysis process, not necessarily in an extensive fashion, for instance by rearranging paragraphs or inserting entire chapters, but at least so that one could attend to trivia such as OCR mistakes, punctuation marks and line breaks. Such an edit feature is difficult to implement in an application that builds on the 'annotation as database'-paradigm and aims to support real-time online collaboration.[23] Recalculating and then re-writing 'on the fly' all subsequent character offsets across all user-specific variants that a team of annotators might have produced for a text corpus using CATMA's collaborative functionality may be possible in theory; in practice it is not feasible. More importantly, taking this route would in fact be paradoxical, for in the 'annotation as database' paradigm the source text is no longer considered as privileged and foundational; rather, it represents one of many nodes in a dynamically evolving network of texts and metatexts. The logical way to address the problem, then, is to consider an edit operation as a versioning of the source document.[24]

Integrating visualisation as a hermeneutic operator: CATMA and the 3DH project

CATMA's initial hermeneutic data model presented in Figure 10.3 lists tags and tagsets as well as theories and models of text as 'hermeneutic operators'. But one very important hermeneutic operator is missing in this list: visualisation.

In her seminal publication *Graphesis*, Drucker refers to 'Visual Forms of Knowledge Production' (Drucker 2014). As far as annotation is concerned, visualisation is indeed one of the most powerful and intuitive conceptual enablers that we may use to correlate, investigate and interpret all types of data that are of relevance to the annotation workflow: source documents as well as their annotations and meta-annotations. Bradley's *Pliny* already demonstrated how one might conceptually emulate the logic of the traditional humanists' inductive, explorative workflow using graphical means: rather than resorting to the engineering science's data-driven approach to 'visualization-as-product' *Pliny* tried to sketch out the option for a 'visualization-as-process'-centred approach that uses the desktop metaphor.

CATMA has contained a visualisation module since version 3.0. Yet its functionality was limited: the user could plot query results as a line diagram, and from version 5.0 onward also in the form of an expandable Double Tree[25] that displays the left and rights contexts of a selected keyword (Figure 10.5).

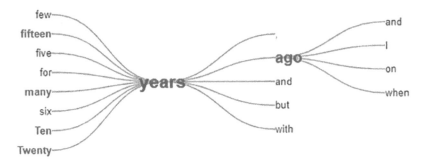

Figure 10.5 Expandable Double Tree visualisation of a keyword in context in CATMA.

These visualisations are essentially based on an archetype, which, as Drucker (2014, 66) has pointed out, we have been culturally conditioned not to 'see' as visualisation any longer: the tabular format which maps the conceptual dimensionality of data sorted into columns and lines onto the two axes of spatial dimensionality inherent to all graphic media. In contemporary DH more fancy and colourful visualisations do of course abound; the choice offered in code libraries such as D3.js is overwhelming. Yet humanists, if anybody, should beware: visualisations can, as Drucker observes, easily become

> a kind of intellectual Trojan horse, a vehicle through which assumptions about what constitutes information swarm with potent force. These assumptions are cloaked in a rhetoric taken wholesale from the techniques of the empirical sciences that conceals their epistemological biases under a guise of familiarity. So naturalised are the Google maps and bar charts generated from spreadsheets that they pass as unquestioned representations of 'what is'. This is the hallmark of realist models of knowledge and needs to be subjected to a radical critique to return the humanistic tenets of constructedness and interpretation to the fore . . . Rendering *observation* (the act of creating a statistical, empirical, or subjective account or image) as if it were *the same as the phenomena observed* collapses the critical distance between the phenomenal world and its interpretation,

undoing the basis of interpretation on which humanistic knowledge production is based. (Drucker 2011)

An uncritical, unreflective use of visualisation can thus on the one hand easily result in a conceptual reification of *capta* (Drucker 2014) as *data*. So how can we empower users of DH tools to use this form of 'knowledge production' while at the same time bringing to their attention the constructedness of it?

Up to version 5 we tried to achieve this by delegating visualisations to a separate functional module. In CATMA 6 we use a different approach: the UI now seamlessly integrates the epistemic functionality of visualisations with that of query-based analyses. But it does so by presenting the user with a choice of four ready-made visualisation options on top of its table of query results, and nothing will be rendered before the user has decided to interact with the system and selected one of these options. This emphasis on user activity as a compulsory trigger is the result of a thorough process of theorising about the requirements of hermeneutic data visualisation up-front. And users who want to take this critical, reflected approach to visualisation of their data one step further are empowered to do so by a unique technological feature in CATMA: an integrated viewer and editor for the VEGA code which constructs but also deconstructs all visual rendering of output data displayed by the system.

Our more reflective approach to visualisation in CATMA is the fruit of the 3DH project, which we ran in parallel to CATMA's ongoing development, from 2015 to 2017.[26] Our aim in 3DH was to lay the foundations for a 'next-generation', critical approach to visualisation in and for the (digital) humanities: an approach in which the concept of 'third dimension' is no longer defined at surface level, that is, in terms of the traditional z-axis of three-dimensionality that turns the flat image into a mimesis of a physical real-world object. For us the third dimension is that of critical, self-referential reflection which the traditional approaches to data visualisation adapted from the empirical sciences lack. The project's conceptual outcome was therefore the formulation of four postulates for hermeneutic data visualisation, summarised in Kleymann as follows:

1. the '2 way screen postulate' (i.e. an interaction focused approach toward visualisation);
2. the 'parallax postulate' (i.e. the idea that visualisation in and for the humanities should not just tolerate, but actively put to use the power of visual multi perspectivity in order to realise epistemic multi perspectivity);

3. the 'qualitative postulate' (i.e. the idea that visualisations should not just 'represent' data, but also offer a means to make and exchange qualitative statements about data);
4. the 'discursive postulate' (i.e. the idea that visualisations should not just be used to illustrate an already formed argument or line of reasoning, but should also become functional during the preceding/subsequent steps of reasoning, such as exploration of phenomena and data, generation of hypotheses, critique and validation, etc.). (Kleymann 2015)

The ready-made visualisation options for query output in CATMA 6 from which a user can choose are KWIC (KeyWord In Context), Distribution Graph, Word Cloud, Double Tree (and potentially also Network). These four types meet the postulated requirements of hermeneutic data visualisation to varying degrees: all use a 'linked screen' approach that allows the user to jump from any point in, say, a line chart directly to the relevant string in the source document (first postulate); some of them also enable the user to express and explore multiperspectivity and add to the database qualitative statements (postulates two and three); none of them can however be directly integrated into a discursive argument (postulate four), for CATMA, unlike Bradley's conceptually more ambitious *Pliny*, is not (yet) a tool or a working environment in which one can in fact *formulate* a coherent metatext.

However, the 3DH project also resulted in a software prototype that demonstrates the more ambitious, argument-centred use of visualisation that we will aim for in the next development phase: *Stereoscope* (http://www.stereoscope.threedh.net) can ingest a CATMA source text and its annotations and meta-annotations. In this prototype all three types of data are automatically visualised. The user can then qualify, discuss and cross-link them; the various annotations generated on a canvas during this process can also be saved as a so-called 'views', that is, as a visual snapshot which can be annotated, commented on, and combined with other such views (see Figure 10.6). Visualisation is thus considered equally from the perspective of process and output and consequently contributes directly toward the formulation of an elaborate visual-textual argumentation.

While *Stereoscope* is not yet integrated into CATMA's production version, another feature already mentioned enables the user to generate, critique, interact with, and even manipulate any type of data visualisation: all CATMA visualisations are coded in VEGA, a high-level visualisation language based on Wilkinson's generic 'Grammar of

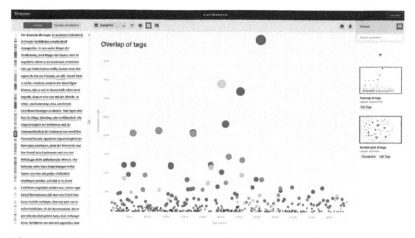

Figure 10.6 *Stereoscope*, a 3DH-compliant prototype that supports the generation, critique and discursive organisation of CATMA-generated annotation and meta-annotation data.

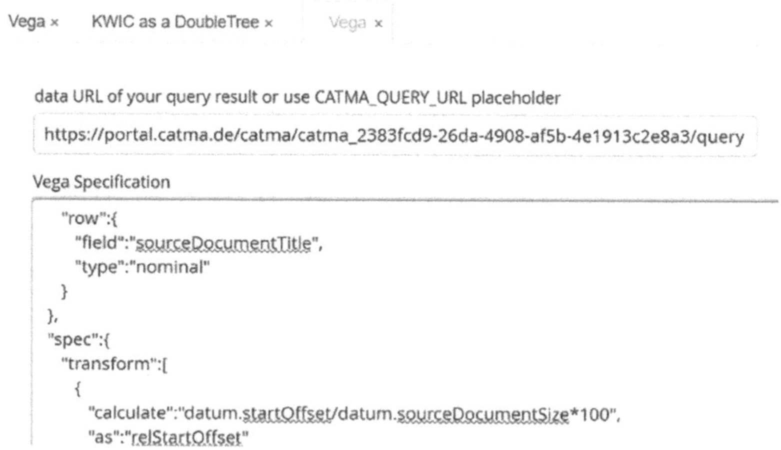

Vega ×   KWIC as a DoubleTree ×   Vega ×

data URL of your query result or use CATMA_QUERY_URL placeholder

https://portal.catma.de/catma/catma_2383fcd9-26da-4908-af5b-4e1913c2e8a3/query

Vega Specification

    "row":{
      "field":"sourceDocumentTitle",
      "type":"nominal"
    }
  },
  "spec":{
    "transform":[
      {
        "calculate":"datum.startOffset/datum.sourceDocumentSize*100",
        "as":"relStartOffset"

Figure 10.7 VEGA code editor in CATMA 6 (prototype).

Graphics' (Wilkinson 2005). This underlying VEGA code can be accessed and manipulated directly from within the CATMA UI. The *techne* of visualisation is thus no longer a hard-coded wizardry that remains opaque to the user, but is rather made transparent in terms of its definitions, parameter settings, data flows, interactions and algorithmic transformations that can be inspected and critiqued – just as one inspects, discusses and critiques the annotations themselves in CATMA (Figure 10.7).

Consensus ex machina? Consensus *qua* machina!

Bradley's TACT and *Pliny* stand out as tools – one robust and applied in numerous text analytical projects in the day and age of humanities computing, the other a prototype which brushes algorithmic logic almost against the grain – that demonstrated in exemplary fashion the significant conceptual dimension of software development in and for the humanities which Ramsay and Rockwell (2012) and others have repeatedly pointed out. However, the painstaking manual interaction with source data in close reading mode is no longer the primary focus in contemporary cutting-edge DH research. The methods which at present enjoy attention are those that can contribute to the automated analysis of large corpora, and they obviously come with different constraints and pitfalls than manual annotation. Yet once they have become more robust and reliable we might choose to integrate one or the other, not necessarily technically, but certainly conceptually with semi-automatic and manual environments for text annotation and analysis like CATMA. Such an attempt to 'mix methods' will of course come with a new risk: that of no longer reifying the data as such, but rather reifying the second-order data patterns and structures that approaches such as topic modelling, word2vec and stylometry may generate. However, this problem is a praxeological one and thus a matter of investing equally in 'doing' DH, and in reflecting on how we do what we do in DH. But more importantly, it is a matter of reminding ourselves of the type of phenomenon that we aim to engage with as humanists.

This is a matter of choice, not of dogma. As for me, the primary object domain of the humanities is that of symbolic artefacts, of man-made signs and meaning-bearing systems that constantly change, adapt, and impact on us, their observers. This is a field that presents us with a unique methodological challenge because it defies objectivist empiricism. Dynamic feedback between observer and observed may of course nowadays be considered a fundamental epistemological principle of all knowledge generation, but if indeed it is, it does not manifest itself in the same way across epistemic domains. In the humanities it is real and measurable on an everyday basis, and the digital humanities are therefore called upon to become more 'realistic' in their critical, self-reflective approach to knowledge. At the same time digital tools like TACT have helped us to re-conceptualise what was once considered to be a matter of 'two worlds' as an epistemological continuum that extends between phenomenological and formal approaches to an object domain. In the practice of textual and language studies this continuum takes on the shape of a methodological triad: that of annotation, analysis and synthesis. CATMA aims to support scholars of text to explore this epistemological continuum, and to practise this triad of methods in an undogmatic, discursive and collaborative manner. To this end our web application employs state-of-the-art computational concepts and technology. Conceptually, though, it remains indebted to Bradley's TACT and *Pliny*.

And so am I. My first contribution to the (then nascent) field of humanities computing was a critical intervention against what I considered to be a naïve programmatic vision, namely that of a *consensus ex machina* – this was the title of the 1994 ACH/ALLC conference in Paris – which we could reach by empiricising the humanities, and in particular by employing digital tools (Meister 1995). Inspired by TACT and my own fledgling attempts at modelling narrated events in PROLOG in terms of what I might nowadays call 'latent actions' I argued that we should rather strive for a *consensus **qua** machina*: digital approaches in the humanities presented us with a unique opportunity to make explicit and transparent, via annotation as well as formal modelling, many of the premises and assumptions that the traditional humanities had hitherto been able to avoid addressing. For the *machina* of the computer is on the one hand uncompromising in its insistence on explication, yet at the same time always willing to engage in a new, slightly differently parameterised iteration and recombination of computationally operationalised concepts and ideas. Humanists, I argued, should therefore begin to use this cognitive *machina* to continuously approximate, question and revisit knowledge rather than as a means to generate automatically finite results. As computing humanists we should always be mindful of the specificity of our object domain, and of our ultimate goal: to understand how humans construct, communicate and interpret meaning using symbolic artefacts and practices.

More than 25 years later my current contribution is essentially an attempt to reiterate this point. In taking up Bradley's suggestion to 'think about interpretation' I have outlined the trajectory from TACT to *Pliny* to CATMA, from text analysis to annotation and (visual as well as argumentative) synthesis, and then ultimately toward (theoretically infinite) re-interpretation. And so it might seem that we have merely gone full circle. But the hermeneutic circle is a spiral. We progress by consciously revisiting where we've already been, be it in theorising, in modelling, or in building tools.

Notes

1. Da observes that '[r]esources unimaginable in any other part of the humanities are being redirected toward it (computational literary studies; JCM), and things like positions, hiring and promotion, publishing opportunities, and grant money are all affected' (Da 2019). Da finds the trend to be problematic not primarily because it disadvantages traditional literary studies, but rather because of a lack of methodological rigor and quality control in CLS's quantitative research practice.

2. Underwood's (2019a) *Distant Horizons: Digital evidence and literary change* has once again sparked a vivid debate on whether quantitative digital approaches offer added intellectual value to literary history. See e.g. Da on 'The Digital Humanities Debacle' (2019) and Underwood (2019b) as reply, both of which form part of an ongoing critical discourse in *The Chronicle of Higher Education* published under the collective title 'The Digital Humanities War'.

3. In our 2016 DFG (German Research Foundation) grant proposal for the DH dissemination project *forTEXT* we analysed the DFG project database GEPRIS in order to establish the proportion of successful funding applications in literary studies that had employed DH methods in the widest sense during the 2005 to 2015 period. We found that the database had recorded a total of 2,825 research proposals in literary studies; in 49 instances the relevant project abstracts had contained the keywords 'digital' and 'literature'. However, on closer inspection it turned out that only 15 of these proposals (0.5%) were substantially related to digital methods: 12 of them were digitisation projects, and a mere three (= 0.11%) had actually applied DH methods in practice.

4. In a witty intellectual *mise-en-abyme*, Bradley (2008) himself uses excerpts from Wittig's 1977 article to demonstrate *Pliny*'s UI and functionality.

5. For documentation on TACT, see https://tapor.ca/tools/199. All websites cited in the notes below were accessed and checked 6 September 2022.

6. A vivid debate on the pros and cons of a hierarchical representation of text was sparked by, among others, Coombs, Renear and DeRose (1987). Galey summarises as follows: 'Specifically, DeRose invokes the idea that all texts have an essential structure in the form of an Ordered Hierarchy of Content Objects (OHCO), a tree structure of non-overlapping nodes that conveniently matches the structure of all XML documents. The debate over the OHCO theory of texts divided critics . . . with DeRose, Alan Renear, and their co-authors on the pro-OHCO side, and opposing them McGann, Hayles, and others with links to textual scholarship. From a textual studies perspective, the OHCO thesis lost in theory but won in practice . . . the OHCO model is everywhere in our digital tools, from the structure of XML documents, to the historical core of the TEI guidelines' (Galey 2011, 112 n24). This debate is far from over, as a more recent (2019) exchange on HUMANIST on 'the McGann–Renear debate' has demonstrated (see https://humanist.kdl.kcl.ac.uk/volume/32/424/et passim). In this context Peter Robinson (2019), after 'years of barking up the wrong "overlapping hierarchies" tree' himself, proposes an alternative model. He invites us to consider 'text NOT being a single stream with multiple overlapping hierarchies. Instead, text is better modelled as a set of leaves, with each leaf potentially present in multiple tree-like hierarchies.' Bradley's TACT could in fact have supported this model to a degree as it used the COCOA tagging convention which knows no explicit closing tags.

7. CATMA 6 power users can also use the Gitlab REST API and the git protocol to access CATMA as a webservice.

8. A brief historical *excursus*: TACT was originally designed and developed by Bradley, with the support of Ian Lancashire, as a desktop suite of programs for DOS computers (see the program's original README-file at http://korpus.uib.no/icame/manuals/TACTREAD.HTM). In order to apply it in my own research, but even more so in my teaching at Hamburg University from 1994 onward, I therefore had to use DOS emulators. This alienating effect was in fact a pedagogical advantage: what happened to and what one did with digital text in TACT was completely transparent and the result of a step-by-step interaction between user and machine where the roles were clearly defined. In 2007 the idea of re-implementing TACT as a desktop

application for Windows was eventually hatched. For further details on its development history see https://catma.de/documentation/history/

9. As a scholarly method the hermeneutic approach built on a tradition of systematic exegesis of scripture that had evolved in practical theology and religious studies since the Middle Ages, which in turn drew on the teachings of classical rhetoric. Up until the Reformation, orthodox biblical exegesis had been based on the claim that correct and true readings of the text can only be determined by the religious authority in power. This is the concept of the authoritative, dogmatic interpretation. Both the religious and the interpretive dogmatic authority were contested by among others Luther, who then proclaimed the principle of *sola scriptura* – a call to revisit the original text and rid biblical scripture of the layers of interpretive appropriation brought about by the Roman Catholic church. If Luther's sixteenth-century paradigm shift was essentially one of radical de-contextualisation, then the eighteenth-century Romantics' counter proposal of hermeneutics was to re-introduce historicity – though this time as a flexible and subjective frame of reference that aims to acknowledge the historicity of the production as well as of the interpretation of a given text.

10. Section 5 of this paper is a translated, expanded and differently contextualised version of parts of sections 2–4 in my (German-language) article 'Annotation als Mark-Up *avant la lettre*' in Jannidis 2022.

11. The typology was subsequently called into question by Renear (2000), who found that 'the descriptive/procedural distinction is flawed'.

12. See e.g. Renear 2004; Rapp 2017.

13. My definition of annotation as a means to communicate a specific 'reading' positions it, in the function of a hermeneutic mediator, between the source document and this document's potential realm of application and relevance. This corresponds to Boot's (2009) concept of *mesotext* which serves as an epistemic springboard from the source text bound triad of *textdata* – *mesodata* – *mesotext* to the fully articulated, medially independent metatext.

14. As an example for the latter see McGann's (2004) proposal for a so-called 'topological markup' which he bases on the idea of patacriticism, i.e. a 'theory of subjective interpretation' which focuses on the reader's engagement with the autopoetic function of an aesthetic text.

15. Which, though of course very efficient, is by no means a technological must: instead of using a generic SGML <b> -tag one could also define a unique hexadecimal code for every bold letter.

16. On the Overlapping Hierarchies debate with particular regard to TEI see Pierazzo (2016, 316–19); for a more general appraisal see Witt (2004), who proposes a 'technique of annotating documents in multiple forms' as an alternative to standoff markup.

17. As an example for this approach see the outcome of the project heureCLÉA in which we used supervised ML to automate narratological high-level annotation of discourse temporality features (Gius and Jacke 2015).

18. The algorithms for these functions are the result of a supervised ML analysis of manual CATMA annotations of a corpus of 100 German nineteenth-century short stories in the project heureCLÉA (http://heureclea.de). For a discussion of the conceptual approach see Bögel et al. 2015.

19. See http://threedh.net

20. For continuously updated information see https://catma.de and https://github.com/mpetris/catma

21. A query constrained by the conditions specified under the last three bullets effectively analyses the free text comment as if it were a primary document. This reflexive application of base-level query constraints is already fully implemented for structured CATMA annotations; its extension to the free-text comments is expected for version 6.1. (In case you are wondering about the annotated word in the original source document mentioned under bullet 1, it is of course the Cheshire Cat in Carroll's *Alice in Wonderland*.)

22. Note that XML is an export/import format only: CATMA 6 stores all tags and annotations internally as JSON data, using the JSON-LD format which is the recommended serialisation format for the Web Annotation Data Model on which CATMA annotations are based.

23. Neill and Kuczera (2019) claim to have developed 'a new approach to the annotation of texts . . . based on standoff properties. These allow for index based multidimensional annotations that can be assigned to the relevant users' (my translation; the original reads: 'einen neuen Ansatz zur Annotation von Texten . . . Grundlage sind Standoff Properties, die indexbasiert mehrdimensionale Annotationen mit Zuordnung zu den jeweiligen Nutzenden ermöglichen'). Moreover, the authors assert that their markup tool has resolved the problem of editing the source documents in a standoff markup approach. Both claims are a misrepresentation. What the 'new' tool actually does (some 10 years after CATMA's first launch as a tool capable of

handling inter-annotator disagreement, and some three years after we introduced a graph database) is recalculate, subsequent to an on-screen source text edit, the affected standoffs *on the client side*. But this transformation pertains merely to HTML-based screen output and local annotation operations performed in isolation on a client machine; it does not address the complexity of the issue as it presents itself in a collaborative, real-time synchronous online web service like CATMA which relies on a host-side graph database architecture and a Gitlab versioning mechanism.

24. To be more precise, the source document edit has to be conceptualised as a *multi versioning* problem: each version of a source document belongs to the corresponding versions of its annotations. A change of source document, i.e. the creation of a new source document version, will therefore also imply the creation of new versions of the original annotations. In a multi-version set-up these versions would thus form a meta version. In short, the implementation of a source document editing function in a collaborative working environment and web application like CATMA necessitates a three-dimensional configuration of the version setup across (a) one or more document versions, (b) all their corresponding annotation versions, and (c) all their corresponding tag versions. This can be achieved as long as the altering operations on the source document allow a computation of the impacts on their annotations, just like the changes of a tag allows a computation of the impacts on the annotations in which the tag has been used. In CATMA 6 we already made the first step towards editable source documents: there is a git container that manages all the corresponding versions and that is versioned itself (the meta version). The next step is to compute the impacts of a source document change on its annotations.

25. The double-tree visualisation was developed by Chris Culy.

26. The core contributors to this project were members of the original CATMA and heureCLÉA teams (Evelyn Gius, Janina Jacke, Jan Christoph Meister, Marco Petris), visualisation experts (Johanna Drucker, Geoffrey Rockwell, Marian Dörk) and 3DH's own Rabea Kleymann and Jan-Erik Stange. In addition, during the summer semester 2016 we gained valuable input from numerous international visualisation experts who addressed particular aspects during a 3DH lecture series programmatically titled 'A word says more than a thousand pictures'; for details see http://threedh.net

27. This might change in the future as we plan to add an algorithm that can adjust associated annotations based upon a versioned journal of (minor!) changes applied to the document.

References

Ast, Friedrich. 1808. *Grundlinien der Grammatik, Hermeneutik und Kritik*. Landshut: Jos. Thomann. Digital facsimile available from the Bayerische Staatsbibliothek digital/MDZ. Accessed 6 September 2022. http://mdz-nbn-resolving.de/urn:nbn:de:bvb:12-bsb10582792-2

Bauer, Matthias, and Angelika Zirker. 2015. 'Whipping Boys Explained: Literary annotation and digital humanities'. In *Literary Studies in the Digital Age. An evolving anthology*. Accessed 6 September 2022. https://dlsanthology.mla.hcommons.org/whipping-boys-explained-literary-annotation-and-digital-humanities/

Blei, David M., Andrew Y. Ng and Michael Jordan. 2003. 'Latent Dirichlet Allocation', *Journal of Machine Learning Research* 3(4–5): 993–1022.

Bögel, Thomas, Michael Gertz, Evelyn Gius, Janina Jacke, Jan Christoph Meister, Marco Petris and Jannik Strötgen. 2015. 'Collaborative Text Annotation Meets Machine Learning: HeureCLÉA, a digital heuristic of narrative'. *DHCommons Journal*. Accessed 6 September 2022. https://zenodo.org/record/3240591#.YoQ7f1RByUk

Boot, P. 2009. 'Mesotext. Digitised emblems, modelled annotations and humanities scholarship'. Dissertation, 20 November. Accessed 6 September 2022. http://dspace.library.uu.nl/handle/1874/36539

Bradley, John. 1996. 'TACT Design'. *Digital Studies/le Champ Numérique* 2. http://doi.org/10.16995/dscn.225

Bradley, John. 2008. 'Thinking about Interpretation: Pliny and scholarship in the humanities', *Literary and Linguistic Computing* 23(3): 263–79. https://doi.org/10.1093/llc/fqn021

Burnard, Lou. 2001. 'On the Hermeneutic Implications of Text Encoding'. In *New Media and the Humanities: Research and applications*, edited by D. Fiormonte and J. Usher, 31–8. Oxford: Humanities Computing Unit.

Buzzetti, Dino. 2002. 'Digital Representation and the Text Model', *New Literary History* 33: 61–88.

Caton, Paul. 2001. 'Markup's Current Imbalance', *Markup Languages* 3(1): 1–13. Accessed 6 September 2022. http://xml.coverpages.org/mltpTOC31.html

Coombs, James H., Allen H. Renear and Steven J. DeRose. 1987. 'Markup Systems and the Future of Scholarly Text Processing', *Communications of the ACM* 30(11): 933–47. https://doi.org/ 10.1145/32206.32209

Da, Nan Z. 2019. 'The Digital Humanities Debacle: Computational methods repeatedly come up short'. *Chronicle of Higher Education*, 27 March. Accessed 6 September 2022. https://www. chronicle.com/article/The-Digital-Humanities-Debacle/245986

Drucker, Johanna. 2011. 'Humanities Approaches to Graphical Display', *Digital Humanities Quarterly* 5(1). Accessed 6 September 2022. http://www.digitalhumanities.org/dhq/vol/5/ 1/000091/000091.html

Drucker, Johanna. 2014. *Graphesis: Visual forms of knowledge production*. Cambridge, MA: Harvard University Press.

Flanders, Julia and Fotis Jannidis. 2016. 'Data Modeling'. In *A New Companion to Digital Humanities*, edited by Susan Schreibman, Ray Siemens and John Unsworth, 229–37. Chichester: Wiley Blackwell.

Frankl, Viktor. 1959. *Man's Search for Meaning*. Boston, MA: Beacon Press.

Frege, Gottlob. 1892. 'Über Sinn und Bedeutung'. In *Zeitschrift für Philosophie und philosophische Kritik* 100: 25–50.

Galey, Alan. 2011. 'The Human Presence in Digital Artefacts'. In *Text and Genre in Reconstruction: Effects of digitalization on ideas, behaviours, products and institutions*, edited by W. McCarty, 93–118. Cambridge: Open Book.

Gius, Evelyn and Janina Jacke. 2015. 'Informatik und Hermeneutik. Zum Mehrwert interdisziplinärer Textanalyse'. Accessed 6 September 2022. http://www.zfdg.de/sb001_006

Jannidis, Fotis. 2022. *Digitale Literaturwissenschaft. DFG-Symposion 2017*. Stuttgart: J.B. Metzler.

Kleymann, Rabea. 2015. 'Visualisation of Literary Narratives: How to support text analysis with visualisations? Creating a narratological use case', *3DH* (blog). Accessed 6 September 2022. https://threedh.net/index.html@p=346.html

McCarty, Willard. 1996. 'Finding Implicit Patterns in Ovid's *Metamorphoses* with Tact', *Digital Studies/Le Champ Numérique* 0(2). https://doi.org/10.16995/dscn.227

McGann, Jerome. 2004. 'Marking Texts of Many Dimensions'. In *A Companion to Digital Humanities*, edited by S. Schreibman, R. Siemens and J. Unsworth, 198–217. Malden, MA: Blackwell Publishing. https://doi.org/10.1002/9780470999875.ch16

Meister, Jan Christoph. 1995. 'Consensus ex machina? Consensus qua machina!', *Literary and Linguistic Computing* 10(4): 263–70.

Moretti, Franco. 2000. 'Conjectures on World Literature', *New Left Review* 1. Accessed 6 September 2022. https://newleftreview.org/issues/II1/articles/franco-moretti-conjectures-on-world-literature

Neill, Iian and Kuczera, Andreas. 2019. 'The Codex – an atlas of relations'. In *Die Modellierung Des Zweifels – Schlüsselideen und -Konzepte zur graphbasierten Modellierung von Unsicherheiten*, edited by Andreas Kuczera, Thorsten Wübbena and Thomas Kollatz. Zeitschrift für digitale Geisteswissenschaften / Sonderbände, 4. https://doi.org/10.17175/sb004_008

Nyhan, Julianne. 2012. 'Text Encoding and Scholarly Digital Editions'. In *Digital Humanities in Practice*, edited by Claire Warwick, Melissa M. Terras and Julianne Nyhan, 117–38. London: Facet Publishing in association with UCL Centre for Digital Humanities.

Pierazzo, Elena. 2016. 'Textual Scholarship and Text Encoding'. In *A New Companion to Digital Humanities*, edited by Susan Schreibman, Ray Siemens and John Unsworth, 307–21. Chichester: Wiley Blackwell.

Piez, Wendell. 2010. 'Towards Hermeneutic Markup: An architectural outline'. Accessed 6 September 2022. http://dh2010.cch.kcl.ac.uk/academic-programme/abstracts/papers/ html/ab-743.html

Pritchard, J.K., M. Stephens and P. Donnelly. 2000. 'Inference of Population Structure Using Multilocus Genotype Data', *Genetics* 155(2): 945–59.

Ramsay, Stephen and Geoffrey Rockwell. 2012. 'Developing Things: Notes toward an epistemology of building in the digital humanities'. In *Debates in the Digital Humanities*, edited by Matthew K. Gold, 75–84. Minneapolis, MN: University of Minnesota Press. https://doi.org/10.5749/ minnesota/9780816677948.003.0010

Rapp, Andrea. 2017. 'Manuelle und automatische Annotation'. In *Digital Humanities*, edited by Fotis Jannidis, Hubertus Kohle and Malte Rehbein. Stuttgart: Eine Einführung.

Renear, Allen. 2000. 'The Descriptive/Procedural Distinction is Flawed', *Markup Languages: Theory and Practice* 2(4): 411–20.

Renear, Allan. 2004. 'Text Encoding'. In *Companion to Digital Humanities* (Blackwell Companions to Literature and Culture), Oxford: Blackwell.

Robinson, Peter. 2019. 'The MacGann–Renear Debate', *Humanist Discussion Group* 32(424).

Schloen, David and Sandra Schloen. 2014. 'Beyond Gutenberg: Transcending the document paradigm in digital humanities', *Digital Humanities Quarterly* 008(4). Accessed 6 September 2022. http://www.digitalhumanities.org/dhq/vol/8/4/000196/000196.html

Thaller, Manfred. 2018. 'On Information in Historical Sources'. *Hypotheses*. Accessed 29 September 2022. https://ivorytower.hypotheses.org/56#more-56

Underwood, Ted. 2019a. *Distant Horizons: Digital evidence and literary change*. Chicago, IL: University of Chicago Press.

Underwood, Ted. 2019b. 'Dear Humanists: Fear not the digital revolution. Advances in computing will benefit traditional scholarship – not compete with it', *Chronicle of Higher Education*, 27 March. Accessed 5 October 2022. https://www.chronicle.com/article/dear-humanists-fear-not-the-digital-revolution/

Unsworth, John. 2000. 'Scholarly Primitives: What methods do humanities researchers have in common, and how might our tools reflect this?', *Symposium on Humanities Computing: Formal Methods, Experimental Practice*. King's College London, 13 May. Accessed 29 September 2022. http://johnunsworth.name/Kings.5-00/primitives.html

van Zundert, Joris. 2016. 'Screwmeneutics and Hermenumericals. The computationality of hermeneutics'. In *A New Companion to Digital Humanities*, edited by Susan Schreibman, Ray Siemens and John Unsworth. Chichester: Wiley Blackwell. Accessed 6 September 2022. http://eu.wiley.com/WileyCDA/WileyTitle/productCd-1118680596.html

Wilkinson, Leland. 2005. *The Grammar of Graphics*, 2nd edn. Cham, Switzerland: Springer. https://doi.org/10.1007/0-387-28695-0

Witt, Andreas. 2004. 'Multiple Hierarchies: New aspects of an old solution', *Extreme Markup Languages 2004*. Montréal, Québec, 2–6 August. Accessed 6 September 2022. https://citeseerx.ist.psu.edu/viewdoc/download?doi=10.1.1.135.2648&rep=rep1&type=pdf

Wittig, Susan. 1977. 'The Computer and the Concept of Text', *Computers and the Humanities* 11(4): 211–15.

Software

CATMA. Computer Assisted Textual Markup and Analysis – https://catma.de

Meister, Jan-Christoph, Petris, Marco, Gius, Evelyn, Jacke, Janina, Horstmann, Jan, & Bruck, Christian. (18 June 2018). CATMA (Version v5.2). Zenodo. http://doi.org/10.5281/zenodo.1470119

Pliny. A note manager – http://pliny.cch.kcl.ac.uk/
John Bradley (2017)

TACT. https://tapor.ca/tools/199 (documentation) and https://github.com/johnBradley501/TACT (Source code for TACT text analysis software, developed 1986–96)

Appendix: The CATMA 6 System Architecture

Marco Petris, Lead Developer CATMA

CATMA 6 (release date: October 2019; for the code and technical documentation see https://github.com/mpetris/catma-core) consists of two main components: a JAVA based servlet web application with a GitLab installation as its backend.

The central organizational unit in CATMA is a **Project**. A Project consists of the following resources: Documents, Annotation Collections and Tagsets. A Project also has a team of one or more users.

A **Document** is the primary object of investigation in CATMA. Each Document can have zero or more associated **Annotation Collections**. The Document cannot and must not be altered after having been uploaded to the system.[27]

A **Tagset** is a set of zero or more **Tags**. Tags form a single rooted tree where a Tag has one or no parent and zero or more children.

A Tag has a name, a colour and an author. Each Tag can have zero or more user defined **Properties** each with a name and a list of zero or more values to be proposed upon application.

An **Annotation Collection** is a collection of Annotations associated with a Document. Each Annotation Collection belongs to exactly one Document and can contain zero or more Annotations. An Annotation is always applied to one or more possibly discontinuous segments of text with character start and character end offsets. It is typed by its Tag and gets zero or more user defined Properties from its Tag. These Properties then receive an annotation-specific configuration of values. The values can be from the list of values proposed by the Tag but they are not limited to those values. An Annotation has an author and a timestamp.

Each Project has an **owner**. Other than the 'owner' role there are the four other GitLab roles (maintainer, developer, reporter and guest) that drive the permissions on the Project and its resources.

Each resource is managed as a **git repository**. In order to manage the versions of the participating resources on the Project level, there is a container git repository that contains all resource git repositories as git submodules.

All Annotations and metadata are stored in JSON format. The Annotations are modelled according to the Web Annotation Data Model.

The GitLab backend provides user management and role-based access control. The GitLab equivalent of a Project is a Group. The Group is the namespace of all resource git repositories. This allows the reuse of resources in different Projects by forking the git repositories into a new Group, i.e. into a new namespace with a fresh setting of users, roles

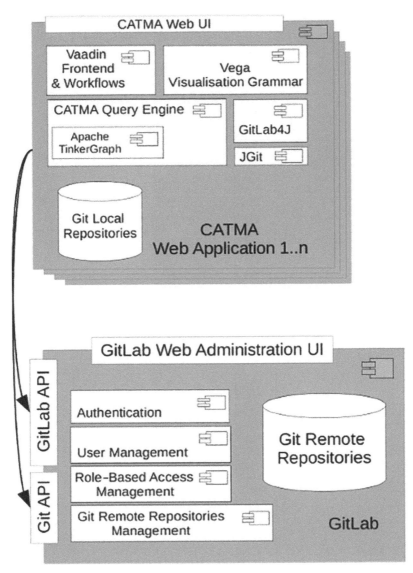

Figure 10.8   CATMA 6 System Architecture.

and permissions. GitLab enables collaborative work on reusable shared resources by ensuring role-based access and by exchanging resources. The heavy work instead is done by the CATMA Web Application.

The CATMA Web Application is able to scale horizontally and in principle also to run as a local desktop client. It talks to the GitLab backend via the GitLab REST API and the GitLab Git API for authentication and collaboration. The Projects are managed via JGit as local git projects, cloned from the GitLab remotes. On opening a Project it gets loaded into an in-memory TinkerGraph graph database that drives the CATMA Query Engine and the Vaadin UI's data models and workflows. The graph database provides a balance between fast indexing and fast retrieval and goes beyond the capabilities of token-based indexers such as Lucene/ Elastic Search.

GitLab and the CATMA Web Application can run on a single machine or on separate machines.

11
Pursuing a combinatorial habit of mind and machine

Willard McCarty

Introduction

Thanks to the development of tools and techniques, we can, after half a century of repeatedly questioning digital scholarship for revolutionary breakthroughs, begin to see 'evidence of value' in results not otherwise obtainable.[1] How and to what extent the academic mainstream has been affected is a matter for debate, discipline by discipline and (don't forget) culture by culture. Here, however, I want to pursue a different but related line of enquiry, one closely attuned to John Bradley's life in digital work. My question is this: at the low-tech end of scholarship, where most scholars spend most of their time, how have digital tools and methods affected habits of work and mind and processes of reasoning? Neurocognitive scientist Michael Anderson has observed that:

> when we invent scales, rulers, clocks, and other measuring devices, along with the specific practices necessary for using them, we are not merely doing better with tools what we were doing all along in perception. Rather, we are constructing new properties to perceive in the world . . . properties that actually *require* these tools to perceive them accurately (Anderson 2014, 181f.)

– or perhaps at all. But, he and many others have argued, cognition is not only or perhaps even primarily in the head; we need to look for it throughout the body, and not only there, but also in the whole person situated in a world of affordances, social interactions and physical consequences, where the digital machine has established a presence.[2] Thus, although there is some truth in the hype of a Digital Age, the machine's 'evidence of value' for the humanities has been a long time emerging out of the infancy or *incunabular* period of the machine. In 1994 Paul Evan Peters announced 'the Dawn of the Meso-Electronic Period'. He was then an optimist; now I would be tempted to agree.

Part of the problem we have had lies in a pervasive disinclination to look for clues in what Philip Mirowski (following Donna Haraway) has called 'the cyborg sciences' (Mirowski 2002), especially those focused on cognition. But there's also the plain fact that the digestive powers of the less technoscientific disciplines and areas of life beyond the natural sciences work slowly. In 1971, in one of my favourite statements on such matters, historical sociologist W.G. Runciman wrote:

> No doubt the rewards of ingenuity, even if coupled with perseverance, are often meagre. They may indeed be particularly meagre in the traditionally less exact sciences. But this may mean that in due course the opportunities for spectacular advance will be all the greater. Every branch of science has had its false starts, its deluded hopes and its naively misapplied techniques . . . But it remains true that habits of mind usually take a generation to be overturned: wasteful techniques, unfruitful hypotheses and misconceived presuppositions are apt to fade out only with the deaths of the protagonists. We may have to wait two or three hundred years before we know what are the most rewarding applications of quantitative methods to the sciences of man, and meanwhile it is irrelevant if not positively unhelpful to carp at the lack of immediate success. (Runciman 1971, 943)

Historian Linda Colley, more optimistic than Runciman, has likewise observed that most 'major changes become apparent within the canonical span of a human lifetime: three score years and ten' (Colley 2018, 12) – a measure which matches almost exactly the period of humankind's cohabitation with the digital machine. So now is an apposite moment for these reflections.

Colley uses the modern derivative of the old Germanic *spann*, which in its modern spelling survived well into the nineteenth century: a distance measured by the hand when fully extended (*OED*). Like other common words in English that measure the world in human terms by relating it to the body, such as 'foot', 'hand' and 'fathom', 'span' is a clue to our physical intimacy inter alia with the machine, which was designed for hands to manipulate and structured (as machine-language programmers of my vintage will know) according to operations of the hand and body, as with the abacus. It's about time, I say, that we looked critically inward, *to ourselves as embodied users of a bodily imprinted device*, for the answer to the big question of significance we keep asking ourselves, or should be.

But we must also look outward, specifically toward the often wild scattering of sources online, whose materials the scholar in interaction with the machine makes into an argument or description of something.[3] Thus the tendency, amplified from the movements characteristic of a physical library, toward Claude Lévi-Strauss's *bricolage*, the assembling of 'structured sets . . . by using remains and debris . . . "des bribes et des morceaux" . . . odds and ends' (Lévi-Strauss 1966/1962, 21f).[4] Similarly, at the turn of the millennium philosopher Richard Rorty (with no mention of anything digital) argued for a fundamental shift in emphasis, from regarding objects as having an intrinsic nature investigated by narrowly specialised techniques and theories, to the idea that 'to understand something better is to have more to say about it – to be able to tie together the various things previously said in a new and perspicuous way' (Rorty 2000, 24). Among other things, the prominent emphasis on interdisciplinary research, now made radically easier to pursue (though not to do well), would seem to follow.

This book is a commemorative offering, a *Festschrift*, but for me and several other contributors it is also and more importantly a *liber amicorum*, a book written by a gathering of friends, stitched together in such a way as to suggest the larger significance of a particular life in the intersection of computing and the humanities. I take this as sufficient justification to write in an informal, personal mode rather than a sociological or media archaeological one, as the initial form of my question might suggest. But I have another reason for writing like this. In 'The Dilemma of Scientific Subjectivity in Postvital Culture', feminist historian of science Evelyn Fox Keller has written of the 'enduring and final erasure' of the knowing subject in scientific writings during the seventeenth to the nineteenth centuries. The individual scientist, she argues, was

> replaced by the abstract 'scientist' . . . who could speak for everyman but was no-man, in a double sense: not any particular man, and also a site for the not-man within each and every particular observer. By the beginning of the last century a hollow place had been carved out in the mind of every actual or virtual witness into which a machine could vicariously be placed. (Fox Keller 1996, 418–19)

Likewise, Nobel geneticist François Jacob has described his colleagues' routine weeding out of the fruitful but all-too-human, agonising uncertainties and confusions he calls 'night science' so that an official 'day science . . . [can call] into play arguments that mesh like gears, results that have the force of certainty' (Jacob 1998/1997, 126).

Through painstaking examination of laboratory notebooks, cognitive-historical studies of experimentation have since the 1980s striven to reconstruct as much of this night science as possible in order to recover moments in which experimenters fashioned experience into communicable knowledge.[5] Perhaps we who are so much preoccupied by the great engine of our age need to pay particular attention to how we ourselves have come to know what we think we know by virtue of our own particular experiences – and to start keeping our own laboratory notebooks. Bruno Latour is on our side in this: he has argued for shattering the illusion of seamless, bullet-proof arguments, where results hold centre-stage, so that the sometimes messy processes by which we figure things out can become visible (Latour 2004). Obviously, such a programme could be carried too far, but the desirability of revealing philosopher Gilbert Ryle's 'knowing how' (Ryle 1945) in digital scholarship – manifested in particular over John's lifetime of puzzling out what to do with the machine – seems undeniable. Make no mistake in this: experimental practice *is* what many digital practitioners do. Even today that which can be learned from tool-use tends to vanish in the rush to display evidence of value to mainstream disciplines, to exhibit the up-to-date or nervously to worry the social organisation and proprieties of our young discipline.

So much for the prolegomenon. The rest comprises a narrative of my experiences and introspections on them, but these are not the gold for which I am panning.

A small *Bildungsroman*

In brief I am panning for the emergence of a combinatorial habit of mind (one that reasons about the world by sorting and re-sorting it) in order to match and harness the inbuilt processes of the digital machine that have urged us to think *combinatorially*. This is a very large subject that I can only hint at here.

Combinatorics is a branch of mathematics that studies *configurations*, that is, groups of objects 'distributed according to certain predetermined constraints. Cramming miscellaneous packets into a drawer is an example of a configuration' (Berge 1971/1968, 1). So is a certain arrangement of words in a text, colours in an image, cards in a hand of poker or milfoil (yarrow) stalks in a *Yijing* divination.[6] Combinatorics 'counts, enumerates, examines, and investigates the existence of configurations with certain specified properties. With combinatorics, one looks for their intrinsic properties, and studies transformations of one configuration into another, as well as "subconfigurations" of a given configuration' (Berge 1971/1968, 2). Claude Berge – the most significant mathematician of the Oulipo (Motte 1998/1986) – goes on to note that 'this particular discipline has developed on the edge of, or away from, the mainstream of modern mathematics'. A playful devotee of such things, he expresses surprise. Unsurprisingly, attention to it has grown since the digital machine became commonly available to mathematicians.

The coming to prominence of combinatorics neatly coincides with the period 1978–84, during which I struggled to put together a large number of biblical and classical references for my PhD dissertation on the archetypal pattern of the Exodus in John Milton's *Paradise Lost*. (This happened at the University of Toronto, where John, two of the editors of this volume and I first met.) Faced by masses of data, I used 3x5 cards to keep notes, several thousands of them. To discover patterns in the scattered data I found myself using the floor or bed to lay out the cards, sort them into thematic piles, arrange these spatially, re-sort, re-group and so on. During this time I discovered that the great lexicographer Sir James Murray had done the same in putting together volumes of the *Oxford English Dictionary*, spreading his slips of paper 'out on a table or on the floor, where [the researcher] can obtain a general survey of the whole . . . [spending] hour after hour in shifting them about like the pieces on a chess-board, striving to find in the fragmentary evidence of an incomplete historical record, such a sequence of meanings as may form a logical chain of development' (Murray 1884, 510). Having constructed my own associational web of relations, the cards went back into boxes. On a hot July afternoon in 1984, frustrated by my inability to find among those cards a reference crucial to the bibliography, I realised that these many boxes comprised not a resource for further work but a graveyard of knowledge. To make sure I would never again have to dig in that graveyard, I wrote software to keep notes – but in later work continued to print out card-images so as to retain the kinaesthetics of sorting. At the time I was ignorant of Gibson's near-contemporaneous theory of affordances. This theory launched work which led to the now commonplace realisation that cognition happens 'beyond the brain', in and with the world (see note 2). I was finding this out by thinking with notecards.

Shortly afterwards, I joined forces with the similarly minded Geoffrey Rockwell in a software-design project to look into the question of how academics take notes. Both the Macintosh and HyperCard, new that year, offered a ready-made platform for development. We interviewed a number of Toronto academics across several disciplines, expecting to find a common denominator easily translatable into a structure of menus and operations – a technologist's classic error (Carlisle 1976). After all, we thought, note-taking is largely mechanical if not algorithmically resolvable. To our surprise we discovered no consensus at all about how or indeed whether to take notes. Rather we found an ad hoc mixture of practices variable by project as well as by person, discipline, circumstance, even whim (Hellenist philosopher Brad Inwood, less riveted to the technology but quite familiar with it, pointed this out to me immediately when I told him about the interviews). So, liberated from the illusion of a methodological universal for scholarly research, even *in potentia*, I was thrown back to my own kinaesthetic use of notecards better to understand what was going on with sorting by means of the digital machine.

In the years that followed, the question of implementing Murray's method became part of a much larger enquiry into the relation between ourselves and our machines in the intimate moments of forming patterns from the (barely) constrained chaos of all that is available. This intimacy, I should point out, happens whether the scholar is working alone or in collaboration with others. Stressing the importance of thinking with others must not obscure the simultaneous need to think privately.

Tacit practices

For me, questions of implementation faded away with the growth of my work on the *Metamorphoses* of Ovid and attempts to understand the field we then called 'humanities computing'. Modelling was my primary focus. The methodological problem of shuffling notecards along with its implications went into hibernation, although my deep interest in modelling laid the groundwork for later work on combinatorics.

By the late 1990s, John and I both found ourselves on the other side of the Pond, at King's College London. He stayed with the question of how to implement note-taking. *Pliny* was the result.[7] Despite its felicity and the intelligence of its design, my own intellectual disorderliness and the infamous problem of 'screen real estate' drove me from *Pliny* back to paper slips and their manual sorting on table or floor. Years and several writing projects later, an invitation in 2018 to speak on annotation forced me to awaken that long-sleeping interest in notecards and consider their sortition once again (McCarty 2020). This invitation came in the midst of the most complex and demanding project I have yet undertaken,[8] so I had a perfect opportunity to look again at that methodological problem under the most demanding circumstances. My conclusions take up the remainder of the paper.

A note-maker's account of actual note-making

Nowadays the note-maker, wanting the benefits of the machine, perhaps looks for and finds an app, then gets to work. In my experience the note-maker who pays close attention to the demands of the sources finds it exceedingly difficult to fit them to the assumptions of the app. Paradoxically, the more facilities an app provides, the greater the chance these limitations will loom large, inducing intellectual claustrophobia, bewilderment or both. For me, at least, the place of the app is invisibly in the background – while I am making notes, that is.

Seeing an opportunity, but before reaching for the toolbox, the properly educated systems designer will consider what's been done and what's available, then talk to many note-makers about their practices, likes and dislikes. As I have already recounted, experience has suggested to me that such anthropological fieldwork and time spent with the relevant literature will *not* converge on a single, one-size-fits-all design, and that the elusiveness of such a design is fundamentally *not* due to the shortcomings of current technologies. The basic problem is that note-making is not itself singular nor does it tend to settle down for good. Indeed, it is not an 'it' but a fluid mode of thinking-by-doing realised in a coupling with one or more of the world's affordances, taken up then abandoned as suits the occasion. Note-making is *not* invariant across research projects, the individuals who pursue them, their subject areas and the physical media and circumstances involved. It may vary, possibly for no identifiable reason, even from one day to the next. The point is not at all that the means are irrelevant – they are indeed essential in their concrete particulars – rather that couplings of human and machine (both being polymorphically perverse) are impermanent, answerable to the variable situations of note-making, not to any particular implementation.

The technologically minimalist style I am about to use in describing how I went about research for the project is not how I always take and use notes, but I have often worked in this way when the project is large in scope and complex. Again, experience has taught me that no one size or even a discrete range of sizes will fit all circumstances or even a majority of them.

We must begin with specific examples, of which this is one. But my point is to exemplify the coupling, *not* promote a particular method or tool.

Cultural and media historian Markus Krajewski comments in *Paper Machines* that despite the undeniably transformative effects of digital technologies, things also 'remain the same': the card-index continues to surface, as it does with me, again and again. As I will demonstrate, it is undoubtedly laborious, but when used well it is nevertheless marvellously efficient (Krajewski 2011/2002, 143). Krajewski cites Niklas Luhmann's account of his card index system, 'the furnace in which the texts are forged'. In an interview for the *Frankfurter Rundschau* in 1985, Luhmann described how his ideas came from a card-box of notes, by sorting and combining them:

> The new ideas . . . arise from the different combinations of the notes to the individual terms. Without the notes, so by reflection alone, I would not come to such ideas. Of course my head is required to write down the ideas, but it cannot be held responsible for them alone. In that sense, I work like a computer, which can also be creative in the sense that by combining input data, it produces new results that were not predictable. (Luhmann 1987, 144f., my translation)[9]

The card-index is 'like a computer' because both are fundamentally combinatorial, hence creative not only within but also *because of* their constraints. 'When ideas are combined in all possible ways,' mathematician Martin Gardner has observed, 'the new combinations start the mind thinking along novel channels and one is led to discover fresh truths and arguments' (Gardner 1958, 17). But the combinatorial apparatus does more than start the mind in a new direction; it also provides a different style of reasoning, as Lévi-Strauss and Rorty have suggested. The question to ask of both digital and paper machines is where and how their *künstliche Intelligenz* arises (the German term for 'artificial intelligence' is a good reminder that 'artificial' means 'made by art', that is, by artisans, and that the result is artisanal). Yes, this AI arises in the coupling with the enquirer, but *what happens there?* Currently we do not have an answer, or not much of one, but we can proceed by not underestimating the power of knowing-by-doing and so pay attention to what changes, especially what is lost when the observable actions of note-making are translated into software. We can draw on those cognitive-historical studies of experiment, among other things. We can ask, for example, what happens when the inchoate, shifting relationships expressed spatially by a desk strewn with piles of cards, with the memory of strewing them, is rendered by screenicons with named links between them?

Much more needs to be known about the space between brain and card, mind and the worldly affordances to mindfulness. The examples I am about to give should help. But note: once again, there is nothing canonical here. I provide only an example. Again, what matters is that we pay attention at a fine-grained level to individuals' actions and experiences on particular occasions, for specific projects.

Typically I do more or less the following.

1. If I am reading a book (which I prefer to do with the codex in hand), I take very brief notes on paper slips to record ideas, keywords and references to other sources I want to come back to later for more detailed note-making. The highly variable circumstances under which I read and the sheer convenience of taking notes in this way while reading a codex make it a very effective procedure. (Figure 11.1)
2. Later I return to the book and make more detailed notes in software from the book,[10] which if at all possible has been digitised and is accessed on screen. For digitised books and articles, I take notes, mostly by cut-and-paste. (Figure 11.2)
3. Once I have finished an episode of note-taking, I print index cards from these notes, four to a page, then cut the sheets into individual cards and stack them for sorting. (Figure 11.3)
4. I then take the stack of cards, sort and resort the cards (as Murray describes) until satisfied with the resulting topical piles, label and clip them together. (Figure 11.4)
5. From each individual pile, I attempt to construct a narrative by writing out summary notes by hand on sheets of paper. (Figure 11.5)
6. If, as sometimes happens, I find that the attempted narrative lacks coherence, or that particular notes require rearrangement, I cut up the offending sheets, paste the resulting strips on blank sheets in revised order, scan and print the replacements. (Figure 11.6)

Writing the paper then follows.

The labour and time involved should be painfully obvious. But note: equally important to the product is *what is not and cannot be shown*: the intellectual-kinaesthetic work of sorting out a highly complex subject and producing that proto-narrative. Perhaps the painful physical work does its cognitive work by distracting the conscious mind so that the rest of the mind can go on with what it does so well? In my experience such labour and the invisible intellectual operations are inseparable.

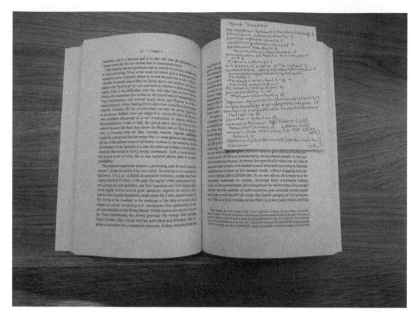

Figure 11.1 Notes written on a 3x5 paper slip while reading a book.

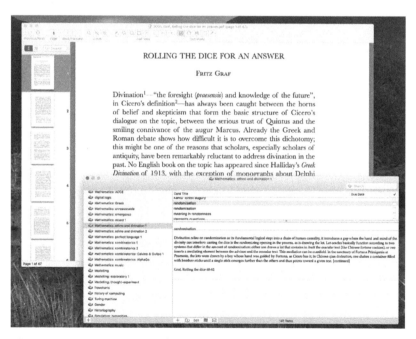

Figure 11.2 Notes copied from a digitised article into NoteCards.

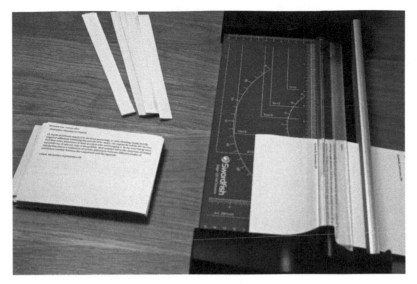

Figure 11.3 Printed notes cut into 3x5 slips.

Figure 11.4 Slips sorted and gathered into thematic groups.

Figure 11.5   Transcription of groups onto pages.

The fact that the implicit links between cards and piles of cards are left implicit – changeable if not fluid, if not tacit, intertwined with inchoate feelings that an idea or cluster of ideas 'belongs with' or 'is far away from' or 'is quite unlike' another, or is a right-handed or left-handed sort of thing – is in my view essential, though I cannot say why. *As a note-taker, I do not need to understand why the procedure works or what is going on cognitively at each step.* I just let it do what it does, then observe that it has somehow worked. But students of note-taking do need to investigate.

On the horizon

For digital humanists attracted by the potential yield from digging into relations of mind, subject matter, machine and note-taking, there is much to be done. Several fields – cognitive history and psychology to begin with – offer valuable help. On the answer(s) to the question of what happens when we take notes turns the design of better software for doing it, and as John, the designers of *NoteCards* and others have shown, writing this software raises new and exciting questions. In a sense I have gone in the opposite direction from those writers of software, to straightforward use of a minimalist app to generate piles of notecards, and as that person am now very close to concluding that I should simply let happen what happens and not fall prey to the centipede's dilemma, of stopping

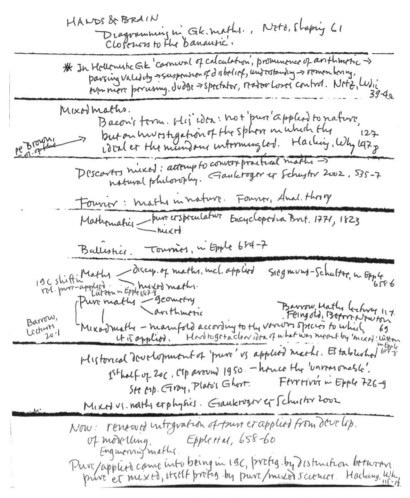

Figure 11.6 Transcribed notes physically reorganised, photocopied and printed.

to figure out how it is that she does what she does, and as a result fall 'exhausted in the ditch / Not knowing how to run'.[11] But having become a digital humanist *circa* 1984, I am also their fellow traveller. The very paper whose making provided me with the evidence for the note-taking practices I've presented here is in fact a prolonged meditation on the artisanal potential of the machine to become a more intelligent collaborative affordance in the web-amplified work of tying 'together the things previously said in a new and perspicuous way' (Rorty 2000, 24).

Here I must stop. I leave you with three suggestions regarding further explorations. The first is to pay critical attention to the sciences of mind and machine, including the anthropology of human–machine interaction (Suchman 2007; Duguid 2012). The second is to turn from mimesis to alterity in thinking about *künstliche Intelligenz*, that is, from imitation of human intelligence to exploration of intelligence differently constituted, not to match ourselves when taking notes but to provide a worthy and not always agreeable interlocutor. My third, last and most adventurous suggestion is to seek analogical help from uses of combinatorial enquiry wherever it is to be found: close at hand culturally, in the natural sciences and mathematics, and further afield, from other people, in other times, places and cultures. What have people done with counting and sorting when, unassisted by computers, they were at a loss to proceed? My title gives a hint of one rather unexpected place to look.

Notes

1. On the phrase 'evidence of value' see McCarty 2012, 117–19.
2. For the extensive literature on embodied cognition and related areas of research, begin with Gibson 2015/1979, especially the Preface and 'The Theory of Affordances', 119–35; Anderson 2014; Anderson et al. 2016; Cowley and Valée-Tourangeau 2013; Chemero 2009; Clark 2008.
3. The same has always been true of the research library, indeed is of its essence. But seen in the context of the web, the library of codices imposes a classification physically in the arrangement of stacks, even of separate buildings, and hence radically slows down and so limits its recombinatorial potential.
4. Thus the *OED*: 'The process or technique of creating a new artwork, concept, etc., by appropriating a diverse miscellany of existing materials or sources.' In Lévi-Strauss's terms, the scholar, like the artist, is midway between the scientist and the *bricoleur* (Lévi-Strauss 1966/1962, 22).
5. See: Gooding 1990; Steinle 2016/2005; Nersessian 2008; Rheinberger 2010/2006; cf. McCarty 2020 and esp. 2021.
6. I make the argument for the relevance of ancient, cross-cultural divinatory practices in McCarty 2021.
7. To my mind, *Pliny* shares with the much earlier *NoteCards* the honour of the most thoughtful and suggestive software environment for note-taking devised to date. Neither *NoteCards* nor *Pliny* made it to market. On *NoteCards* see Halasz et al. 2001; Brown 1985; and Halasz, Moran and Trigg 1987; on *Pliny*, Bradley 2008, cf. 2012; for a survey of annotation systems, Hunter 2009. See also DeRose 1989. For Vannevar Bush's *Memex*, grandfather of all, see Nyce and Kahn 1991 and Engelbart 1962, 48ff.
8. I refer to an ongoing series of workshops at Cambridge, 'Science in the Forest, Science in the Past' (2019–), for which see Lloyd and Vilaça 2019; McCarty, Lloyd and Vilaça 2022. A third workshop was held in June 2022, proceedings of which are to be published in *Interdisciplinary Science Reviews* (forthcoming, 2024).
9. 'Die neuen Ideen ergeben sich dann aus den verschiedenen Kombinationsmöglichkeiten der Zettel zu den einzelnen Begriffen. Ohne die Zettel, also allein durch Nachdenken, würde ich auf solche Ideen nicht kommen. Natürlich ist mein Kopf erforderlich, um die Einfälle zu notieren, aber er kann nicht allein dafür verantwortlich gemacht werden. Insofern arbeite ich

wie ein Computer, der ja auch in dem Sinne kreativ sein kann, daß er durch die Kombination eingegebener Daten neue Ergebnisse produziert, die so nicht voraussehbar waren'.

10. The software I happen to use for the above steps is QwikCards (https://www.qwikcards.com/), which I prefer for its elegant simplicity – precisely for its minimalist restraint. But any program that makes printing out cards on paper would leave my description more or less unchanged.

11. From a poem attributed to Katherine Craster (1841–74), https://en.wikipedia.org/wiki/The_Centipede%27s_Dilemma (accessed 6 September 2022).

References

Dates given as X/Y refer to the publication date of the work used (X) and that of the first printing or work in the original language (Y).

Anderson, Michael L. 2014. *After Phrenology: Neural reuse and the interactive brain.* Cambridge, MA: MIT Press.

Anderson, Michael L. et al. 2016. 'Précis of *After Phrenology: Neural Reuse and the Interactive Brain*' followed by 'Open Peer Commentary', *Behavioral and Brain Sciences* 39: 1–45.

Berge, C. 1971/1968. *Principles of Combinatorics*, trans. from *Principes Combinatoire.* New York: Academic Press.

Bradley, John. 2008. '*Pliny:* A model for digital support of scholarship', *Journal of Digital Information* 9(1). Accessed 6 September 2022. https://journals.tdl.org/jodi/index.php/jodi/article/view/209/198

Bradley, John. 2012. 'Towards a Richer Sense of Digital Annotation: Moving beyond a "media" orientation of the annotation of digital objects', *Digital Humanities Quarterly* 6(2).

Brown, John Seely. 1985. 'Idea Amplifiers – New kinds of electronic learning environments', *Educational Horizons* 63(3): 108–12.

Carlisle, James H. 1976. 'Evaluating the Impact of Office Automation on Top Management Communication', *Proceedings of the National Computer Conference*, American Federation of Information Processing Societies (AFIPS), 7–10 June. New York: ACM Press.

Chemero, Anthony. 2009. *Radical Embodied Cognitive Science.* Cambridge, MA: MIT Press.

Clark, Andy. 2008. *Supersizing the Mind: Embodiment, action and cognitive extension.* Oxford: Oxford University Press.

Colley, Linda. 2018. 'Can History Help?', *London Review of Books* 40(6): 12–16.

Cowley, Stephen J. and Frédéric Valée-Tourangeau (eds). 2013. *Cognition Beyond the Brain: Computation, interactivity and human artifice.* 2nd edn. London: Springer-Verlag.

DeRose, Steven J. 1989. 'Expanding the Notion of Links', *Proceedings of ACM Hypertext 89 Conference*, 249–57. New York: ACM Press. Accessed 6 September 2022. https://www.interaction-design.org/literature/conference/proceedings-of-acm-hypertext-89-conference

Duguid, Paul. 2012. 'On Rereading. Suchman and Situated Action', *Libellio* 8(2): 3–9. Accessed 6 September 2022. http://lelibellio.com/category/uncategorized/le-libellio/page/5/

Engelbart, D.C. 1962. *Augmenting Human Intellect: A conceptual framework.* Stanford Research Institute Project No. 3578. Menlo Park, CA: Stanford Research Institute.

Fox Keller, Evelyn. 1996. 'The Dilemma of Scientific Subjectivity in a Postvital Culture'. In *The Disunity of Science: Boundaries, contexts, and power*, edited by Peter Galison and David J. Stump, 417–27. Stanford, CA: Stanford University Press.

Gardner, Martin. 1958. *Logic Machines and Diagrams.* New York: McGraw-Hill.

Gibson, James J. 2015/1979. *The Ecological Approach to Visual Perception: Classic edition.* New York: Psychology Press.

Gooding, David. 1990. *Experiment and the Making of Meaning: Human agency in scientific observation and experiment.* Dordrecht: Kluwer.

Halasz, Frank G., Kate Dobroth, Richard Furuta, Catherine C. Marshall and Elli Mylonas. 2001. 'Reflections on NoteCards: Seven issues for the next generation of hypermedia systems' [followed by four commentaries and a reply], *ACM Journal of Computer Documentation* 25(3): 71–114.

Halasz, Frank G., Thomas P. Moran and Randall H. Trigg. 1987. 'NoteCards in a Nutshell', *CHI '87 Proceedings of the SIGCHI/GI Conference on Human Factors in Computing Systems and Graphics Interface*, Toronto, Ontario, Canada. New York: ACM Press.

Hunter, Jane. 2009. 'Collaborative Semantic Tagging and Annotation Systems', *Annual Review of Information Science and Technology* 43(1): 1–84.

Jacob, François. 1988/1987. *The Statue Within: An autobiography*, trans. Franklin Philip. Cold Spring Harbor, NY: Cold Spring Harbor Laboratory Press.

Latour, Bruno. 2004. 'Why has Critique Run out of Steam? From matters of fact to matters of concern', *Critical Inquiry* 30(2): 225–48.

Lévi-Strauss, Claude. 1966/1962. *The Savage Mind (La pensée sauvage)*. London: Weidenfeld and Nicolson.

Lloyd, Geoffrey E.R. and Aparecida Vilaça (eds). *Science in the Forest, Science in the Past*. A special issue of *HAU: Journal of Ethnographic Theory* 9(1): 36–182.

Luhmann, Niklas. 1987. *Archimedes und wir*. Berlin: Merve Verlag.

Krajewski, Markus. 2011/2002. *Paper Machines: About cards & catalogs, 1548–1929*, trans. Peter Krapp. Cambridge, MA: MIT Press.

McCarty, Willard. 2012. 'A Telescope for the Mind?'. In *Debates in the Digital Humanities*, edited by Matthew K. Gold, 113–23. Minneapolis, MN: University of Minnesota Press.

McCarty, Willard. 2019. 'Modeling, Ontology and Wild Thought: Toward an anthropology of the artificially intelligent'. In *Science in the Forest, Science in the Past*. A special issue of *HAU: Journal of Ethnographic Theory*, edited by Geoffrey E.R. Lloyd and Aparecida Vilaça: 147–61.

McCarty, Willard. 2020. 'Making and Studying Notes: Towards a cognitive ecology of annotation'. In *Annotating Scholarly Editions and Research: Functions, differentiation, systematization*, edited by Julia Nantke and Frederik Schlupkothen, 271–97. Berlin: Walter de Gruyter.

McCarty, Willard. 2021. 'As Perceived, Not as Known: Computational enquiry, experimental science and divination'. In *Science in the Forest, Science in the Past II*, edited by Willard McCarty, Geoffrey E.R. Lloyd and Aparecida Vilaça. Special issue of *Interdisciplinary Science Reviews* 46(1).

McCarty, Willard, Geoffrey E.R. Lloyd and Aparecida Vilaça (eds). 2022. *Science in the Forest, Science in the Past: Further Interdisciplinary Explorations*. London: Routledge.

Mirowski, Philip. 2002. *Machine Dreams: Economics becomes a cyborg science*. Cambridge: Cambridge University Press.

Motte, Warren F. 1998/1986. *Oulipo: A primer of potential literature*. Normal, IL: Dalkey Archive Press.

Murray, J.A.H. 1884. 'Thirteenth Address of the President, to the Philological Society, delivered at the Anniversary Meeting, Friday, 16th May, 1884', *Transactions of the Philological Society* 19(1): 501–27.

Nersessian, Nancy J. 2008. *Creating Scientific Concepts*. Cambridge, MA: MIT Press.

Nyce, James M. and Paul Kahn. 1991. *From Memex to Hypertext: Vannevar Bush and the mind's machine*. Boston, MA: Harcourt Brace Jovanovich.

Peters, Paul Evan. 1994. 'Digital Libraries '94 Keynote Address', *Proceedings of the First Annual Conference on the Theory and Practice of Digital Libraries*, 19–21 June, College Station, Texas.

Rheinberger, Hans-Jörg. 2010/2006. *An Epistemology of the Concrete: Twentieth-century histories of life*, trans. G.M. Goshgarian. Durham, NC: Duke University Press.

Rorty, Richard. 2000. 'Being that Can be Understood is Language', *London Review of Books* 22(6): 23–25.

Runciman, W.G. 1971. 'Thinking by Numbers: 1', *Times Literary Supplement* 3623 (6 August): 943–4.

Ryle, Gilbert. 1945. 'Knowing How and Knowing That: The Presidential Address', *Proceedings of the Aristotelian Society* NS 46: 1–16.

Steinle, Friedrich. 2016/2005. *Exploratory Experiments: Ampère, Faraday, and the origins of electrodynamics*, trans. Alex Levine. Pittsburgh, PA: University of Pittsburgh Press.

Suchman, Lucy A. 2007. *Human-Machine Reconfigurations: Plans and situated actions*, 2nd edn. Cambridge: Cambridge University Press.

12
Historians, texts and factoids

Manfred Thaller

First observation

In 2014 John Bradley started a paper on the usefulness of GIS and database approaches for historical research with the following observation:

> It says something interesting that although tools for structuring digital data have been available for historians for almost twenty years (for example: Access has been part of Microsoft's suite of programs since 1992, and FileMaker even longer than that), they have not really found a place in the repertoire of tools for most historians. Why is this so? (Bradley 2014, 13)

This paper tries to answer – or at least comment upon – John's question, augmented by comments on another question from his œuvre.

This observation is certainly true. But more to the point, it is in fact surprising, when you notice that almost 20 years before John Bradley wrote this – 1996, to be precise – a monograph on how to use databases in historical research was published with a bibliography of 22 pages (Harvey and Press 1996). In 1990, when the then Macintosh-only FileMaker was still exotic, a systematic *Comparaison théorique des Système de Gestion de Bases de Données Relationnelles (SGBDR) Oracle, Informix et Ingres* (Pasleau 1990) was available, directed explicitly at historians using computers. McCrank's admittedly massively overblown bibliography of around 5,700 entries on *Historical Information Science* lists at least 500 titles relating to databases and (an extremely broad conception of) the historical disciplines (McCrank 2002, 634–975). In the abortive conference series with which Joseph Raben tried in the 1980s to express his opinion that Computing in the Humanities should include more disciplines than the prevalent view of ACH/ALLC at that time maintained, historical topics were among the more frequent ones (Raben and Marks 1980; Allen 1985; Moberg 1987; McCrank 1989). And of the 56 papers contained in the first volume of the History and Computing series, out of which the Association for History and Computing arose, at the very least one third was dealing with database applications (Denley and Hopkin 1987).

Let me stop before this turns into a bibliography. But let the evidence given so far suffice to justify rephrasing John Bradley's question *why such tools have not really found a place in the repertoire of historians* into *why does there seem to be a decline in the use of such tools*, against fashionable trends?

Rephrasing the question does not immediately require giving an answer, though a rephrasing of the answer as well may be appropriate. Speaking bluntly: Many of the practitioners of database approaches in historical research would never have taken Hayden White (as in Bradley 2014, 14) seriously; nor would he in his turn probably have recognised many database-related projects as significant contributions to history. That is not so much a question of methodology in a narrow sense, but more a reflection of some unspoken assumptions about what a methodology should achieve in history. John Bradley himself recognises that.

> By embracing the wonderfully evocative and slippery nature of words historians are best able to represent their interpretation of the past. Indeed, a good historian can even apparently write in ways that exploits language in ways similar to how literary writing works. (Bradley 2014, 15)

This is indeed the understanding of Hayden White: historians are different, by interpreting the past differently. If you follow this premise, comparing the literary style of Michelet and Ranke (White 1973, ch. 3 vs ch. 4) makes eminent sense. Focusing on the literary style of the representation of their interpretation of course means that we implicitly assume that these interpretations are applied to a phenomenon that is well understood and generally known. If we ignore that no two historians would probably agree what *exactly* 'understood' means: macro-historical phenomena like the French Revolution or the system of diplomatic relations between early modern powers are well known. So, the question, where we take the assurance from, that the existing body of knowledge represents the past as well as possible, is quite irrelevant.

If you look at the types of historical research that are represented by the projects John Bradley quotes, particularly in Pasin and Bradley 2015, that assumption becomes impossible, however. While there is an eagle's view of what happened roughly in the French Revolution, there is no such thing on the life of 'Eucharius 4' (Pasin and Bradley 2015, 87). And, indeed, the eagles find it rather difficult to understand why one should bother about a gentleman like this. Not without reason, Frank R. Ankersmit finds it extremely difficult to integrate *Alltagsgeschichte* (roughly: anthropological interpretations of the daily life in the past) into his view of history, or possibly even recognise it as historical study (Ankersmit 2001, 146f, 270f). And while subdisciplines of history like *Alltagsgeschichte* or historical demography usually study periods at least a thousand years later than the life of 'Eucharius 4', they are based on the re-construction of individual micro-biographies from a vast array of sources, exactly as classical prosopography is. And *these* fields of study were responsible for a large part of the glut of historical database projects in the 80s and 90s, being the primary example underlying Harvey and Press 1996.

One answer to John Bradley's question, at least in the rephrased form given above, could therefore be: Exactly at the time when software for the handling of structured data became more easily accessible some 30 years ago, at a time when methods and research problems from the social and economic sciences were very much in the focus of the methodological debates in history at large, they were eagerly picked up by the historical disciplines. As the focus of these debates has shifted elsewhere to a stronger appreciation of quite traditional topics, methods or narratives, these tools have moved into the background. The reasons for this change of focus within historical research shall not concern us here.

Second observation

Within the seemingly hidden past of database applications in historical research there has also been a tradition of discussing the relationship between loosely structured sources and the requirements of software expecting structured data, as presented with admirable clarity in Pasin and Bradley 2015. Indeed, the discussion about the basic problem of how to convert data contained in a natural text into something fit for data processing, or rather: how best to do so technically, can be traced to at least 1977 (Ginter et al. 1977).

More significant, though almost unknown due to the obscure place of publication, is a short methodological piece from 1980, which presents very clearly many ideas which became more prominent much later, so I think it deserves to be summarised in some detail (Baum and Sprandel 1980). It describes the technical solutions for the handling of a typical late medieval/ early modern source, a *Lehensregister* (a register of fiefs handed out and the income due from them). Being in principle a list, the source contains a set of descriptions of individual pieces of property in natural language. While obviously in the late 1970s not envisaged in XML, let alone an ontology in the sense created by the semantic web discussion, there is a clear separation between the full text described and inserted normalisations of such parts of the terminology as are needed for computational analysis. Computational analysis; not a *specific type of* analysis. This way was chosen, according to the authors, as the information contained in the documents is so rich that it is pointless to optimise it for just *one* specific form of analysis. They therefore should be prepared in such a way that they are open for all types of unforeseeable questions that might arise during the research process. This approach is called 'source conservative' and connected back to a French discussion (Genicot 1977) between uses of computers following either a model of *recherche fermée* (encoding for one specific analysis) or *recherche ouverte* (encoding – or rather: markup – for all possible sorts of analysis). The normalised items prepared in such a way – personal names, topographic names, amounts – are strikingly like the factoids as defined in Pasin and Bradley 2015.

Another early attempt to augment a transcription with markup for factoids has been the Earls Colne project at Cambridge (Macfarlane 1977). Here a machine-readable verbatim transcript of the complete surviving pre-1870 documents from one English village was created. Macfarlane transcribed the whole text of each document, adding additional markup to delimit specific categories of information. A description of the technical solutions was unfortunately published in very brief form only (King 1981).

Again, looking at the bibliographic record, John Bradley's question comes to mind, probably again slightly reformulated: *Why have these approaches left so few traces, not only in the historical mainstream, but even in the digital history or digital humanities tradition?*

In 1991 I tried to systematise the approaches taken by historians to the task of processing information extracted from historical sources by current software (Thaller 2018). I distinguished between four generic approaches at that time: (a) coding for statistical software; (b) extraction of textual snippets into fields of databases; (c) marked up text; and (d) what I described in 1991 as 'image-bound', referring to the then brand new 'hyper' software; today one probably would speak of annotated media. There is no point in following the full argument of this paper. Let it suffice to say that I considered the task of extracting processable data from historical sources as an effort which had to negotiate between two requirements: to extract chunks of information with an appropriate semantic precision while trying to preserve the form in which that information had been transmitted. Coding something into statistical variables has the advantage that there is a truly clear operational model of how to derive analytic rewards from the exercise. But checking the reliability and validity of the coding is next to impossible from the statistical data. Connecting links to scanned manuscripts allows permanent control of the conceptual decisions taken; but whether an analysis of such annotated material can be supported for any analytic approach beyond facilitating hermeneutic inspection was – and is – difficult to answer. And the other two approaches listed above just represent two other attempts to balance the requirements mentioned.

The process of negotiation between the two goals described above has led to frustrating results for many historians. One of the reasons that databases were as popular in the 1980s/early 1990s as they were, was probably that many historians found it a wonderful idea that you just could type textual snippets into the fields of your database 'without bothering about how to press them into a Procrustean coding system'. Unfortunately, many researchers feeling enthusiastic about 'entering just what the source said' found out, after a year of intensive data entry, that when they started counting terms, so many orthographic variances turned up that it was almost impossible to make any sense of the counts. And categories of data for which computational tools could provide obvious advantages – say calendar dates – left much to desire for processing, if you had entered the 'second Tuesday after Easter' just as you encountered it. Without entering the intricacies of processing temporal expressions in historical sources, let me just notice that they have been a permanent topic of computer scientists with an affinity to historical studies for an exceedingly long time (Zarri 1984; De Tré 2016). Trying to document more modest and pragmatic solutions to this class of problems in individual projects would, again, turn this into a bibliographic exercise. What is a bit puzzling is that on both levels – formal approaches somewhere in or close to the sphere of AI, as well as pragmatic how-we-have-handled-temporal-information-in-the-only-software-package-we-happen-to-know reports – there seems to be no progress over the years.

Theorists are not aware of previous work; projects solve the same question again and again for yet another database or processing system, without obvious profit from their forerunners.

Bluntly speaking, therefore: if you enter data as they occur in sources, it becomes extremely difficult to process them; if you enter them in a consistent notation that eases processing but still remains as close to the text as it is possible, your investment – be it your own time, or staff time – is heavy. That a markup standard has existed for a long time has not changed this. Indeed, the TEI has provided since P3 (TEI P3, 598–603) a standard for encoding temporal data, which was expanded extensively until P5 (TEI P5, 445–7). As in other cases, these recommendations assume, implicitly, however: (a) that the transfer from the information encoded in the text into a standardised representation that facilitates processing happens manually; and (b) that the users are themselves responsible for implementing a technical solution to process this standardised representation. The example: '<residence from="1857-03-01" to="1857-04-30">Lived in Amsterdam during March and April of 1857.</residence>' is followed by the statement 'Normalization of date and time values permits the efficient processing of data (for example, to determine whether one event precedes or follows another)' (TEI P5, 447). This is undoubtedly true. But it means that PhD students working on data collection for their thesis first have to enter the markup, then convert the temporal expression manually, and finally find a software solution for deciding which of two overlapping periods precedes or follows the other. Which means that the harassed PhD student quite likely will simply enter the dates into a database without the detour via markup – or avoid the database completely and just quote such dates as are unavoidable for the argument. 'Unavoidable for the argument' . . . which is a breach of the promise that employing information technology would allow one to handle easily types and amounts of sources, which could not be handled without them.

This might be another partial answer to the question of John Bradley's that we started with. And a similar problem applies to the brilliant factoid model presented in Pasin and Bradley 2015. In a world where researchers, particularly young ones, have to economise their working hours, applying such highly evolved standards, only to learn that afterwards you have to solve all sorts of technical problems for processing them, is rather prohibitive – unless you have a whole team which produces a database as the digital equivalent of a printed prosopography, rather than as a tool for a project, which derives its merit not from the database, but from the analysis put on top of it. And for a discipline like history, not so much interested in the text as such, but rather in the factoids derived from it, the distance between machine-readable source and final product is greater than in literary studies.

The factoids, argued for so convincingly in Pasin and Bradley 2015, could be highly attractive for historians (at least for the non-Hayden-White type), if:

(a) marking up the raw material for factoids in a natural text would be supported by feature extraction software;
(b) the conversion of textual expressions in the markup into processable representations would be supported by software modules implementing knowledge about individual categories of such expressions;
(c) using (a) and (b) factoids of the type under discussion could be constructed by suitable tools; and
(d) factoids form a class of digital objects, which could be processed with the same ease as images can be today.

That is, factoids would have to be supported as 'objects' in the full sense of software technology – where an object is defined *not* as a bundle of data in some format, but as a collection of data, together with *methods supporting their processing*. In other words: for factoids to flourish among historians, we need a technical implementation which does for them what TACT (Bradley 1989) did to text retrieval/concordances.

References

Allen, Robert F. (ed.). 1985. *Data Bases in the Humanities and the Social Sciences* 2. Osprey: Paradigm Press.

Ankersmit, Frank R. 2001. *Historical Representation*. Stanford, CA: Stanford University Press.

Baum, Hans-Peter and Rolf Sprandel. 1980. 'Die Erforschung von Lehensregistern in Verbindung mit der EDV. Ein sozialgeschichtliches Projekt der Universität Würzburg', *Jahrbuch der historischen Forschung* 6: 49–55.

Bradley, John. 1989. *TACT*. University of Toronto.

Bradley, John. 2014. 'Databases and GIS: A critical approach', *International Journal of Humanities and Arts Computing* 8(1): 13–27.

De Tré, Guy and Jeroen Deploige. 2016. 'Time Modelling in Digital Humanities. Challenges posed by the development of a database of medieval charters', *it - Information Technology* 58(2): 97–103.

Denley, Peter and Deian Hopkin. 1987. *History and Computing*. Manchester: Manchester University Press.

Genicot, Léopold. 1977. 'Le Traitement électronique des textes diplomatiques belges antérieurs à 1200', *Informatique et histoire médiévale (= Collection de l'Ecole française de Rome (31))*: 97–104.

Ginter, Donald E., Peter Grogono and Frederick A. Bode. 1977. 'A Review of Optimal Input Methods: Fixed field, free field, and the edited text', *Historical Methods Newsletter* 10(4): 166–76.

Harvey, Charles and Jon Press. 1996. *Databases in Historical Research*. London: Macmillan.

King, Timothy. 1981. 'The Use of Computers for Storing Records in Historical Research', *Historical Methods* 14: 59–64.

Macfarlane, Alan. 1977. *Reconstructing Historical Communities*. Cambridge: Cambridge University Press.

McCrank, Lawrence (ed.). 1989. *Databases in the Humanities and the Social Sciences 4*. Medford, NJ: Learned Information.

McCrank, Lawrence J. 2002. *Historical Information Science*. Medford, NJ: Information Today.

Moberg, Thomas F. (ed.) 1987. *Data Bases in the Humanities and the Social Sciences 3*. Osprey: Paradigm Press.

Pasin, Michele and John Bradley. 2015. 'Factoid-Based Prosopography and Computer Ontologies: Towards an integrated approach', *Digital Scholarship in the Humanities* 30(1): 86–97.

Pasleau, Suzy. 1990. 'Comparaison théorique des Système de Gestion de Bases de Données Relationnelles (SGBDR) Oracle, Informix et Ingres', *Revue informatique et statistique dans les sciences humaines* 26: 183–202.

Raben, Joseph and Gregory Marks (eds). 1980. *Data Bases in the Humanities and the Social Sciences*. Amsterdam: North Holland.

TEI P3 – C. Michael Sperberg-McQueen and Lou Burnard: *Guidelines for Electronic Text Encoding and Interchange (TEI P3)*, version quoted: 8 April 1994.

TEI P5 – TEI Consortium: *TEI P5: Guidelines for Electronic Text Encoding and Interchange*, Version 3.4.0. Last updated 23 July 2018, revision 1fa0b54.

Thaller, Manfred. 2018. 'The Need for Standards: Data modelling and exchange [1991]', *Historical Social Research* Suppl. 29: 203–20. https://doi.10.12759/hsr.suppl.29.2017.203-220

White, Hayden. 1973. *Metahistory*. Baltimore, MD: Johns Hopkins University Press.

Zarri, Gian Pierro. 1984. 'An Overview of RESEDA. An artificial intelligence question answering system dealing with a biographical database'. In *Computer Applications to Medieval Studies*, edited by Anne Gilmour-Bryson, 177–94. Kalamazoo, MI: Western Michigan University, Medieval Institute Publications.

Part IV:
In Memoriam

13
If Voyant then Spyral: remembering Stéfan Sinclair*

Geoffrey Rockwell

Humanities research tends to be thought of as solitary practice. We recognise that humanists might work together on tools like dictionaries or concordances, but our image of the thinking that is *really* research is that of a solitary thinker like Rembrandt's *Philosopher in Meditation* (Figure 13.1), where the thinker is lit up by the warm sunlight from above while a spiral staircase of thought winds upwards, into the darkness.[1]

Figure 13.1   Rembrandt's *Philosopher in Meditation*.

We could blame René Descartes who, in his 1637 *Discourse on Method*, tells a story of a moment of solitude that allowed him to talk to himself about his thoughts and to develop a method for thinking correctly. This is how he describes the solitude he needed to realise that solitary work was the best:

> As I was returning to the army from the coronation of the emperor, I was halted by the onset of winter in quarters where, having no diverting company and fortunately also no cares or emotional turmoil to trouble me, I spent the whole day shut up in a small room heated by a stove, in which I could converse with my own thoughts at leisure. Among the first of these was the realization that things made up of different elements and produced by the hands of several master craftsmen are often less perfect than those on which only one person has worked. (Descartes 2006, 12)

Descartes would probably have welcomed the isolation forced on us by the COVID-19 pandemic, which, at the time of writing, we are experiencing here in Canada as Descartes did, in winter.

By contrast, in hybrid fields like the digital humanities we are often required to think together, in interdisciplinary teams. We have to bring together different crafts, from graphic design to scholarly editing to programming, in order to develop digital things. The image of our work might be reflected in an illustration of craft workers collaborating from, for example, Diderot's *Encyclopédie*. Diderot, it should be added, not only celebrated the crafts, but mocked the myth of solitary genius in his dialogue *Le Neveu de Rameau* (1956).

What does this have to do with remembering Stéfan Sinclair?[2] For Descartes the work of many hands is less perfect because error can creep in more easily. Certainty comes from clear and distinct ideas which are held in the mind – one mind; a mind locked down like Descartes's was, in a small room heated by a stove. For Stéfan the potential of the digital humanities came from thinking together with others and looking through crafted tools at the gyre of texts and ideas. If Voyant was an instrument for looking differently at texts, then Spyral is a way of sharing the looking with others. Which is why, in this concluding chapter, I want to challenge the image of the solitary thinker we have inherited for humanities practice. I want to tell a different story – a story of collaborative practice rather than a methodology of doubt. It is about the practice of thinking-through the development of text analysis tools that Stéfan Sinclair and I engaged in from about 2008, that led to a series of hybrid interventions combining tools like Voyant 2.0 (2016) with reflections on the making like those written up in *Hermeneutica* (2016).

Specifically I will discuss thinking-through as the practice we used to develop Voyant. Next I will talk about the notebook programming environment Spyral, which extends Voyant, and finally I will conclude with a discussion about notebooks and replication as practice.

If the reader will indulge me and allow a play on words, this discourse, unlike that of Descartes which was on method, is on practice. Method is what we say we do or aspire to do; practice is what we actually do. Therefore this chapter looks at a different spiral of thought; not the solitary turn of the philosopher in meditation, but the doubled practice of thinking-through.

Thinking-through

When one looks closely at the *Philosopher in Meditation* one sees a second figure in the lower right tending a second source of light – a fire for heating the room or perhaps for preparing food. Rembrandt lets us discover that the solitary thinker is not really alone, but is in fact supported by a servant whose carework makes it possible to meditate in the first place. He can meditate, or fall asleep and dream, because he is comfortable and cared for.

In 'The Carework and Codework of the Digital Humanities' (2015), Lauren Klein talks about another type of carework – namely the often invisible work of building and maintaining infrastructure like libraries and tools that make research possible. Voyant is one such infrastructure. Stéfan and I found ourselves in a situation that is common in the digital humanities, whereby one can get a one-time grant to develop a tool like Voyant, but then struggle to obtain support to care for it continuously and, furthermore, find it hard to get academic credit for what, after all, is seen as 'tool building'.

Digital humanists know what it is like to end up overlooked in the corner. This is in part due to the logic of software; a well-designed interface does not draw attention to itself the way academic work should; it becomes transparent in the way a telescope does, so that the researcher can see through it. The tool becomes a lens for interpretation, or a telescope for the mind as Margaret Masterman put it in 1962, but no one pays much attention to the lens grinder. The thinking-through of the tool follows the carework of design and maintenance that the developer of the tool engages in. It is only when the tool needs to be developed, or tuned, or breaks down that it and the practices it enables are presented to us to think about. To draw attention to the practices, you need to interrupt its use. Let's look again at Voyant.

Voyant evolved out of a long collaboration that began when Stéfan and I were both at McMaster University, supported by a CFI-funded project called the Text Analysis Portal for Research (TAPoR) which, among other things, had funded a lab there.[3] Stéfan had developed HyperPo, a brilliant in-browser text analysis tool, as part of his doctoral work; I had been working on various tools. TAPoR, which was meant to bring together text analysis services, gave us reason to collaborate on something new and a warm lab in which to do it. We decided to try an experiment where we would take a small text analysis project through from conception to write-up in a day. We would meet in the lab and, over a day, pick a challenge, find the texts, hack away and see how far we could get with the tools at hand. This first experiment eventually led to a chapter in our book *Hermeneutica* (2016), entitled 'Now Analyze That'.

From the outset we decided that this was to be a reflective experiment, in the sense that we were going to not just experiment with tools but also reflect back on how the tools worked, what tools were needed, and even how the collaborative research worked. We decided to adapt what was then a new method in programming practice called Pair Programming, where all programming is done in pairs with only one person actually programming while the other is free to reflect, comment, guide, plan, get coffee, research and document. We therefore always had one person not using tools and thus free to think about them. In short, we took a day off from all the other things we should have been doing and spent it playing and talking about the playing.

Needless to say, we did not get the project done by the end of the day, but we got far enough to know that this was more generative than working alone. Errors are less likely when you have to talk everything through with someone else. We also discovered that none of the tools at hand really did what we wanted them to do, which led to a tool agenda. We were going to have to weave into our practice the ongoing development of new tools. We were going to have to bootstrap the research and tools. We could also see a way to a paper (and eventually a book) which would help with the problem of getting no credit for tool work. From this collaborative start it was not a big step to start planning a set of experiments that had the following features.

- We would take real projects through to completion to test the whole lifecycle of text analysis, from ideation to publication.

- We would reflect on the practices of working together, like the practice of Pair Programming.
- We would use the experiments to drive the development of a new set of tools. Thus these experiments became a development and usability practice. Many of the features of Voyant came from what we found we needed in our experiments.

We could only tackle such a multifaceted project because Stéfan was a brilliant programmer who was also interested in interpretation. He possessed a rare combination of professional programming skills and academic training in literary text analysis. My role was more that of the gadfly asking questions – the Watson to his Holmes – reflecting stories like this one about what we did.

Having found our one-day experiment so generative, we decided to build a praxis around such experiments. We would develop a series of experiments of different sorts and through those hybrid projects we would both develop Voyant 2.0 and write papers illustrating Voyant's use and reflecting back on the practice. Inevitably Voyant became a reflection of our collaboration – almost a ghost third collaborator.

Later on, when writing *Hermeneutica* we settled on the phrase *thinking-through* as a description of our practice. There are number of reasons for this.

- Thinking-through is an alternative translation for the Greek *dia-logos*. Many think the '*dia*' in *dialogos* means two, but in fact '*dia*' means *between* or *through*. Thus one can think of dialogue as a thinking that happens between people or through conversation. In our case the dialogue was a thinking-through both in the form of conversation and through crafting hermeneutical tools.
- As part of our reflection on practice we were reading a lot about tools and instruments and how they could be scholarly artefacts that bear, or hide, theory. We were particularly taken with Davis Baird's 2004 discussion of demonstration instruments like the orrery in *Thing Knowledge*. The notion of things bearing knowledge captured what we felt we were developing. The question was how a tool might bear knowledge, and 'thinking-through' described the way a practice using tools would be shaped by the scholarly instrument. Tools frame the thinking done through them the way telescopes change seeing.
- I should add that the digital humanities has had to deal for decades with the hierarchy of value in academia that treats tool building as service work that is of less value than other forms of production like

theorising through books. We wanted to challenge this through a double move of both building a tool as theory and writing a book that reflected on how our tools could be read. There was, to be frank, a defensive side to this – if we did not get credit for the development, at least we would get credit for the conference papers, workshops, journal articles and book.

- The thing we were most proud of was how we designed Voyant so that you could export the interactive panels – the hermeneutical things you made and which we called the *hermeneutica*, and then embed them in your online papers. This was one of the outgrowths of reflecting on the whole cycle of a project right up to publication. We wanted to be able to embed interactives directly into our papers and then we wanted others to be able to do the same. Ironically the interpretative paradigm we were theorizing and developing for – that of publishing papers with embedded interactive hermeneutical things – was perhaps the feature few actually used. Publishing papers online was a practice too far. Users love Voyant; it is used by hundreds of thousands of people around the world, and a few nice people read the book, but almost no one embeds *hermeneutica* into their interpretations.

Which leads me to Spyral and how we returned to the idea of weaving projects out of code and reflection.

Reflecting with/on Spyral

After developing Voyant and writing *Hermeneutica* we started a second project that like the first involved developing tools through experiments and reflecting on them. In this case the tool we developed/are developing is called Spyral and it is an extension to Voyant that provides a notebook-style programming environment.

In Spyral you create a (spiral) notebook made up of text cells and code cells. The text cells are where you can document what you are trying to do and reflect on the results. The code cells are where you can write code to process text and/or open Voyant panels as output. The Voyant panels like the Cirrus panel in Figure 13.2 are fully interactive. We chose to spell the tool Spyral with a 'y' to connect it to Voyant and to carry on the visual metaphor of seeing or spying on the text.

Spyral follows the 'literate programming' paradigm that Knuth (1984) proposed where the programming environment encourages writing out a literate narrative of what you are doing. In literate programming

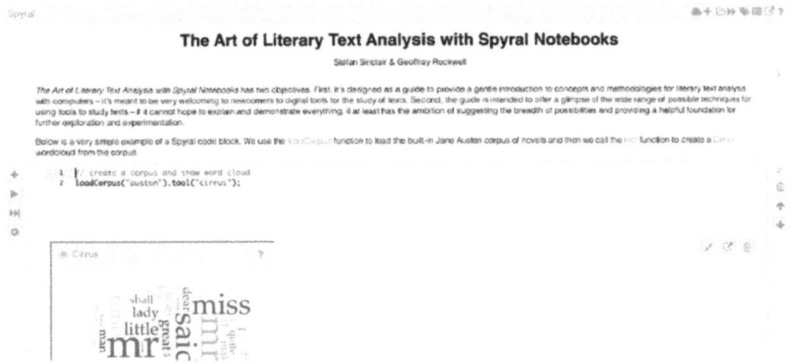

The Art of Literary Text Analysis with Spyral Notebooks

Stéfan Sinclair & Geoffrey Rockwell

The Art of Literary Text Analysis with Spyral Notebooks has two objectives. First, it is designed as a guide to provide a gentle introduction to concepts and methodologies for literary text analysis with computers – it's meant to be very welcoming to newcomers to digital tools for the study of texts. Second, the guide is intended to offer a glimpse of the wide range of possible techniques for using tools to study texts – if it cannot hope to explain and demonstrate everything, it at least has the ambition of suggesting the breadth of possibilities and providing a helpful foundation for further exploration and experimentation.

Below is a very simple example of a Spyral code block. We use the loadCorpus *function to load the built-in Jane Austen corpus of novels and then we call the* tool *function to create a* Cirrus *wordcloud from the corpus.*

```
1  // create a corpus and show word cloud
2  loadCorpus("austen").tool("cirrus");
```

Figure 13.2   Spyral notebook from the Art of Literary Text
Analysis series.

you are not writing only code, but keeping a notebook that, like a scientist's notebook, documents through text, code and panels, what you have seen. Programming in a notebook environment starts with describing what you want to achieve and what the code should do for others. You then add the code that generates Voyant panels that make your point. This paradigm overturns the usual relationship between coding and commenting. You do not code and then reluctantly add comments afterwards. Literate programming also recognises that programs are often read and re-read by humans as well as run on a computer, so you are encouraged to write for future readers like yourself. Our added turn is that you can use Spyral to write a paper communicating the results of thinking-through text analysis with the relevant Voyant panels showing results embedded live in the flow of your argument.

Literate programming with notebooks has been around for a while. Wolfram Mathematica (http://www.wolfram.com/mathematica/) and now Jupyter notebooks (http://jupyter.org) are some of the best-known examples of such literate notebook environments and they are both used widely for data science and scientific computing because they encourage the writing out of the thinking behind analysis. Figure 13.3 shows a Mathematica notebook.[4]

This notebook model has become popular in digital humanities text mining, for the same reasons it is popular in other fields where researchers want to share their thinking. A notebook is an easy way to explain the reasoning behind a project. A notebook lets you weave together explanation, code and results, in a fashion that others can use to replicate your results or try your methods on other texts. In effect, it brings together into one spiral-bound notebook two tools important to the digital humanist,

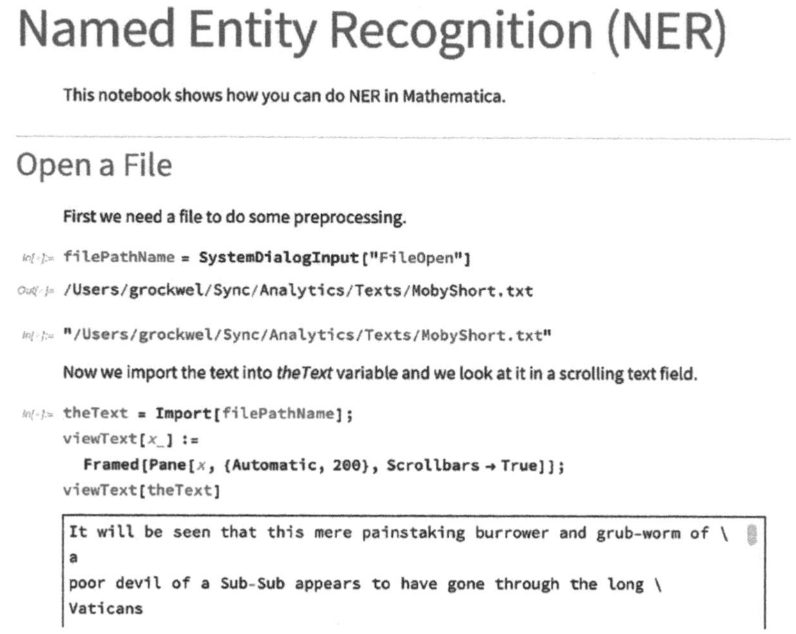

Named Entity Recognition (NER)

This notebook shows how you can do NER in Mathematica.

Open a File

First we need a file to do some preprocessing.

```
In[·]:= filePathName = SystemDialogInput["FileOpen"]
```

```
Out[·]= /Users/grockwel/Sync/Analytics/Texts/MobyShort.txt
```

```
In[·]:= "/Users/grockwel/Sync/Analytics/Texts/MobyShort.txt"
```

Now we import the text into *theText* variable and we look at it in a scrolling text field.

```
In[·]:= theText = Import[filePathName];
viewText[x_] :=
   Framed[Pane[x, {Automatic, 200}, Scrollbars → True]];
viewText[theText]
```

```
It will be seen that this mere painstaking burrower and grub-worm of \
a
poor devil of a Sub-Sub appears to have gone through the long \
Vaticans
```

Figure 13.3   Mathematica notebook.

the editor for writing and the programming environment for analysing data. Intertwined, one can think-through writing and coding or coding as writing.

Notebooks also provide useful learning tools where the tutorial text, example code, and exercises can be woven together and read while running. Figure 13.2 above shows an edited version of the first notebook in the series *The Art of Literary Text Analysis*. This is an example textbook that we wrote first in Jupyter IPython notebooks and that we are now reimplementing in Spyral.

Equally important is the way notebooks provide a pathway for users to go from playing with Voyant to writing about and with text analysis. In this way users can replicate the generative practices of taking a project from ideation to sharing or publishing online. Key to this is a feature Stéfan added to Voyant so that you can export any interactive panel you like to a Spyral notebook with the associated corpus (Figure 13.4). This lets you see the code needed to get your panel so you can start adding to it or experimenting with the parameters. In this, Stéfan was designing Spyral not just for research but also for teaching. He set it up so that it would be easy for students to share their thinking through text analysis. They could start by playing with Voyant and *if* Voyant showed them

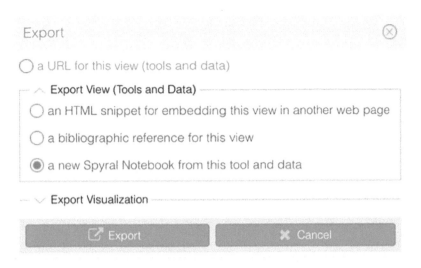

Figure 13.4 Voyant Export panel.

something interesting *then* they could tell the story through Spyral. As such he was imagining a different type of term paper that could have embedded interactive panels. We were again trying to support the practices we have found so generative, but support these practices for students first experiencing text analysis. We both had extensive experience trying to teach students more than how to use text analysis, now we wanted them to think beyond the tool. With Spyral we could give them a programming environment that extends Voyant and that doubles as a place they could share their results back in an interactive form.

Next steps

To conclude I spiral back to the *Philosopher in Meditation*. The painting actually has a third figure that has disappeared over time. In the dark of the spiral staircase there is a ghostly figure facing us that has been obscured by the ageing varnish. You can see it in the nineteenth-century engraved reproduction in Figure 13.5.[5] This third figure is climbing the spiral staircase and seems to turn to us and invite us to follow. It could be Anna if the painting is in fact supposed to be Tobit and Anna waiting for their son. Or it could be Philosophy herself inviting us, not the snoozing Cartesian, up into the spiral of thinking-through. Given the play of light and dark one is tempted to see this staircase as lit by, on the one hand, both the light of the heavenly sun and books next to the philosopher and,

Figure 13.5 Engraving of the *Philosopher in Meditation* by Devilliers l'aîné after Rembrandt (1814).

on the other hand, by the modest and artificial light of the fire of technology tended by the caretaker. Like Spyral notebooks the staircase, as a representation of thinking-through, is braided from these two sources of light: the light of thinking from above and the warmth from below of technologies also used for thinking.

Remember that the spiral staircase is not just a metaphor for thinking – it is itself a technology – a technology that provides a pathway up and around. A technology that the third figure invites us to explore. I think of Stéfan in the spiral inviting us to continue the careful work. If Voyant then Spyral.

In memory of Stéfan Sinclair who passed in August 2020
https://csdh-schn.org/stefan-sinclair-in-memoriam-2/

Notes

* This paper evolved out of a talk given online to colleagues of Stéfan Sinclair at McGill in November 2020. Ideas in the paper were also adapted for a paper for the INKE project under review. All websites cited in the notes below were accessed and checked 6 September 2022.
1. Recent research actually suggests that the painting is not of a philosopher, but that it is Tobit waiting for his son. Nonetheless this painting has been taken to be paradigmatic of the

meditating philosopher. The image was sourced from Wikipedia at https://en.wikipedia.org/wiki/Philosopher_in_Meditation and is in the public domain.

2. Stéfan Sinclair, one of the original editors of this collection, passed away in August 2020. See https://csdh-schn.org/stefan-sinclair-in-memoriam/ for an obituary. This chapter is based on a presentation that G. Rockwell gave to his department after Stéfan's passing.

3. The TAPoR project was funded in 2002 by the Canadian Foundation for Innovation. TAPoR funded labs at the participating universities and served as a central portal. This portal has changed over time, but is still available as a tool discovery tool; see http://tapor.ca

4. William Turkel has created a great textbook in the notebook programming environment Mathematica called *Digital Research Methods with Mathematica*, https://williamjturkel.net/digital-research-methods-with-mathematica/. The book shows how a text can have live code panels woven into it for learning by doing.

5. See the Wikipedia page on the Philosopher in Meditation for more: https://en.wikipedia.org/wiki/Philosopher_in_Meditation

References

Baird, D. 2004. *Thing Knowledge: A philosophy of scientific instruments*. Berkeley, CA: University of California Press.

Descartes, R. 2006. *A Discourse on the Method of Correctly Conducting One's Reason and Seeking Truth in the Sciences*, trans. I. Maclean. Oxford: Oxford University Press.

Diderot, D. 1956. *Rameau's Nephew and Other Works*, trans. J. Barzun and R.H. Bowen. Garden City, NY: Doubleday.

Klein, Lauren F. 2015. 'The Carework and Codework of the Digital Humanities', conference paper presented at *The Digital Antiquarian 2015*. Accessed 5 September 2022. http://lklein.com/archives/the-carework-and-codework-of-the-digital-humanities/

Knuth, D.E. 1984. 'Literate Programming', *The Computer Journal* 27(2): 97–111.

Masterman, M. 1962. '"The Intellect's New Eye". Freeing the mind: articles and letters from the *Times Literary Supplement* during March–June, 1962'. London: Times Pub. Co., 38–44.

Rockwell, G. and S. Sinclair 2016. *Hermeneutica: Computer-assisted interpretation in the humanities*. Cambridge, MA: MIT Press.

Index

abduction 180–4, 191, 193
Abrahamsson, Pekka 185
abstract ideas 32, 253
academic work 6, 45, 129, 136–7
access to museum collections 167
adaptive systems 183–8
'administrators' 158, 160
affordances, theory of 255
agile development 183–5
Albert of Saxony 196
'algorithmic facts' 224–5
ambiguity, textual 191–3
American New Criticism 214
analyst role 158–9, 180
Andersen, Chris 173, 179
Anderson, Michael 251
Ankersmit, Frank 106, 117–18, 269
annotated source documents 235–6
annotation process 40, 223–9, 242
    digital 228–9
Anselm of Canterbury 194, 198
Apple Macintosh computers 11, 19
apps 257
Aquinas, Thomas 139
archiving 171
Armstrong, Guyda 19
ARRAS system 19
artificial intelligence (AI) 179–82, 258
    symbolic 182
artificial sciences 181–3, 187
Arts and Humanities Research Board
    (AHRB) 60, 62
Arts and Humanities Research Council
    (AHRC) 38, 68
assertiveness 194
Ast, Friedrich 219
autopoiesis 5, 186, 190, 204–5
axes
    of *method, function* and *procedure* 229
    of *process, discourse* and *context* 218–19

Baird, Davis 281
Barnes, Jonathan 194
Barwise, Jon 191, 194, 197–8
Bauer, Matthias 227
Baum, Hans-Peter 270
Bauman, Syd 153
Baxter, Stephen 62
Beech, George T. 53
Berge, Claude 255
Berners-Lee, Tim 75

bibliography 271
'big data' 15, 179, 207, 214, 217
'big tent' DH 15–16
Bird, Otto 195–6
Blair, Ann 38–9
Blei, David M. 215
Blevins, Cameron 23–4
Boast, Robin 168–9
Bodard, Gabriel 91
Bodenhamer, David 27
Boot, P. 226
Borgman, Christine 179
Borgolte, Michael 55
Boyle, Robert 135–6
Bradley, John v, vii, 1–2, 6–12, 21, 23, 29, 37,
    58–64, 66–70, 74, 78–81, 87–92, 96–100,
    105–7, 116–18, 129, 136–8, 213–18, 230,
    236, 239–42, 251, 254–6, 262, 267–73
'Breaking of Britain' project 109
brieves and brieve-charters 109
British Museum 164, 171
Brockman, W.S. 38
Broun, Dauvit v, vii, 89
Brown, Susan 69
Browning, Robert 57
Buckner, Cameron 179
Bullough, Donald 54–5
Burghart, Alex 60
Burnard, Lou 232
Burns, Arthur 60, 88
Busa, Roberto 1–2, 131–4, 138–43
Buscema, Massimo 187
Buzzetti, Dino vi–vii, 187, 200, 227

Cameron, Averil v, vii, 54, 58, 60
Canadian Writing Research Collaboratory
    (CWRC) 69
canonical figures 133
Cardon, Dominique 181–2, 189
Carroll, B.A. 135
Carruthers, W. 143
cataloguing 29, 165
category-mistakes 194
Caton, Paul 223
Centre for Research in the Humanities
    (CeRch) 83
'chiasm' concept 207
Ciula, Arianna v, vii, 97
civil rights movements 164
Clergy of the Church of England 1540–1835
    (CCEd database) 88–90

Clifford, James 165, 168–9
code libraries 237
cognition 251–2
collaborative work 8–9, 26, 69, 75, 121, 129, 149, 236, 256
collegiality 80
Colley, Linda 252
combinatorics 254–5, 264
commas 199
Community of the Realm in Medieval Scotland 110
Companion to Digital Humanities 131–2
complexity, levels of 225
computational analysis 187–8, 192, 198, 207, 270
computational literary studies (CLS) 214–15
criticism of 214
computationality 224
Computer Assisted Text Markup and Association (CATMA) 10, 218, 230–40
analysis module 230
hermeneutic data model 231–2
versions of 230
conceptualisation 228
Concordance Generating System (COGS) 17–18
configurations 254–5
connectionist procedures 180–2
contact zones 168–9
conversational cycle 201–2
Coombs, James H. 222–3
copyright restrictions 68
Cornwall, Andrew 169
Correspondence Analysis (CA) 21–5
COVID-19 pandemic 278
cross-collection searching 70
cultural heritage 164–7
cybernetics 204–5
'cyborg sciences' 252

Da, Nan Z. 214
Dante Alighieri 12
data creators 158–9
data-driven procedures 215
data entry 30
data sovereignty 174–5
database technology 70
databases 5, 8, 32–3, 62, 105–13, 116–21, 130, 166, 267, 269
and historical theory 195–7
de re statements 198
decision-making 169
deduction theorem 193–4
degree programs 161
Denton, William 35–6
Depreux, Philippe 55
Descartes, René 278
'developers' 156–9
Di Clemente, Valeria 110
Diderot, Denis 278
digital artefacts, skills and tools needed for dealing with 3–6
digital editions 27, 31, 33, 35
digital humanities (DH) 3–17, 26–7, 31–3, 37, 42–5, 54, 63, 78–83, 86–8, 92–6, 99–101, 129–38, 142–3, 148–59, 180, 213–18, 223–5, 237–8, 241, 262–3, 278

careers in 148
definition of 2
hybrid specialists in 6
impact of 44
making in 1–5, 9–11
options for 217–18
scope and shaping of 2, 4
vulnerability of 149
worth of 5
digital humanities centres 148–9, 152
digital projects 4–8, 11
developed by teams 6
individuals working on 7
space for and primacy of 4–5
digital technology 55–6, 59, 61, 258
'digital turn' 216
digitisation 165–6
Dinsman, Melissa 44–5
Django framework 30, 84, 86, 90
Domesday Book 62
Dorn, Sherman 117
Drucker, Johanna 96, 237–8

Earls Colne project 270
Early Modern London Theatres (EMLoT) 68–9, 73–5
e-books 70
Eclipse platform 39
Egyptology 143
Einstein, Albert 181–2
Ekwall, Eilert 72
Eliot, T.S. 12
Elizabeth 1, Queen 71
Ellis, John 25
embedding 282
empowerment and disempowerment 169, 238
encoding, interactional 223
'end of theory' 179
Engelbart, Douglas 39–40
'English Royal Administration' (ERA) 109
enthymematic argument 196
entity relationship diagrams 30
epistemology 203
eREED 73–4
Etchemendy, John 191, 194, 197–8
Eurocentrism 166, 171
'evidence of value' 251–2
expert systems 187–9
experts 164
Exploratory Data Analysis 23

facetted searching, facetted classification and facetted browsing 35–7
factoids 28–9, 32, 43, 59–63, 105, 112, 270
derived from the text 273
Feibleman, James 18
feminism and feminisation 135, 142–3
Ferguson, Brinker vi, viii
Fincham, Ken 88
first- and *second-order* statements 201
Fish, Stanley 14–16, 23–4, 38, 44
Flanders, Julia vi, viii, 6–8, 100, 228
follow-on projects 5
formalization 188
Fortune Theatre 69
Fox Keller, Evelyn 253

Frankl, Viktor 219
Freeman, Jessica 69
Frege, Gottlob 220–1
Froeyman, Anton 107, 117–21

Gadamer, Hans-Georg 221
Galileo 24
Gallacher, Gordon 56–9
Gardin, Jean-Claude 188–202
Gardner, Martin 258
Garson, James 179
Geismar, Haidy 167
Gelzer, Matthias 51
gender stereotypes 135
Gerbaudo, Paolo 42
Gibson, James J. 255
Gigenzer, Gerd 181
Gitelman, Lisa 166
Gold, Matthew K. 15
Google Scholar 132
Gray, Jonathan 92
'great men' 134
Greenacre, Michael 21
Grundy, Lynne 58

'hack and yack' 2
Hacking, Ian 24–5
Hakiwai, Arapata vi, viii, 7, 10
Hall, Elliott 61
Hammond, Matthew (and 'Hammond
    numbers') 108, 110
Haraway, Donna 252
Harris, Aroha 171
Hawthorne, Mark 19
Hegel, G.W.F. 220
helicoidal cycle 202–3
heritage practices 164
'hermeneutic circle' 220, 222, 232, 242
hermeneutica 22, 282
hermeneutics 219–24, 227–8
Herstein, Israel Nathan 187
Hestenes, David 192
heuristics 181
Highsmith, James A. 184–5
Hinton, Geoffrey 180
Hire, Pauline 54
Hirschheim, Rudy 185
historical theory 195–7
historical thinking 33
historicisation of DH 131
historiography 120
    inversion of 105
history
    as an activity 117–21
    of DH 130–6, 143
    digital 107, 116, 120
    medieval 55
    nature of 105–6, 111, 114
    of Parliament 72–3
    written 106, 117, 121
human-computer interaction (HCI) 19–20
humanities computing 150–1, 213–16, 242,
    256, 277; see also digital humanities
Hume, David 21
Hunnisett, R.F. 70
Hutchins, Edwin 93, 98
hypotheses, interpretive 23

IBM computers 18–19
Ife, Barry 58
Index Thomisticus 133, 138–43
indexing guidelines 70
indigenous communities 164–5, 172–5
inductive machines 181
inference, rules of 194
'inference-ticket' theory 194–6
information management 158
infrastructure 9–10, 85
intellectual property 173–5
intelligent machines 182–3
interaction between humans and
    machines 264
interdisciplinarity 6, 8, 58, 64, 129,
    253, 278
interoperability 70, 76, 92
interpretation
    textual 220
    versus reading 220–2
interpretive theory 226
Ito, Joichi 183

Jacob, François 253–4
Jakacki, Diane 69
Jannidis, Fotis 228
Jeffreys, Elizabeth 61
Jeffreys, Michael 60–1
Jenkins, Keith 106
Johnstone, Karl vi, viii, 169–70
Jones, A.H.M. 52–3
Jordan, Michael 215

Kaltenbrunner, W. 130
Keynes, Simon 60
keypunching 139–42
Kierkegaard, Søren 21
King's College, London 16, 25–9, 38, 42, 45,
    55–63, 69, 74, 79–83, 86–8, 92–4, 100,
    129, 137–8, 151, 256
    Department of Digital Humanities (DDH)
    79–80, 83, 92
King's Digital Lab (KDL) 5, 78–93,
    96–101
    career development in 80–1
Klein, Heinz K. 185
Klein, Lauren 15, 279
Kleymann, Rabea 238–9
knowledge generation 217
Knuth, D.E. 281
Krajewski, Markus 258
Kruse, Susan 56–60

laboratory support staff 136
labour, devaluation of 3
Lancashire, Anne 68
Lancashire, Ian 17–18
language
    natural 206–8
    subjective and objective 205–6
Latour, Bruno 254
Lavagnino, John 58
LDA algorithm 215
LeCun, Yann 181
legacy projects 84, 87–92, 97, 100
Leicester, Earl of (Robert
    Dudley) 72–5

leveraging potential 216
Lévi-Strauss, Claude 253, 258
Liar sentence 191
lifecycle of a project 96
Linked Open Data (LOD) 37
'linked screens' 239
literary criticism 22–5
literary studies 130, 215, 225
lived experience 117–18
logical foundations 193–8
'logicism' 188–9
Lonetree, Amy 169
Luhmann, Niklas 258
Lynch, Bernadette 169

McCarthy, Conal 169
McCarty, Willard vi, viii, 9, 14–15, 43, 58,
    94–5, 132, 181, 216, 259
McCrank, Lawrence 267
McCulloch, Warren S. 180
McGann, Jerome 43, 186–7, 190–2, 200
McGavin, J. 68
Machiavelli, Niccolò 19
machine learning 224, 229
McKinnon, Alastair 21–3
MacLean, Sally-Beth v, viii
McLuhan, Marshall 186
Mahoney, Michael Sean 129–30
maintenance of digital resources 9
Mandal, Anthony 15
Mandelbaum, Maurice 193
Mandouze, A. 53
Mango, Cyril 54, 57
Manovich, Lev 166
Māori culture and rights 169–70, 174
mapping 72, 110
Marche, Stephen 15
markup 198–202, 216–17, 222–8, 231–5
    types of 225, 227
Maron, Nancy 148–50
Marrou, H.I. 52–3
Martindale, J.R. 53, 57–60
Masterman, Margaret 279
Maturana, Humberto R. 189
maxims 196
Mazurs, Edward G. 203
Mead, Moko 170
meaning-making 219, 221
measuring devices 251–2
Meister, Jan Christoph vi, ix, 7, 10–11
Meister, Malte 230
Mellon Foundation 41, 69–70
Merleau-Ponty, Maurice 203–4
mesotext 226
meta-annotation 232
metaknowledge 153, 157–8
metalanguage 192
metatext 226
methodological reductionism 223
methodology, use of the
    word 184, 279
Micheloud, François Xavier 23
microscopes 20, 24–5
Milton, John 38, 255
Mirowski, Philip 252
mixed methods 241

modelling 32–3, 93–101, 216, 227–8, 242, 256
    of the hermeneutic cycle 222
Mommsen, Theodor 51–2
Moretti, Franco 214, 216
Morus, I.R. 143
Munslow, Alun 106
Münzer, Friedrich 52
Murray, James 255–6, 259
museum collections and museology 164–9
music 98–9

Nagel, Ernest 196
Namier, Lewis 52
National Gallery of Australia 171
navigation between online resources 35
Nelson, Janet L. v, ix, 56–7, 60
neoliberalism 165
Nerur, Sridhar 185
Neumann, L. 38
neural networks 180–2
New Zealand 162–3, 173
'Newtonian neurosis' 184
Ng, Andrew Y. 215
Nietzsche, Friedrich 220
Norrish, Jamie 74
Northeastern University 152
note-taking 39–40, 255–64, 283
Nowviskie, Bethany 27, 43–5
Nyhan, Julianne v, ix, 45, 132, 138, 222

objective observation 25
Ong, Tiffany 97
'open access' 170
open data 91
oral history 140
Ordered Hierarchy of Content Objects (OHCO)
    217, 227
organic computing 183, 186
originality, concept of 135
overloading of junior jobs 160
Ovid 256
Oxford Concordance Program (OCP) 17
Oxford Dictionary of National Biography
    (ODNB) 52, 70–3
Oxford English Dictionary 255

Palmer, C. 38
Parker-Rhodes, Frederick 201–2
Parkinson, David J. 68
Pasin, Michele 105, 107, 115–18, 269, 272–3
Patrons and Performances 71–6
peer review 133
peerage 71, 73
Peirce, Charles Sanders 181–2
Pelteret, David 60
People of Medieval Scotland (PoMS) database
    8, 28, 89–90, 93, 106–21
People of Northern England (PoNE) 110
Peters, Paul Evan 252
Petrie, Flinders 134
Petris, Marco 230
philology 227
piano-playing 99
Pickle, Sarah 148–50
Pierazzo, Elena 27, 31, 35
Piez, Wendell 223

Pitts, Walter 180
place-names and place-date 113
Pliny system 11, 38–42, 213–16, 236,
    239–42, 256
    limitations of 41
Plutniak, Sébastien 188
poetry 190–1
postmodernism 106
postnarrativism 106–7, 120
Potter, Rosanne G. 21–5
Pratt, Mary Louise 168
Presutti, Lidio 18
priming effects 233
professional expertise 81
professional identity 148–9, 156
'Project Augment' 39
Prosopographia Imperii Romani (PIR) 51–3
Prosopographie der mittelbyzantinischen Zeit
    (PmbZ) 58–9
prosopography 28–9, 32, 51–60, 66, 75,
    105, 269
    digitised 54–5
    at King's College 56–9
    of social interactions 108–9
    structured 43
Prosopography of Anglo Saxon England (PASE)
    36, 43, 60–3
Prosopography of the Byzantine Empire (PBE)
    26, 28, 54, 57–63
Prosopography of the Later Roman Empire
    (PLRE) 5
Prosopography of the Roman Republic
    (DPRR) 37
punctuation 199

query languages 35, 230

Raben, Joseph 138, 267–8
Ramsay, Stephen 20, 43, 153, 155, 241
rangatirantanga systems 172–4
Rathbone, Dominic 56
Raymond, Darrell Ronald 199
reading 220–1, 226
    kinds of 35
re-conceptualisation of objects of study 216
Records of Early English Drama (REED) project
    8, 17, 66–76
    Handbook for Editors 67
    online version of 74, 76
reflection machines 182–3
Rehbein, Malte 31–2
re-interpretation 242
relational databases 32
relevance 221
Rembrandt 277, 279, 286
Renear, Allen 199
reorientation 214
repatriation of objects 10
    digital 163–75
    types of 228
research evaluation 79, 137–8
Research Software Engineers (RSEs) 78, 80–3,
    90, 93, 98
Research Unit in Humanities Computing
    (RUHC) 57
resources, ephemerality of 149

reward systems 160
Rich Prospect Browsing 35
Rockwell, Geoffrey vi, ix, 3, 6, 10, 19–24, 133,
    155, 241
roles attached to specific jobs 150–4, 160
Rongowhakaata 162–75
Rorty, Richard 253, 258, 264
Roueché, Charlotte v, ix, 91
Ruecker, Stan 35
Runciman, W.G. 252
Russell, N.C. 136
Ryder, Judith 62
Ryle, Gilbert 194–5, 254

Sahle, Patrick 27, 31
schemata, referencing of 222
Schleiermacher, F.E.D. 219, 221
Schloen, David and Sandra 228
scholar-perception approach 23
scholarly work and scholarly associations 133,
    138, 141, 156–7
scholarship
    humanistic 38–9, 42
    digital 154–5
Scotland, boundaries of 108
self-organising systems 183–6
sense, making of 221
Service Level Agreements
    (SLAs) 84, 90
SGML 226–7
Shapin, S. 135–6
Short, Harold 16, 26, 38, 56–60
short-term jobs 160
SIMWEB 21–2
Sinclair, Stéfan 3, 10, 19, 22, 133,
    278, 281
skills required 150, 153–4, 159
Smith, LauraJane 164
Smithies, James v, ix–x, 44, 80, 83–4,
    91, 94, 97
Smithsonian institutions 164
Smythe, Dion 58
social constructionism 135–6
Social Network Analysis (SNA) 110–13
software development 185
solitary work 278
Somerset, J. Alan B. 68
'source conservative' approach 270
spatial proximity 227
Spence, Paul 92
Spencer-Brown, George 189–92
Sperberg-McQueen, C. 198
Sprandel, Rolf 270
SQL 35
Stambovsky, Phillip 193
Stanley, Henry (earl of Derby) 74
Stereoscope 239–40
Stewart, Mark 56
Stiegler, Bernard 186–7
Stone, Lawrence 52
succession planning 161
sustainability 148–9
    of digital scholarship 9
Svensson, Patrik 2
Syme, Ronald 52
Szczecin (Poland) 111

tags and tagsets 232, 236
Tahu Kukutai 172
Taylor, Alice 89
Taylor, John 172
Taylor, Stephen 88
Te Hau-ki Tūranga 162–7, 170–1, 174
Te Mana Raraunga (TMR) 173
Te Papa 163–4, 171
teamwork 7, 130, 183
techies' and technical work 7, 129, 131,
    136–8, 141–3
technical systems 81–6, 92, 98, 100
technology studies 142
telescopes 20, 24
text
    analysis of 19–20, 24, 56, 231, 280
    concept of 214–15, 223
    commentaries on 225–6
    meaning of 220
    as a system 189–91
Text Analysis Computing Tool (TACT) 10–11,
    18–21, 217–18, 230–1, 241–2, 273
Text Analysis Portal for Research (TAPoR) 280
Text Encoding Initiative (TEI) 11, 27–8, 34,
    94, 220–3, 233
    functional aspects of 216
Textual Big Data methods 15
textual editions 32
textual studies, semantics of 226
Thaller, Manfred vi, x, 5, 218
themes of research 63
theoretical bases 25
thinking through 281
Thomas, St see Aquinas
Thomson Klein, Julie 2
Tidline, T.J. 38
Tinti, Francesca 60
tools and tool building 18, 23, 38–9, 99, 150,
    153–9, 216, 227, 229, 231, 268, 279–81
Topic Modelling 23–5
TOPICS 215
Toulmin, Stephen 195–6
training pipelines 152
transactional documents 109
transcription 67, 69, 262–3
Transformation of Gaelic Scotland in the
    Twelfth and Thirteenth Centuries 110

Tredinnick, Luke 119–20
Tucker, Joanna v, x
Tuhiwai-Smith, Linda 173
turnover of staff 149, 160

Ullmann, Walter 54
United Nations 172–3
University of Maryland 160
Unsworth, J. 132, 225

Van Den Akker, Chiel 117
Van Hyning, Victoria 137
Van Zundert, Joris 224
VEGA code 238, 240
'versioning' 225
'views' 239
visualization 236–9
von Foerster, Heinz 203, 205
Voyant Tools 22
Vuillemin, Jules 182

Waitangi Tribunal 169
Wajcman, J. 135
Walter, Maggie 173
Web 3.0 69
Weizsäcker, Viktor von 204
Whaitiri, Lewis 170
White, Hayden 268
Wickham, Chris 107
Wiener, Norbert 183
Wilkinson, Leland 239
Williamwood High
    School 111
Wisbey, Roy 55–8
'wise eclecticism' 25
Wittgenstein, Ludwig 224
Wittig, Susan 214–15
women's work 51, 135, 140–1
world wide web 3
writing 284

XML 33–4, 159, 270

'yack and hack' 7

Zirkier, Angelika 227
Zorich, Diane 148

CPSIA information can be obtained
at www.ICGtesting.com
Printed in the USA
BVHW010249220623
665971BV00001B/1